RESTAURANTS of SAN FRANCISCO

NEW REVIEWS FROM THE

SAN FRANCISCO CHRONICLE

PLUS MORE THAN FIFTY

CRITICS' CHOICE RESTAURANTS

PATRICIA UNTERMAN
AND STAN SESSER

CHRONICLE BOOKS ■ SAN FRANCISCO

First published May 1988.

Printed in the United States of America.

Library of Congress Cataloging in Publication Data

Unterman, Patricia.
     Restaurants of San Francisco : new reviews from the San Francisco Chronicle plus more than 50 critics' choice restaurants / Patricia Unterman, Stan Sesser.
     p. cm.
   Includes index.
   ISBN 0-87701-495-7 (pbk.)
    1. Restaurants, lunch rooms, etc.—California—San Francisco Bay Area—Guide-books. I. Sesser, Stan. II. San Francisco Chronicle. III. Title.
TX907.U68 1988
647'.95'7946—dc19   88-5027
                                            CIP

Cover design by Karen Pike
Typography by TBH/Typecast, Inc.

10 9 8 7 6 5 4 3 2 1

Chronicle Books
San Francisco, California

Contents

Dedication

For our constant dining out companions:
Tim, Anne, and Harry

Preface

Restaurants can change—sometimes dramatically, sometimes overnight.

This can pose a big problem for a restaurant critic. The very week your review appears, the chef could walk out the door and the food could become entirely different. The owner could decide to coast along on a good review and not pay as much attention to the food. Alternatively, the restaurant could get so inspired by a favorable review that the food gets even better.

Publishing a restaurant review book complicates the problem even more, since it takes several months between the time the manuscript is handed in and the book appears. Even if we managed to sprout a dozen extra stomachs and eat at every restaurant just before the manuscript deadline, inevitably some of the things would change at some restaurants.

What to do?

In this book, we've adopted a solution we think is the most fair and the most accurate. We've reprinted all the reviews of restaurants we've written for the *San Francisco Chronicle* since our last book appeared. This includes new looks at old favorites and our appraisals of the latest restaurants to open in the Bay Area. The basic information, such as hours of operations and reservations policy, has been updated, but the reviews themselves are as they appeared in the paper.

Then we offer a second section: capsule reviews of more than fifty of our favorite restaurants from our previous restaurant review book—restaurants we don't want you to forget about in choosing a place to eat. Here, many of our appraisals are based on relatively recent meals, since these restaurants are places we go on "nights off." Again, the basic information is updated.

The nationality and geographic indexes include all the restaurants from both the full reviews and the capsules. So, in scanning the indexes, you're looking at the entire spectrum of our choices for the best places to eat in the Bay Area.

We depend on you, our readers, to tell us when you think a restaurant has changed, or to share with us a restaurant discovery of your own that we haven't reviewed. Write us in care of the *San Francisco Chronicle*, 901 Mission Street, San Francisco, California 94103. If we learn that one of our reviews is no longer accurate, we'll revisit the restaurant a couple more times, and you'll see our new appraisal in the Friday or Sunday edition of the *Chronicle*.

Finally, a word about prices. As far as restaurant menus are concerned, they've only been going in one direction—up. So, instead of mentioning specific prices of dishes, which could be out of date before the ink dries, we've characterized most prices in general terms. For most restaurants listed as "inexpensive," you can probably get out for under $15 per person, sometimes $10, unless you order extravagantly. "Moderate" is that vast middle category from $15 to about $40 per person. (This assumes that you order one of the less expensive bottles of wine to be split between two people.) For "expensive," the sky's the limit. At an expensive French restaurant these days, it's not unheard of for two people to run up a tab of over $200.

We hope you enjoy eating at these restaurants as much as we've enjoyed reviewing them. From a restaurant critic's standpoint, the great ethnic variety and the high quality of so many San Francisco restaurants turn reviewing into a real pleasure.

■ Editors' note: As this book went to press three restaurants had closed—Bridge Creek, E Street Restaurant and Tapas Bar, and Krung-Kao.

About the Authors

Patricia Unterman and Stan Sesser are both transplanted Midwesterners, and both combine in restaurant criticism an interest in journalism and food. Ms. Unterman grew up in Chicago. She studied English at Stanford University and journalism at the University of California, Berkeley, but soon after started a small Berkeley restaurant. She's now a partner in Hayes Street Grill, a fish restaurant, and the adjacent Vicolo Pizzeria, which specializes in deep-dish pizzas. For many years Ms. Unterman has reviewed restaurants, first for *New West* (now called *California* magazine), then for the Sunday *San Francisco Chronicle and Examiner*.

Stan Sesser grew up in Cleveland. He studied American history at Columbia but quickly succumbed to journalism as a reporter for the *Wall Street Journal* in New York, San Francisco, and Chicago, and for the Associated Press in London. He now writes consumer-oriented articles for a national magazine. Before joining the *San Francisco Chronicle* as Friday restaurant critic, he wrote a monthly restaurant column for *San Francisco* magazine.

Some Advice About Coping with San Francisco Restaurants

For anyone who loves eating out, few cities in the world can duplicate the attractions of the San Francisco Bay Area. Paris may have better French food, Taipei better Chinese food, Florence better Italian food. But few places combine the wide variety of eating experiences that are available right here. You can have a marvelous meal night after night without repeating the same ethnic type twice. The diversity of San Francisco's population, the bounty of the Pacific Ocean, the abundance of California's farms, and the great wines of the nearby Napa Valley all contribute to making San Francisco unparalleled for dining out.

Before you plunge in, we want to offer a few words of advice. Since we go to restaurants anonymously, we've encountered every sort of frustration you can imagine—and some you probably never thought of. We've been insulted, overcharged, and doused with everything from wine to beet juice. In one restaurant we couldn't even get a meal; two hours after we ordered, the kitchen hadn't even yet bothered to start on it, although the place was only half full. Since eating out should maximize pleasure and minimize frustration, we've distilled from the cumulative difficulties we've encountered a few nuggets of advice, intended to guide you in avoiding some of these problems yourselves. Here they are:

1 ▪ **When they say you have to reserve ten weeks in advance, they don't necessarily mean it.** These days, when restaurants seem to have surpassed movies as our favorite form of entertainment, phones can be ringing off the hook as soon as word gets out that a restaurant is great. For a fancy French restaurant with limited seating, this can mean the intimidating prospect of booking further in advance than you would a trip to Europe.

Fortunately for us, a lot of people reserve but don't show up. So call the day you want to go and ask what the prospects are. Even better, call at seven that night and ask if the restaurant can squeeze you in. You'd be amazed how often a table unexpectedly turns up empty.

2 ▪ **When a crowded restaurant seems to accept reservations readily from all comers, be wary and book a table for early in the evening.** We've found a number of places—many of them Italian—where a reservation does little more than get you in the door to stand in a seemingly endless line. Go to these places when you have play or symphony tickets and want to eat early. The later in the evening your reservation, the more backed up things will be.

3 ▪ **Don't sit there passively and accept an endless recitation of "specials."** This is a rapidly growing method of separating you from the maximum possible yield from your wallet; you're handed a printed menu, but that's only the beginning of the decision making. The waiter than launches into an interminable list of "specials" that evening, sometimes so many you can't possibly begin to remember them. Conveniently the prices are omitted, with the restaurant assuming most people will be too embarrassed to ask. Then the bill comes, and you discover the "specials" are priced far higher than anything else on the menu.

There's a very fair way of dealing with this, if the restaurant is so inclined; Hayes Street Grill and Fourth Street Grill, among others, put all their specials (and all the prices) on a blackboard. If the restaurant you're eating at insists on the oral list, do some insisting yourself. Tell the waiter at the outset that you want the price of each dish mentioned. And if the list is too long to remember, ask the waiter for pencil and paper so you can write each item down.

4 ■ Ask carefully what's fresh and what's frozen. Increasingly, restaurants are recognizing that their patrons don't want something that has been sitting in a freezer for months. But some well-known old-time San Francisco restaurants, particularly fish places, still rely extensively for their basic menu on frozen food, supplementing that by whatever happens to come in fresh that day. If in doubt, ask the waiter. And if the answer sounds suspicious (we were once told that every single thing on about a fifty-item fish menu was fresh), call over the maitre d' and ask again.

5 ■ Don't let them talk you into an expensive bottle of wine. To you, wine is simply something pleasant to drink with your meal. To the restaurant, wine is a major profit center. That $20 bottle of chardonnay on the wine list typically might have cost the restaurant about $8 wholesale. Often you're better off sticking to the lower-priced wines on the list. These are the ones restaurants sell in huge quantity, so they'd be reluctant to offer something most people don't like. Remember that while great French wines can be superb, inexpensive California wines are often of higher quality than mediocre wines from France. And Italian red wines, particularly those with some age on them, are often extraordinary values.

Because the weather is less variable in California, vintages aren't as important. Young white wines can be fresh and delightful; there's no particular need to look for age. But, in red wines, the zinfandels and cabernets of recent vintage can be overwhelmingly heavy and tannic. Be sure to consult the waiter closely about these. A less-expensive California red wine might be a better choice than a higher-priced cabernet that is years away from maturity.

If you're ordering a French wine, remember that prices of bordeaux and burgundies have soared in recent years. And beaujolais, while much cheaper, are often mediocre. You might want to look for a red or white from the Rhone, which can be an excellent wine and a good value, or for a white from a district outside Burgundy, such as Sancerre or Muscadet.

If you know that the wine list is inferior or a clear rip-off, ask about bringing your own. Most San Francisco restaurants offer corkage privileges, meaning you can bring you own wine and pay something, often $5 a bottle, to drink it there. And remember an alternative: Rather than having to pay $25 for a $6 bottle of wine, you can always drink beer.

A Word about Food

Here, in a nutshell, are a few bits of advice on some of the types of cuisine you're likely to encounter in San Francisco restaurants.

Fish ■ Many of the relatively new restaurants specializing in the kind of food that has come to be called California cuisine do fish in a style rarely found a decade ago. The fish is either grilled over mesquite or sauteed simply, and what you're served is moist, even juicy, never dried out. But at some of the old-time fish restaurants, like Tadich Grill and Sam's Grill, you'd do well to order your fish "rare." And avoid at all çost any fish preparation in a gloppy sauce, particularly a cheese sauce.

French ■ Among the Bay Area's best French restaurants, there are two distinctly different styles of cooking. Masa's and Fleur de Lys are examples of the classic style. The sauces often rely heavily on butter and cream, which you'll want to mop up with lots of bread. The food is delicious, but it won't be a light meal. On the other hand, Chez Panisse exemplifies the newer style of light, innovative cooking using mainly local ingredients. If you were expecting a rich, classic dinner with lots of pastry crusts and sauces, you could walk away disappointed. We love both kinds of cooking, but understanding the difference will make the meals more satisfying.

Italian ▪ Each region of Italy has its own distinct style of cooking. But these differences tend to become blurred in San Francisco Italian restaurants, which frequently fill their menus with "everybody's old favorites," an amalgam of dishes and techniques crossing regional lines. If you want more authentic Italian cooking, try Vivande or the Wednesday Italian meals at Square One. La Lanterna and Il Fornaio in Marin prepare regional dishes.

Chinese ▪ Here there are true regional differences in San Francisco restaurants. Cantonese food, which predominates, includes such things as egg rolls, won ton soup, sweet-and-sour pork, spareribs, and chow mein. We can do without these, but we can't do without the great Cantonese Hong Kong–style fish restaurants springing up throughout the Bay Area, since superb fish preparations are what these places do best. Yuet Lee is the classic of this genre. The cooking at northern Chinese or Peking restaurants tends to be spicier, with wheat as well as rice used as an ingredient in some dishes. Here the stir-fried dishes, including duck, red meat, and all sorts of vegetables, tend to be excellent. Then there are the Szechuanese and Hunanese restaurants, the spiciest yet, where many dishes include red-hot chili peppers.

The greatest single contribution San Francisco makes to the world's Chinese food scene comes with dim sum, the Chinese tea pastries for which our city is a mecca. Only two cities, San Francisco and Hong Kong, offer such a wide choice of excellent dim sum parlors. So if you can have only one Chinese meal in San Francisco, make it dim sum for brunch or lunch, at Tung Fong, Harbor Village, or Yank Sing.

Thai ▪ The rapid mushrooming of Thai restaurants throughout the Bay Area is making this once-exotic cuisine a staple of lots of neighborhoods. In its complexity, variety of seasonings, and innovative preparations, Thai restaurants are frequently our number-one choice for Asian food. If you eat at Plearn, Marnee Thai, or Royal Thai, you'll see that the pervasive use of chili peppers never overwhelms the exotic bouquet of flavors.

Latin ▪ Everyone knows that San Francisco's Mission District is lined with inexpensive and often first-rate Mexican restaurants. It's not the elaborate, almost continental food you get in Mexico itself, but rather the Tex-Mex variety; the tacos, burritos, enchiladas, and the like that predominate in Texas and California. That's no reason to knock it, though, as you'll quickly discover if you have a burrito at La Cumbre or Taqueria Morelia. For more stylish Mexican food, try the Cadillac Bar. And be sure to sample the wide variety of other sorts of Latin restaurants, including Cuban, Salvadoran, Peruvian, and Spanish.

American ▪ Finally, let's not forget our own authentic native cuisines, which more and more restaurants are taking seriously. Campton Place offers gloriously elegant and innovative American food; Cafe Beaujolais and JoAnn's fabulous brunches; and Taxi and Fog City Diner deliciously rethought old classics.

Key to the Ratings

★★★ Extraordinary food combined with a very pleasant atmosphere. One of the handful of the Bay Area's greatest restaurants.

★★ Excellent food, worth going out of your way for. But the ambience can vary from plush to bare-bones, so read the review first.

★ Very good food, a restaurant well worth eating at.

The Bay Area's Best Restaurants
(in alphabetical order)

Expensive
Campton Place ★★★
Chez Panisse ★★★
Fleur de Lys ★★★
Masa's ★★★
Square One ★★

Medium-Priced
Broadway Terrace Cafe ★★
Chez Panisse Cafe ★★★
China Moon ★★★
Flower Lounge ★★★
Greens ★★★
Janot's ★★
Kabuto ★★★
Vivande ★★
Wolfdale's ★★★
Zuni Cafe ★★

Inexpensive
Bombay Cuisine ★★
Cafe Latte ★★★
Golden Turtle ★★★
Harbor Village ★★
Nan Yang ★★
Pat O'Shea's Mad Hatter ★★
Plearn Thai Cuisine ★★★
Royal Thai ★★★
Sanppo ★★
Yujean's ★★

Restaurants

Alejandro's Sociedad Gastronomica

★

1840 Clement Street (between Nineteenth and Twentieth avenues), San Francisco. 668-1184. Open Monday through Thursday 5 to 11 P.M., Friday and Saturday 5 to midnight, Sunday 4 to 11 P.M. Full bar. Major credit cards. Reservations recommended. Moderate.

I'm sure you know this already, but I'll say it anyway: Mesquite-grilled monkfish, formerly the signature dish for people of the yuppie persuasion, is out—now as much an anachronism as beef wellington.

In its place, sweeping the restaurant world, has come the newest fad: tapas. Once defined as little snacks that Spaniards ate on the way home from work, restaurants trying to be trendy now consider tapas almost anything that precedes an entree. Do you want some pasta or pizza tapas? Step right up.

What's wrong with trendy food? Restaurants do best when they create something, not when they try to duplicate a dish that sells well down the street. And critics can quickly lose their sanity if they have to taste the same things week after week.

I got through 1986 without reviewing a single plate of mesquite-grilled monkfish, and I was determined to do the same for 1987 with tapas. But then I faced a quandary when I decided to do a new review of Alejandro's Sociedad Gastronomica, an old favorite I hadn't been back to in years.

The problem was this: Since my previous visits, Alejandro's had introduced an extensive tapas menu. But Alejandro's also happens to be a Spanish restaurant, not one serving Italian food or California cuisine. If they want tapas, they're entitled to them, and I'm forced to break my vow.

So now you actually have the novel option of going to a Spanish restaurant for your tapas. And these particular tapas happen to be terrific, establishing themselves as the highlight of Alejandro's menu.

But before we get to that, let's consider the mysterious Sociedad Gastronomica, which appears liberally sprinkled throughout the menu as "SG" in a circle, indicating that the society approves of that particular dish.

I long had fantasies of the sociedad as the eating arm of Opus Dei, the secret Spanish society that by some accounts controls a large chunk of the world. But Alejandro Espinosa, the restaurant's owner and chef, has a much more mundane explanation: It's a group of South Americans now working in San Francisco restaurants who get together occasionally for dinner.

Espinosa came from a Spanish family that lived in Peru, and when he arrived in the United States, he cooked in a Mexican restaurant. That accounts for the multiethnic nature of Alejandro's menu, which has a page of Mexican food and several Peruvian dishes mixed in with the Spanish ones.

Forget about the Mexican food; it's basically leaden and dull. You can do as well in any neighborhood Mexican restaurant and, for the floury and bland "SG" *chiles rellenos*, you can do better.

But the Spanish food is another story. The great dishes I remember from years back hadn't lost any of their charm, and, in the case of the rabbit, had actually gotten better.

The gigantic portion of rabbit (you won't walk away hungry from Alejandro's no matter what you order) has been marinated overnight in garlic, wine vinegar, thyme, and orange. The juices of the marinade are thrown in with onions, cilantro, white wine, and lots of ground peanuts to make a fantastic sauce. It's accompanied by saffron-coated rice and carrots and also, unfortunately, by frozen green beans that taste like shredded plastic.

The other great dishes all involve seafood, and here a word of warning is in order. Alejandro's is one of those restaurants that hasn't caught up with the higher expectations many people have eating seafood today. The fish, scallops, and squid are fine, but the shrimp is frozen, and some of the clams and mussels taste considerably less than impeccable. You play a game of seafood roulette when you eat a clam or mussel, not knowing whether you'll swallow it or spit it out.

If you can accept that, you can eat seafood in some beautiful preparations. The *zarzuela de mariscos* is a seafood stew in an irresistibly rich sauce of fresh tomatoes, tomato sauce, sherry, garlic, onions, and oregano. The *pescada a lo macho* is a fillet of Pacific red snapper smothered in a dark, spicy tomato-based sauce and buried under a heap of seafood, including what must be a pound of squid.

Then there's the *paella a la valenciana*, one of the few edible versions of paella in a San Francisco restaurant. The saffron-coated rice isn't a bit greasy, and chunks of chicken and chorizo sausage are added to the seafood.

But it would be easy to make a meal on the tapas alone. The twenty-five tapas on the menu range from common things like fried chicken to rarities like pig ears. Both, incidentally, were excellent, the chunks of chicken freshly fried and greaseless, served with a peppery dipping sauce, and the shreds of pig ears marinated to tenderness.

Among the tapas, don't miss the *conchitas* — scallops with butter, wine, and grated cheese put under a broiler — and the *papas*, the classic Peruvian dish of potatoes with cheese sauce. Above all, order the "alejandrinos," a sort of Spanish won ton that's stuffed with cheese, eggs, and jalapenos and then deep fried.

There's an infectious enthusiasm among the staff at Alejandro's that makes eating there fun. There's a funky Spanish decor — one that would be improved by pulling up the carpets, which are beginning to reek with age. The Spanish waiters are clearly enjoying their job, and they're unflappable.

Too often in San Francisco, restaurants become popular for a couple of years, then hit the skids. In the case of Alejandro's, it's good to see a place that's still just as I remembered it years back. ■

—Stan Sesser, March 8, 1987

Allegro
★

1701 Jones Street (at Broadway), San Francisco. 928-4002. Open Monday through Saturday 5:30 to 10:30 P.M. Beer, wine. Major credit cards. Reservations essential. Moderate.

Rapallo
★

365 Nineteenth Street (near Franklin), Oakland. 763-1310. Open for lunch Monday through Friday 11:30 A.M. to 2:30 P.M.; for dinner Wednesday and Thursday 5:30 to 8:30 P.M., Friday and Saturday 6 to 9:30 P.M. Beer, wine. MasterCard, Visa. Reservations accepted. Moderate.

No one would create much controversy by saying the Bay Area has lots of mediocre Italian restaurants. But how many good ones are there? Particularly compared to other popular cuisines, there are distressingly few.

It is a mystery of major proportions in a city that loves food and has a large Italian population. What I can do is redouble my efforts to review Italian restaurants and find the good ones.

So this week I'm revisiting Allegro on Russian Hill and Rapallo in downtown Oakland, places I wrote about when they first opened a couple years ago. Allegro has a new owner, and Rapallo has become increasingly popular.

Allegro
When I first reviewed Allegro, I pointed out how wonderfully Italian the atmosphere was, a bit ironic since the owner was Armenian. No one will have to ask about the ethnicity of the new owner, Angelo Quaranta, a big bear of a man who dominates this cute little restaurant.

Quaranta's business card reads "insurance and business consultant and cook." He bought the building that houses Allegro, set himself up as executive chef as a "hobby," and set out to make the restaurant resemble the kind of place he'd want to eat in.

In ambience, what emerges is as close to Italy as you can find outside its shores. This place is fun, and the waiters don't miss an opportunity. When our waiter, for instance, came with espresso in a big cup because they were out of small ones, he first apologized, then launched into an effusive explanation of how lucky we were, because we were getting a much bigger portion. "It's beautiful, it's beautiful," he exulted as he patted the cup.

And the new menu Quaranta created also remarkably resembles those in Italy, a far cry from the usual San Francisco leaden Italian menu with lasagna, veal parmigiana, and the like. It emphasizes instead simple grilled meats, served plain with the lightest possible sauce. For once, here's an Italian restaurant where you can have a full-course meal and not stagger out.

I tried three of the grilled meats: a rack of lamb, thinly sliced veal, and half a chicken that had, according to the menu, been grilled under a brick. All were okay but nothing more. Both the grilled veal and another dish, veal rolled around cheese, suffered from meat that was dried out and not very tender. The flavor of the veal and the other meats simply wasn't very intense. I don't know what the brick did to the very plain grilled chicken, but I would have happily traded that brick for evidence of a tasty marinade with fresh herbs.

The appetizers maintained the theme of lightness, and you can sample several of them in the *bocconcini* plate for two. There is a simple grilled eggplant and zucchini, marinated calamari tossed with celery, and slices of mozzarella and tomato. All were fine—no puddles of oil here—but, like the entrees, nothing really sparkled.

The pastas, and a glorious frothy zabaglione for dessert, were the most interesting courses. *Penne arrabbiata*, translated as "angry pasta," had fiery red peppers in its simple sauce of olive oil, garlic, and tomatoes. Angel hair pasta proved a dieter's delight with cherry tomatoes and other vegetables tossed with the thin noodles.

For a surprisingly elegant restaurant on Russian Hill, Allegro is quite a bargain. You won't be bowled over by the food, but the restaurant is pleasant and fun.

Rapallo

Again the theme is lightness. In a big, airy, art-filled room in downtown Oakland, Rapallo presents a menu that's a total departure from standard Italian fare. Instead it attempts much more interesting Italian dishes, incorporating elements of California cuisine.

When I tasted the appetizers, I was in three-star heaven. The waiter brought three innovative dishes, each one fabulous. Flavorful eggplant mousse in grape leaves was served cold in a tangy, garlicky tomato vinaigrette sauce. A pancake of polenta and fresh corn stuffed with melted goat cheese couldn't have been fluffier, more delicate, or more wonderful. Deep-fried, saffron-scented rice balls filled with gorgonzola and mozzarella cheeses proved as interesting as they sound.

Fettuccine with smoked chicken kept up the performance—loaded with chicken, reeking of garlic, and featuring an unusual sauce that included mustard. Angel hair pasta with tomatoes and zucchini was excellent, too, with a very light sauce tasting of vinegar.

How could the same kitchen produce entrees that quickly brought me to earth with a thud? I don't know, but suddenly the magic and lightness disappeared. Overly cooked and overly floured veal scallopini was close to inedible. Braised rabbit in a heavy sauce was dry and boring, without a hint of seasoning. A lovely sausage stuffing wasn't enough to redeem flavorless and dried-out grilled quail.

Nor did the kitchen do better with desserts. Lemon pound cake, heavy and none too fresh, was quickly renamed by a dinner companion "five-pound cake." Homemade chocolate and vanilla bean ice creams were appallingly tasteless.

So what started out as a three-star dinner inexplicably ended up at one star. I'd go to Rapallo in a minute; the service is excellent, the setting is pleasant, and it's not crowded for dinner. But I'd fill up on antipasto and pasta, and stop there. ∎

—Stan Sesser, August 28, 1987

American Chow

★ ★

340 Division Street (at Brannan), San Francisco. 863-1212. Open for breakfast Monday through Friday 7 to 11 A.M.; for brunch Saturday 9 A.M. to 3 P.M.; for lunch Monday through Friday 11 A.M. to 3 P.M.; for dinner Monday through Saturday 5 to 10 P.M. Beer, wine. MasterCard, Visa. Reservations for six or more at dinner only. Inexpensive.

To bring off a good, inexpensive American diner is no piece of cake. I've been to too many of them that serve garbage—greasy, sloppily prepared food, some of which is so wrong and so pretentious in its reinterpretation of the old favorites that you wonder how it could have found its way onto any plate. Yet these American diners are popular, evidence that people want to eat familiar, comforting dishes at casual, inexpensive restaurants. After many frustrating meals at resurrected diners and coffee shops, I stumbled upon American Chow and understood what all these places should be going after.

American Chow is a new diner in a redone clapboard shack underneath the freeway. Having taken over the none-too-savory quarters of the old Cottage Kitchen, owner Albert Sun kept the structure intact but rebuilt and refurbished everything. The result is understated but clever, personal but immediately identifiable as a member of the diner genre. American Chow is intended to be used every day for breakfast, lunch, and dinner by a broad spectrum of the South of Market population. Its simplicity and low prices make that possible.

The outside boasts an eye-catching neon sign, but the structure itself is plain white with a cheerful red and blue trim, a motif that is continued inside. Banks of new multipaned windows add a surprising degree of architectural distinction, and blue-green shades emphasize them even more.

At one end of the cabinlike dining area, there is a small counter with five stools, and an open kitchen. The small dining room has sturdy gray carpeting, aluminum-trimmed Formica tables, and blue vinyl-seated wooden chairs. Horizontal pine wood wainscoting and pine trimming on the windows give American Chow a cozy cottage feel. San Francisco policemen grab dinner at the counter; single men and women sit comfortably reading, waiting for their food as if American Chow were a home away from home.

The food is as clean and honest as the decor. A bellwether of any restaurant is its salads, and American Chow's are treated with respect. A hearty spinach salad gets a creamy garlic dressing and a generous sprinkling of real bacon bits, hard-boiled egg, and blue cheese. The mixed green salad brings floppy greens and some horrible tomatoes in a well-balanced vinaigrette, a far cry from the typical coffee-shop iceberg salads. One evening the special salad was a caesar, but it wasn't special enough. It takes expensive parmesan, anchovies, croutons, and a lot of fiddling around to make this kind of salad taste right.

Both the potato salad and the coleslaw that accompany many of the sandwiches are made with crisp fresh cabbage and sweet red potatoes. Their bland sour-cream dressing tastes clean and wholesome. It doesn't mask the main ingredients, but connoisseurs might think both salads need more zip. (I don't discourage the occasional underseasoning because so many restaurants that season with abandon turn out inedible food.)

The thinnish charcoal-crusted hamburgers on soft sesame buns are totally satisfying. The fries are cooked in clean oil. There's no stinting on the bacon in a classic BLT on white toast, and milk shakes in vanilla, chocolate, and coffee flavors are just about the best around—milk and ice cream blended to a thick but drinkable consistency.

At both breakfast and lunch, American Chow serves the kind of corned beef hash that I adore. Finely ground corned beef with soft shredded potato seasoned with lots of black pepper and onion, it fries up crisp with a soft interior. Topped with a perfect sunny-side-up egg and grilled tomato slices, it's a great dish. The greasy spoon has been wiped clean; this hash, like everything else I've tasted there, was cooked with a modicum of oil.

Clam chowder one day was full of tender clams, halves of soft red potato, celery, and onion in a creamy clam broth. It's worth dropping by on Fridays to get a bowl, though a pale green zucchini soup prepared on another day lacked character. The thick red bean and ground beef chili is mildly spicy and sweet from lots of onion.

One evening a soothing beef pot roast came with whole roasted potatoes, a sea of pleasant brown gravy, and nicely cooked zucchini and carrots. A pair of moist, deliciously charred pork chops came with cinnamon applesauce and a heap of corn bread pan stuffing. What a great plate! Another day, the kitchen put out a gently curried pork stew on rice with raisins and onions, accompanied with zucchini and red peppers. A thin New York steak with acrid burned garlic butter was my only disappointment.

For those Californians who now require a glass of wine with their meal, there are fruity wines by the glass, such as Clos du Bois merlot.

Finally, American Chow makes its own desserts, with a special aptitude for pies. The crusts are crisp, the fillings not too sweet, and the portions reasonably small, so don't hold back. The pumpkin pie is spectacular; the coconut cream a model of its coffee-shop kind. Fresh apple cranberry is no small achievement, either. The house-made cakes are a little heavy for my taste, with almost as much frosting as cake.

Considering that the prices are truly cheap, American Chow puts out the whole repertoire of American coffee shop food and then some, with integrity, restraint, and real skill. It's a terrific neighborhood restaurant. ∎

—Patricia Unterman, November 15, 1987

John Ash and Co.

★★

4330 Barnes Road (Highway 101 at River Road), Santa Rosa. 707-527-7687. Open for lunch Tuesday through Friday 11:30 A.M. to 1:45 P.M.; for dinner Tuesday through Thursday and Sunday 6 to 9:30 P.M., Friday and Saturday 6 to 10 P.M.; for brunch Sunday 10:30 A.M. to 2 P.M. Full bar. Major credit cards. Reservations highly recommended. Expensive.

John Ash and Co., an ambitious, luxury-class restaurant that used to be located in a rustic, ranch-style wing of a Santa Rosa shopping center, has moved into stunning quarters in the brand new Vintners Inn complex. The new restaurant provides an elegant but regional dining-out experience, unduplicated anywhere else. This uniqueness is its charm and perhaps a bit of a problem as well.

The new quarters define the current romantic, wine-country look with their location in the middle of vineyards. Tall arched windows and trellised patios are but a yard away from rows of vines, and there's nothing more exciting for wine lovers than eating in the middle of the plants that produce their favorite drink. The interior of the building draws from Auberge du Soleil in St. Helena and the Sonoma Mission Inn. High ceilings and terra cotta tile floors, miles of stucco walls painted ecru with a warm pink glow, oversized ceramic pots with tall arrangements of dried grasses, large tables, and comfortable upholstered chairs conjure up the aura of wine-country luxury. Large commissioned canvases of Sonoma county landscapes, all successfully evocative of the surrounding countryside, add a local touch.

A large and well-trained staff of waiters, sommeliers, and maitre d's, mostly women on my two visits, keep the reservations and dining room running precisely. Everyone, without fail, is genuinely glad that you're there. On both occasions we were late for our reservations and the women handling the seating post couldn't have been more forgiving. The service proceeded flawlessly, if a bit slowly on the busy weekend evening we were there, and right up to tempo at a lunch. John Ash has succeeded in drawing together a dedicated staff, one, it seems to me, that reflects old-fashioned community values of taking pride in their work. There's none of the cynicism or brusqueness that you find in so many San Francisco restaurants.

The menu, in a folder decorated with original artwork, is set up so it can be changed often to reflect seasonal availability of foods. The list of dishes can only be described as singular, and in fact, many of them are original to the point of being odd. Every single dish I sampled was made of impeccable ingredients—the freshest, brightest produce, fresh fish and absurdly generous portions of excellent meats—but John Ash is working awfully hard to create a signature cuisine. Whether you like his ideas or not is a matter of personal taste. There aren't technical flaws to the cooking, but you have to like sweet sauces and accents in your main courses and appetizers to be an adherent of this restaurant.

At dinner one evening the tiny slices of quiche laid at the table, topped with golden caviar, had sugar in their cornmeal crust. This unexpected sweetness was indicative of what was to follow. Half the dishes took me by surprise.

A black bean chowder, a chunky mixture of whole beans, tomatoes, and onions in a clear stock, was aggressively seasoned with clove. A soup of sweet mulled wine sported slices of raw pear and ravioli stuffed with roquefort cheese. I understand where the inspiration for this dish might have come from, stilton cheese, pears, and port being an English trinity, but this reworking sent me to the bread basket, filled with three different, delicious house-made breads, for sustenance.

I loved a lusty, thick puree of fresh tomatoes full of garlic and basil topped by a toast slathered with basil aioli, but tired in front of a hillock of barely warm scallop mousse in a pond of extremely thick chive beurre blanc, simply too much of a rich thing.

Main courses were monumental. Loin lamb chops at least three inches thick were slathered in toasted hazelnuts and honey, strong treatment for some otherwise succulent, naturally sweet lamb. A veal chop of even greater proportions sat on a sweet, intense, much-reduced red wine sauce that, if eaten with the meat, masked its best qualities. The distinctly blackberry-flavored sauce accompanying a breast of muscovy duck tasted more appropriate with the gamy red meat of the duck, but it actually wasn't as strong as the sauce served with the veal. My favorite dish was the most modest, a moist chicken breast on a bed of creamy fresh corn and chives. The flavors melted into each in a comforting, logical way.

All the plates look lovely. They're dramatically garnished with fruits and vegetables, fresh herbs, and edible flowers that evoke the Sonoma countryside.

Desserts need some refining. I would prefer the crusts on the tarts to be crisper, lighter, and baked longer, and the fillings to be less sweet and strong. An overpowering marzipan presence subverted a fresh peach tart; a pale, heavy crust diminished the fun of a caramel, chocolate, and macadamia nut tart. An unnecessary shot of Grand Marnier in the chocolate sauce detracted from my pleasure of a whimsical sundae made with house-made vanilla ice cream, toasted filberts, and a praline cookie. Strawberry sorbet prettily presented in a cookie cup with raspberry sauce gets my nod.

I returned for lunch with some trepidation and ended up liking the restaurant much better when it was serving on a less-grand scale. A handsome salad of local baby greens came with a fine walnut-oil dressing on the bottom of the plate. I guess you're supposed to toss it yourself. Onion soup with a tender cheese and crouton hat on a nutmeggy broth brought back memories of Paris. A plate of juicy ripe melon, raspberries, prosciutto, and watercress came with a ramekin of sweet, clear chili-infused dressing, a combination that still mystifies me.

For main courses there were tasty, chunky crab, sole and shrimp cakes with a perky mayonnaise; a single, crisp soft-shell crab in an opulent beurre blanc; and some cold poached salmon that was cooked a little too long and needed a livelier sauce.

What indicated the potential of John Ash to me was a fixed-price meal called Today's Light Lunch. It began with a clear, saffron yellow lobster-scented broth with four sweet and tender poached scallops and a bouquet of julienned vegetable; moved on to a skillfully grilled chicken breast with a fresh tomato-cilantro salsa; and finished with a plate of ripe melon and raspberries. Forget that this lunch was only 650 calories. It showed that John Ash could put out a meal of both complex technique and clean, integrated flavors.

At dinner, I get the feeling that John Ash and Co. is trying to be the Carnelian Room of Santa Rosa. It wants to establish itself as a destination restaurant, as an enclave of sincerely luxurious dining in the country and a distinctly individual culinary voice. It has achieved all that, but the effort shows as far as the cooking style is concerned. The food at dinner seems a little too fancy for the sake of being fancy—and that, after all, is just what a sophisticated restaurant wants to avoid. ■

—Patricia Unterman, October 4, 1987

The Avenue Grill

★

44 East Blythdale Avenue, Mill Valley. 388-6003. Open Sunday through Thursday 5:30 to 10 P.M., Friday and Saturday until 11 P.M. Beer, wine. MasterCard, Visa. Reservations accepted. Moderate.

The Avenue Grill is a bustling, enthusiastically run neighborhood restaurant that caters to people who want a good feed. A cross between an American diner and a California grill, this restaurant serves up big plates of meat and potatoes, substantial salads and appetizers, and gigantic desserts. It's all prepared with a sure hand and served in rather posh surroundings for this type of eating.

The Avenue in both menu and decor has borrowed bits and pieces from other restaurants, past and present. Its most striking feature is a white-tiled open kitchen with a charcoal broiler and a beautiful vertical rotisserie. If you want a very close look, you can sit at the counter in front of it. A dark green and cream color scheme, a floor of linoleum squares, old-fashioned venetian blinds, mirrors, handsome hanging light fixtures, and some upholstered benches have all been juggled into the right places. The tables covered with crisp white linen add a tone of dressiness, but The Avenue Grill is patronized by casually dressed man and child alike. It's noisy enough to muffle even the shouts of young children.

The cooking explores the earthy side of California cuisine. Portions are huge, presentations straightforward, seasoning broad. One unique feature of the menu is that it acknowledges producers. Living Foods and Green Gulch Farms supply produce; the Niman-Schell Ranch in Bolinas naturally fed beef. In these days of pesticide and chemical abuse on vegetables and animals, I applaud restaurants that specially seek out untainted food.

I'm a fan of Avenue Grill's green salads. Their caesar made with small, whole, inner romaine leaves sprinkled with garlicky croutons and freshly grated parmesan cheese has all the bite and richness of the best. A plate of mixed lettuces with a pleasant, creamy vinaigrette stays interesting from first bite to last. Indeed, California is the land of the green salad, and The Avenue Grill respectfully carries on the tradition.

Heartier appetizers are also featured with varying ethnic overtones. Peppery prawns get a Cajun treatment with a cayenne-and-melted-butter sauce and a California presentation that includes lots of greens and avocado. Two huge griddled crab cakes are loaded with crab meat but need more seasoning. They sit atop an unripe-tomato salsa that tastes mostly of lemon juice. The combination doesn't work. Neither did the elements in spaghettini tossed with cherry tomatoes, scallions, and canned black olives. The flavors didn't merge; there was no reason for those ingredients to be on the same plate.

My very favorite dish at Avenue Grill is the Avenue burger, made of ground natural prime beef that stays amazingly juicy and full of flavor when ordered medium rare. It is deliciously charred on the outside. As you bite into the soft, poppy-seed bun piled with grilled onions, the juices run out onto the plate. A pile of french fries accompanies.

I'm also an advocate of the "green plate special," which changes nightly. One time a pile of sliced house-cured ham, really a brined leg of pork with a moist texture and slightly sweet and aromatic flavor, came with sweet potatoes, green beans, and authentic coffee-flavored redeye gravy. The house-made applesauce that was supposed to be served with it never arrived. Another evening the special brought slices of delicately smoked and roasted turkey with garlic mashed potatoes, fresh cranberry sauce, sagy bread stuffing, and made-from-scratch gravy—Thanksgiving in February.

The "all-American meat loaf" serves as a model of its kind. Loosely packed, moist, well seasoned, it's too bad it gets a winy gravy that detracts from its virtues. A heap of the garlic mashed potatoes and crisp vegetables come with it. Timing is all important when you order rotisseried half chicken. If you can get it right off the rotisserie, it will be delicate and juicy with a crisp skin. But as roast chicken sits, it loses its charm. The Avenue chicken I had was fine, but not great. Good coleslaw and fries are heaped on the plate.

Desserts carry on the style of simple abundance. A big bowl of fresh apple crisp could be a meal in itself, though I would have liked the apples to have more flavor. Individual lemon meringue pies look mountainous with their caps of fluffy meringue, but they deflate into a soggy heap when you cut into them. Though the lemon filling is tart and bright tasting, the crusts are wet and sugary.

The wine list struck me as being too small and pricy for the kind of food being served. I would expect some choices in both red and white in the $12 range, but only one good red (1982 Calera Cienega Valley zinfandel) fit the category. Most of the wines cost over $20.

Also, the food comes out of the kitchen sporadically. One evening we suffered a forty-five-minute wait between first course and meat loaf. On another visit, some appetizers came before others and the wait for main courses was again long. The Avenue's menu is large and the plates get a lot of different foods, for which I'm willing to wait, but I sensed, on both occasions, that the kitchen was falling behind.

Matters of timing aside, The Avenue Grill does an admirable job of turning out American favorites with their own signature. They capture the heartiness and comfort of the originals without being fussy, a philosophy that sets the tone of the whole restaurant. If you're hungry and want something homey that you know will be made with high-quality ingredients, head for the Avenue. ∎

—Patricia Unterman, February 22, 1987

The Bayon

★ ★ ★

2018 Lombard Street (near Webster), San Francisco. 922-1400. Open for lunch Tuesday through Friday 11:30 A.M. to 2 P.M.; for dinner Tuesday through Saturday 5:30 to 10:30 P.M., Sunday 4:30 to 10 P.M. Beer, wine. Major credit cards. Reservations advised. Moderate.

By latest count, I've written reviews of restaurants of thirty-four different nationalities and ethnic varieties. Enough is enough; that sort of choice should keep the most adventurous eaters in the Bay Area happy indefinitely.

But it turns out we've now got to consider number 35. It's so good there's simply no way to avoid it.

The cuisine can be called Franco-

Khmer: French food as cooked by the Cambodian aristocracy. The French, as any world traveler quickly discovers, liked to take their cuisine with them when they extended their empire. But Cambodia posed a particular problem, since it lacked two of the staples of French cooking, butter and cream.

So the French colonialists improvised a substitute cuisine, using coconut milk instead of dairy products and plugging Cambodian spices into traditional French recipes. This food quickly spread into the homes of wealthy Cambodians who wanted to adopt the French life style. And it just as quickly died with the disintegration of Cambodia in the 1970s.

Miraculously, San Francisco a couple of months ago got itself a Franco-Khmer restaurant, perhaps the only one in the world. The sign in front says "Cambodian," but don't believe it. Only a few of the dishes, mostly appetizers, are traditional Cambodian. The rest is food the likes of which you've never tasted before.

The restaurant is called the Bayon (named after Cambodia's most famous temple), and its owner is 35-year-old Sary Leng, who learned about Franco-Khmer cuisine from the cooks at his family's home in Cambodia. Leng came to U.C. Berkeley in 1973 to study political science, and adopted the first name "Dean" because he wanted an American name that reflected his love of academia.

Leng works in the kitchen of the Bayon with a woman who was chef to Lon Nol, the American-backed Cambodian prime minister in the early 1970s. Using only fresh ingredients, including organic vegetables bought directly from farmers, they cook everything from scratch when it's ordered. This can mean a long wait between courses, sometimes so long you wouldn't have minded a little preparation done in advance.

While the food is wonderful and extraordinarily sophisticated, the dining room displays a problem common to lots of restaurants with French pretensions but a non-French staff: The waiters (in this case Cambodians) shuffle around your table uneasily trying to be very formal, and constantly asking you whether everything is satisfactory. Yes, it is, but they should relax and let the food speak for itself.

The wine list is a second problem. It's reasonably priced, but there are only a few French wines and the vintage years aren't listed. Oddly enough, the list is half Italian, the heritage of the Italian restaurant that previously occupied the Bayon's Lombard Street site.

But all complaints end when you pick up the menu, which is a fascinating trip through previously unexplored terrain. There are dishes routine on French menus but almost never seen on Asian ones, including veal, calf's liver, lamb chops, and brains. But in each there's a Cambodian accent in the spices, marinades, and sauces. It elevates some of the dishes to culinary heights rarely reached in French restaurants themselves.

Take what's called "veal majestique" as an example. Tender slices of veal, along with mushrooms, onions, and carrots, are simmered in a magnificently rich and aromatic sauce of coconut milk, lemon grass, shallots, garlic, three different roots of the *galangal* family, and enough chili pepper to produce just a tingle of heat. I've never had a blanquette of veal in a French restaurant nearly as wonderful.

Then there's the grilled lamb. Baby rib chops are marinated in a mixture of East (lime leaves, lemon grass, *galangal*) meets West (lemon juice, rosemary, thyme). The meat itself is magnificent, and the marinade brings out its flavor perfectly.

Other spectacular entrees include succulent boneless roast quail stuffed with ground pork, bean threads, peanuts, lotus seeds, and black mushrooms; tender fat-free duck in a citrus sauce that for once isn't sweet and syrupy; and fresh salmon in a rich, creamy sauce of coconut milk and lemon grass. One entree is pure Cambodian, but it can't be ignored: absolutely the best chicken curry around, boneless chunks of chicken in a sauce perfumed with a whole bouquet of perfectly balanced flavors.

Except for the escargots—snails never tasted so good as they do in this version, combining lemon grass and coconut milk with garlic and shallots—the appetizers are more Cambodian than French. But they're equally spectacular, particularly the papaya and the tripe salads, each crunchy, very fresh tasting, and only lightly dressed. In the first, shredded green papaya is mixed with carrots, chopped peanuts, a few chilies, and fresh prawns. The second combines tripe and calamari; I've always considered tripe a real test of a restaurant, and this one passes with flying colors.

Prices are reasonable—and by French standards absolutely cheap. For $20 you get a degustation dinner that includes a variety of appetizers, a choice of the two excellent soups (one is a sour chicken soup, the second a combination of sea-food in a tamarind-flavored broth), and a choice of any entree.

To my mind the Bayon is the most exciting new restaurant to open in San Francisco this year. By the yardstick of interesting and innovative food, it's miles ahead of those places featuring the latest twist on California cuisine. ■

—Stan Sesser, November 20, 1987

BeauSejour

★ ★

170 State Street, Los Altos. 948-1388. Open Monday through Friday 11:30 a.m. to 2:30 P.M., Monday through Saturday 5:30 to 10 P.M. Full bar. MasterCard, Visa. Reservations recommended; essential on weekends. Moderate a la carte; inexpensive fixed-price dinners.

There's a new restaurant on the Peninsula that's so authentically French, with sauces so perfect, you'd swear the chef had just stepped off the boat from France. In fact, there *was* a boat trip involved in the history of this restaurant—but one of a very different kind.

I've heard some astonishing stories of how restaurants get started, but that of BeauSejour in Los Altos should win some sort of award. It's one of the few French res-

taurants in the Bay Area where the food is so skillfully prepared you could close your eyes and think you were eating in France. But the classic French dishes that come out of the kitchen turn out to have been done by a Vietnamese refugee—who learned French cooking in the United States.

Back in Vietnam, Huynh Trung Lap owned a ranch, an agricultural processing business, and a Saigon French restaurant. He was also a political official, and he and twelve family members fled two hours before the fall of Saigon in 1975. They boarded a barge with only the possessions they could carry, drifted for two days, and were lucky enough to be picked up by an American destroyer.

Although Huynh (this family name is pronounced "win") had never actually cooked at his restaurant in Saigon, he decided a restaurant was the best venture here because it could employ his whole clan. So now there are eighteen Huynh family members working at BeauSejour. They moved here in April after selling their French restaurant in Santa Monica.

Santa Monica's loss turns out to be our gain—particularly for the Peninsula, which doesn't have an abundance of first-rate French food. Not only is the food at BeauSejour consistently excellent—with the only weak part being desserts—but the place is also extraordinarily pleasant. It's divided into small rooms, each with thick carpets and elegant wallpaper and furnishings.

But the first thing you're going to notice are the prices. The entrees are reasonable enough, but the "bistro menu" is out of another era. For a reasonable fixed price, there's a choice of five main courses, all with soup and salad.

I sampled two of these dinners, and from the first taste of soup I knew this restaurant was going to be something special. The cream of mushroom soup was so light, yet so perfectly captured the intensity of mushroom taste, that I could hardly believe what I was eating. And then came the salad—an assortment of crisp lettuces in an absolutely splendid dressing combining oil, vinegar, shallots, mustard, and a touch of honey.

And the entrees proved impressive, too. Duck in red wine sauce presented a stew of very tender, fat-free duck in a thick, aromatic sauce of reduced duck stock, red wine, onions, tomatoes, carrots, and cognac. And *osso buco* was excellent, also—not only the huge portion of veal shank, but also a heap of fresh noodles flavored with a sauce of cream, shallots, butter, lemon, and a creamy French cheese.

I'd imagine these dinners are special enticements to draw customers while the restaurant is new, since the ingredients alone must cost almost as much as the charged price. But even things from the regular a la carte menu are so good you'll feel they are a bargain.

Foremost among Huynh's skills are his sauces. There must be stockpots going twenty-four hours a day in the kitchen, because everything is based on reductions that capture a bouquet of flavors. A tender roast saddle of lamb has a sauce based on stock from lamb bones; delicious shelled lobster meat rests in a rich sauce flavored by lobster shells. I couldn't begin to guess what was in this sauce until I called Huynh. Besides the shells, it included fish stock, cognac, white wine, onions, carrots, butter, cream, and rice blended in for thickening.

Another entree to consider is the lemon chicken. With its crisp skin and rich lemony sauce, it manages to be both light and satisfying. The kitchen also does a great job with some of the appetizers. Number one on my list are the oysters and mussels baked in puff pastry.

Surprisingly, in view of all this wonderful food, desserts proved to be nothing special. Chocolate and Grand Marnier souffles were nice and puffy, but they didn't have very much taste. A fruit tart had a thick, unpleasant crust. Raspberry mousse was more like a square of flavored gelatin.

The wine list was another negative. Many of the wines are overpriced, sometimes three times retail, and they're not particularly well selected.

Service at BeauSejour is attentive—even a water guzzler like myself never had to think about asking for more—but the waiters tended to be a bit too stiff.

I have friends in Los Altos who for years have been starved for good non-Asian food that didn't require a long drive; they're now eating at BeauSejour several times a week. For anyone on the Peninsula who cares about good food, this place is a godsend. ■

—Stan Sesser, June 6, 1986

Blondie's Pizza

★

2340 Telegraph Avenue (a block from the U.C. campus), Berkeley. 548-1129. Open Monday through Thursday 10:30 A.M. to 1 A.M., Friday and Saturday 10:30 A.M. to 2 A.M., Sunday noon to midnight. No reservations. No alcohol. Cash only. Inexpensive.

The Cheese Board

★

1504 Shattuck Avenue, Berkeley. 549-3183. Open for pizza Tuesday through Thursday 11:30 A.M. to 1:30 P.M., Friday 4 to 7 P.M. No alcohol. No reservations. Cash only. Inexpensive.

Remember in the good old days when a pizza was a pizza and you didn't have to think about what style you wanted? It was all mozzarella cheese, tomato sauce, and the same basic choice of toppings; the only question was who did it best.

Today, pizzeria pizzas are only one segment of an industry. There's also yuppie pizza—something on the order of goat cheese, rose petals, and pickled shallots.

In Berkeley there is one of each variety that I've long wanted to review. Here they are, in one indigestible column.

Pizzeria Pizza—Blondie's Pizza

To call Blondie's seedy is an understatement. Remarkably, when it recently shut down for a couple of weeks and expanded in size, it emerged looking even seedier than before. I wonder whether an architect was called in to ensure that they didn't alienate their clientele by spiffing up the place. This clientele can best be characterized as teenagers who reject the Hard Rock Cafe because the crowd there is too straight. A smattering of college students is mixed in, but basically Blondie's customers lead you to suspect that pizza makes your hair turn orange.

Yet few things look as appealing as the slices of Blondie's pizza constantly being carried up and down Telegraph Avenue. The cheese is piled on high, the crust doesn't sag, and the aroma is intoxicating.

In fact, if you stick with the thick-crust version and the vegetable toppings, the pizza tastes almost as good as it looks. The pillowy-soft mozzarella cheese is of high quality, and there's lots of it. Tomato sauce is dabbed on sparingly, as it should be. The crust is light, tasty, and crisp all the way through. And even if you order a slice instead of a whole pie, it's served to you piping hot.

There's just one defect: a lack of seasoning. Parmesan, oregano, and pepper flakes are offered in shakers, but a pizza is vastly improved if the spices are baked in rather than scattered on afterward. As for your choice of toppings, the mushrooms, tomatoes, and green pepper are all nice and fresh, but the sausage tastes like a greasy American hot dog.

Yuppie Pizza—The Cheese Board

If you pass Shattuck and Vine on a Friday evening, you'll see, directly across from Chez Panisse, a line that makes the lines for the latest hit movie seem short. I'd wager that lots of people join the line having no idea what it's for, just on the theory that if so many people are waiting in Berkeley's Gourmet Ghetto, whatever it is they're waiting for has got to be great.

What they're waiting for are the pizzas turned out by The Cheese Board, a couple of doors down from the store, in what used to be Pig by the Tail charcuterie. The Cheese Board is the Bay Area's best, and certainly most politically correct, cheese store. It's cooperatively owned, it closes for nuclear protest marches, and it bakes

what's got to be the greatest sourdough baguette in history.

Here, as at Blondie's, there are a few tables, and there's also an upright piano that customers frequently sit down at and play. But most people get slices to eat on the street, or whole pizzas to take home. As part of The Cheese Board's philosophy of not ripping people off, the pizza is about half the price of some of the yuppie places in San Francisco.

Unfortunately, good politics—and indisputably good ingredients—don't necessarily make good pizza. The Cheese Board offers just one variety of pizza each day, loaded with interesting-sounding things. But the pizzas vary in quality from near-great to near-inedible.

If there's one defect, it's in the crust. The three pizzas I sampled for this review all had crusts that were unpleasantly hard and chewy; in the worst case, it almost resembled stale bread.

As for the toppings, it depends on what day you're there. One day a topping that included mozzarella, goat cheese, fresh tomatoes, onions, and pesto was outstanding. But another day the topping (three cheeses, fennel, romano beans, garlic, and other stuff) was a total loser; it was much too dense, and so overcooked that the cheese had hardened into a crusty mass. ∎

—Stan Sesser, September 5, 1986

Bombay Cuisine
★★

2006 Ninth Street (at University), Berkeley. 843-9601. Open Sunday, Tuesday, Wednesday, Thursday from 11:30 A.M. to 9 P.M., Friday and Saturday until 9:30 P.M. Beer, wine. Major credit cards. Reservations recommended. Inexpensive.

Ever since I was a reporter in London eighteen years ago, I've been particularly fond of neighborhood Indian restaurants. When I was faced with eating British food, they were all that stood between me and virtual starvation.

While the Bay Area certainly doesn't lack alternatives, it still has been nice during the past couple of years to see little Indian restaurants springing up all over the place. Now I've found one of the best: an unpretentious, insanely cheap Indian restaurant in the flatlands of Berkeley, with spicing so sophisticated it would be more appropriate for a maharajah's palace.

How do you know you're eating great Indian food? One test is if you find yourself enjoying dishes that include spinach or peas, which Indians traditionally cook to the point where they taste like they came out of a can. At Bombay Cuisine, the seasonings blend so well with the vegetables that it almost makes the overcooking (by our al dente Western standards) seem appropriate.

Bombay Cuisine is owned by Haresh Parmar, who last October took over a failed Vietnamese restaurant next door to his spice store on University Avenue. If you get to the restaurant early enough, you can get your taste buds in the right mood by walking through the spice store, where the wafting aromas of fifty-five-gallon drums of Indian spices will bowl you over.

Parmar hired as his chef China Sawami, who had cooked at Moti Mahal in Sausalito. Although Sawami is from southern India, Parmar and his wife taught him to cook in the Gujarati style, which is popular in Bombay.

The menu is tiny; four people can go through almost everything. But while there aren't many dishes, several are ones I've never seen before, and they were fabulously successful.

Consider, for instance, two appetizers: *khaman dhokla* and *patra*. The former is squares of pureed garbanzo beans, blended with chilies, turmeric, and ginger, then steamed, then topped with mustard seeds, coconut, and fresh coriander. It comes out like a wonderful version of polenta, and a spicy dipping sauce makes it even better. *Patra* is even more unusual: taro leaves are battered with garbanzo flour and spices and deep fried, emerging to taste like an exotic vegetable.

Then there's something called *masada* chicken. Boneless chunks of chicken are deep fried and served in a spicy sauce of cilantro, carrots, and onion. Just as with the *samosas* (turnovers stuffed with potatoes and peas) and the *pappadums* (big lentil flour wafers that resemble potato chips), nothing at Bombay Cuisine turns out greasy or heavy.

All the entrees are curries—vegetable, chicken, lamb, or prawns. But every one is so delicate, and with such beautiful and complex aromas and flavors, that you won't mind the lack of choice. *Palak* lamb, with tender fat-free chunks of lamb in spinach; chicken curry scented with cinnamon and including cloves, bay leaves, fresh ginger, garlic, chilies, and cilantro; and an eggplant curry that isn't the least bit oily or mushy, were my favorites.

With the curries you can have some wonderful breads, including the big puffy *puri* and the fried whole-wheat *paratha* that again has not a speck of grease. Then there's basmati rice fragrant with saffron, excellent chutneys, and a creamy, spicy *raita* of homemade yogurt and cucumbers.

There's even a wonderful dessert called *rasmallai*, a ricottalike cheese served in milk and flavored with saffron, cashews, almonds, cardamom, and rosewater.

The prices are extraordinarily low. The combination dinners seem like a great bargain, too—but everything comes on a big tray with compartments and it has the feel of eating a giant TV dinner.

With Indian music, tapestries on the walls, and pink tablecloths, Bombay Cuisine is a cute little place, too. The only negative is one shared by many Indian restaurants: the tables are tiny, and even if you ask for things one at a time, you'll inevitably get all the appetizers together, then all the entrees. Each time they serve something, the waiters are befuddled, since there's never a place to put all the dishes.

Bombay Cuisine offers something only Asian restaurants seem able to pull off: delicious, sophisticated meals for less than it costs to cook at home. ∎

—Stan Sesser, June 26, 1987

Bon Temps

★ ★

1963 Sutter Street, San Francisco. 563-6300. Open Tuesday through Thursday 6 to 9:30 P.M., Friday and Saturday 6 to 10:30 P.M., Sunday 5 to 9 P.M. Beer, wine. American Express. Reservations accepted. Moderate.

Ever since people started lining up on Chartres Street in New Orleans to share a linoleum table in Paul Prudhomme's funky K-Paul's Louisiana Kitchen, Cajun and Creole cooking have been the cultural phenomenon of the eighties. Here, hidden away in geographically isolated, semitropical bayous off the Gulf of Mexico was a native American cuisine so unusual, so spicy, so soulful, that the first time you tasted it done right, you never wanted to stop eating it.

What happened is that Prudhomme, a culinary genius, took the Cajun food he grew up on, refined it just a little, and started cooking it in a restaurant for the first time. Yes, you could get some fancy Frenchified Creole cooking at places like Galatoire's and the Commander's Palace, but no one had brought authentic Cajun cooking out of the swamps to the public. It seemed too difficult.

Alex Patout, chef-owner of Patout's in New Iberia, told me that a dish like crayfish *étouffée* would take a whole family—and when you're talking family in the bayou, you're talking about five or six kids, aunts, uncles, their kids, and grandparents—three days to make. First the crayfish had to be trapped. Then the tails had to be shelled. Then the roux had to be made and finally the sauce put together. The only dish more labor intensive might be something like stuffed crayfish heads in redfish court bouillon. As you can imagine, this kind of cooking was reserved for special occasions.

So when Prudhomme opened his K-Paul's, he not only managed to develop a set of recipes that could be executed in a restaurant kitchen, but he founded a whole food industry along with it. Pretty soon producers started shelling the crayfish and selling the tail meat by the pound. Prudhomme himself made *andouille* and *tasso* commercially because he wasn't satisfied with anyone else's. The whole fishing industry along the Gulf Coast hit boom times—times so good that the gulf redfish is almost fished out. Once these ingredients became nationally available, Cajun restaurants started spreading all over the country. San Francisco was not immune.

The Elite Cafe on Fillmore opened to immediate crowds, as did an even better restaurant, Gulf Coast Oyster Bar on Washington Street in Oakland, which still flies most of its ingredients up from La Place, Louisiana. Five or six others opened, closed, or are still going, while Cajun dishes proliferate on local menus like mushrooms after a rain.

What I found as a critic was that most of the Cajun cooking in the Bay Area only suggested the taste of the real thing. California Cajun turned out to be a shallow imitation. It lacked guts, proper preparation, and the right ingredients. Eating it was so frustrating, it was like being teased to death.

Just three months ago, a Louisiana restaurant called Bon Temps opened, which changed my mind about Cajun cooking in San Francisco. [Though opened under the name Borel's, the restaurant changed its name to Bon Temps shortly after.] Brad Borel had no formal restaurant experience before he opened this immaculate little restaurant, yet his food has the depth of real Louisiana home cooking combined with professional meticulousness. His cooking is just plain delicious.

Whoever put together the front of the house knew what they were doing too, because that same attention to detail, along with graciousness and warmth, presides. Both the small front and back dining rooms (with the kitchen in the middle) have snowy white tablecloths, polished wood parquet floors, and wooden wainscoting. Small original ink drawings hang on the walls. Fresh flowers and candles decorate each table. The waiters are personable, well trained, and well informed. A single-page wine list is right in proportion with the small menu.

Borel does a pure repertoire of Louisiana dishes, without, I am happy to say, any "blackened" preparations. Don't pass up the superb gumbo, full of big pieces of crab, chicken, and velvety sausage. Stuffed shrimp have a thick, peppery, crunchy batter that seals in a juicy shrimp and a moist corn-bread stuffing. They come with a cinnamony salsa. Bon Temps's shrimp remoulade is light and refreshing, notable for flavorful chilled shrimp in a mustardy tomato relish. It's the best shrimp cocktail in town. If you want to ease into Louisiana cooking slowly, there's a fine green salad full of crisp radishes, carrots, and ripe tomatoes tossed in a creamy roquefort dressing that would do many California restaurants proud.

The jambalaya, a rice dish in which the rice absorbs the spectrum of flavors in smoky *andouille* sausages, sauteed vegetables, and good stock, would make an Acadian homesick. This northerner would have liked it to be hotter in temperature. I suggest ordering it in an appetizer-sized portion, and the superior gumbo, so thick a spoon can stand up in it, as a main course.

One of my favorite dishes at Bon Temps, chicken Laree, is a chicken breast stuffed with a magically light corn bread, shrimp, and *andouille* mixture that melts in your mouth. A stuffed pork chop didn't have as much of the fabulous stuffing as I would have liked.

In his version of *coubouillon*, Borel takes boneless fillets of catfish, simmers them in an aromatic tomato sauce perfumed with cinnamon and peppers, and presents them over rice. Catfish never had it so good.

Shrimp Creole suffered one night from tasting rewarmed. The shrimp became tough and the dish never got hot enough. Much better was a special, another night, of crayfish *étouffée*, in which the tiny crayfish tails stayed tender as lumps of butter and the sauce had the energy of a zydeco combo. The crisply sauteed apples slices served with it were a little stroke of genius.

Most of the saucy main courses are served over rice with two buttery vegetables. The zucchini on every visit has been well cooked but bitter. A basket of warm, light, crumbly corn bread precedes dinner.

Desserts are a letdown. The bread pudding is too sweet and boozy. The peach cobbler made with canned fruit cannot be ordered a la mode because the restaurant doesn't serve ice cream. The filling of the pecan pie is certainly not too sweet, but somehow dull, as is the crust. I'd be willing to pay several dollars more for desserts just to finish off the meal on the same level as the appetizers and the main courses.

When you really get down to it, Bon Temps succeeds because it is such a personal restaurant. Borel comes around in his spotless whites, giving everyone a big smile and taking real pleasure in their comments. His restaurant feels a little too new now and the small menu needs time to expand, but I predict that Bon Temps will get better and better with time. He has to figure out how to half-cook some of his dishes and finish them off to order. I suspect that this chef learned how to cook at home when he was young, because he loved to do it, and that he opened his own restaurant because he thought his dishes were better than anyone else's. Whoever taught him did a great job but now he's got to adjust to the restaurant kitchen. ■

—Patricia Unterman, March 2, 1986

Bridge Creek

★ ★ ★ Breakfast

1549 Shattuck Avenue (at Vine), Berkeley. 548-1774. Open for breakfast Saturday 8:30 A.M. to 1:30 P.M., Sunday until 2:30 P.M.; for dinner Tuesday through Saturday 6 to 10 P.M. Beer, wine. No smoking. Cash and personal checks only. Reservations accepted for dinner. Expensive for breakfast; moderate for dinner.

Meat loaf dry as sawdust, cooked until the kitchen filled with smoke. A Jell-O mold with canned peaches. Iceberg lettuce brown at the edges, drowned in Wishbone french dressing. Wonder Bread, slathered with margarine. These are foods I remember all too vividly growing up in Cleveland. Today it's fashionable in the food world, or "warm and comforting," as the articles put it, to resurrect our nostalgia trips and re-create what we ate in our youth. I considered it for a while, but decided in the end that cooking a feast like the above would simply be too self-indulgent.

I was thinking about this after a recent dinner at Bridge Creek, the Berkeley restaurant that has gained a national reputation for dipping into the annals of Americana and coming up with sensational breakfasts. But breakfasts alone can't fatten a restaurant's bank account, particularly when they're so expensive ($15 a head at Bridge Creek wouldn't be unusual) that most people will come only on weekends.

A year ago, Bridge Creek tried to supplement their breakfasts with fixed-price $25 dinners, but they went back to breakfasts exclusively this spring. Now there's a new format once again: American dinners—steaks, chops, and other foods of our youth—Tuesday through Saturday, and breakfasts only on weekends.

I can report that the breakfasts are still wonderful, but the dinner format raised some real questions. Take, for instance, the vegetable that came with each entree: green beans cooked with bacon so long that the beans turned gray and floated in a puddle of bacon grease.

I was so surprised to be served this at Bridge Creek that I called the manager and asked her what was going on. Overcooking them "was the whole idea," she replied. "Mother used to stew them to death."

Is Bridge Creek trying to re-create authentically *bad* American food as well as good? The answer seems to be yes and no. Yes because their home-baked crackers resemble Ritz, not only in taste but in salt and grease content. Yes because of the terrible California canned olives on the relish tray. Yes because of the gloppy mayonnaise-based dressing on the house salad, the sort of salad I remember from coffee shops in New York.

But then how do we explain the Acme bakery breads; what American mother used to serve baguettes and *pain levain* with dinner? Or the lemon-parsley butter on the grilled swordfish? There were no trendy flavored butters in my house, just an overcooked piece of fish on a plate.

In short, thematically the Bridge Creek dinners are about as muddled as you can get. They don't work on another level, too: If you're going to base a menu on steaks and chops, served without sauces, you'd better have the best-quality meats. But the New York steak, the lamb chops, and the pork chops were all just so-so, not particularly enjoyable or flavorful.

What elevates Bridge Creek dinners to one star are the impeccable fresh fish from Monterey Fish Market, a very decent roast chicken with sage dressing and gravy, and an absolutely ethereal deviled crab casserole. We might not be talking authentic (no Campbell's cream of mushroom soup in this casserole), but we're talking fresh dungeness crab meat, diced onions, celery, and red peppers, baked together delicately with spices that convey just a hint of heat.

Dinner started with a choice of two appetizers, both disappointing. That relish tray with olives and crackers centered around potted smoked tuna, but there was virtually no tuna taste in the very buttery concoction. A mulligatawny soup was too rich and creamy, and too boring; it desperately needed more spicing.

There were two interesting desserts: a bread pudding that had much more custard then bread, but delicious eggy custard if you like that sort of thing, and ice cream served with thick huckleberry puree and crisp, tasty homemade chocolate chip cookies.

So the dinners proved a mixed experience, with many things far below Bridge Creek's reputation. But the breakfasts were another story entirely. Although you now have no choice but to face the weekend mobs, the Bridge Creek breakfasts are as fine as ever.

The light and flavorful waffles are just on the edge of crispiness. There's a version of *huevos rancheros* that beats anything in a Mexican restaurant, with shreds of pork, a spicy green sauce, two fried eggs, and jack cheese on a crisp flour tortilla. You can order two eggs baked in cream, served alongside three buttermilk pancakes. And a side order of biscuits will put you in heaven.

In fact, except for some boring omelets that aren't at all fluffy (you get the grand choice of ham, cheese, or ham and cheese, hugely overpriced), there isn't a loser on Bridge Creek's menu. And the restaurant's intimate setting is all the more wonderful during the day, when light floods in the big windows.

It's clear from the breakfasts that the people at Bridge Creek know how to capture some of the best elements of American cooking. But at this point, their new dinner concept falls flat. It needs a lot more work and a lot more thought. ■

—Stan Sesser, December 4, 1987

Broadway Terrace Cafe

★★

5891 Broadway Terrace (Broadway Terrace starts near the intersection of College and Broadway), Oakland. 652-4442. Open Wednesday through Saturday 5:30 to 10:00 P.M., Sunday 5 to 9 P.M. Beer, wine. Cash and personal checks only. Reservations required. Moderate.

The name of Jeremiah Tower's famous restaurant, Stars, is certainly appropriate because Tower and many other Bay Area chefs have become celebrities. But one restaurant that has been around for five years serves California cuisine as trendy and innovative as any place, although it has gone unrecognized by all but its regular customers. Its chef is as inventive as Tower—and far more consistent—yet he's never mentioned on any list of great Bay Area cooks.

I'm talking about Albert Katz, owner and chef of Broadway Terrace Cafe, a little restaurant in the hills of Oakland near the Berkeley line. The obscure location probably has limited Broadway Terrace's fame.

I think it serves better food than Stars, and at substantially lower prices.

You notice the differences between the two restaurants when you walk in. Stars reverberates with noise, while Broadway Terrace, with just thirty-eight seats and three dining rooms, is quiet and relaxed.

There's also a difference, symbolic of things to come, when the bread appears at the table. At Stars you get the kind of mediocre sourdough you find on some supermarket shelves. At Broadway Terrace you're served Acme bakery's *pain au levain*, among the best breads in the Bay Area.

This bread is just one reflection of a feeling I get throughout the meal: that Katz is interested in doing everything right, in putting together a dinner that shines from beginning to end. Some of his dishes fail, as is expected with anyone who experiments a lot, but there's none of the hit-and-miss inconsistency that marred my dinners at Stars.

To get an idea of Katz's ingenuity, consider his grilled leg of lamb. In the California cuisine style of cooking, where you want the basic flavors to predominate, it's difficult to do anything to lamb that doesn't muck it up. Pan juices are all it needs.

But Katz manages to introduce complexities without making the dish heavy and without masking the basic flavor. He serves the lamb on a delicate, aromatic bed of lentils, pomegranate seeds, and bits of walnut, with a sauce of lamb stock, walnut oil, and pomegranate juice, and the scent of lightly applied cumin, coriander, and marjoram. With lots of vegetables, it's delicious and a bargain.

Swordfish is another example of how an ordinary dish is made to shine. The fish is cut into noisettes, mesquite grilled, then topped with pesto and served on a bed of buttery polenta surrounded by bits of yellow tomatoes and red peppers. It works only because every component is perfectly cooked.

Lots of other entrees sparkled. Wild boar featured a thick loin chop served on a bed of spinach, surrounded by an interesting garnish of figs and onions stewed in orange juice, sherry, veal stock, and mint.

A pasta with smoked sturgeon, cucumbers, grilled yellow peppers, arugula, and garlic couldn't have been more delicate.

There were wonderful appetizers, too. Mexican fish soup turned out to be a spicy broth filled with mussels, squid, chunks of cod, toasted tortilla pieces, and a cilantro-tomato puree. Squid sauteed with tomatoes, olives, capers, and garlic had a bouquet of flavors and a light tomato sauce scented with olive oil. A market salad, with olives and jack cheese pureed into the dressing, was an array of beautiful baby vegetables and butter lettuces.

I know I'm eating great meals when the negative comments in my notes are more quibbles than anything else. Sweet-potato soup was much too peppery, stuffed buckwheat crepes were overwhelmed by too much goat cheese, and baked mozzarella on green tomatoes was a combination that just didn't work.

Samantha Greenwood, the Broadway Terrace's pastry chef, who's all of twenty years old, puts out a good array of desserts, particularly her ice creams and sorbets. Cinnamon ice cream in fruit sauce with raspberries, pears, and figs couldn't have been better. The same can be said for apple crisp with vanilla ice cream and a fig-pear spice cake.

Service at the Broadway Terrace is friendly and knowledgeable. But the waiters are compelled to recite a long list of daily specials. That's the only thing that mars the dinner, since you hear the constant drone repeated at every table. It's ridiculous because no diner can remember all the special dishes when deciding what to order.

I first reviewed Broadway Terrace several years ago when it was already popular enough to fill up every night. Katz could easily have rested on his laurels. But each year, the restaurant seems to get better and more inventive. Today it should be on anyone's list of the best restaurants in the Bay Area. ∎

—Stan Sesser, November 28, 1986

Butler's

★★

625 Redwood Highway, Mill Valley. 383-1900. Open Monday through Saturday 5:30 to 10 P.M., Sunday 5 to 9 P.M. Full bar. MasterCard, Visa, American Express. Reservations advised. Moderate.

Everything that Perry Butler decides to do, he does well. His original Perry's on Union Street was the hottest spot in town shortly after it opened seventeen years ago. Under the onslaught of hundreds of the city's singles, the place stood out as a model of good management, consistent food, and high spirits (in more ways than one).

Four years ago, Butler opened a second Perry's in Mill Valley with an identically designed bar, but light-filled, airy dining rooms with a view of Mount Tamalpais and Richardson Bay. The old pub food menu from Union Street didn't seem right for this new location, so he hired two young women chefs with impressive cooking credentials to revamp it. The result was a fresh interpretation of the classic bar menu, with more emphasis on fish, salads, and ethnic dishes.

A few months ago Butler's opened upstairs in the Perry's Mill Valley building, and this restaurant drifts further into the territory of California cuisine. Butler's may be what Mr. Butler has been working toward all these years, a comfortable but more formal restaurant that concentrates on first-class food.

Butler's is a separate entity from the operation downstairs. You enter up a ramp from the parking lot into a little waiting area with sofas, a collage on the wall, and a maitre d' station from which you are led upstairs into a glowing white space with picture windows on one side and an open kitchen on the other. The windows frame the sunset over the Marin hills if you hit it right. Tables, chairs, and soft upholstered benches are spaced generously far apart. The noise level is humane; the waiters and waitresses intelligent and helpful; the surroundings clean-edged, cheerful, sophisticated but not intrusive. Just walking into the dining room for the first time you sense that something appealing is going to come out of that kitchen.

And it does. The hand-written menu offers a manageable list of appetizers and grilled items with all sorts of interesting twists. In the new food arena of the eighties, where the quality and freshness of the ingredients take precedence over complicated preparation, the cleverness of the accompaniments, the pairings, and the presentation give a restaurant its style. At Butler's, the style borrows eclectically from a number of local restaurants and ethnic cuisines, but the result is unified by good execution and common sense.

One of the best parts of the meal are the house-baked breads like the dense, tasty rye and crusty Italian white bread served on both of my visits. Nothing gets a meal off to a better start than good bread and fresh butter. It's one of the first tip-offs about the quality of a restaurant.

Standbys like a caesar salad, light on the anchovies with lots of lemon and freshly grated parmesan cheese on top, or green salad made with young lettuces and herb vinaigrette share the appetizer menu with more exotic dishes. One day we had a smoky eggplant soup, a little too thick, garnished with tomato and basil; another time, a long anaheim chili stuffed with goat cheese, battered and deep fried, and surrounded by a terrific pureed tomato sauce alive with onion and cilantro. It was more of a meal than a first course. You have to be careful not to order a first course that repeats ingredients with the main course you choose. The menu needs to be sorted out so that it's easier to put together a whole meal.

One of the most glorious dishes on the menu is Butler's fresh fettuccine ever so simply but elegantly dressed with cream infused with roasted garlic, fresh tomato, and a little basil.

The heart of the menu comes from the grill. I've had grilled chicken on two different occasions, one time accompanied by spicy Thai noodles sprinkled with peanuts and smoky mashed egg-plant; and another time accompanied by sauteed corn and pepper pancakes, sauteed greens, and cream biscuits. The half chickens were juicy and well grilled, but what made them memorable were the accompaniments. I would have taken the ethnic theme a step further and given the chicken different marinades to match— an American barbecue sauce for one, a spicy Thai marinade for the other.

Fish gets the kitchen's full attention here. It starts out fresh, is stored correctly, and comes off the grill perfectly cooked. Swordfish one night was as fine a specimen as I've tasted, and a gingery tomato basil vinaigrette set it off nicely. Crisp shoestring potatoes and sweet green beans made it an exemplary plate of grill food. A fillet of salmon received the same respectful treatment.

In many restaurants fish stews end up with all the stale odds and ends of fish, but Butler's shellfish curry, loaded with scallops, mussels, clams, and shrimp in a sweet coconut milk curry with lots of hot green chilies was made with only the freshest seafood. Served over nutty basmati rice, it's my favorite dish on the menu.

Meat dishes take up the rest of the menu. There's a well-aged, tasty, tender prime New York steak, and carne asada, a thin skirt steak served with black beans, avocado, tortillas, and two fresh salsas. Fork-tender lamb shanks braised with fresh tomatoes and whole cloves of garlic sit on a bed of house-made noodles sprinkled with artichokes. Sauteed pork scallops and a mixed grill present further choices.

Another sign of a serious restaurant is that it doesn't let down for dessert. Butler's pastry chef has come up with a breathtaking hazelnut daquoise, many layers of crisp meringue, apricots, and hazelnut butter-cream glazed in dark chocolate. A plate of assorted butter cookies, gingersnaps, chocolate cookies, and sugar cookies go with intense toasted almond and rum raisin ice creams, among many other choices.

Butler's is achieving its goal of bringing city standards of dining to Marin County, but it's also bringing some of Marin to serious dining with the wonderful view, the comfortable, airy dining room, and the relaxed feeling of the restaurant. ■

—Patricia Unterman, August 24, 1986

Cafe Latte

★ ★ ★

100 Bush (at Battery), second floor, San Francisco. 989-2233. Open Monday through Friday 7 A.M. to 3 P.M. Beer, wine. MasterCard, Visa. Reservations accepted for six or more only. Inexpensive.

Lunch in a Financial District cafeteria? Sounds like a date you'd try to avoid. The very word "cafeteria" conjures up memories of bad school meals—of soggy spaghetti in tinny tomato sauce and meager tuna sandwiches on flavorless bread. The idea of the cafeteria implies institutional feeding, the American solution to serving the masses with the greatest efficiency. The problem with cafeteria food is that it is cooked in advance and kept either hot or cold while waiting to be chosen. It's a degrading process; held food is invariably tired food. These were my thoughts as I was trying to find Cafe Latte, a Financial District cafeteria that was supposed to be different.

You'd never stumble into this place by chance. It's hidden away on the second floor of the handsome old Shell Building, ostensibly to serve its tenants, though obviously many others from neighboring buildings use it. During the heart of the lunch hour you have to pray that a place to sit will come free before your plate of just-made pasta emerges from the kitchen.

The dining area, which faces on a light well, is packed as tightly as a sardine can with tiny glass-topped tables. Mirrored walls make Cafe Latte seem larger than it is, but even so, the din at peak hour is ferocious. The cafeteria line itself is elegantly fitted out with a marble tray ledge and counters that match an expanse of marble

floor. A vaguely art deco theme was used in the conversion of the space from Shell commissary to public restaurant.

There's very little that's institutional about this cafeteria line. Colorful cold foods ready to be served are dished from glass salad bowls. You can watch pasta being rolled out and stuffed at one station and sandwiches being made to order at another.

Cafe Latte disproves every prejudice I have against cafeterias. As a matter of fact, it's one of the best places to get fresh pasta in the city. Due to an efficacious system of hot food delivery, you can get plates of freshly stuffed *tortelloni* dressed with butter and sage or hot noodles tossed with seafood a few minutes after you sit down. When you order the pastas you get a color-coded flag that stands on your tray. When your dish is ready, it's brought to you from the kitchen by runners who are adept at scanning a forest of flags and pinpointing the right table. There's some kind of magic going on here, but the system never seems to fail.

The menu changes every day, though the format, happily, stays pretty much the same—a small section of appetizers, salads, homemade pastas, sandwiches, and house-made desserts. At one lunch we began with a hot cup of unthickened clam chowder, and Cafe Latte's signature appetizer of paper-thin slices of grilled eggplant finished off with three melted cheeses and tomato sauce, a very sophisticated version of eggplant parmigiana. It arrived just as we found a table.

The cafeteria tuna sandwich I so dreaded was reworked here by putting it on a soft, crusty roll and garnishing it with a fresh salsa, spicy with hot peppers and cilantro. Quickly made to order, it was one the tastiest tuna sandwiches I've ever had. Also delicious was a warm chicken salad with balsamic vinaigrette, a succulent grilled breast sliced over a bed of lettuce. For dessert, a thin walnut tart with a flaky, buttery crust was served on a small dollop of sour cream. The combination was serendipitous.

On another occasion we stuck to the pastas, which come with a green salad topped with crisp carrots, cauliflower, and other seasonal vegetables. The most wonderful of the pastas is the *tortelloni* stuffed with ricotta and chard, finished off with butter, parmesan, and sage leaves. Another satisfying dish is Cafe Latte's exceptionally juicy marinated and grilled chicken breast served with red and white noodles simply tossed with butter and freshly grated parmesan. A plate of these same noodles sauced with shrimp, bay scallops, and cream was uncharacteristically bland and the noodles were stuck together—perhaps from being cooked in advance.

A smoked salmon appetizer, appealingly presented over tissue-thin slices of cucumber and sour cream was subverted by low-quality smoked salmon. However, a chicken pasta salad in an oriental dressing revived what I had thought was a dead-horse dish. Far from being bland or oily or texturally dull, this combination of al dente bow-tie and corkscrew pasta, chopped celery, and big chunks of moist chicken, in a dressing fragrant with ginger, sesame oil, and cilantro, hit the spot.

For dessert, there was a spectacular chocolate tart on a ground-nut crust served with caramel sauce that surprised me by its lightness.

The young chef behind this new kind of cafeteria cooking, Faz Poursohi, is no newcomer to the restaurant business. He worked for an upscale Chicago group called Lettuce Entertain You, which currently owns the Pump Room, and then came out here to be head chef at Spectrum's MacArthur Park in Palo Alto. Not only did he pick up a lot of tricks as a chef along the way, but he learned the importance of good management. Cafe Latte is run like the best sit-down restaurants. An eager floor staff serves the dining room as if they were being tipped for it. If they see you need a napkin, they run and get it for you. Empty plates are whisked away, as are cumbersome trays. Mr. Poursohi has been very much in attendance on all my visits. He greets his regular customers, bringing them glasses of wine. He urges them to try his favorite dishes and brings them over to taste. You can tell he loves the business and he has infused his own personal gra-

ciousness into it at every turn.

He is soon to open a much larger operation almost next door at 132 Bush [see Faz Restaurant and Bar] that will feature his own smoked fish, meats, and game. A lot of us can hardly wait. ■

—Patricia Unterman, February 2, 1986

Cafe Majestic

★ ★

1500 Sutter Street, San Francisco. 776-6400. Open Tuesday through Saturday 7:30 to 10:30 A.M., 11 A.M. to 2:30 P.M., 5:30 to 11 P.M. Full bar. MasterCard, Visa, American Express. Reservations recommended. Moderate to expensive.

When a local boy makes good, everyone celebrates. Stanley Eichelbaum, former theater and movie critic for the *Examiner* for twenty years, the "oldest student" in his class at the California Culinary Academy, chef-owner of Eichelbaum's for five years and now chef-owner-creator of the stunning Cafe Majestic, certainly doesn't consider himself a boy, but he is a real success story. His elegant new restaurant in the fastidiously renovated Majestic Hotel has all the earmarks of a San Francisco tradition without any of the mustiness.

Approached by a couple of "developers with taste," as he put it, Eichelbaum took to the idea of launching a restaurant in a meticulously restored Victorian hotel. Visions of London's Connaught Grill flashed through his mind. Understanding the magnitude of the undertaking, he enlisted John Struer, a fellow classmate at the Culinary Academy and veteran of Wolfgang Puck's Spago and Chinois in Los Angeles. Together they put together a menu that evokes an older, more gracious era, yet incorporates all the culinary breakthroughs of the past six years. The handsome dining room, the elaborate hotel setting, the theatrical ambience, and the menu all come from similar ideas about quality. Everyone was on the same wavelength right from the beginning.

The experience begins when you walk into the lavishly decorated period lobby of the hotel and then into the clubby bar room, hung with a remounted antique collection of butterflies and moths. The dining room, gently divided into three areas, eases up on decor. Though there's no shortage of pillars, wainscoting, and ornate plasterwork, the scale of the room, filled with light from tall framed windows, saves it from Victorian oppressiveness. Textured walls in mysterious shades of grayish "sea foam" with peach trim do not diminish the masculine aspects of the dining room. For a change, the decor of a new restaurant doesn't intrude; rather, it quietly and graciously supports its function.

Both the lunch and dinner menus are studded with dishes that have been inspired by old recipes from turn-of-the-century San Francisco restaurants. Though reinterpreted, it's fun to taste them in a room carefully restored from photographs taken in 1902.

Hearts of palm Mission Dolores, a fanciful arrangement of asparaguslike palmetto hearts garnished with sliced black olives, a fresh tomato salsa, and a delicious creamy vinaigrette, never tasted so good. Olives must have been used often in old recipes. They form the stuffing and contribute to the sauce of moist grilled "gold rush chicken," served at lunch on a plate loaded with colorful vegetables—three kinds of beans, baby turnips, beets, carrots, three colors of peppers. Also served at lunch is a tender grilled flank steak cut into strips and piled onto a crusty bun with lots of sauteed onions, a modern idea with old-fashioned heartiness.

The soups have been full-flavored and interesting, like a creamy, tan mushroom soup full of chopped dried mushrooms and a naturally sweet, intriguingly seasoned red pepper puree.

Though the title "special designer pizza" should be subjected to some of the editing skills from Mr. Eichelbaum's years of writing, a pizza full of house-made sausage and sweet peppers on a chewy crust couldn't have been more delicious.

Tortellini with gorgonzola and cream were heavy for a first course, but elegant lobster ravioli lavished in classical lobster sauce showed off the sophistication of the kitchen.

Dinner entrees all come with platefuls of beautiful, perfectly cooked vegetables and I find this one of the most endearing aspects of this restaurant: you're given lots of food to eat and it's satisfying without being heavy.

A generous portion of medium-rare leg of lamb in natural gravy infused with rosemary and garlic, accompanied with all the vegetables, made for an ideal modern grill-style plate. The unexpectedly savory combination of litchis and chanterelles in a buttery sauce served over grilled chicken Nellie Melba qualifies this old San Francisco dish for a modern run. A thick veal chop topped with melted fontina cheese and fresh sage came off the grill in top form, but a fillet of salmon had charred a bit too much. I wasn't quite sure about its presentation on a bed of pureed garlic potatoes—the textures didn't work. Also not quite right was a simple dish of sea bass cooked in parchment with julienned vegetables and lemon zest. The lemon dominated and the whole creation came out too austerely.

On the opposite end of the scale, a special of grilled duck breast with fresh fig sauce turned out to be a lush pairing of fruit and game, albeit domestic.

Desserts are confined to pastries, most of them made by Mr. Eichelbaum himself when I tasted them (his pastry chef had walked out). Mr. Eichelbaum threw together all sorts of individual tarts filled with nuts and chocolate and caramel, a rich lemon pound cake that took off when sauced with a fresh strawberry puree, a moist German chocolate cake topped with coconut frosting, and a dramatic nectarine tart topped with phyllo pastry pressed into accordion pleats. I hope his replacement does as well.

A practical, serviceable, small wine list and intelligent service contribute their part to the meal, as does the refined piano playing of Don Asher, who knows how to modulate for a crowded restaurant.

Though Cafe Majestic has only been open for a few months, it has so captured the spirit of San Francisco that I would bring visitors there to show them what this city is like. Perhaps it takes a man who has covered the arts for a daily newspaper, who has dedicated himself to matters of taste as well as two crafts and who loves theater, to put together a restaurant that reflects both his own personality and that of his city. ∎

—Patricia Unterman, August 31, 1986

Cafe Pastoral

★

2160 University Avenue, Berkeley. 540-7514. Open for lunch Tuesday to Friday 11:30 A.M. to 2:30 P.M.; for dinner Tuesday through Thursday 5:30 to 10 P.M., Friday and Saturday 5:30 to 10:30 P.M., Sunday 5 to 9:30 P.M. Beer, wine. Cash or personal checks only. Reservations recommended, essential on weekends. Moderate.

A couple of years ago, I had dinner at a new little neighborhood restaurant in Berkeley called Cafe Pastoral. The food was quite decent, but the experience made me think that the time might have finally arrived to pack up and leave town.

The problem was with the waiters, who seemingly had memorized a guidebook on how to serve yuppies. From the "Is everything satisfactory?" starting before the food had even arrived to the "Have a nice day" at the end, every sentence was a cliche, spoken as the waiter stood stiffly by the table. I got so frustrated I started asking outrageous questions to crack the veneer, but nothing helped. If this is happening at a neighborhood restaurant in Berkeley, I thought, can there be any hope for life as we once knew it in the Bay Area?

Well, I have some good news. In its new larger quarters, around the corner from the old location, the service at Cafe Pastoral has changed dramatically enough to give us all hope a counter trend is setting in. The waiters laugh and talk like real people. They apologize if everything doesn't come from the kitchen in proper order, and joke about it. Not once do they wish you a nice day.

Pastoral is one of a growing number of East-meets-West restaurants, one of the happiest food trends around. The idea that Western and Asian cooking can be improved by borrowing ideas from each other's cuisines is so obvious that you wonder why it hasn't become widespread until so recently.

In this case, the borrowing is done by two young Koreans, Sanju Dong, the chef, and her husband, Hi-Suk. When I asked him to attach a tag to what he was cooking, Hi-Suk replied, "I would call it Korean-French, but no one knows what Korean-French means, including ourselves."

I'll take a stab at it and call Cafe Pastoral's cooking California cuisine with an oriental touch. Sanju is a painter (she has a studio above the restaurant) and Hi-Suk an architect, and their Asian-based sense of aesthetics shows in the food. Everything is beautifully arranged on the plate, and there's a marvelous contrast of colors, textures, and tastes.

There's one thing that can be said definitely about Pastoral's food: No restaurant uses vegetables with greater abandon, and no one makes more of an effort to see that the vegetables are fresh. The salads are a virtual tour through a produce store, and with one of the entrees I counted seven different vegetables on the plate.

But beyond that, Pastoral is one of those restaurants that bedevils critics. Though some of the dishes are excellent, others are flawed in major ways despite the excellence of both the concept and the ingredients.

Let's start with the salads, because so few restaurants make an attempt to create interesting salads, and those that do frequently give you three-bite portions. At Pastoral, the half dozen salads on the menu are loaded with wonderful things, and they're actually big enough to eat, not just pick at. Here's an example: The smoked poussin salad, which you'd expect to be served just on a bed of greens, also included macadamia nuts, slices of fresh peach, sugar snap peas, jicama, and blueberries. Everything was fresh and very subtle.

The salad combinations were always innovative and pleasant, like slices of fresh pear combined with walnuts and endive. But a duck salad was marred by being drowned in soy sauce, and the Pastoral salad—a marvelous array of avocado, tomatoes, and other fresh vegetables—rested in a pool of indifferent olive oil, with no other tastes in the dressing to perk it up.

The entrees are a strange lot—a combination of trendy California cuisine with some puzzlingly hack dishes. Who would expect to see on the same small menu a fettuccine with pine nuts, feta cheese, and garlic, and chicken cordon bleu, that old standard of microwave French restaurants?

In this case, the chicken was clearly homemade rather than home thawed, but it was still disappointing. The meat itself, stuffed with ham and cheese, was both tough and dried out. But another old standard, veal scallopini, proved much better. The very tender meat came in a pleasantly light marsala wine sauce.

Among the California cuisine entrees, the fettuccine was perfect, managing to be light and delicate, despite a creamy sauce that included parmesan and feta cheese. Salmon was nicely grilled but served on a plate swimming in soy sauce, making everything unpleasantly salty. Hawaiian ono (a fish also known as wahoo) was very fresh but needed a minute less on the grill. And delicious grilled poussin was marred by a redcurrant sauce that was much too sweet.

Desserts were a mixed bag, too, but not if your order was the chocolate torte. The two that I had, one with walnuts and one with lots of pecans ground in, were exceptional. But strawberry shortcake had hard and unpleasant-tasting biscuits, and Irish-coffee cheesecake tasted much more of whiskey than of cheese.

Such flaws didn't ruin the meal, but they indicated to me that the chef lacked expertise in certain areas—something that will probably come with more experience. Meanwhile, Cafe Pastoral is a very pleasant place to eat at very fair prices. It's a particularly good choice if you like lots of very fresh vegetables. ■
—Stan Sesser, August 22, 1986

Cafe Pranzo

★

706 Third Street, San Rafael. 495-3553. Open Monday through Thursday 11:30 A.M. to 10:30 P.M., Friday and Saturday 11:30 A.M. to 11 P.M., Sunday 4 to 10 P.M. Full bar. MasterCard, Visa, American Express. Reservations accepted. Moderate.

Alice Waters really got to people's hearts through their stomachs when she opened the upstairs cafe at Chez Panisse in Berkeley. By extending the downstairs restaurant's philosophy of using the best and freshest ingredients to more casual cooking, she convinced everyone that they wanted to eat pasta and pizza again. And now numerous restaurants have jumped on the bandwagon.

In fact, a Californian who is about to open a 120-seat American grill on the Rue Franklin Delano Roosevelt in Paris just gave me a ring. He is looking for a chef. I asked him what his menu was going to be. "Oh, you know," he said, "Chez Panisse pizza, grilled chops, some Italian things." So pretty soon we can travel to Paris and feel as if we were in Berkeley.

A short trip over the Golden Gate Bridge, however, can get you to the newest pasta-pizza-grill spot, a five-month-old restaurant in downtown San Rafael called Cafe Pranzo—roughly translated as "cafe dinner." The restaurant offers a large and promising list of the above-mentioned dishes. A beautiful brick oven at the center of this busy restaurant turns out fire-branded pizzas. Bright salads glow on a glass service counter where they await delivery to the tables, and big, flat bowls of colorful pasta come steaming out of the kitchen.

Yet, although the sets, the action, the

script are all there, the kitchen needs some time to figure out how to act it out. Restaurant owners think it's easy to put out good pasta and pizza, but it's not. Both are really tricky. A pizza crust has to be chewy, flavorful, and crisp. Pranzo's crust didn't have the right elasticity. It needed salt and more yeast. Good ingredients, such as chunky vegetables in a *pizza primavera* or roasted garlic and yellow tomatoes on a special pizza, were used on the tops, but there weren't enough herbs to pull them together. The pizzas needed focus and spiciness. Discordancies, such as canned artichoke hearts on a pizza full of fresh vegetables, didn't sit right.

On the other hand, the two pastas I sampled had lively, well-seasoned sauces. The balance of cream, butter, and cheese that so smoothly coated the noodles in fettuccine Alfredo would have pleased the inventor himself, but he would have been disappointed by the doughy texture of the noodles.

Pasta jambalaya tried to bring together the best of two ethnic cuisines with a smoky, spicy tomato sauce, but dry chunks of overcooked chicken and shrimp and matted and doughy fettuccine made the dish unpleasant.

I liked some of the appetizers very much. Singapore chicken salad with spicy peanut dressing was a huge portion of shredded moist chicken on a bed of chopped lettuce in a light, tasty sauce full of chopped peanuts. A bibb and butter lettuce salad sprinkled with roasted pecans and gorgonzola would have succeeded if the lettuces had been dry and the salad thoroughly tossed. A delicious special appetizer one night consisted of roasted red and yellow peppers stuffed with warm ricotta and melted mozzarella cheese.

Main courses were hit-and-miss. A fresh piece of swordfish came off the grill juicy and tender, but a couple of bratwurst were dry and mealy. Both were accompanied by half-raw oil-slicked Japanese eggplant. A sauteed rabbit special had a marvelous sauce full of fresh tomato and mushrooms, but the rabbit was tough and

lackluster. On another evening, a spiced chicken breast was scored with deep burn marks from a fire that was too hot. The vegetables this evening, buttery snow peas and yellow squash, were the best part of the meal.

A dense, rough-textured chocolate nut torte topped with a scoop of vanilla ice cream was our most dependable dessert. An overripe pear poached in white zinfandel turned out to be brown and mushy, though the *crème anglaise* and raspberry sauce that dressed it were tasty.

Despite all the criticism of the food, I had fun at Pranzo. There's a full bar and a reasonably priced wine list with two or three drinkable wines poured by the glass. The restaurant is a noisy, friendly, unpretentious place. Prices are kept down, portions are large, and you can order a lot or a little without anyone's batting an eye. There's something on the menu for everyone in the family, and there are even curtained wooden booths in the back to accommodate larger parties.

Conscientious management of the dining room goes a long way to elevate the experience of eating at Cafe Pranzo. The service by fast-moving young women and a cadre of bus people is organized and efficient. I admire the ambitiousness of this undertaking, and the fact that the restaurant offers so many choices. I do think the kitchen will get better with time. They've got the right equipment and ideas, but they have to work on the details, with special attention to the pastas and pizzas, the most popular dishes on the menu. I have a hunch that a second look at this restaurant in six months will show marked improvement. ■

—Patricia Unterman, September 8, 1985

Cafe Violeta

★

3105 Shattuck Avenue (just south of Ashby), Berkeley. 843-0662. Open Tuesday through Sunday 5:30 to 9:30 P.M., Friday and Saturday until 10:30P.M. Beer, wine. No smoking. Cash or personal checks only. Reservations accepted. Inexpensive.

Anyone turned off by the trendiness of the Bay Area restaurant scene should try Cafe Violeta. It's an honest restaurant, with heaps of good, fresh food at rock-bottom prices. It's also the perfect place if you want to discuss Oliver North and the Contras over a plate of Central American food. Violeta is part of Berkeley's La Pena Cultural Center, whose fund-raising activities include helping victims of repression in Latin America.

I first wrote about Violeta a few years ago when you had to order your food at a counter, a situation that could produce long lines and chaos on busy nights. Now there's table service, which makes significantly more pleasant a meal in the attractive room, with its brick walls, tile floor, and track lighting.

The menu is a culinary tour of Latin America, and a particularly rewarding one for anyone who likes vegetables. There are beautiful salads, casserole dishes that include lots of vegetables, and a couple of satisfying vegetarian entrees. The *ensalada California* is the best of the lot, a crisp flour tortilla basket piled high with cheese, avocado, hard-boiled eggs, cauliflower, broccoli, and lots of other vegetables, all tasting impeccably fresh.

The *pescado frito*, a Chilean-style red snapper, was perfect, deep fried in a tasty light batter without a speck of grease. The *pastel de chocolo* was another winner, a casserole of chicken, beef, olive, raisins, and hard-boiled egg topped with creamy corn.

Some dishes, however, suffer for lack of seasoning. Cuban black bean soup was distressingly bland; another Cuban dish with simmered shredded beef had first-rate ingredients, but cried out for some heat and spiciness. ■

—Stan Sesser, July 24, 1987

Caffe Esprit

★

Sixteenth Street at Illinois, San Francisco. 777-5558. Open Monday through Saturday 11 A.M. to 3 P.M. Beer, wine. MasterCard, Visa. Reservations accepted. Inexpensive.

Caffe Esprit is a restaurant about style. Every aspect of the operation—the menu, the seating, the service—is subordinate to its design. That it happens to be an appealing one is lucky and not surprising. Esprit, a gigantically successful clothing manufacturer, has made its mark knocking off the cleverest designs in the fashion world and reproducing them relatively inexpensively. The Esprit style aspires to a look of offbeat privilege, of personal freedom, of colorfulness, which seems to appeal most strongly to the preteen set, as evidenced by the demographics in the two-hour line in front of the stunning Esprit factory outlet one day.

The food in the cafe is a knockoff too, of the most sophisticated casual food around today. The small menu offers four salads, four pizzas in small and large sizes, four sandwiches, a Double Rainbow soda fountain, and an espresso bar. The principles of freshness, lightness, good quality, and color are adhered to with a fair amount of rigor. Many people whom I respect in the restaurant business are excited by Caffe Esprit because it makes philosophically correct food fun and accessible; it introduces a way of eating to a new market in the same way wine currently is being sold on TV, to "regular" people. But I think that the cafe doesn't go far enough in executing its vision. Though outwardly impressive, the Esprit food outlet remains an idea of a clothes manufacturer, not a chef. The concept is shallow and imitative, but most of all it misses on the most important things—tastiness, comfort, and pleasure.

I couldn't find the cafe on my first attempt, a problem many are having who don't shop at the Esprit outlet. It turns out that they are both west of Third Street on Sixteenth Street, right up against an expanse of railroad tracks and the bay where you don't think anything could be.

The second try another evening with a two-and-a-half-year-old child and husband proved successful. My husband, who finds it hard enough getting through a meal with me, let alone his fidgety son, consented to Caffe Esprit because, fashion maven that he is, he knew it would be casual enough for children. He was right. Children were running around a cement courtyard with outdoor tables, benches, and saillike umbrellas. They were climbing up and down the curving metal stairway that leads to mezzanine seating inside the caffe. They were grabbing apples from a wire basket set out on a metal cart at the entryway structure. The industrial, indestructible side of Caffe Esprit appeals to children, who like the climbable fixed benches and round picnic tables downstairs and the feeling of open space, contributed to by a retractable wall of windows. The elegance of the materials—three-inch thick white ash tabletops, stone composition floors, a sparkling exhibition kitchen—and the structure's conceptual design make it interesting and dramatic for adults at first.

On the evening I was there, the place was almost empty and the artificial light softened the hardness of the interior. [The cafe is now open only at lunchtime.] We sat upstairs in quiet, except for the synthesized Wyndham Hill music burbling over the sound system. At a lunch visit, every seat was taken. The cafe roared with noise; the insipid music was turned up even louder to stay above the din. We sat downstairs at the playground structure picnic tables, eating with a shifting group of strangers and feeling as if we were den mothers in an institutional eating hall. The oversized scale of the ground floor tables made me feel like part of the decor, a unit in the Esprit schematic. Indeed, most of the people around us were wearing the same uniform and looked to be about twelve to fourteen.

They ordered pizza, the great crossover food, and left the salads to the older women. One evening the doughy crust on a *pizza margherita* had not baked long enough, but its simple topping of cheese and fresh tomatoes with a sprinkling of fresh basil tasted fine. A *pancetta* and garlic pizza at lunch had a terrific crisp, sweet, white crust, but the combination of provolone, sun-dried tomatoes, and Italian bacon was annoyingly salty.

At evening a huge plate of assorted young lettuces strewn with edible blossoms and fresh herbs, ever so lightly dressed with good olive oil and pear vinegar, tasted intriguing. The salad greens themselves and herbs had lots of flavor, so the barest whisper of dressing was all that was needed. Its size baffled me; no one wants to eat a huge plate of lettuce, no matter how lovely, as a meal. A nicoise salad, made mostly of lettuces with a chunk or two of none-too-fresh grilled tuna, a few underdone potatoes, and not enough green beans, needed a much livelier dressing and more of it than was applied. The cooks weren't tasting. At lunch, an antipasto plate called *insalata mista* also lacked conviction. There were some great marinated mushrooms, but the broccoli tasted only of raw garlic. An insipid dressing did nothing for a pile of small white beans. Where's all that good extra virgin olive oil the menu boasts about when it is needed? Mealy, out-of-season pear tomatoes, paper-thin slices of salami, and a slice of marinated fresh mozzarella filled out a plate that looked gorgeous but disappointed on the tongue.

I loved the sandwiches. A grilled chicken breast club constructed on three pieces of airy, toasted brioche bread layered with excellent bacon and flavorful lettuces is amply moistened with chive mayonnaise. The hero starts with a fine crusty roll and gets stuffed with paper-thin slices of prosciutto and salami, dry jack and provolone, tissue-thin slices of pickle and onion, shredded lettuce, and roasted peppers, with vinaigrette and mayonnaise for lubrication. The net effect of all these paper-thin ingredients is juicy, fruity, and savory, if again, a little too salty.

The soda fountain puts out a spritzy lemonade in place of soda pop, an enlightened practice, and a handsome hot fudge sundae with softly whipped cream and roasted pecans. The fudge sauce, however, is too corn syrupy and not chocolaty enough.

I know I should be cheering for this cafe because it is a missionary effort, an attempt to convert young Esprit followers to Esprit's supposedly enlightened idea of food. But there's more style than substance here, and maybe it's just that "join the Esprit club" ambience that puts me off. I can see Caffe Esprit with its formula menu and its oppressive decor and its slick, halfway-there food opening next to Esprit sections in department stores or as adjuncts to Esprit stores in shopping malls. I would be glad to have them there instead of commercial fast-food outlets, but I wouldn't seek them out. ■
—Patricia Unterman, January 11, 1987

Caffe Quadro

★ ★

180 Pacific Avenue Mall (at Front and Pacific), San Francisco. 398-1777. Open Monday through Friday 11:30 A.M. to 2:30 P.M. Beer, wine. MasterCard, Visa. No reservations. Moderate.

I'm no great fan of restaurants slavishly doing something because it's supposed to be "trendy," but there's one trend I think is terrific. This is when a successful restaurant starts a low-priced, informal "cafe" nearby.

A cafe gives those of us who don't want a long expensive meal an attractive alternative: without dressing up, without spending much money, we can eat, if not identical food, at least food that's in the same spirit and style.

Chez Panisse started this trend several years ago, and there have been occasions over the years when the Cafe at Chez Panisse was actually offering better and more interesting food than the restaurant downstairs. Now the latest cafe has come to Square One, Joyce Goldstein's popular restaurant at Pacific and Front.

It's called Caffe Quadro, and physically it shares the same problem of its next-door neighbor. During the day, there's a pleasant view out the floor-to-ceiling window of a vest-pocket park, but at night the stark modernity of the building prevails, and both Square One and Quadro become reminiscent of the scene in an office building lobby. [The cafe is now only open at lunchtime.]

The coldness of Quadro's decor doesn't help. The polished granite tables and tile floors are tasteful in themselves, but a room like this needs something for warmth, and nothing is offered.

Worst of all, the food is served on paper plates and in paper bowls, an incredible indignity. This isn't a barbecue joint—it's a restaurant, charging at least $5 for a sandwich and over $10 for a pizza. Since plenty of money has clearly been put into Quadro's decor, the paper plates have got to be some sort of affectation, and it doesn't work.

Once you get past the atmosphere and plunge into a pizza, however, things brighten considerably. This is absolutely, positively the best yuppie pizza in San Francisco. Moreover, it has the rarest of rare features: crust that's both tasty and crisp, and consistently so. I managed to work my way through four pizzas and two calzones, and none of the crusts was less than perfect.

Each day there's a calzone and three pizzas, and a couple are always different from the day before. If you don't want a whole pizza, you can get a very generous slice, served hot, for just a few dollars. In short, Quadro is a pizza lover's heaven.

The toppings are innovative, the ingredients fresh and good. One night, for instance, there was an astonishingly tasty Mexican pizza of chorizo, peppers, onions, cilantro, and fresh basil. Particularly if the sausage is greasy, such a pizza can degenerate into a gloppy mess, but somehow this one managed to remain light and delicate.

With a pizza, you can get a first-rate green salad, lightly dressed and dusted with parmesan cheese. And, miraculously, there were even two good house wines (Calera's chardonnay and zinfandel) sold both by the bottle and by the glass.

With pizzas this good, you'll be tempted to skip the sandwiches, which will definitely prove a wise decision. They sound remarkable on paper ("grilled flank steak with parmesan, capers, lemon, arugula, hot pepper oil on rye" or "grilled chicken with tarragon mustard mayonnaise, cucumbers, watercress on semolina bread"). But more often than not they turned out to be simply a thin slice of meat on dry-tasting bread. You could open them up and see little smears of the advertised ingredients, but you couldn't taste anything but meat and bread.

Desserts at Caffe Quadro, as at Square One next door, are nothing less than fabulous. I tasted nine desserts over two dinners, and there wasn't anything that approached being a loser. The homemade ice creams and sorbets, in flavors like blood orange, pear-chocolate swirl, and strawberry-passion fruit, can't be duplicated at the best of our boutique ice cream stores. And pastries like the rhubarb crisp and a velvety chocolate cake match the ice cream in quality.

While the decor might be cold, service at Quadro goes a long way toward warming the place up. When it's crowded, you order and pick up your food at the counter. But the very helpful and concerned people who work there provide elements of table service when time allows.

In short, Quadro is a great place for pizza, salad, and dessert. It's also the restaurant of choice in San Francisco if you just want to stop in for dessert and an espresso drink. (Fortunately, they drew the line at coffee drinks, which are served in regular cups rather than styrofoam.) If you avoid the sandwiches, there's nothing wrong with Quadro that some china plates wouldn't cure. ∎

—Stan Sesser, March 7, 1986

California Culinary Academy

625 Polk Street (at Turk), San Francisco. 771-3500. A la carte lunches on balcony Monday through Friday, fixed-price lunches Monday through Thursday, buffet lunch Friday, fixed-price dinner Monday through Wednesday, buffet dinners Thursday and Friday. Full bar. Major credit cards. Reserve one month ahead for buffets, one day ahead for fixed-price meals. Moderate.

What is the most popular restaurant in San Francisco, judging from how long in advance you must make reservations? If you've never been there, you'll never guess. The answer is the California Culinary Academy, the cooking school whose graduates populate the kitchens of so many Bay Area restaurants. To get into the academy's Thursday and Friday Grand Classical Buffet dinners, you actually must make reservations two months ahead.

Why would people be breaking down the doors to spend over $20 (plus wine, coffee, and tip) for a dinner cooked by students? I was curious to find out, and also to see how the academy, which is owned by McKesson Corporation, is doing in its new Polk Street headquarters. So I went to a buffet, and also to one of the Monday-through-Wednesday fixed-price dinners.

For anyone who remembers the academy from its South of Market days, with the light and airy dining room and the glassed-in kitchens, the new location is going to come as something of a shock. The dining room is in an old building that once was an auditorium, renovated so that glassed-in kitchens replace what used to be the stage.

It sounds like a neat idea to eat in a former auditorium with sixty-foot ceilings, but that's not the way it works out. The decor is so dreary, and the building itself so undistinguished, that you feel like you're in the banquet hall of an old, slightly seedy hotel. The room is so big and the kitchens so far away that the feel of intimacy between students and diners is lost.

I was depressed by the setting, but even more depressed by the food. San Francisco is one of the premier cities in the world for experimentation with new and exciting dishes—chefs are outdoing each other to create things that are light and interesting and that capture the intensity of flavor and wonderful fresh ingredients.

But the Culinary Academy seemed locked in a time warp. There were leaden sauces, overcooked meats, and gooey desserts tasting of nothing but sugar and whipped cream. Even though some of the dishes on the buffet were quite decent, it was the sort of thing you'd expect from a cruise ship, not from a San Francisco school that trains chefs. Almost everything was bland, and almost everything would have been more appropriate on a buffet table thirty years ago.

The buffet procedure itself can be a stomach-wrenching challenge. First you make as many trips as you want to two huge tables overflowing with food. Then, when you're about ready to be dragged out in a wheelbarrow, the waiter brings the last thing you feel like tackling: a sit-down entree. (Everyone gets the same dish; my night it was veal scallopini.) Finally, if you can stagger back to your feet, there's a table of desserts.

The buffet table is the place to both start and stop. It had the only good food in my two dinners at the academy. There are no Jell-O molds here, no steam tables, no skimping on ingredients. You choose from pâtés, seafood mousses, poached salmon, and even chunks of fresh lobster buried under mounds of bay shrimp on a salad.

But except for the cold pasta with a first-rate pesto sauce, the one defect that ran through the buffet was lack of seasoning. Chinese chicken salad had nothing that made it taste Chinese. Celery root salad with ham and mushrooms tasted of little more than its boring, gloppy remoulade dressing. Blandness characterized everything from roast turkey to a squid salad.

The buffet could still be enjoyed because of the quality of the ingredients.

But there was little I could enjoy in what came after. The entree featured overly floured veal in a brown sauce that had separated by the time it reached the table. And the desserts were a disaster. The cakes and pastries seemed to be competing over which could contain the most sugar and whipped cream. Even the coffee was weak and foul tasting.

The fixed-price dinner provided a much more relaxed atmosphere. Instead of hordes of people elbowing each other, you're waited on by friendly students trying very hard to please, and you have time to talk with them about their training.

The fixed-price menu offers three or four choices for each course, and again I have no quarrel with the ingredients. But the food again was uniformly bad.

Each entree was hugely overcooked, and that was only the start of the problem. Veal medallions, topped by wild mushrooms cooked to mush, were overwhelmed by a sauce that resembled canned brown gravy. Mallard duck had been so overcooked that the slices of breast meat were gray and devoid of taste. And good-quality prawns were not only overdone, but came in a thick cheese-laden cream sauce that turned them into an intolerably heavy dish.

Appetizers and desserts were no better. An interesting pasta of agnolotti (round ravioli) stuffed with spinach and prosciutto was so salty it was hard to eat. Lemon chiffon cake offered no hint of lemon taste.

Normally, after a meal like this I'd walk out feeling ripped off. But at the Culinary Academy I instead felt sad that a new generation of chefs is apparently being taught nothing about the light innovative cooking that's proving to be so popular today. The students should demand more for their tuition. ■

—Stan Sesser, May 2, 1986

Calzone's

★

430 Columbus Avenue, San Francisco. 397-3600. Open daily 11 A.M. to 1 A.M. Full bar. MasterCard, Visa, American Express. Reservations accepted for six or more only. Moderate.

Nothing smells more delicious than a pizza pulled from a wood-burning brick oven. The pie, blackened around the edges, has absorbed the fragrance of the fire. Whatever toppings adorn the pie have been transformed by the moist, aromatic heat that comes from burning wood. Unfortunately, most of the fire-baked pizzas in the Bay Area come from California-inspired restaurants instead of old-world Italian joints with atmosphere. Now there's a new bar and cafe in North Beach that turns out wood-fired pizzas in an ambience so right for the neighborhood that it feels like it's been there forever.

Calzone's moved into a highly coveted spot on Columbus, right next to Caffe Roma, previously filled by Dante's. It's a shallow space that runs parallel to the street, giving every table in the house a closeup view of the passing parade on the sidewalk. When the sliding windows let in the breezes on warm days, Calzone's feels like a European outdoor cafe, but whoever designed it had pure North Beach in mind.

The outside facade is resplendent with black tile, like a number of buildings along Columbus. Red-and-black linoleum floors, green-and-black marbleized Formica tables trimmed with aluminum on black metal bases, and ceiling fans are not oddities to North Beach either. Weathered, dark, polished wood in the dining room and small bar area contribute to the vintage look. Glassed-in cabinets above the bar have been stocked with thousands of miniature liquor bottles, while shelves high on the dining room walls display a colorful array of Italian groceries. The whole grocery store scheme looks so natural and eye-catching that you want to sit there and take inventory. The brick pizza oven and a cramped cooking area framed by more black tile reminds me of trattorias I've seen in Italy. It makes me hungry just imagining what might come out of a kitchen that looks like this.

Some good pizzas do. They're about ten inches in diameter with thin, elastic crusts crisped by the fire. You don't choose your own toppings here, but select from a long list of house-created combinations, the most successful of which use salamis, sausages, prosciutto, and *pancetta* from Iacoppi butcher shop a few blocks away. "Sausage trio" pizza gets a layer of three crumbled sausages seasoned with nutmeg and chopped tomato beneath a creamy layer of mozzarella. It comes out tasting like a pizza covered with bolognese sauce. In the meatball version, tiny, light, well-seasoned Italian meatballs and fresh tomato are nestled under the cheese. A ground cover of pepperoni and tomato or a savory combo of anchovies with roasted red and yellow peppers make for two other fine pizzas. As a porcini lover, I appreciated the generous carpeting of these meaty, rehydrated mushrooms on porcini pizza. The other flavors on the pizza, some mild Italian bacon and a whisper of roasted garlic, were kept intentionally quiet.

Calzone's cheeseless pizzas turn out like vegetable tarts, as did a ratatouille pizza thickly spread with a tomatoey stew of roasted yellow squash and eggplant. Oddly enough, only four namesake calzone, or folded pizzas, are offered, and the one I sampled, filled with anchovies, raisins, black olives, pine nuts, and ricotta, tasted bland in spite of the intriguing list of ingredients.

Calzone's makes a fantastic appetizer composed of three shrimp, wrapped in prosciutto and then radicchio, marinated in garlic and olive oil, and then sauteed. There are a number of other creative appetizers, but I found them menacingly rich, like big slices of a torta made with mascarpone (Italian cream cheese) and basil served on oil-rich garlic toasts and thin slices of tomato with vinaigrette poured over all. It's delicious but hard to integrate into a meal. If one or two of the "colors" were forsaken in "grilled polenta tricolore," like the white gorgonzola or the green pesto melted into the polenta, already strewn with sauteed sausage, peppers, and radicchio, it would be a manageable appetizer. Fontina-stuffed squash blossoms were wonderfully crisp but, for once, needed an extra ingredient, an herb or a little bit of prosciutto, to make them into something.

A crunchy house salad of curly endive, carrots, cucumbers, and tomato with a good vinaigrette makes for a simple starter, as does an attractive and generous antipasto of roasted peppers, salami, and provolone with pitted black olives. Be sure you don't order a pizza with the same ingredients on it, though.

I did not care for the pastas. The noodles in every one I sampled were soft and mushy and flagrantly oversauced. The sauces, too, seemed odd. A room-temperature pasta soaked in a sauce of mushy fresh tomatoes, herbs, olives, and fontina tasted garbled instead of clean and summery. An unusual pasta with cilantro, peppers, tomatoes, tuna, and peas with two poached eggs cooked in the sauce came off as a tasty, Italian tuna-noodle casserole. I liked it but it was soggy. *Tortelli* of the day, made of green noodle dough stuffed with a passive ricotta filling, was slathered in a strange textured butter sauce with cheese melted into it, jarringly seasoned with tarragon.

After dishes as rich as these, you don't want dessert, but one afternoon my two-year-old blackmailed me into getting him a piece of truffle cake he spotted in a glass case. He ate the chocolate ribbons off the top and I polished the rest of it off with pleasure and an exceptionally good espresso. The airy, cream-filled layers were the lightest part of the meal.

I happen to live in North Beach and Calzone's is one of the few restaurants I visit in my neighborhood. I go for the pizzas, the shrimp appetizer, and the resonance of the place. It's open throughout the day and I love the way the room looks when the sun shines through the open windows in the quiet late afternoon. ■

—Patricia Unterman, July 27, 1986

Campton Place

★ ★ ★

340 Stockton Street, San Francisco. 781-5155. Open for breakfast Monday through Friday 7 to 11 A.M., Saturday 8 to 11:30 A.M.; for brunch Sunday 8 A.M. to 2:30 P.M.; for lunch Monday through Friday 11:30 A.M. to 2:30 P.M., Saturday noon to 2:30 P.M.; for dinner Sunday through Thursday 5:30 to 10 P.M., Friday and Saturday 5:30 to 10:30 P.M. Full bar. Major credit cards. Reservations advised. Expensive.

As the highly visible chef of nationally acclaimed Campton Place, Brad Ogden often must feel like a target in a shooting gallery. Every day he has to live up to his notices, which can be more difficult than getting them in the first place. Not only are restaurant critics eager to find lapses, but his customers walk into the dining room with high expectations. They're paying a lot of money for the cooking of this hotshot chef, and they want to be impressed. It's not easy being at the top. If you slip a little, it can be very embarrassing.

A chef of Brad Ogden's caliber has it harder than an actor, or a soloist of similar stature, let's say. These artists are judged on one or two performances. The play closes, the concert ends, the scrutiny is over. Their next endeavor gets a new set of notices. Ogden, on the other hand, has to put out three meals a day every day of the week and he's judged each time a plate is brought to the table. And most of the time, he's not actually cooking himself. His art as an inventive chef can only be gauged by his skill at kitchen management. He has to get a staff to turn out his food the way he wants it day after day. He fails as a restaurant chef if he can't grind it out.

Recently, Campton Place has been garnering some disgruntled reviews, easy enough to do when you serve bacon, lettuce, and tomato sandwiches for $12.50 and $50 breakfasts for two. Some surmise that the cause is because Odgen is too often away from the restaurant in his role of celebrity chef.

I wanted to judge for myself whether Campton Place was slipping. I made reservations for brunch, lunch, and dinner under an assumed name at busy hours. At brunch and dinner, Ogden was actually in the dining room, and I was recognized midway through those meals. I acknowledge that I know Ogden personally, but as a restaurant critic, I was at Campton to do my job: to judge the meals as objectively as possible. If the food coming out of his kitchen was sloppy, I was out to bust the restaurant.

I couldn't. All three meals were as meticulously prepared and served as befitting a three-star restaurant. What's more, the dinner menu had just been changed the night I was there, so it was the first time the kitchen staff had produced many of these dishes for a full dining room.

The dinner was the most brilliant of the meals at Campton Place. The substantial dinner dishes best express Ogden's style of including many different ingredients on one plate. Many of these food combinations are traditional in American cooking, but Ogden puts them together in a new way. For example, liver and bacon at Campton Place comes as a thick steak, grilled, topped with crisp strips of delicate Italian bacon, and placed on a bed of swiss chard, Italian mushrooms, and tiny, crusty red "creamer" potatoes. It really is the best and most elegant plate of liver you've ever eaten.

Ogden knows how to make the premier lamb chops in town. He trims, marinates, and grills them so that they turn out miraculously succulent. The tiny potato-and-wild-onion pancakes, the grilled baby corn ears, and red peppers make the plate look like a miniature garden. A grilled veal T-bone chop travels in a completely different direction with a finely cut ratatouille of eggplant and black olives and a creamy sauce infused with sharp sun-dried tomatoes.

In contrast to Ogden's natural ease with meats, his fish dishes seem fussy. There's too much going on, with sauces, relishes, and vegetables that ultimately don't enhance the fish, as was the case of a special preparation of grouper with shrimp salsa, three different kinds of mushrooms, and a basil-cream sauce. However, the two seafood appetizers at dinner are superb. A carpaccio of halibut in a sesame-scented vinaigrette made with Chinese black vinegar is the centerpiece of a stunning composition with anchovy toasts and a salad of pungent flat-leaf Italian parsley.

In another inspired creation, Ogden stuffed a snappy *pasilla* pepper with chunks of lobster and mild cheese, lightly battered and deep fried it, sauced it with a puree of roasted garlic, and garnished it with a blackbean salad flecked with lemon peel. Both a white corn soup with smoked-salmon cream and ravioli stuffed with goat cheese and smoked chicken were notable for their clean, forthright flavors.

For dessert, a plate of fresh figs arranged around nut-thick pistachio ice cream on caramel sauce wins my award for the loveliest seasonal dessert. The tingling fresh fruit sorbets and refreshing peach melba parfait made with juicy peaches and fresh raspberry puree also speak of summer.

At brunch, served on the weekends, look for the warm berry brioche pudding, buttery egg bread soaked in lemon custard garnished with fresh blackberries and raspberries. It's crisp on top, creamy on the bottom, and absolutely irresistible. If you like something resembling an ice cream sundae for breakfast, you'll be delighted with feather light peach pancakes rife with big chunks of ripe fruit, topped with a scoop of blackberry butter, and garnished with fresh berries. A rasher of thick-sliced bacon mysteriously goes well with the pancakes.

The signature breakfast dish at Campton Place, two poached eggs atop a flaky scone and prosciutto-thin slices of Missouri ham, all blanketed in orange hollandaise, was perfectly executed the day I had it. You have to like eggs benedict on the sweet rather than savory side to really love this dish. Your Wedgwood coffee cup is endlessly refilled and fresh-squeezed orange juice is poured into your glass as you sit down.

Lunch is the least interesting of the meals. Plates are scaled down in a way that doesn't allow all the Ogden twists and turns. No one could nitpick about the crunchy fried salt-and-pepper squid served with saffron aioli, but a corn crepe stuffed with shredded duck in a sweet-and-sour barbecue sauce didn't make sense; you couldn't tell what you were eating. Mundane linguine bathed in pesto was topped with whole grilled shrimp and piled into an unattractively small bowl. A wonderful crisp potato pancake was the highlight of a plate of rare slices of leg of lamb on a bed of vinegary wilted spinach.

One reason to eat at Campton Place any time is to dig through the basket of house-baked breads until you find the warm, buttery corn sticks, sometimes laced with jalapenos, sometimes with kernels of fresh sweet corn. What heaven!

I purposely visited Campton Place right after a two-week stay in Paris. That way, I felt I wouldn't be too shocked by the prices and my French three-star dining experiences would serve as a comparison. Well, the prices at Campton Place are painful, but comparable to those in New York and Paris, and you really do get something unique, highly refined, and delicious. On my three visits, there was never any question about the quality of ingredients, the carefulness of preparation, or that every dish had been rigorously thought through with an unifying aesthetic in mind—the mark of all great restaurants. ■

—Patricia Unterman, August 16, 1987

Capp's Corner

★ ★

1600 Powell Street, San Francisco. 989-2589. Open for lunch Tuesday through Friday 11:30 A.M. to 2:30 P.M.; for dinner Monday through Saturday 4:30 to 10:30 P.M., Sunday 4 to 10 P.M. Full bar. MasterCard, Visa. Reservations accepted. Inexpensive.

The family-style North Beach restaurant has suffered its ups and downs over the years in both quality and attendance. When La Pantera on Grant Street closed recently, I felt it was a bad omen for the genre. And when I heard that Joe Capp had sold Capp's Corner, I thought the end had arrived, until I heard that nomad chef Willy Bishop, famous within professional cooking circles, was working at Capp's. I rushed over for dinner, and sure enough, the food was wonderful. It satisfied the way only simple, hearty cooking made from real ingredients can. For a modest price, you walk out of Capp's Corner feeling like a million bucks.

Thankfully, Capp's decor hasn't been changed one bit. The old Victorian bar at the front of the restaurant still stays active all day with a neighborhood clientele presided over by Joe Capp in brown pinstripe suit, open collar, matching brown hat, and a twelve-inch stogie. He hasn't abandoned his place even though he sold it. The Celebrity Corner has remained intact with photos of the All Time Italian American Baseball Team, Italian boxers in action poses, and autographed star photos of actors like Jack Lord and Lorne Greene. This gallery is hung above an alcove of red-and-white-checked Formica tables with red vinyl banquettes and matching vinyl-seated wooden chairs. Ancient linoleum floors, acoustic ceilings, and plywood veneer walls give Capp's that authentic North Beach look. Modest though it is, Capp's dining room on weekday nights is sprinkled with sportscasters, private eyes, journalists, and guys who like to eat big.

What has changed is the food, not the

family-style format or the menu, but the quality. What before used to be standard steam table, poured-out-of-cans fare, is now fresh, lively, and infinitely better tasting.

One night dinner began with a tureen of fine minestrone soup made with real stock, lots of cabbage, celery, beans, and pasta tubes. The vegetables weren't cooked to death and the broth had a deep natural flavor. I could have made a meal out of the soup alone and I practically did, ladling myself three portions from the generous serving bowl. A crisp, hand-torn romaine salad that you toss and serve yourself was dressed in a basic, tart Italian vinaigrette amplified by garlic. A big slice of lasagna followed, homey, not too rich, but substantial with cheese and a good tomato sauce.

You get to choose your main course from seven or eight items and, believe it or not, you will not be let down even after all that preliminary eating. We were served tender, succulent slices of gently garlicked roast pork, half a baked chicken with a crisp skin and moist flesh, and spicy, lean Italian sausages in a chunky tomato-and-green-pepper sauce. Rosemary-scented roasted potatoes and the most delicious freshly cooked chard and zucchini accompanied the meats.

At early dinner one Sunday, a fabulous, peppery mushroom-barley soup made with the rich stock began the meal, which moved on to al dente *penne*, tube-shaped pasta, bathed in a beautiful light-green basil sauce made with butter and lots of parmesan. A large, thin veal T-bone chop was carefully grilled and served with a provencal-inspired sauce of peppers, mushrooms, and tomatoes, all finely minced and incorporated into reduced stock. The sauce tasted like something I'd just had at Fleur de Lys, where the same price would have bought just an appetizer.

Whenever Willy Bishop's calamari is posted on the blackboard, order it. He quickly sautes it with fresh tomatoes, red peppers, spicy green chilies, and whole leaves of basil with a sort of bolognese-sauce base. It's a Sicilian squid dish by way of Thailand. The squid stays indisputably fresh and delicately tender, bathed in the spicy vegetable stew.

The braised dishes can taste a little tired, like rabbit in tomato sauce, which had lost its spunk from spending too long in the stewing pot. *Osso buco*, a thick slice of veal shank simmered with mushrooms, tomatoes, and stock satisfied without thrilling. If you stick to the roasted meats, cooked-to-order chops, and sautes, you can't go wrong. These dishes were accompanied with the extraordinary sauteed vegetables, again freshly and crisply cooked. All meals end with passable coffee and commercial spumoni.

Willy Bishop might be the most knowledgeable cook that Capp's Corner has ever cornered in its antiquated kitchen. He started his career washing dishes in the early days of Chez Panisse, but soon started prepping and cooking. He left to run the excellent Wim's, the first of the nouveau diners, on the ground floor of Francis Ford Coppola's triangular building on Columbus and Kearny. Then it was off to Siam Cuisine on University Avenue in Berkeley, the Boonville Hotel, Pig by the Tail charcuterie, stints at Enrico's, Washington Square Bar & Grill, and Fourth Street Grill. He alternates travel with work. I think he considers cooking a form of travel and entertainment. At any rate, he taught himself how to cook. He knows quality ingredients and where to get them. He understands how to make something taste good by using fresh ingredients. He doesn't take shortcuts and you can taste this honesty in this amazingly inexpensive food. What's interesting is that these gargantuan, San Francisco-style Italian meals seem to express Willy Bishop's personal voice best of all. The meals I ate at Capp's Corner recently had character I never noticed before in "family-style" venues. Capp's Corner is the right place for Bishop and the new owners are lucky to have him.

I noticed, walking by the Capp's kitchen door on Green Street, some fresh sausages dangling from a rafter in the kitchen. Never have I seen a more positive sign of the rebirth of a restaurant than a chef making his own sausages. ■

—Patricia Unterman, November 9, 1986

Carmen & Family Bar-B-Que

★ ★

3252 Adeline Street (near Alcatraz), Berkeley. 652-RIBS. Also 692 West A Street, Hayward. 887-1979. Berkeley branch open daily 6 A.M. to 11 P.M.Hayward branch open Sunday through Thursday 11 A.M. to midnight, Friday and Saturday till 1 A.M. Beer, wine in Hayward; license pending in Berkeley. MasterCard, Visa, American Express, Carte Blanche. Reservations accepted in Berkeley. Inexpensive.

I get a lot of letters from readers recommending restaurants, and if the letters sound knowledgeable and enthusiastic, I put them in my "to be reviewed" pile. Sometimes it takes me six months to get around to trying the place.

But recently a letter came from a Berkeley architect that sent me flying out the door. It was three typewritten pages, single spaced, devoted entirely to extolling the virtues of a Berkeley barbecue called Carmen & Family. A few months ago, I had had some not-too-unkind words to say about Flint's Bar-B-Q in Oakland, and here's how the architect responded to that:

"You say that Flint's hot sauce is the reason for human existence on this planet. Ha! Carmen's explains the cosmos from beginning to end. Say Hallelujah."

But when I walked into Carmen's on a Sunday night, I immediately encountered what I'll call an "ambience problem." The place was clean; "60 Minutes" was playing on the television. Most shocking of all, when I ordered the brisket of beef, the counterman looked up at me and asked, "Would you like that beef well trimmed, sir?"

This is a barbecue? If I can alter the famous line of Calvin Trillin a bit: "Patronizing a shiny-clean barbecue with a polite counterman is like going to a gentile internist. It might all work out okay in the end, but the odds are against it."

Well, it all worked out okay in the end. If you want links, continue going to Flint's. Flint's links remind you of your transgression as much as three days later, while Carmen's, although meaty and totally grease free, lack that extra zip.

But for ribs, I have to admit that Carmen's beats out Flint's hands down. Carmen's ribs have been done to perfection, just to the point where the fat vanishes but the meat doesn't start drying out. They're relatively small, totally tender, and free of grease and gristle.

Then there's the hot sauce. I described Flint's hot sauce as being capable of taking the bark off trees. That's a good start for a hot sauce, but in retrospect I think Flint's fails in one key characteristic: It has an unpleasantly acrid aftertaste, to my palate a sign of overdoing it on the Liquid Smoke.

Carmen's hot sauce, I swear, is even more fiery than Flint's. You scream, cry, blow your nose, gasp for air—then plunge in for more. But it also has a wonderfully pleasant balance, if "pleasant" can be a proper word for something that makes you clutch your throat, jump up and down, and bang your head against the wall.

I called the proprietor, Abe Kelly (who runs it along with his wife Carmen), and asked him the secret of the sauce. He started out talking about "three different peppers." Then there was silence, much like the CIA agent at a bar who suddenly realizes he has been spilling defense secrets.

If that hot sauce sounds just a shade too hot for you, I'll give my blessing to the medium sauce, too. It's not as sweet as most, and its heat level is actually quite impressive.

Now let's deal with the rest of the menu. The chicken is delicious, the first really good chicken I've had at a barbecue place whose main draw is ribs. The two are generally incompatible, since an oven capable of blasting away the fat on ribs will turn the much more delicate chicken into sawdust. But Carmen's chicken remains juicy, with a nice smoky taste.

The ham and beef simply can't compete with the ribs and chicken. They're decent, with the beef commendably free of fat and gristle. But great brisket of beef is the hardest thing to get. My last two times at Flint's the beef was disappointing, and even when a friend brought me some from Sonny Bryant's in Dallas, it was a bust. The first time I had tasted Sonny Bryant's brisket, I thought I had gone to heaven.

As for the potato salad, if anyone has ever had a good potato salad from a barbecue joint, they're one up on me. And for bread, Carmen's offers homemade corn bread instead of the usual balloon bread, a nice alternative had the corn bread not been so dry.

If Abe and Carmen Kelly run an unusual barbecue place, it might be because they have an unusual background for it. They grew up in Jamaica and lived for twenty years in England, where he was an engineer and she a nurse. Six years ago they opened their first barbecue in Hayward. They started the much larger place in Berkeley (it has lots of tables and counter stools) because so many of their Hayward customers were driving down from Berkeley.

Instead of a conventional brick barbecue oven, the Berkeley branch has a newly developed 2,000-pound steel cooker mounted on wheels. It comes from, of all places, Mesquite, Texas, but the Kellys fuel it with black oak. They say that one of its virtues is that it gives them control over the final product; the ribs come out tasting the same each time.

So now, with the appearance of Carmen and Family, we can resurrect our great barbecue debate all over again. When I recommended Flint's, half the letters I got were ecstatic, and the other half dismissed me as a madman. I'm curious to see what the mail on Carmen and Family will bring. ∎

—Stan Sesser, November 1, 1985

Celadon

★★

881 Clay Street, San Francisco. 982-1168. Open daily 8 A.M. to 3 P.M., 5:30 to 11 P.M. Full bar. Major credit cards. Reservations accepted. Moderate.

After the holiday season with its hams and rib roasts and pounds of butter cookies, many of us want a respite from rich, fatty foods. Sushi or steamed fish and vegetables take on new appeal. The Celadon, an elegantly appointed Chinese restaurant, allows you to slide into a little post-holiday austerity without giving up all the fun.

This is one of the dressy Chinese restaurants in Chinatown. The mysterious gray-green color of celadon pottery, after which the restaurant was named, makes its appearance in the carpeting, the napkins, and on interior columns. The white-linen-covered tables are set with rice-shot porcelain teacups, silver soup spoons, candles in lamps, and a clever little silver rack upon which to lay chopsticks and other utensils between courses. Upholstered banquettes and solid, tall-backed lacquered chairs provide dignified seating. The front door of Celadon, a huge piece of cast bronze, lets you know right off that money was spent on building this restaurant. Yet for all its flourishes and amenities, Celadon remains a moderately priced restaurant, less expensive and more satisfying than the older Grant Avenue contingent of high-priced Chinese restaurants.

You can get a meal made up of delicacies like Peking duck, steamed lobster, and deep-fried squab for about $25 a person, and this is with formal table service in which dishes are brought out sequentially, presented, and then carefully arranged on individual plates. Warm towels appear after courses that require the use of fingers. The whole experience is carefully orchestrated. Everything is done for you at a leisurely pace that allows for good talk around the table. You feel pampered and civilized at your meals at Celadon.

The menu is reassuringly small by the standards of most Chinese restaurants. Dishes from a number of different provinces are represented, though the kitchen seems most at home with Cantonese-style cooking. Celadon reminds me of restaurants in Hong Kong that cater to the prosperous and demanding middle class.

The lobster dishes are unique here, especially "steamed lobster, Celadon style," which is served in a small amount of intensely flavored broth infused with garlic and actually thickened with melted scallions and lobster fat. The tender meat, which easily came out of the shell, and the sweet lobster tomalley were tip-offs that the lobster was alive seconds before it was steamed. My only regret was that I didn't have a piece of french bread to soak up the fantastic liquid. A similar dish, "lobster steamed in garlic sauce," was more delicate. Its light, clear, aromatic sauce had the pungent but nonintrusive quality of long-simmered garlic.

Another unusual dish at Celadon, a soup called coconut nectar that is cooked and presented in a coconut, tastes and looks like a chowder except that the milk comes from fresh coconuts instead of a cow. The brewing in the coconut produces a lovely white, aromatic broth that is studded with tiny shrimp, bits of winter melon, and pine nuts. I've had something like it only in Hong Kong, where another featured Celadon dish, squab Shatin, originated. This is a preparation for squab lovers, for those who like the gamy quality of pigeon. The aged birds are deep fried with absolutely no spices or aromatics. The skin emerges dark and crisp, the flesh deep brown and creamy. You dip the pieces into finely ground white pepper and salt for seasoning.

There are plenty of familiar dishes on the menu as well. Pot stickers are just about perfect here, with thin, tender noodle coverings and juicy meat fillings. Oddly enough, the cured-ham-filled spring rolls were way too salty and soggy with oil. A better appetizer choice was "minced squab in a green purse," a crunchy dice of squab, fresh water chestnuts, pine nuts, and black mushrooms quickly stir-fried and presented in iceberg lettuce cups. You roll up the leaves and eat them with your fingers.

Seafood is fresh and sensitively cooked here. Clams in black bean sauce were big but tender with an assertive sauce, musky with fermented black beans, aromatic with ginger and scallion. The powerful sauce well matched the strong-flavored Pacific clams. "Prawns of three provinces," much recommended by the staff, were indeed magically plump, juicy, and translucent while still being cooked all the way through, but their sauces were tame, even the spicy and hot provincial representatives. This is a dish mostly about texture for shrimp lovers.

One of the most addictively tasty dishes in all of Chinese cuisine is Peking duck, and Celadon makes a worthy production of it. Both soft white steamed buns and thin white pancakes serve as receptacles for the burnished ducks, skillfully sliced at tableside by the white-gloved maitre d'. Bits of skin with crisply rendered duck fat and velvet-textured meat are stuffed into the buns and crepes along with a swipe of sweet black bean sauce and wisps of scallion. What a combination! The dish is so rich that one scrawny-looking duck serves four easily, making it affordable to order it as the centerpiece of your meal.

After lobster and duck, it's always nice to eat some simply steamed vegetables. Celadon finishes off both steamed Chinese broccoli and bok choy with a quick turn in the wok in the lightest of sauces. Bowls of rice are served at the end of the meal unless requested sooner. Share Celadon's coconut custard for dessert. It has the flavor of real coconuts.

I encountered a few problems during my visits and most of them had to do with the formal tone of the restaurant. There were some embarrassing rough edges in the dining room—tablecloths were not smoothed down, plates and silver were smudged. Also, the food was consistently not hot enough. The considerable amount of time the waiters spend at tableside presenting and serving means that they must pick up food from the kitchen the second it is done and serve it on very hot plates. If Celadon is going to provide all this table service, they need better organization. I'd like to see more equilibrium between the kitchen and the dining room. ■

—Patricia Unterman, January 4, 1987

Cha Cha Cha

★

1805 Haight Street, San Francisco. 386-5758. Open for lunch Monday through Saturday 11:30 A.M. to 3 P.M.; for dinner Monday through Thursday 5 to 11:30 P.M., Friday and Saturday 5:30 to 11:30 P.M., Sunday 5:30 to 10 P.M. Wine, beer. No credit cards. No reservations. Inexpensive.

Every time I visit the Haight these days, I'm delighted by it. The neighborhood is blossoming with a bunch of colorful small restaurants, shops, and clubs intermingling with the old, firmly rooted places. The area boasts a clientele as diverse and imaginative as to be found anywhere in the city. Gay, straight, young (um, fortyish), the Haight has cast off its seventies drug-culture-turned-nasty image to become a meeting place for those who want to dress, eat, drink, bowl, and dance casually, relatively inexpensively but with style. I know that the Haight Ashbury Neighborhood Council feels that the neighborhood is falling prey to soulless gentrification, and the opposing Haight Ashbury Improvement Association thinks there are too many drug rehabilitation centers, but whatever standoff these two active neighborhood groups achieve, their community remains one of the most unique in the city.

I had dinner one night at a vibrant little place called Cha Cha Cha, which represents the best of the Haight. It's a complete original. Half of a storefront, the dining room has one tall brick wall stenciled with palm trees and a high ceiling with green latticework that sprouts spotlights in different colors. The whole place must have been put together on a shoestring, but the ideas all work. When you walk in, smells of spicy grilled meats whet your appetite, the best effect of all.

Most likely every seat will be taken, so you move to the back of the restaurant, past three wooden booths painted red and blue and five or six tables to a tiled tapas bar with a few stools. A bulbous glass jar of sangria sits at one end, afloat with orange slices. You can wait there agreeably for a table, eating tapas and drinking glasses of sangria.

As our group ate charred, grilled, marinated whole sardines, which were absolutely delicious, and succulent marinated chicken wings, which had picked up a wonderful flavor from the grill, bathed in a dusky garlic sauce, I learned that one of my party happened to be the chairman of the above-mentioned improvement association.

Over thin strips of beef coated with searing hot, cracked black pepper in a cream sauce and peeled shrimp in a fantastic, hot Cajun sauce pink with cayenne, I found out about neighborhood struggles to keep a Round Table Pizza franchise out of the former site of the Grand Piano.

At a booth set with abstract black-and-white plastic place mats we continued with conversation and tapas. Piquant cold mussels on the half shell topped with a fresh tomato-and-onion relish had an authentic Caribbean-Creole flavor. Thinly sliced scallops were chewy but full of the pungent flavors of garlic, red and yellow peppers, and white wine with which they were sauteed. Because the kitchen was out of squid baked in onion and beer, we ordered New Orleans–style BBQ shrimp that were overcharred and acrid with a gritty, spicy-hot sauce, the only tapa I didn't like.

The main courses are not as much fun as the little dishes, though several are excellent. A Spanish-style panfried trout, crisp and succulent, got a sprightly sherry-and-browned-butter sauce. I also like a blackened hamburger that stayed moist and rare, with a side of creamy sauce infused with Cajun spices. A thin breast of chicken dijon came off the grill burnt and juiceless, as did a fillet of blackened red snapper from the frying pan. All this blackening can get tedious if it means that the food to be darkened loses all its character. A New York steak smothered with sauteed red peppers was okay, a little tough, a little watery, but certainly priced well. All these entrees come with mashed potatoes and carrots and a medley of vegetables sauteed with too much dried oregano. You also get a tiny cup of soup with them. A cilantro-and-chili-spiked chicken soup that was hot, lemony, and full of big chunks of chicken was so good it should be offered as a separate course.

And there's even something satisfying for dessert, a chocolate mousse cake with raspberry sauce that's creamy, light, and not too sweet. A flan had industrial-strength texture.

The unifying theme behind all the food seems to be a Caribbean-Creole mix of Spanish, Cuban, African, and Latin American flavors. The emphasis is on spices and hot chilies. Most everything has a kick to it, just like the cha cha.

A young French waiter felt right at home with the cuisine and the ambience. He guided us straight to the best tapas, which change often. With ironic detachment, a sense of humor, and complete efficiency, he kept things rolling, never intruding yet projecting a whimsical personality. I wish American waiters could figure out how to do it, especially without having to tell us their names and social security numbers.

As we strolled down Haight Street afterward, reminiscing about the apartments we shared, the clothes we bought from stores that we were passing, and old books we'd found in the used bookstores, I happened to notice a new, clean, white cafelike space with bentwood chairs and wooden tables.

"Hey, what's that?," I asked the Haight Street resident.

"It's the Round Table Pizza that I told you about," he said.

It was the most disguised, homegrown Round Table branch I'd ever seen. In fact, it blended right into the neighborhood. I don't know how popular it will be if places as terrific as Cha Cha Cha are around, but it proves that a neighborhood can mold its businesses to suit its tastes. ■

—Patricia Unterman, February 16, 1986

The Cheese Board
★

See review for Blondie's Pizza.

Chevys
★★

2400 Mariner Square, Alameda (take the first right after the Alameda tunnel). 521-3768. Open Monday through Thursday 11:30 A.M. to 3 P.M. and 5 to 10 P.M., Friday to 11 P.M., Saturday 11 A.M. to 11 P.M., Sunday 11 A.M. to 10 P.M. MasterCard, Visa, American Express. Full bar. Reservations for eight or more only. Inexpensive to moderate.

I recently read an article that claimed restaurants have replaced movies as the leading form of entertainment. People don't want just a meal now; they want an evening of fun. And restaurateurs are responding to this trend with "theme" restaurants—little Disneylands of dining that do for adults what Chuck E. Cheese Pizza Time Theaters tried to do for kids.

My reaction to all this is not exactly positive. Such restaurants tend to have proprietors who spend millions on decor, then try to get it back by cutting corners on food—if they even give their food that much thought.

So I was less than inspired by the letters I got from Warren (Scooter) Simmons, owner of two fish restaurants on Pier 39 and son of the original owner of the Tia Maria chain, about his new Mexican restaurant in Alameda called Chevys. "We'll use bare light bulbs with hub caps for light fixtures," one letter promised, "rumble seats for some of our booths, and maybe a radiator grill or two thrown in for effect."

Nor was I convinced by Simmons's claim that the food would be authentic and would reflect "my time and effort traveling throughout Mexico gathering local recipes." You wonder a bit about authenticity when you learn that the two head chefs are French Canadian and American.

In some ways, Chevys realized my fears. With the cutesy decor and funny Spanish signs, and with the mobs of people being shunted upstairs to the bar (in business terminology known as the "profit center"), it had all the hallmarks of a theme-restaurant operation. Nothing about the place—including the waiters, who were definitely not Mexican and who knew little about the food—promised an authentic Mexican meal.

Amazingly, unlike what you see in most Mexican restaurants in these parts, Chevys has actually taken care to procure fresh first-rate ingredients, and not to cook them to death in heavy sauce. It works beautifully, making a new taste experience out of what so often can be a leaden cuisine.

Take the roll-your-own tacos, for instance. You get a basket of hot flour tortillas made fresh by an impressive Rube Goldberg-like machine that's smack in the middle of the restaurant. Then, instead of the usual indifferent ground or shredded beef, comes a red-hot platter of sizzling slices of skirt steak and chicken breast that have been marinated and mesquite grilled. (Simmons claims the steak comes from Texas and costs three times as much as the California equivalent, and when you taste it you won't disagree.) There's also a mound of very fresh-tasting guacamole and beans that have been delicately simmered in an aromatic sauce rather than being refried. When you wrap all this in a tortilla, it adds up to heaven—the best taco ever.

The quality of the ingredients is reflected in more than the tacos. The salsa is made hourly from fresh-chopped tomatoes. The chips are fried every fifteen minutes and often come to the table hot. The *chile relleno* is actually made from a fresh poblano chili and stuffed with a fluffy Monterey jack cheese that's superb.

What Chevys does extraordinarily well is the mesquite grilling. There are several dishes involving the skirt steak, and they're all wonderful. Two dishes that come more from California cuisine than from Mexico—grilled swordfish and quail—are perfect, juicy, succulent, and not over-cooked. I can't remember eating better or fresher swordfish in any fish restaurant.

As for the traditional Tex-Mex food, everything could use a bit more spicing up, but the ingredients make it worthwhile. It's all so delicately prepared that you can load up on enchiladas, tamales, and the like and not feel queasy.

Appetizers generally were much weaker than entrees. The ceviche featured lots of marinated raw fish, but it tasted as if it had been sitting in the refrigerator far too long. *Chile con queso* was a disgusting bowl of melted Velveeta-like cheese with a few little pieces of tomato and chili thrown in. Tortilla soup was inedibly salty. I'd stick with the *queso fundido*, a great combination of melted jack and chorizo (sausage) that you roll in a tortilla.

There's an added bonus at Chevys. While the building is only ten years old, it looks like a funky restored old house and provides a very pleasant place to eat. The back wall is glassed in, with a spectacular view of the Oakland estuary. Outside are shoreline footpaths.

The service adds to the pleasant experience. The waiters are uniformly friendly and helpful, and constant refills of salsa, tortillas, and chips come without asking. Nor will the prices cast a pall on the evening. Portions are huge.

In short, Chevys is one theme restaurant that works. It shows what can happen when someone remembers that the purpose of a restaurant is to serve good food. ∎

—Stan Sesser, September 19, 1986

Chez T.J.

938 Villa Street, Mountain View. 964-7466. Open Tuesday through Saturday 5:30 to 9:30 P.M., Friday 11:30 A.M. to 2 P.M. Beer, wine. No smoking. MasterCard, Visa. Reservations essential, two weeks in advance for weeknights, three weeks for weekends. Moderate.

So many French restaurants in the U.S. have such intimidatingly formal service that you'd suppose they were imitating what goes on in France. But that isn't true; the best restaurants in France try to make everyone feel completely comfortable, no matter how idiosyncratic the customer might be.

Consider by contrast what happened at Chez T.J., a fancy French restaurant in Mountain View so popular that you have to reserve two weeks in advance even for weeknights. I ordered for all of us, and the waiter asked who was having which dish. I said it didn't matter, since we were splitting everything. But the waiter flatly refused, saying he couldn't offer proper service unless he was told where each dish was to be placed. He ended up walking away looking shaken by our boorishness.

That was the atmosphere that prevailed all evening, formal enough to make you squirm. A tuxedo-clad busboy stood stiffly by the table. At least eight times during the dinner various people asked us whether everything was satisfactory, and I think each would have gasped and expired on the spot had we said anything but a formal yes.

But in fact, with just a couple of exceptions, everything turned out to be considerably less than satisfactory. Other than an exemplary cheese course and one excellent entree, I found that everything else ranged from mundane to seriously botched. My experience was dramatically different from that depicted in a rave review in the January issue of *Gourmet*.

It's too bad, because Chez T.J., named after the chef, Thomas J. McCombie, has a lot going for it. The first is the setting, a beautiful old house with tables in several rooms, so that the dining experience becomes wonderfully intimate.

Second is the limited menu. Too many French restaurants try to be all things to all people. Chez T.J. offers an elaborate fixed-price dinner changing every two weeks, with no more than three choices in any category. You can't order a la carte, but there are two slimmed down versions of the fixed-price dinner, costing proportionately less.

With so few things to concentrate on, I'd expect the kitchen to send out dishes that were little jewels in taste and presentation. But instead the experience was more like a walk down the costume jewelry aisle of a dime store.

Consider, as a prime example, "Chez T.J.'s special smoked salmon with lemon dill sauce." It's a simple matter to make bright-colored smoked salmon slices look beautiful on a plate. But in T.J.'s version, the salmon was hacked into tiny little bits and served in a mound. Then the dill sauce was spooned over it.

Although the hacking ruined the salmon, the sauce did have lots of fresh dill flavor. But that was about the only flavor present in any appetizer.

A miserably tough, underdone artichoke came with what was advertised as goat cheese stuffing, but it had absolutely no taste and the consistency of Cool Whip. There wasn't a hint of pea flavor in the chilled split-pea soup, just a vague sort of bitterness. Sliced marinated beef was totally innocuous. Mediocre bread and butter that tasted slightly rancid didn't help get the appetizers down.

While I normally welcome creativity, two of T.J.'s dishes went beyond innovative to the weird. A dry, overcooked, flavorless piece of halibut was served in a sauce of red wine and cherries. And a salad, ice cold as if it had just been taken out of a refrigerator, mixed spinach and strawberries. Spinach and strawberries?

There were a couple of odd touches among the entrees, too. Rack of lamb, which was actually a nice piece of meat, had yogurt spooned all over it—not a sauce that included yogurt, but what tasted like pure yogurt, so that the sourness of the yogurt overwhelmed the lamb's flavor. As for the chicken quenelles with pasta, no one at the table got anything more out of them than the sensation of flour.

How, then, can I explain the peppered beef sauteed with foie gras? Tender beef with a crisp, peppery crust was served over delicate sauteed slices of goose liver and a beautiful sauce. It was perfect, and so was the cheese course that followed—as nice a selection of imported cheeses as I've seen in the U.S.

Desserts were back to the more familiar pattern. Boring orange slices were doused with burned-tasting caramelized *crème à l'anglaise*. A chocolate-walnut torte, with stale-tasting walnuts, was dense as a chocolate bar. Grand Marnier ice cream had an icy texture, and tasted much too strongly of the liqueur.

The beef entree and the skillfully selected cheese gave at least a hint that someone in Chez T.J.'s kitchen knew how to do things right. But that hint was swept away by a flood of boring or flawed dishes. It's too bad, because the lovely old building provides such an ideal setting that you're hoping for a great meal. ■

—Stan Sesser, June 5, 1987

Chiang Mai

★

5020 Geary Boulevard, San Francisco. 387-1299. Open Monday through Saturday 11:30 A.M. to 3 P.M., 5 to 10:30 P.M., Sunday 4 to 10 P.M. Beer, wine. MasterCard, Visa, American Express, Diners Club. Reservations accepted. Inexpensive.

Chiang Mai is a cheerful little Thai restaurant decorated with large fans, carved wood statues, delicate hanging light fixtures, and a window that looks up into a cymbidium garden with a fountain. A visiting raccoon uses the water to moisten his food. He probably wants to get his claws around some of the good stuff being cooked inside.

Chiang Mai is named after a city in northern Thailand where the food is heartier, simpler, and less sweet than the cooking of Bangkok. The area around Chiang Mai is the home of sticky rice, so firm you can eat it with your hands, and searing-hot beef and pork stews and "dips."

Though most Thai restaurants in San Francisco list the same dishes on their menus, including Chiang Mai, each kitchen interprets them differently. Some cook with more chilies, others with more fragrant Thai herbs. And everyone uses the Thai version of soy sauce, called *nam pla* or fish sauce, their own way. As a Westerner who adores the hot and spicy food, I don't happen to like a strong, fermented fish sauce flavor. The Southeast Asian restaurants I prefer use fish sauce subtly, much like good Western cooks use salt. You shouldn't notice either its absence or presence.

At Chiang Mai, the main-course curries, seafood-studded coconut custard, and the noodle dishes were well-balanced, but the appetizers and Thai salads weren't as skillfully made as the rest of the menu. Beef salad and squid salad were dominated by fish sauce and too much raw red onion. The deep frying of stuffed chicken wings and dry Thai egg rolls wasn't clean enough. However, the few regional dishes on the menu were particularly vigorous and intriguing. The staff is trained to take orders by number, and the numbers I've listed here signify the northern Thai dishes.

Number 31, *num-plik-onge*, a rich, fiery stew of minced pork simmered with chili paste and tomatoes, is meant to be eaten like a dip, scooped up by big slices of cool cucumber and chilled raw cabbage. The contrasts in temperature and texture are exhilarating. Number 51, *kao-soy* Chiang Mai, is a wonderful northern noodle dish that you can regulate yourself. The heart of the dish is a stew of tender sweet-and-sour beef, long cooked in a delicious coconut milk curry sauce. The chunks of meat come on a bed of soft egg noodles, the top scattered with crisp deep-fried noodles. You toss in at table some of the hottest, most-innocent-looking, clear chili sauces and a plate of raw bean sprouts. This net result is absolutely delicious.

Another standout at this restaurant is a seafood dish called *hor-mork*. If you see it posted on the blackboard, order it, because it's one of the most captivating Thai dishes I've tasted. Coconut milk and curry paste is cooked for hours to form a silky, eggless custard. A mixture of diced seafood and fresh basil is folded into it and then it's steamed to order in banana leaf bowls. The flavors are subtle and the texture as tender as the most delicate crème brûlée.

Number 48, a stir-fry of spinach, green beans, Chinese cabbage, and bean cake topped with curried peanut sauce, employs the freshest of vegetables and the lightest of sauces, and a roast duck curry gets a lovely, orange coconut milk sauce.

For dessert you must order a tropical Thai banana split with a deep-fried banana, with exotic palm fruit and jackfruit taking the place of pineapple and strawberries. It's perfect after a meal of searing northern Thai specialties. ■

—Patricia Unterman, March 29, 1987

China Moon Cafe

★★★

639 Post Street, San Francisco. 775-4789. Dim sum lunch served Monday through Saturday 11:30 A.M. to 2:30 P.M.; dinner Monday through Saturday 5:30 to 10:15 P.M.; late-night supper Friday and Saturday 10:15 to 11 P.M. Wine, beer. MasterCard, Visa, American Express. Reservations accepted. Moderate.

Barbara Tropp, the diminutive non-Asian Chinese chef and cookbook author, garnered so much publicity for her first restaurant, which literally never got off the ground, that the actual opening of her more modest China Moon almost seemed anticlimactic. Her followers, among which I number, were expecting a restaurant on the scale of Square One or Stars. What opened, instead, was a small, wittily resurrected Chinese "cafe" with Formica booths and a lunch counter. The odd thing about this place is that its miniature size and informality suits Tropp's hearty cooking and meticulous personality better than any other imaginable venue. China Moon is one of those brilliant, eccentric, personal restaurants that happen once in a blue moon.

Tropp takes a fresh look at Chinese cooking as we know it in San Francisco. She uses predominantly Chinese ingredients and cooking techniques, except for desserts, but her dishes do not come off as traditional Chinese food. It is Tropp Chinese, an invented cuisine, a cuisine filtered through the taste and imagination of this intense, perfection-seeking chef.

My most recent dinner there was stunning. A tender, perfumed breast of five-spice duck served as the centerpiece for a Peking antipasto plate. The succulent meat was balanced by very hot, juicy cabbage pickle and a pile of fragrant, elegantly thin chili-orange noodles. Crisp, sweet white pastry buns were stuffed with a melange of wild and domestic mushrooms stewed together in oyster sauce. The filling tasted like some kind of rich, exotic meat. Little plates of spicy red-onion pickles, sweet and sour, hot and garlicky, went beautifully with everything. "Twice-wrapped sausage on a bed of leeks, red bell peppers, and onions" came in a parchment packet that enclosed thick slices of aromatic, greaseless Chinese pork sausage.

The soup that evening, "cosmic chaos," looked as poetic as its name. Fat, gossamer-skinned won tons, filled with a rough, flavorful fish mousse, chunky with bits of water chestnuts and shrimp, shared a bowl of clear, peppery, not too gingery chicken broth with carrot threads and tiny spinach leaves.

The main courses present more of a challenge to Tropp than the appetizers. She's trying to force big plates out of the entrees and the result can be tiresome, especially after the liveliness of the first courses. However, everyone that evening was excited by a vibrant, spicy, velvety stir-fry of lamb shreds, red pepper, and snap peas in hoisin sauce thrown over a crisp, brown noodle pancake. As a matter of fact, it disappeared immediately, as did two deep-fried soft-shell crabs in a disconcertingly sweet lemon sauce. (As far as I'm concerned, soft shells should be sauteed and finished off with a little butter. Any other treatment is travesty.) Wonderful stir-fried baby bok choy and some dull, greasy almond fried rice came with them. I have found that there are never enough greens on the entree plates and too much rice. Why not offer everything a la carte — rice, vegetables, main courses — and let people decide how they want to put their meal together? Most of the kitchen-chosen matchups have not been all that profound. I also miss not having a bowl of clean, high-quality steamed rice to eat with the saucy stir-fried dishes. The rice bowl presents a hearty way of eating that I don't like to give up.

For example, that night there was a tasty dish called "spicy lettuce-wrapped chicken" that came on a big plate with lettuce leaves and almond fried rice. The delicate, celery-scented, chilie-spiked chicken stir-fry seemed to get lost among the leaves and the rice. Everything should have been presented in separate bowls and plates to maintain its integrity.

A beef and vegetable stew in a sand pot had the opposite problem. The big chunks of lean beef, carrots, turnips, and whole red potatoes in a thin, cassia-blossom-scented gravy had not cooked together long enough to develop into a stew. The juices of the different ingredients didn't enrich each other.

Desserts are frankly Western and sweet. House-made ice creams like refreshing lime rum or vibrant olallie berry are heavy with cream and full of flavor, the scoops so big they can be shared. There are delicious berry tartlets with bright lemon-cream fillings and a tongue-startling sundae that uses peppery ginger ice cream and a lovely bittersweet chocolate sauce. My favorite dessert is the selection of thin, delicate cookies and buttery bars that come in seven different flavors. When all seven are fresh, they finish off the meal perfectly, better than any other of the desserts.

Each time I visit China Moon it gets better, more assured, more satisfying. Yes, there are things that annoy me about it—the carafes of tepid chlorinated tap water placed on the tables, the music turned up too loud, the uncomfortableness of the benches in the booths. But these seem like quibbles in light of the creativity, thought, and continual striving for improvement that goes on in this restaurant. China Moon is a rare beast, a one-of-a-kind restaurant that deserves to be nurtured, forgiven, and put up with so that it will continue growing. You can't tell how good this restaurant will turn out to be; it shows endless potential. ■

—Patricia Unterman, June 15, 1986

Dim Sum Lunch

★★★

Barbara Tropp recently has abandoned her regular menu at lunch and instituted a dim sum menu that provides one of the most remarkable dining experiences in the city. Rarely have I seen so many current eating trends converge in one place so comfortably. Here you eat only starters and small dishes of spicy food presented with a great deal of style.

The dim sum format, hardly an innovation of Tropp's, fits today's new lunching habits perfectly because you can eat lightly or substantially by choosing from twenty or so little dishes of food. The dim sum dishes, as expressed at China Moon, are varied and colorful. Some are hot and spicy, some cold and clean, others rich, simple, complicated, smooth or crisp, but always exotic. Though many strong and unusual flavors characterize these dishes, they're never awkward or unexpected. Tropp's cooking shows solid technique, learned from studying traditional Chinese cooking. Foods are not taken out of context, as they are in the new Chinese-French marriage, yet each dish is a personal creation. I think China Moon has been working toward this clarification all along.

The meal starts with a bamboo tray of cold dishes, each in a celadon leaf-shaped bowl. The gay colors of the foods and the ceramics make the tiny portions of food irresistible. There are deep-brown glazed pecans; pale-green peking pickled cabbage; sweet, hot, and crisp japanese cucumber fans; aromatically spiced red onion pickles; fat tan triangles of caramelized tofu; mysteriously seasoned strange-flavor eggplant; and pearly white cubes of fresh water chestnuts, a simple delicacy. The pickling on these cold dishes is something to admire. Each pickle has a different flavor and texture and none is too sour.

Unlike Chinese dim sum houses, the

next tier of foods is ordered off the menu. They're brought all together and assembled on the table, forming a lush, brilliantly colored landscape.

The chicken salad looks like an exotic bird of paradise with its bright-orange carrot threads, swirled white daikon radish threads, paper-thin slices of green chili, black sesame seeds, creamy-white chicken breast, and whole chinese parsley leaves all in a tangy dijon mustard vinaigrette, with the plate separated in the middle by whole chives. Fried-noodle pancakes are cut in wedges and lavished with gorgeous stir-fried peppers, yellow and green beans, miraculously tender strips of marinated pork, tree ears, scallions, and triangles of wok-grilled white onion in a dark, delicious, unthickened sauce. The portion is huge but you'll eat every bit of it, especially as the crispy noodles soak up the stir-fry juices.

Strange-flavor sparerib nuggets, a stew of thick meaty pork bones in a dusky black bean sauce, goes with riotously colorful shanghai vegetable rice, smoky pearl rice studded with carrots, egg ribbons, decoratively cut snow peas, and bok choy flowers. Lively by itself and superb with the ribs, there's nothing in town like this rice dish.

I know people who slip into China Moon to sit alone at the counter and eat the fantastic spring rolls, either filled with curried chicken and glass noodles or with pork and jalapenos, with sprigs of chinese parsley rolled into their impeccably crisp wrappers. The tart, bright-green dipping sauce that comes with them is made of pulverized fresh anaheims, yellow wax peppers, and pickled ginger.

I am addicted to China Moon's preparation of a rather bland home-style Chinese dish called pearl balls. They're long-steamed pork balls studded with water chestnuts, coated in pearl rice, and served on a bed of chervil. They must remind me of something my mother cooked, because they never fail to give me pleasure. The little bed of green underneath, an original Tropp touch, and the fresh water chestnuts give them distinction.

Crescent moon turnovers have flaky pastry and explosive, aromatic lamb curry fillings. They're better than ever. Buddha's buns, a crisp brown bun with a soft vegetarian filling, is the only dish I wouldn't order again. It lacks the punch of the other dishes. Mandarin dumplings, soft pot stickers filled with spicy pork, come in a bowl of chili-infused sauce, and they're wonderful. For those who like fried chicken, China Moon puts out its very own chicken nuggets of tender marinated breast in a sharp, clean sauce seasoned with balsamic vinegar.

For dessert, there's peppery ginger ice cream with dark chocolate sauce and an array of delicate cookies to be eaten with espresso or different kinds of tea. I'd like to see some fresh fruit, perhaps marinated or poached, to end what invariably turns out to be a spicy meal. With dim sum, I drink China Moon's iced peach ginger tea, which tastes like fruity ginger ale.

It takes time for any kitchen to hit its stride, to be able to get out its ideas. Tropp had plenty of ideas when she opened China Moon. She had produced an excellent, very detailed cookbook with all her recipes laid out in meticulous detail, but she had never worked in a restaurant. With 1½ years of professional cooking behind her, she's executing with new assurance. It's very exciting to eat this dim sum lunch, the down-scaled proportions of which express Tropp's sensibility the best of all. Though practically every dish is laced with chilies and garlic, they taste and look refined. They boast the detail, brilliant color, and strength of Chinese silk tapestry. ∎

—Patricia Unterman, November 8, 1987

Circolo

161 Sutter Street (at Crocker Galleria), San Francisco. 362-0404. Open Monday through Saturday 11 A.M. to 11 P.M. Full bar. Major credit cards. Reservations advised. Moderate.

No, the waiter insisted, he didn't have to write down our order; he could remember it.

So I told him what we wanted and he repeated it—getting several items wrong. I listed them again, but he still didn't get everything right. So I went through them a third time.

Five minutes later he was back at our table. "Was that prawns you wanted as your third entree?" he asked. Actually, I replied, it was a veal chop. Miraculously, we ended up getting the veal chop—but when the check came, we had been charged for prawns.

I suppose something like that could happen on a given night in any restaurant. But when I encountered it at Circolo, the slick new Italian restaurant at downtown San Francisco's Crocker Galleria, I felt it symbolized what the place was about.

At Circolo, you play Italian roulette with the food and service. Despite the occasional appearance of a very decent dish, you walk away wondering how a restaurant could be so incredibly haphazard. Consider:

■ Just in case you missed something on your plate the first time around, you might very well see it in a subsequent dish. The marinated seafood in the salad part of the menu included the identical squid dish we had had as an appetizer, and the same herbed mayonnaise that had come with a stuffed artichoke. I had eggplant with cheese and tomato sauce as an appetizer, and identically prepared eggplant appears with two lamp chops sitting on it as the "lamb loin with eggplant." And the first night, our coffee order was delivered to the table twice by two different waiters.

■ The same type of meat can be both good and bad at the same time. Delicious tender slices of smoked breast of duck sat on a plate next to a leg of duck that was a tough, fatty, impenetrable heap.

■ Not everything appears as advertised. The menu said fettuccine with wild mushrooms. But there wasn't a speck of wild mushroom on the plate; they were all the commercial variety you'd buy in a supermarket.

Those events took place in an odd setting: a modestly priced Italian restaurant that's housed in the splendor of high-tech plush, complete with a brass elevator that whisks you to the second floor, where a maitre d' standing behind a lectern greets you. Circolo occupies what was the Old Poodle Dog, a pricy French restaurant that reportedly spent $2 million on its quarters.

Circolo was created by Fazol Poursohi, who also owns two very successful Financial District restaurants, Cafe Latte and Faz. He kept not only much of the Poodle Dog's decor, but also the dinner plates, which have a little depiction of a dog on them.

Unfortunately, that's an apt characterization of some of the food. The menu seems strictly hit-or-miss in each category. For instance, while that pasta with the non-wild "wild mushrooms" was fine, a linguine with scallops, mussels, and sun-dried tomatoes featured tough scallops, an unpleasantly biting sauce, and a mussel so foul that even though I spit it out immediately, I felt as if I could still taste it the next day.

Worst of all was the calzone from Circolo's wood-burning pizza oven. I've never understood why wood-burning ovens have become so trendy, since they make it difficult to get the precisely regulated heat that's necessary for a good pizza. The calzone I had was soggy on the bottom, burned on the top, and had a mushy cheese filling that tasted strangely waterlogged.

That calzone, like several of Circolo's dishes, left a layer of grease on the plate. So did a veal chop with basil butter; although the big fatty chop was OK, the basil butter had no taste but salt, and the accompanying vegetables were drowned in oil.

Several of the dishes, by contrast, were quite decent. The marinated calamari, very tender, fresh-tasting rings of squid tossed with tomatoes and green onions, is a good appetizer. Another good starter is the antipasto, which includes a slice of smoked salmon from Faz, also with nice crisp green beans and cold pasta.

For entrees, that lamb with eggplant was outstanding and a bargain. Two pink double lamb chops come on a bed of very thin eggplant slices, which have been cooked with tomato sauce and three kinds of cheese. Nothing else I ate at Circolo came close to matching that dish.

The desserts—at least the three different cakes that I tried—were good also. But two of the cakes came in a blueberry sauce that tasted unpleasantly fermented. The blueberries appeared to have been frozen, and the cherries in the sauce with the smoked duck tasted canned. What's wrong with using fresh fruit of the season for sauces?

If you stick with the calamari and the lamb, you can do quite well at Circolo, and you'd have a chance to dine in a setting so plush you'd think you were on Manhattan's East Side. But with haphazard and some-times painfully slow service, and with so many disappointing dishes, this restaurant has a long way to go before it matches the reputations that Faz and Cafe Latte have established. ■

—Stan Sesser, April 24, 1987

Clift Hotel—French Room

See review for Neiman-Marcus The Rotunda.

Colette: A Restaurant

802 Second Street, Davis (take the Davis exit off I-80, make a sharp right after the bridge, and go to the first stop sign). 916-758-3377. Open Monday through Friday 11:30 A.M. to 2:30 P.M., Monday through Saturday 5:30 P.M. to 10 P.M. Beer, wine. American Express. Reservations recommended. Inexpensive to moderate.

Ma Tante Sumi

4243 Eighteenth Street (at Diamond), San Francisco. 552-6663. Open daily 5:30 to 10 P.M. Beer, wine. MasterCard, Visa, American Express, Diners Club. Reservations accepted. Inexpensive to moderate.

This is an era when you could be justified in suspecting that the restaurant industry is run by computers. First the computer decides which theme is the most popular: Cajun, California cuisine, or whatever. Then it spews out individual names and designs to disguise the fact that they're really part of a chain.

In short, impersonality is becoming rampant. And that's why it's such a delight on occasion to find a restaurant that's a unique product of the owner and the chef, that reflects their instincts rather than the instructions of a business text-book. Here are two such places.

Colette: A Restaurant

The drive between San Francisco and Sacramento is boring enough, but doubly so if your stomach tells you it's time for dinner. The leaden Mexican food along the route might be fairly grim, but it's heaven by comparison to some of the al-ternatives.

That is why I could hardly believe Colette, a nine-table restaurant in Davis, just two minutes off Interstate 80. In stark contrast to the plastic food found in so many places along the freeway, eating at Colette feels almost like being invited into someone's home.

Tom Fries is the owner, chef, busboy, and everything else. Although other peo-ple work there, he seems to be doing everything all the time. He supervises the kitchen, chats about the food, recom-mends wine—and meanwhile replaces every bread basket and refills every water glass.

If the food tastes like home cooking, there's a reason. Fries's background is in family counseling. When he decided to open a restaurant, he simply brought with him the recipes he had been cooking for years for himself and friends.

The small menu, which changes every week, offers nothing fancy, but it's all tasty. The portions are huge, and the entrees, which include soup or salad, are a bar-gain. Fries seems to make a big effort to have only the freshest ingredients; while Davis isn't exactly on the ocean, it's safe to order fish here.

The highlight of my dinner at Colette was sensational pasta, filled with slices of venison sausage and hot Italian sausage, and made aromatic with fennel and pepper. The portion was big enough to make an ample dinner, or else appetizers for two or three people.

Two other starters were also superb. Mussels, bathed in a light cream sauce scented with pernod, were fresh tasting, and lentil soup with slices of *linguiça* managed to be bursting with flavor without being heavy.

The flaws are the same sort of flaws you might see at someone's home: One entree might be a bit overcooked; one sauce might be interesting but just not work. A pork tenderloin with mustard cream sauce had too sharp a mustard taste. Rabbit with chili and caper sauce was pleasant, but it had been on the stove for too long. But a boneless breast of chicken with raspberry butter sauce was juicy and tender.

With the entrees, you get perfectly cooked vegetables and rice pilaf or wild rice. And if you're lucky, they'll have a silky and intense chocolate mousse cake for dessert.

When a friend asked if they had wine by the glass, Fries handed her a very nice wine list and told her to pick any bottle, that he'd open it. She chose an over-$20 chardonnay, got a healthy glass, and was charged $4, not much more than you'd pay for a glass of jug wine at some other restaurants. Colette is that sort of place.

Ma Tante Sumi

It looks like your typical Japanese restaurant: blond wood, a menu that offers miso soup, sashimi, and teriyaki dishes, and a mostly Japanese staff, including a waiter who speaks very little English. But when you read the menu, you also find prosciutto, lamb curry, sweetbreads, and sole meunière.

This new Noe Valley restaurant, called Ma Tante Sumi, is run by Japanese who happen to be French-food freaks. The owner, Sumi Hirose, was a waitress at a French restaurant and a friend of several San Francisco French chefs. The chef, who came from Japan, was trained at a cooking school in France.

It isn't a fancy East-meets-West restaurant with elaborately conceived dishes. Instead you get simple food—roast duck, baked breast of chicken, sauteed rabbit—prepared with both Japanese and French ingredients and cooking styles. Like Colette, the menu is an astonishing bargain: the meal includes soup, an entree with three vegetables, and a good nutty-tasting brown rice.

Duck here is outstanding. We had half a roasted duck, a bit overcooked but with crisp skin and no fat, accompanied by fresh turnips, carrots, and green beans. The duck was in a very pleasant raspberry sauce that was neither sweet nor cloying. Oddly enough, I found the French sauce on the duck far better than the Japanese teriyaki sauce with the rabbit. The teriyaki sauce was both much too sweet and much too salty, and the rabbit itself was on the scrawny side.

Start with the sauteed scallops, brought in from Japan. They're frozen, which detracts from the texture, but they have a wonderful flavor. If you want to begin with a salad, ask for the dressing on the side. A very nice three-lettuce salad, which included radicchio, endive, and enoki and shiitake mushrooms, was swamped by a dressing with far too much soy sauce. ■

—Stan Sesser, March 13, 1987

The Courtyard

★ ★

1026 Alma Street, Menlo Park (take the Marsh Road exit off 101, left on Middlefield, right on Oak Grove, left on Alma). 326-6666. Open for lunch Monday through Friday 11:30 A.M. to 2:30 P.M., for dinner Tuesday through Saturday 6 to 9 P.M. Beer, wine. MasterCard, Visa, American Express. Reservations advised. Moderate.

Maybe it's just my bad luck in picking places to eat, but when I think of the Peninsula, I think of a seemingly disproportionate number of restaurants that offer the "Continental dining experience."

In one way or another, this revolves around dim lighting, red plastic banquettes, pretentious waiters, and unspeakable food, much of it frozen, submerged in thick, floury sauces. A meal like this can make mesquite-grilled monkfish in a San Francisco restaurant with hanging ferns seem innovative by contrast.

Now, at long last, I've found a Peninsula restaurant that dramatically breaks this pattern. It's a delightful new California cuisine restaurant in Menlo Park called The Courtyard, and it could stand up favorably next to similar places in San Francisco.

The Courtyard isn't just another of those formula mesquite grills, trying to capitalize on the latest trends by imitating other restaurants. It's a place that seeks to be unique by making a virtue of its location, by molding itself to the Peninsula's life style.

The Peninsula's warmer weather and suburban informality make dressing up for dinner a bit ridiculous. At The Courtyard, the climate is reflected by a huge and wonderful outdoor eating area, and by dishes carefully designed to be light and interesting. As for informality, this jewel box of a restaurant manages a sort of short-sleeved elegance.

This is about as pretty a restaurant as I've ever seen. Inside is a charming room with flowered wallpaper and linened tables accented with flowers and candles. Outside is a big stone courtyard retaining a giant gnarled oak tree where you can eat at lunch, or if the weather's warm enough, at dinner.

The chef and co-owner is Larry Elbert, who comes from three years as executive chef at the Sonoma Mission Inn. Though a couple of appetizers and a couple of desserts at The Courtyard were seriously flawed, every entree we had was a winner. There's nothing dramatically innovative, just the satisfaction that comes from fresh ingredients, light and interesting sauces, and lots of beautifully prepared fresh vegetables.

Among the entrees, the duck stood out. First roasted and then finished off on the mesquite grill, it offered everything you'd want from a duck: crisp skin, tender,

succulent meat, and not a hint of fat. The sauce—a reduction of white wine, duck and veal stock, cream, and (perhaps a first) Anchor Steam beer—was so expertly handled it managed to be light and intensely flavorful at the same time.

Other successful entrees included chicken zinfandel, a boneless marinated chicken breast brought alive by oyster, shiitake, and chanterelle mushrooms, and another spectacular wine-based sauce. Rack of lamb, four double chops presented rare as ordered, was not only tender, but also came with a little cup of mint sauce that tasted of fresh mint and vinegar for once, not sugar.

What accompanied the entrees was equally impressive. Instead of rice, two dishes came with a remarkably inventive combination of wheat berries, wild rice, and mushrooms. Every plate had a bouquet of fresh vegetables—enough to eat, not just to look at.

Appetizers, however, included a couple of disappointments. A cream of cauliflower soup tasted strangely tinny. Pasta was overcooked, underseasoned, and swimming in gloppy sauce. Crab cakes were so fishy tasting that the crab could just as well have come from a can.

But two spectacular appetizers almost made up for these. Vegetable raviolis, stuffed with spinach, ricotta, and mushrooms and served in a tomato and basil sauce, was a marvel of airy lightness, with the flavoring of fresh herbs. For the second dish, hot oysters were topped with a spicy barbecue sauce, made just subtle enough so that the oyster taste also came through.

If you're offered a pecan tart, it's clearly the choice for dessert. The crust was crisp, the filling remarkably not sweet or gooey, and a light, rum-flavored cream sauce was perfect. Two cakes, however, one of them orange-flavored chocolate and another layers of chocolate and vanilla, each proved to be a sugary mess.

When you see the prices, you won't believe you could eat so well in such a pretty setting. In addition to the entrees, there's also a fixed-price dieter's menu that's a tremendous value—an appetizer, main course, and dessert. Service is consistently friendly and informed.

When I think about The Courtyard, I immediately want to get in my car and make the hour-long drive to the Peninsula. I never thought I'd find a restaurant there that would inspire me to that. ∎
—Stan Sesser, October 8, 1985

Crescent City Cafe

★

1418 Haight Street, San Francisco. 863-1374. Open Tuesday 5 to 10 P.M., Wednesday through Friday 10 A.M. to 10 P.M., Saturday 8 A.M. to 10 P.M., Sunday 8 A.M. to 3 P.M. No alcoholic beverages. No credit cards. No reservations. Inexpensive.

Cooking that comes from the heart never seems shallow. The Cajun and Creole dishes served at Crescent City Cafe, a small, unpretentious neighborhood diner in the middle of the Haight, have that heartfelt quality. The food here is homegrown and inexpensive, a re-creation of the cooking that Louisiana folks grow up with daily. The people who run Crescent City Cafe, in fact, make this small piece of Haight Street real estate feel like a southern enclave with their openness and friendliness. Though there are rough edges to both the cooking and the decor, they only seem to add to the charm of this casual cafe.

In business just four months, you can tell that Crescent City opened on a shoestring budget. The bright, skylit room with five booths and a counter with stools was touched up with green paint, fresh flowers on the tables, and a few mementos of New Orleans on the walls. The plywood veneer wainscoting and old linoleum floors were left untouched. But the place is sparkling clean and neat. During the day, light streams in through big picture windows trimmed with pots of chrysanthemums; at night, the little cafe turns cozy. Whoever figured out the simple lighting system got it just right. All the funkiness recedes into the shadows and the Crescent City Cafe feels romantic.

One problem I have with New Orleans cooking is that it's so rich you tire of eating it. As served in local restaurants, it's not the kind of food you want every day. At Crescent City, which is set up to be an everyday kind of place, the food is kept simple and digestible. In old-fashioned coffee shop style you can order breakfast until 5 P.M., as well as grilled Wisconsin cheddar cheese sandwiches or hamburgers and milk shakes, but what makes Crescent City Cafe so much fun is their reasonably priced Cajun specialties.

You can start your day out with eggs, creamy grits glazed with melted butter, delicious, flaky, warm biscuits, and a Creole crab cake, just about the best home-style breakfast you can get. The crab cakes are different here—they're flat, about a quarter of an inch thick, and made of soaked bread, celery, onions, and good Louisiana crab meat. They remind me of a savory crab stuffing, and when the cook leaves them on the griddle long enough, they become crisp and irresistible. The lunch chef does them perfectly. The breakfast cook tends to rush them. Tell the waitress you want them nice and brown. The other high points of breakfast are some lovely, light buckwheat pancakes stuffed with bananas or walnuts.

Wonderful Cajun sandwiches await you at lunch and dinner. The BBQ shrimp sandwich on a soft bun never fails to please. The tender shrimp have been gently sauteed in a smoky, mildly hot sweet-and-sour barbecue sauce and then piled onto the bun with lettuce and tomato. The same shrimp are served in the evening as an appetizer with piles of toasted, buttered baguette to mop up the terrific sauce.

You expect any New Orleans–style restaurant to know how to deep fry and Crescent City is no exception. Briny fresh oysters emerge from the fryer crisp and greaseless encased in a crunchy cornmeal crust. When served on a soft french roll, buttered and grilled, they make an exemplary "oyster po-boy." These seductive oysters can be ordered without the roll for dinner, though I'd hate to give up the sandwich. Cornmeal-coated catfish fingers are deep fried as an appetizer with equally gratifying results.

Some of the long-cooked dishes want for deep flavor. Crescent City's seafood gumbo is loaded with juicy shrimp and crab meat and thickened with okra, which gives it a pleasant slippery texture. However, the stock doesn't have body. It lacks the intense smoky flavors that come from a brown roux loaded with vegetables and smoked meats. The same thing happens with Crescent City's misguided vegetarian red beans and rice, which taste flat without the perfume of ham hocks. Even with a good Louisiana hot sausage plunked on top, the beans don't absorb enough succulence to balance out the handfuls of thyme that must have gone into the pot. I don't think red beans and rice can succeed as a meatless preparation.

For dinner, four entrees are added to the menu, along with a couple of pastas. One of them, pasta with garlic shrimp and oysters in a cream sauce, is one of those dishes that you can't stop eating even though you know it's too heavy. It is this kind of dish that made Paul Prudhomme the man that he is. The noodles are an afterthought in a creation made of quarts of cream and butter, oyster liquor, shrimp, and chopped oysters, all carefully cooked into a slightly reduced sauce.

A deep-fried stuffed chicken breast filled with ham, swiss cheese, and an interesting herb mixture, comes out a little dry though still tasty. A simple iceberg and romaine salad comes with it, as do some sauteed vegetables and rice topped with a tomatoey Creole sauce. Big chunks of tough, juiceless poached redfish are unappealing if you're thinking about ordering something light.

For dessert there has been fresh peach cobbler with a soft, buttery brown top and unsweetened fruit underneath that is authentic and good. I don't think it should be microwaved to the boiling point before it is served, however.

In this day and age when it's so hard to find good inexpensive American food with any sort of character, the opening of a neighborhood cafe like Crescent City makes me want to celebrate. This is a serviceable restaurant, a place to visit often when you're just plain hungry. There are no gimmicks or throwback glitter. Best of all, you're treated well. When you walk into Crescent City, that mythical southern hospitality takes over and it makes everyone feel very, very good. ■

—Patricia Unterman, October 12, 1986

Dakota Bar and Grill

★ ★

2086 Allston Way (at Shattuck), Berkeley. 841-3848. Open for lunch Monday through Friday from 11:30 A.M. to 2:30 P.M.; for brunch Sunday 10 A.M. to 2 P.M.; for dinner Tuesday through Saturday 5:30 to 9:30 P.M. Full bar. Major credit cards. Reservations advised. Moderate.

Some chefs have the ability to change dramatically, particularly when they get a challenge they never had before.

I twice wrote reviews panning the food at Cafe Americain in North Beach when Daniel Malzhan was chef there. The restaurant seemed to be trying to copy the upstairs cafe at Chez Panisse. Now Malzhan has a chance to be creative and he has succeeded. He has made the Dakota Grill in the Shattuck Hotel in downtown Berkeley one of the most exciting and innovative restaurants to open in the Bay Area in years. At the Dakota, he has taken on one of the most difficult food assignments: running a restaurant that's open for two meals a day and that produces wildly imaginative food, including a long list of nightly specials. The Dakota turns out Southwest cuisine, something that could easily be a cliche. But Malzhan has resolutely steered the Dakota's kitchen away from anything remotely resembling a cliche. There's a gas grill instead of mesquite; there are virtually none of the standard Southwest dishes.

There's also a dessert chef named Barbara Ury, whose creativity is not to be believed. Imagine, for instance, bananas and toasted coconut stuffed into taco shells made from graham crackers; or coconut ice cream frozen inside cream puff dough, deep fried, and served on a bed of fresh pineapple sauce, so the ice cream spurts out over the pineapple when you cut into the puff ball. I haven't been this excited about desserts since the days of Nancy Silverton at Spago in West Hollywood.

Before I discuss the food at the Dakota, let's get the negatives out of the way. When new dishes are being created every night—often from the chef's head and not from a cookbook—some of them are bound to fail. In the joy of discovering preparations resembling nothing you've had before, you can forgive that. Also, the fixed menu tends to be a little less interesting and a little less successful than the daily specials.

And the waiters mar the experience by spouting all the standard syrupy restaurant cliches. You're asked so often whether everything is okay that you wish you had a sign to put on your table with your response. With food this interesting to talk about, why can't they discard the rehearsed lines?

As for the food, there's nothing rehearsed about that. With unusual ingredients such as *anejo* cheese, *calabacitas*, and *chile guajillo* sauce, Malzhan conducts a fascinating exploration of American Southwest and Mexican cooking. When elements of California cuisine appear, as they do often, they're plucked from their usual settings and fashioned into a Southwest mold. So you have salmon caviar and crème fraîche served with fried black-bean cake, or grilled rabbit on a bed of spicy pinto beans and smoked chorizo sausage. This is a restaurant where goat cheese and wild mushrooms share a place in the kitchen with Mexican chilies.

It's not surprising, then, that a meal at Dakota can be an exciting gastronomic adventure. Consider, for instance, some of the specials I tasted at just one of the three dinners I ate there:

Eggplant soup, light on cream and salt and rich in intense flavor, was made even more interesting by grilled peppers, fried tortilla strips, and Mexican cheese. Then came a huge portion of a sensational appetizer. It was tender grilled sweetbreads, wrapped in crispy bacon and served on a bed of black chanterelles set on fire by serrano chilies. No wonder the bacon was so wonderful: it had first been blanched of most of its fat, then seasoned with black pepper, crushed juniper berries, and coriander seeds.

Grilled sturgeon was so perfect it would have been fine alone, but it was enhanced by a sauce that included fresh juniper berries, and served with a delicate gratin of potatoes smothered with black chanterelles. There was also a juicy and flavorful grilled squab, served on a remarkably interesting compote of dates, kumquats, and grilled red onions, along with the nutty couscouslike grain called quinoa.

Hope that you get to the Dakota on a night when they're offering Navajo fry bread; the Dakota's version of this puffy Indian bread was far superior to any I had in Arizona. When I tried it, it accompanied a fabulous spicy pork and red chili stew. At lunch the fry bread is a regular on the menu, served with a lamb stew.

There were a few disappointments, too. I had cornmeal fashioned into a thick, pancakelike *gordita*, a boat-shaped *chalupa*, and puff pastry—and in each case it came out unpleasantly heavy and tasteless. Although some of the Mexican sauces, such as a pumpkin-seed *mole verde*, are stunning, a few tasted bitter and medicinal. Two meats were disappointing: sliced loin of pork was tough, and sautéed leg of venison had been overly floured and had a mushy texture.

The Dakota's prices are reasonable, particularly considering the large portions. And there's an added plus: What was once a barren, barnlike hotel dining room has been brilliantly restored into one of the most pleasant and comfortable restaurants around.

With inventive Southwest cooking and three-star desserts, the Dakota is proving to be one of those rare new restaurants that impart genuine excitement. ■

—Stan Sesser, March 20, 1987

Doidge's

2217 Union Street (near Fillmore), San Francisco. 921-2149. Open Monday through Friday 8 A.M. to 2 P.M., Saturday and Sunday 8 A.M. to 3 P.M. MasterCard, Visa. Reservations essential on weekends, well in advance. Inexpensive to moderate.

Breakfast is something you don't read much about in restaurant columns, but it seems to be on more people's minds than I thought possible. I received an avalanche of replies to my request two months ago for a good breakfast place in San Francisco—far more mail than I've ever gotten on a single subject.

What the replies made clear is that everyone has a different idea about what constitutes a good breakfast. There was a staggering total of sixty-two San Francisco restaurants nominated, and only five had more than two votes. The big winners were Doidge's on Union Street (nine votes), Sear's downtown on Powell Street (six), and Mama's at Washington Square, Brother Juniper's Breadbox on Sutter Street, and Home Plate on Lombard Street with three each.

Some of the recommendations were astonishing. International House of Pancakes and a couple of hotel coffee shops got votes. One reader was apparently into morning masochism, because he wrote about a place as follows: "The cooks are two dishwashers turned short-order cooks. The food they put out is worthy of a sewer, maybe. One employee told me confidentially that in the time he had been there, he had gotten sick off the food a dozen or so times. They have a roach problem in the kitchen. Anyway, try it for yourself." That is a man who knows how to rouse a restaurant critic's enthusiasm. Regrettably, I had to put the sewer aside and head off to the big winner, Doidge's.

I first ate at Doidge's in 1970, and the place today looks every bit as attractive as it did then. With the homey tablecloths and decor, the friendly service, and prices reasonable for Union Street, it's easy to see why the tables are in such demand. (You can't get in the door on weekends without a reservation.)

Why did Doidge's appeal to me fifteen years ago? You could get fresh fruit on your french toast instead of sugar syrup, you had a choice of more than cheese for your omelet, and such interesting things as corned beef hash with poached eggs were on the menu. All these were rarities in a world where breakfast normally meant fried eggs or a Velveeta omelet with balloon-bread toast.

But the world has changed in fifteen years, and all the things that made Doidge's innovative then are commonplace for breakfast now. So I now have to judge Doidge's by today's standards, and here I find it wanting.

Doidge's has remained essentially fixed in its old formula. There are still no espresso drinks, and the coffee is nothing to rave about. Orange juice is squeezed far enough in advance to have turned sour by the time you get it. In a city where wonderful homemade breads are commonplace, Doidge's still uses for both toast and french toast the same Oroweat breads you can find in any supermarket.

All of that could be overlooked if the basic breakfasts were consistently good. But in the three meals I had at Doidge's, I found the food was more often than not a disaster.

Buttermilk pancakes with fresh strawberries, a pleasing enough prospect on a breakfast menu, were the absolute rock bottom. The pancakes were thick and doughy, stuck to the roof of your mouth, and had an unpleasant flavor. The strawberries looked rotten and tasted worse. Our waitress didn't bat an eye when she whisked away our plate of three big pancakes with just two little bites taken out of one of them. She didn't ask a question, and the charge appeared on our bill.

Two omelets, one vegetable with swiss cheese, the second herb and mushrooms, were the opposite of fluffy; the eggs came out thick and hard. It's too bad, because the sauteed mushrooms were juicy and flavorful, the single best thing I tasted at Doidge's.

Compared to the pancakes and omelets, that Oroweat french toast didn't taste bad at all. But it was drowned in butter, and these days not everyone considers a heap of butter the perfect way to start off a day.

I remembered the corned beef hash rather fondly, but this time it was an undistinguished heap tasting of too much salt and pepper. The eggs benedict were much better, with a good light lemony hollandaise sauce, but they were marred by greasy potatoes and an English muffin that bore a strong resemblance to cardboard.

If you hit the right day, you can do well at Doidge's with a fruit bowl, although topping it with an unpeeled slice of kiwi is one of the silliest affectations ever. You can also do well with some excellent breakfast meats, particularly a thick slice of smoky, meaty Motherlode bacon.

But it's still a far cry from what I would define as a decent breakfast, and I'm going to hit the trail in the next few weeks checking some other places. ■

—Stan Sesser, February 6, 1987

Donatello

501 Post Street (at Mason in the Donatello Hotel), San Francisco. 441-7182. Open daily for breakfast 7 to 10:30 A.M., for dinner 6 to 10:30 P.M. Full bar. No smoking. Major credit cards. Reservations recommended, essential on weekends. Expensive.

I've often pointed to Donatello, the elegant and well-known northern Italian restaurant in downtown San Francisco, as providing a model of what Italian food should be. The judgment was based on three spectacular meals—a special wine-tasting dinner in a private room and two meals cooked by visiting chefs from Italy.

But I realized that I had never been to Donatello for a regular dinner from the menu. What are the people getting who eat there when nothing special is going on, and who pay top dollar for the privilege? With Donatello's relatively high prices, it's a question worth asking.

So I returned to Donatello for two dinners. Architecturally, the confusing warren of little rooms would win no awards; there's no real entrance hall, and when you walk in, it's hard to tell where to go to get seated. But in the bustle of downtown, the intimate and lavishly decorated dining rooms proved to be pleasant and relaxing.

When contrasted with my expectations, the food at Donatello ranked as perhaps the letdown of the year. Both the fixed-price dinner and the bulk of our a la carte selections were a world away from the three special meals I remembered so fondly. So dramatic was the difference, it was hard to believe it was all cooked at the same stove.

The first dinner was nothing less than a disaster. It would be redeemed only if you had a fondness for salt, since that was the predominant taste—sometimes the only taste—in most dishes.

An appetizer of scallops sauteed with ginger and orange peels provided a prime example. The light butter-and-cream sauce had not a hint of ginger, just the intense taste of salt. But even the saltiness couldn't disguise the fact that the scallops had a distinct off-taste.

Among the other starters, a salad of lettuce and smoked duck seemed totally without dressing, and two dollops of goat cheese sitting on the duck slivers were an inappropriate attempt to capitalize on a trendy California cuisine ingredient. Ravioli stuffed with seafood had absolutely no seafood taste and a salt content we could hardly believe. Only a simple dish of shiitake mushrooms in garlicky olive oil succeeded.

If anything, the entrees slid even further downhill. Overly floured sauteed sweetbreads had the flavor of salt and the texture of mush and rested in a pool of what appeared to be pure butter. Roast rabbit, in a sauce of almost undiluted cream, was chewy, overcooked, and dried out. Veal medallions were completely tasteless.

The next dinner I tried the fixed-price meal, which includes all you can drink of three Italian wines, a white, a red, and a sweet wine with dessert. A friend ordered a la carte but got the same three wines for a $22 supplement.

One improvement was immediately evident—in the wine service. At the first dinner, when three of us had ordered a bottle of white and a bottle of red, the waiter opened the red while we were still on our appetizers, and poured me a taste while I was eating scallops—ignoring the fact that our white wine glasses were empty and the bottle was still half full. With the fixed-price dinner, by contrast, glasses were constantly refilled with a minimum of ceremony. The wines were excellent choices, too.

There was some improvement in the food, also, particularly in the pasta. Tagliatelle with prosciutto and parmesan cheese, which began the fixed-price dinner, was actually splendid—al dente spinach noodles with meaty shreds of prosciutto and a rich cheese-laden sauce. The a la carte tortellini with spinach and ricotta was marred only by the old nemesis, too much salt.

The fixed-price dinner continued with sea bass in a very fresh-tasting tomato sauce scented with thyme; the fish, however, seemed distinctly too long out of the ocean. Then came tender, high-quality lamb medallions in a boring and much too buttery red wine sauce. Dessert was homemade rum ice cream, the only satisfying dessert of the four I tried.

On balance, my meals at Donatello were far removed from the light and innovative food I remembered at the special dinners. It was much more like the leaden Continental cooking of many expensive restaurants a couple of decades ago. While the fixed-price dinner clearly outshone the a la carte selections, the price was much too steep for a meal that was still several notches below superb.

While Donatello's food was often disappointing, the management receives three stars for their recently instituted policy banning smoking in the restaurant. When I reviewed the restaurant, both meals were marred by overly smoky conditions and a seemingly unconcerned maitre d'. The smoking policy was already being discussed at the time of my visits, and I am pleased to report that Donatello now allows smoking only in the lounge area. This news is a major victory for those who want to taste their food and wine and not inhale other people's cigarette smoke. Other restaurant owners have told me they feel such a move is the only way to avoid endless confusion and controversy, but they fear acting alone. Now that Donatello, one of San Francisco's best-known restaurants, has taken the lead, it should be easier for others to follow this courageous decision. ■

—Stan Sesser, September 4, 1987

Doug's Bar-B-Q

★★

3600 San Pablo Avenue, Emeryville (take the MacArthur exit off I-580). 655-9048. Open Monday through Thursday 10 A.M. to midnight, Friday and Saturday to 2:30 A.M., Sunday to 9:30 P.M. Takeout only. No alcohol, reservations, credit cards, or any of that stuff. Inexpensive.

Move over, Flint's.

I never thought I'd see those words in print, much less be the author of them. But the poetic barbecue served up by the three branches of Flint's in Oakland has now definitely been surpassed.

For a barbecue lover, Oakland has become something of a mecca, a Kansas City of the Pacific. The appetite of Oaklanders for barbecue rivals that of Berkeley for Thai food or San Franciscans for California cuisine.

So far, none of the competitors had succeeded in ousting Flint's as the favorite of barbecue aficionados.

Then I started getting letters about Doug's. Doug's Bar-B-Q is housed in a tired old building nestled alongside the I-580 San Pablo Avenue freeway overpass in Emeryville. While some purists might object that it's a bit too clean, no one could otherwise fault Doug's for its classic barbecue joint ambience. It's carpeted in linoleum and bathed in fluorescent light.

Although Doug's is strictly a takeout, there are several mismatched chairs for the inevitable long wait. Just as at Flint's, efficiency here is a foreign word. But the wait makes everything taste even better once you get it home—assuming you can resist the wafting fumes of barbecue sauce in your car.

Doug's is a winner on three fronts: It does the standard stuff terrifically; it offers some unusual choices like barbecued goat and smoked turkey; and it dishes out the rarest of rarities for a barbecue joint—potato salad and baked beans that are actually good.

But for many visitors, the experience will begin and end with the signature dish of barbecue, the pork ribs. And no one serves up ribs juicier and meatier than Doug's. They're wonderful, and made even better by an unusually sophisticated hot sauce, a sauce that for once isn't drowned out by the reek of Liquid Smoke. The hot sauce, which has some zing but won't set you on fire, is the only sensible choice here; medium is much too sweet.

The menu at Doug's travels the usual path of beef ribs, brisket of beef, links, and chicken, but also branches out to lamb, smoked turkey, and goat. Depending on what you order, you can get a large portion, or a smaller portion (in barbecue parlance, a "sandwich") for a couple of dollars less. The sandwich is more than enough to send you for a roll of Tums.

Next to the ribs, my favorite is the smoked turkey, which is astonishingly moist, tender, and tasty. Because it's low in fat, it's healthy—almost a contradiction in terms for barbecue. I shuddered when I saw Doug's counter woman take the turkey and goat out of a refrigerator and heat them in a microwave oven, but the explanation actually makes sense. Unlike other items, turkey and goat have so little fat that they have to be removed from the barbecue while they're still juicy or else they'd dry out.

The goat was very nice too, although this particular goat had been around enough years to develop the same pungent taste you find in goat cheese. If that turns you off, try the brisket—very tender, smoky slices of beef. Disciples of the Calvin Trillin School of Barbecue can get some wonderful burnt ends when they order brisket at Doug's.

There were two disappointments on the menu. The lamb was old and fatty, beyond mutton to oblivion. And the chicken was dry and overcooked; I think it needed the same treatment as the turkey and the goat.

With your barbecue comes balloon bread (skip it—it just soaks up sauce that's better on the meat) and potato salad that, unlike that of any barbecue I've ever been in before, actually tastes fresh. A side of homemade baked beans is well worth ordering; they have a subtle smoked bacon taste and aren't objectionably sweet. The pies are homemade too, and the sweet potato pie is nothing less than remarkable—flaky crust and sweet potato flavor that's not drowned out by sugar.

In short, Doug's qualifies as a great barbecue, with but one caveat: Barbecue is made for paper plates; Flint's uses one on the bottom, one on the top, and wraps the whole thing in paper. But Doug's serves up your order in a styrofoam container, relegating great barbecue to the aesthetic level of Burger King. It's an atrocity.

Who was the mastermind who ousted Flint's from its number one position? Doug Keyes didn't exactly go the culinary academy route; he was a cowboy in Texas who moved to Oakland to become a diesel mechanic. "I barbecued all the time on the side anyway," he explains. "I cook a lot of Cajun food, too. That's all I am anyway, a Cajun, but just a black one."

The affable Keyes will regale you with stories of his youth if you get him started. And if you want an unusual dinner party, you can bring him a whole goat, lamb, or pig and he'll smoke it for you. I couldn't think of a better dinner than one catered by Doug's. ∎

—Stan Sesser, June 12, 1987

E Street Restaurant and Tapas Bar

★ ★

824 E Street, San Rafael. 459-7007. Restaurant open Tuesday through Friday for lunch 11:30 A.M. to 2:30 P.M., Tuesday through Sunday for dinner 6 to 9:30 P.M., until 10 P.M. Friday and Saturday; for brunch Sunday 10:30 A.M. to 2:30 P.M.; tapas cafe open Tuesday through Friday 11:30 A.M. to 10 P.M., Saturday 4 to 11 P.M. Beer, wine. Major credit cards. Reservations accepted. Moderate.

E Street is the most exciting and original restaurant to open in Marin County since the founding of the now-defunct Maurice et Charles' Bistrot in 1973. Not a suburban version of a San Francisco restaurant, E Street has its own persona, its own look, and its own very unique style of cooking. Though the starting weeks of E Street were shaky with major changes of kitchen staff, the new regime is putting out captivating dishes that break most of the rules of culinary logic but still end up tasting delicious.

You may recognize the opulently refurbished Victorian house that E Street is in as the old Andalou. One of the former partners of that restaurant, Joyce Heinke, reacquired the building and tore it apart, installing a handsome tile-and-wood-beamed tapas bar downstairs that looks onto a patio and garden, and elegantly furnished and decorated dining rooms upstairs. The tapas bar, hung with strings of garlic, stocked with sherries, and displaying dishes of colorful marinated vegetables and cured meats, has the cave-like feeling of tapas bars in Spain. The upstairs restaurant inhabits small, luxurious parlorlike rooms with six or seven tables in each. All the surfaces have been meticulously redone. Luscious shades of pink have been sponged onto the walls and shiny white lacquer applied to all the trim and plasterwork on the ceilings. The gray tablecloths and napkins look stunning against this background. Tall-backed lacquered chairs and thick carpeting contribute to the lush look. Gorgeous marble fireplaces and effusive flower arrangements grace the rooms, with miniature pumpkins and fall flowers set at each table. You get the feeling that Ms. Heinke herself proudly tends her dining rooms as if they were rooms in her own home that she opened to guests. For once, you get to dine out in intimacy and quiet in the civilized ambience of this dreamy pastel house. It's worth a trip to Marin just for that.

The food matches these lofty surroundings. One evening we began with a selection of tapas from the downstairs bar that included a fruity nicoise olive spread served with fantastic toasts made out of herbed bread brushed with olive oil and a lively antipasto plate with fresh, local goat cheese as a centerpiece flanked by roasted pearl onions, grilled marinated eggplant, peppers, and yellow squash, and slices of prosciutto.

Both the tapas and the restaurant menu change daily, so you won't necessarily find the dishes described here on the menu.

One evening a striking grilled duck breast salad was offered, with thin slices of rare grilled duck breast dressed in plum sauce on an assortment of lettuces tossed with crisp bits of Italian bacon, roasted onions, and shiitake mushrooms. Despite the plethora of ingredients, the salad tasted as complete, satisfying, and intriguing as any version I've tasted. The successful balance of Asian and Western flavors made it unique.

A similar pairing of Eastern and Western ideas worked well in a decadent but irresistible dish of Chinese sausage and spinach wrapped in pasta, sliced into a pinwheel, and sauced with a beurre blanc infused with ginger and basil. A little bean sprout salad dressed in sesame oil helped lighten it.

Usually rich shellfish bisque, oddly enough, was comparatively austere, with an appealing saffron-scented broth enriched with just the tiniest bit of cream. I liked it very much. The kitchen does not throw off something as commonly prepared as caesar salad. Even though I take issue with using delicate baby romaine leaves instead of the crisp, inner leaves of mature heads, I liked the creamy, lightly anchovied dressing with lots of good parmesan and tasty croutons.

Some of the main courses were brilliant. A breast of moist roast pheasant, wrapped in bacon, stuffed with savory apple, pecan, and bread dressing, and swathed with a velvety sauce perfumed with sage and port, was served with mildly gingered sweet potatoes, a cornucopia of fall vegetables, and whole cranberry relish. It was the kind of plate you pray for at Christmas dinner. Everything seemed to melt together, to enhance everything else on the plate. All the textures were right; how did they get that pheasant to be so miraculously succulent? As elegant as the plate looked, the flavors suggested the best of the holiday home kitchen. You'd better call ahead to make sure it's on the menu if you like this kind of dish.

Another stunner inspired by a different part of the world had the generic title of stir-fried chicken with black bean sauce, but what a glorious stir-fry it was! The tenderest chunks of chicken breast were heaped with brilliantly colorful vegetables dotted with black beans in a red-tinged sauce that was hot, sour, and salty in just the right proportions. Not entirely Asian, this stir-fry was finished with a butter sauce. Served with nutty basmati rice, this dish reminded me of the dishes I'd had at Wolfgang Puck's Chinois on Main in Santa Monica.

A thick chunk of baked sea bass was gently cooked and moist, but a thick coconut milk curry sauce perfumed with lemon grass was too heavy for it. A handful of sauteed pecans strewn on top of the fish did not make the dish any lighter. For those who want something simple and uncomposed, there's a tender, buttery New York strip steak with golden brown roasted potatoes.

The dessert choices pale by comparison to the wild and wonderful dishes on the rest of the menu. Chocolate and vanilla ice creams refresh the palate after the culinary work out, but an apple tart was topped with tough raw apples, and a chocolate-pecan tart had that candy bar heaviness that becomes cloying after a few bites.

The head chef behind this iconoclastic menu is a young man named Ed Walsh who came to California via La Français, Jean Banchet's bastion of haute cuisine in suburban Chicago, the Ritz in Paris, and the Pierre in New York. Along the way he worked at his father's restaurant on Long Island and Gordon's in Chicago. He's one of a group of young professional chefs who have learned French technique in demanding French kitchens and are fearless about applying it to any combination of ingredients. The work entailed in making these dishes turn out right does not faze him. If he needs a sauce based on a reduction of roasted bones in a long-simmered stock, why he puts it right up. If he has to bone and stuff pheasant and then cook it perfectly, no problem. If a dish calls for a beurre blanc seasoned with Asian ingredients, he'll figure out the proportions. The food has a glossy, professional finish and that deep, back-of-the-mouth flavor that is achieved only from lots of training and experience.

Where the restaurant errs, perhaps, is in overall conception. You have to be a juggler to pull together a meal that makes good sense. A little restraint and some marshaling of all that professional skill into creating dishes that taste good without using pounds of butter will put E Street into the realm of a great restaurant. Now it's one of the most daring, even if it falls down once in a while. The young chefs in this kitchen have to define their style and then develop it, whether it be chinoise, California grill, nouveau French, Spanish, or indeed an eclectic mix. Some sorting out with a whole meal in mind is the next step. ■

—Patricia Unterman, November 16, 1986

E'Angelo

★ ★

2234 Chestnut Street, San Francisco. 567-6164.
Open Tuesday through Sunday 5 to 11 P.M.
Beer, wine. No credit cards. No reservations.
Inexpensive.

These days, when it takes a small fortune to build a restaurant kitchen sophisticated enough to put out state-of-the-art food, the small, homey, inexpensive neighborhood place is becoming a thing of the past. Though small Asian restaurants abound, the vitality of the old-style Italian, French or Basque restaurant wanes. Either too many corners are cut to produce an inexpensive meal or prices rise above the neighborhood level. And what passed ten years ago as good, hearty food now seems a bit dull and tired in light of the cooking revolution that has taken place in the Bay Area.

So it was with trepidation that I revisited a small trattoria on Chestnut Street that I used to like years ago when it was owned and operated by Eduardo Morettoni and his wife Marcella. Eduardo still markets his excellent, eponymously named pasta around town but sold the restaurant to Ezio Rastelli. The only thing Mr. Rastelli changed about the place was the name, and as much as I admired the restaurant ten years ago, I admire it more today. Not only has E'Angelo kept up its standards and low prices over the years, but the very same dishes that this restaurant served ten years ago are still appealing and delicious today.

Getting into E'Angelo is the only trying part of the experience if you come during peak mealtime hours. A long semiopen kitchen shares a small dining room with ten or twelve tables that fill up fast. You have to wait your turn in a tiny lobby since no reservations are taken. Luckily, service by two good-natured waiters is efficient.

The tables are tiny and pushed very close together, covered with blue-and-white-checked oilcloth. The wall along the table side of the room is festooned with framed garage-sale reproductions; otherwise, there's a fortuitous lack of decor in what is a very cramped room. The feeling, however, is just right for the kind of restaurant E'Angelo is. Without any pretensions, the real charm of the place comes from its solid neighborhood trattoria style.

E'Angelo specializes in house-made pastas, the old-fashioned kind with meat sauces and lots of cheese and savory stuffings. The pasta dough itself has a distinctive flavor and texture, thick, toothsome, satiny, and full of character but never heavy. It tastes like the handmade pasta you might get in an Italian home and E'Angelo does robust things with it.

Green spinach noodles are layered with mushroom and chicken liver sauce, fontina, and mozzarella and finished off under the broiler in a mouth-watering version of green lasagna. The same hearty meat sauce with a recognizable chicken liver presence is tossed into egg noodles in *fettuccine ciociara*. The eggy fettuccine also get a copious white sauce, skillfully constructed with only gruyere and cream. Simple and rich, yes, but balanced perfectly.

Cannelloni usually have such bland, dreadful fillings, but here, you can actually taste the chicken and veal that are rolled into white noodle dough and topped with tomato and mushroom sauce and parmesan cheese. One of my favorite dishes here is another oft-abused dish, eggplant parmigiana, which melts in your mouth when prepared by E'Angelo's kitchen. Paper-thin slices of eggplant are layered with mozzarella, tomato sauce, and grated parmesan in just the right proportion.

The ricotta-and-spinach-stuffed ravioli are some of the best in the city. They get a haunting cream sauce infused with a demiglace and mushrooms. None of those all too prevalent tough edges mar these plump ravioli.

For gnocchi lovers, E'Angelo's little dumplings of soft, egg-rich dough poached in salted water and then napped with tomato sauce and a sprinkling of parmesan cheese are properly light and soft.

Starters are limited to an antipasto of paper-thin slices of mortadella, prosciutto, and *bresaola* (dry-cured beef) with some snappy house-pickled vegetables in the center, or prosciutto and melon, a dish well worth ordering now when melons are in season. A mixed green salad gets a brisk dressing of vinegar and oil, as does a plate of tomatoes covered with thinly sliced red onions and dried-out anchovies. Despite the anchovies, the tomato salad is a good one.

Another way to start a meal at E'Angelo is to split a small pizza made only with mozzarella, fresh tomatoes, and either mushrooms or salami. These individual-sized pizzas on sweet, meticulously baked, thin crusts were part of this menu way before the pizza craze swept the country, and you'd be hard pressed to find a better version. The crisp and chewy crusts are always cooked through. Sogginess or oiliness never afflict an E'Angelo pizza. They're about as simple a pizza as you can make, and just about the best.

I've never seen the point of ordering E'Angelo's meat dishes when the pasta and pizza are so exceptional, but if you have a yen for a plate of baked lamb served with brown gravy with a dish of buttery vegetables on the side, E'Angelo's got it.

The small wine list on the back of the menu offers plenty of appropriate bottles for reasonable prices, the foremost being a delicious 1981 Vino Nobile, Montepulciano, a red wine full of fruit, life, and body that enhances the food. I could drink bottles of it.

For dessert there's Stella Bakery's lovely sacripantina cake, with its delicate layers of genoise and zabaglione cream, and a house-made *tiramisu*, that generic dessert of coffee-soaked cake with mascarpone or Italian crème fraîche. Served in a goblet here, the *tiramisu* was a little icy.

To know that E'Angelo is alive and well on Chestnut Street is a comforting thought. Being able to depend on a restaurant year after year makes me, and a lot of other people who jam into E'Angelo every night, particularly happy. ■

—Patricia Unterman, June 28, 1987

Eddie Jacks

★

1151 Folsom Street, San Francisco. 626-2388. Open for lunch Monday through Friday 11:30 A.M. to 2:30 P.M., for dinner Tuesday through Friday 6 to 10 P.M., Friday and Saturday until 10:30 P.M. Beer, wine. MasterCard, Visa. Reservations advised. Moderate.

It's unusual, to say the least, to discover a new restaurant by eating someplace else. But that's what happened a couple of months ago when I dined at Wolfdale's in Tahoe City, a restaurant so wonderful that I look for any excuse to get up to the mountains.

Wolfdale's was giving out business cards for a new place in San Francisco called Eddie Jacks. It turns out that Eddie Jacks is operated by three of the four original Wolfdale's partners. They set up shop on Folsom Street in a south-of-Market commercial area where the number of new restaurants threatens to exceed the number of residents.

Despite their last names, I knew that the presence of Tim Dale, Deborah Dale Wolf, and Jerry Wolf wasn't automatically going to make Eddie Jacks into a Wolfdale's West. The genius of Wolfdale's lies with the chef, Douglas Dale, who remains firmly ensconced in the mountains. No one, not even his siblings, could hope to imitate his application of a Japanese aesthetic to California cuisine.

But I nevertheless hurried to Eddie Jacks to see what was going on. And I found a restaurant that needs no review to point out its existence: solely by word of mouth, it's already jammed.

The three partners have created a restaurant that's instantly likable. Eddie Jacks, named after their fathers, manages to look trendy without being the least bit pretentious, and without the big decorating budget that would necessitate high menu prices. It's a handsome and friendly little place, and, despite the noise when it's filled, everyone seems to be happy and comfortable.

As for the food, it isn't a restaurant that had everything elaborately planned the day the doors opened. Instead, the partners chose to begin with a relatively small menu to see what people liked, tinker with the menu, slowly expand the list of daily specials, and then eventually—although that time hasn't yet come—make their own desserts instead of bringing them in.

The result is a kitchen still in evolution. The ideas come from the three partners as well as the chef, Tom Fox, who previously worked at Fog City Diner and China Moon. The food is something of a mishmash thematically, basically California cuisine with trendy Italian and East-meets-West mixed in.

I found most of the dishes good or excellent, although a few didn't come off. But judging from the improvement in the month between my first and second dinners, I think Eddie Jacks could quickly become a two-star restaurant as the kitchen gets experience and the menu becomes more coherent.

Meanwhile, there are lots of satisfying things to eat. If you're not counting calories, start with the fried polenta sticks, a very clever variation on french fries, served with a dipping sauce of gorgonzola cheese and sour cream. Equally good but much less guilt-producing is a piece of very fresh tuna, marinated in soy sauce, and barely grilled so that it's still raw in the center. Tuna, which has little fat and can quickly dry out, is best done sashimi style. Then move on to the soup of the day. The two that I had were the highlight of each meal, absolutely brilliant. One was red cabbage and potato chunks in a broth that included caraway seeds and sour cream, the second an extremely delicate and flavorful split pea scented with bacon.

My favorite among the entrees on the regular menu is the seafood stew, a very competent presentation of fresh-tasting seafood in a garlicky broth with sliced carrots. The broth cried out for some good bread; getting rid of the mediocre french bread that Eddie Jacks serves would improve the restaurant immensely.

There's also a very decent mixed grill of quail, an aromatic sausage made of pork and fennel, and tasty polenta. Order on the side the panfried vegetable pancake, which normally comes with the grilled flank steak. The steak was tough and listless, but the pancake a sensation.

The regular menu also features an interesting open-faced lamb sandwich that is plenty for dinner. It includes feta cheese, sweet onions, olives, and a coleslaw of red cabbage that puts the more usual variety to shame.

Several things at Eddie Jacks were much less successful than those items. Among the appetizers, a basket of sweet-potato chips was a great idea on paper, but the greasy chips tasted of little more than cooking oil. An asparagus and shiitake mushroom salad, with virtually no mushrooms and an unpleasantly salty soy sauce dressing, was a rip-off.

For entrees, the grilled chicken chow mein was a real disappointment: the chicken was dry and bland and the noodles too oily. The grilled fish of the day was monkfish, hugely undercooked and accompanied by a variety of vegetables that were more raw than al dente.

With moderately priced entrees and a California boutique wine list that includes several good choices in the $12 range, Eddie Jacks is a very reasonable place for an enjoyable evening out. Though not all the food is great, it's such a pleasant restaurant that no one seems to mind. ∎

—Stan Sesser, April 17, 1987

Enrico's
★

504 Broadway, San Francisco. 392-6220. Open every day 11:30 A.M. to 3 A.M. Full bar. Master-Card, Visa, American Express. Reservations accepted. Moderate.

The loyal staff at this beloved San Francisco cafe say that Enrico's closed to remodel; Herb Caen reported that Enrico's was closed down by the feds for nonpayment of payroll taxes. Whatever happened, a spruced up and beneficially remodeled Enrico's has reopened to everyone's relief.

Enrico's, after all, is one of the few restaurants in town with outdoor seating on an important cultural thoroughfare. Lunch or late-night seats under the outdoor heaters at white-linen-covered tables offer a unique city tableau—politicians, writers, entertainers of all sorts, entertainment lawyers, politically connected lawyers, business lawyers, real estate lawyers, personal-injury lawyers, and dentists all saying hello to each other.

However, now that the inside has been nicely opened up, it's perfectly acceptable to sit indoors, away from the noise and fumes of traffic, and out of the cold that penetrates even when the heaters are on. The ice cream counter has been removed from the center of the dining room, affording every table indoors an unobstructed view outside. The two parts of the restaurant have been brought together.

Things are about the same in the kitchen, where Enrico Banducci still cooks. Though the menu is huge, don't expect it all to be available or trustworthy. Highlights have always been and still are chicken thighs, the most delectable part of the bird, deboned, marinated, and crisply grilled, served with vegetables and mashed potato. Fish can be excellent here, especially the Friday special of four filleted rex sole lavished in parsley and brown butter.

Mr. Banducci's delicate homemade pasta called angel wings, with spinach, basil, and avocado worked into the dough, are always a treat. Another unusual combination, fettuccine with dried porcini and prawns, somehow tastes Asian and delicious. Very thinly sliced tomatoes and red onions piled high on a plate and dressed in a fine, old-fashioned "french dressing" are seasonally on target, but a spinach salad is ruined by a topping of smelly canned shrimp.

I have tried now, on three occasions since the reopening, to order a piece of Mr. Banducci's delicious fresh apple pie, but it has not been available. If there is one thing that Mr. Banducci should do differ-

ently in his kitchen, it is to teach the cook on duty how to make his apple pie. After a mediocre dish like tired cross-rib of beef in artificial gravy, you need the apple pie to end the meal on a high note. Mr. Banducci's new partners should have insisted on the availability of the apple pie as part of their deal. ∎

—Patricia Unterman, September 5, 1986

Erna's Elderberry House

★★

Highway 41, at the southern end of Oakhurst (from Fresno, take 41 north for forty miles; from Highway 140 toward Yosemite, take Highway 49 south at Mariposa to Oakhurst, a distance of twenty-six miles, then continue to Yosemite by going north on 41). 209-683-6800. Open for lunch Wednesday through Friday 11:30 A.M. to 1:30 P.M.; for brunch Sunday 11 A.M. to 1:30 P.M.; for dinner Wednesday through Monday 5:30 to 8:30 P.M. Beer, wine. MasterCard, Visa. Reservations suggested. Moderate fixed-price dinner.

Taking a long drive for a great meal is a concept much more widely accepted in Europe than in America. In France, for instance, elegant and expensive restaurants flourish in little villages hours away from major cities, patronized by people who consider a day in a car a small price to pay for gastronomic adventure.

Such a restaurant is a rarity in California. I can only think of two, and one of them, the New Boonville Hotel, perished a year ago amid newspaper headlines, as its debt-ridden owners, Vernon and Charlene Rollins, fled to France.

The second is Erna's Elderberry House in Oakhurst, a tiny town in the Sierra foothills on the highway between Fresno and Yosemite. I had gotten occasional letters from readers about it for the last three years, and six weeks ago Craig Claiborne wrote an admiring *New York Times* piece about it. So after a backpacking trip in Mineral King, I stopped to see what the fuss was about.

If ever a restaurant was misnamed, this is it. If you expect to find a folksy American woman in the kitchen baking berry pies, you're in for quite a surprise.

Instead, you find yourself in Erna's Valhalla, the palatial realization of the dream of a Viennese woman named Erna Kubin. Imagine a town that's little more than a collection of gas stations and fast-food places lining a highway. At one end is the astonishing sight of a sprawling hilltop chateau of rock and stucco walls and a red tile roof. To enter, you pass through a gate whose stone pillars bear the sign Le Domaine du Sureau, "the estate of the elder tree."

Inside, the three sumptuously decorated dining rooms could just as easily house a three-star restaurant in France. When you hear about the oil paintings, the tapestries, the framed mirrors, and the French ceramics, you fear it might all border on kitsch, but everything is done with impeccable taste.

Kubin, a gregarious woman, greets you at the door, appears constantly at the table, and also acts as co-chef with her partner, Fernando Madrigal. The two have worked together since 1979 when they ran a restaurant in Yosemite.

Their food can best be termed Continental cooking adapted to California cuisine, but it's really much more. If the dinner I had is any indication, Kubin and Madrigal are far more interested in inventing exciting dishes than in reproducing what they've come across elsewhere. My meal was exceptional by the standards of San Francisco; except for the bread (which isn't served unless you ask), there isn't a sign of what must be the enormous difficulties of getting good ingredients in such a remote location.

Each night, there's a different fixed-price dinner, a real bargain at around $30. Just as during the early years at Chez Panisse, you're given no choice except for being able to substitute a steak if the entree doesn't appeal to you.

Although I had come from six nights of eating freeze-dried mush in the mountains and was looking forward to any sort of real food, the entree for my dinner sounded like a recipe for disaster. It was tuna on a bed of sauerkraut in roquefort sauce, a most improbable combination if there ever was one. Besides, even in a San Francisco fish restaurant, it's hard to find a piece of tuna that both tastes very fresh and isn't overcooked, since it dries out so quickly.

But Erna's pulled it off magnificently. The sauerkraut had first been soaked to take the bite out, then sauteed in bacon fat to give it flavor, and finally sauteed with apples. A delicate and fruity taste replaced the usual heavy sauerkraut flavor. And the sauce of brown butter, flambeed brandy, and crème fraîche had only a hint of roquefort taste, enough to enhance the tuna instead of drowning it out.

Finally, the tuna itself, delivered that day from Monterey, was perfectly fresh and wonderfully moist. The huge plate looked magnificent, with the tuna surrounded by an array of interesting vegetables, including spaghetti squash and oyster mushrooms.

But that wasn't all. The meal started with what was called beef roulade, but was a clever adaptation of Hungarian goulash to the lightness and delicacy of French cooking. Filet mignon pieces had been sauteed with onions, shallots, and paprika, baked in puff pastry with a bit of spinach and cheese, and then served with a seductive sauce of tomatoes and paprika.

Next came a yellow squash soup that was as good as a pureed vegetable soup can get. Besides chicken stock and cream, the ingredients included finely chopped onion and caraway seeds to enhance the flavor and body. On top were pieces of duck crackling, chopped-up crisp duck skin, another unlikely marriage that worked beautifully.

A salad dressed with fruit vinaigrette, a nightly feature at Erna's, also deserves mention. For my dinner, a mixture of baby lettuces was dressed with a sensational pear vinaigrette; pears had been marinated in vinegar, then pureed with salt, pepper, and herbs, then blended with safflower oil.

Complaints? The magnificent-looking dessert plate had a chocolate-orange souffle and a goat cheese tart, but both fell short on flavor. A honeydew sorbet between courses needed sweeter melon. Although there were some decent California wines, the wine list was amateurish, with only a couple of French wines, and the word "vintage" given instead of the actual year. Finally, there was an unpleasantly long wait between a couple of the courses.

But those are minor quibbles compared to what Erna Kubin and Fernando Madrigal have pulled off. In a gastronomic no-man's-land, they've created an elegant country restaurant with the feel and tastes of Europe. It's just half an hour out of the way if you take the most popular route, Highway 140, from San Francisco to Yosemite, and it's well worth the trip. ■

—Stan Sesser, August 21, 1987

Esther's Ironworks Cafe

★

See review for Moshi Moshi.

Fatapple's

★

1346 Martin Luther King Jr. Way (old Grove Street), Berkeley. 526-2260. Also 7525 Fairmount Avenue, El Cerrito. 528-3433. Berkeley branch open Monday through Friday from 6 A.M. to 11 P.M., Saturday and Sunday 7 A.M. to 11 P.M. El Cerrito branch open Sunday through Thursday 7 A.M. to 10 P.M., Friday and Saturday until 10 P.M. Beer, wine. Cash only. No reservations. Inexpensive.

When I got back from Asia, I decided I was tired of all the usual stuff like snake soup and monkey meat. It was time for a change, to taste something exotic, to do a type of restaurant I've hardly ever reviewed before: a hamburger place.

I don't write about hamburgers for the same reason I haven't done a comparative tasting of TV dinners. There are simply too few meals in life to waste some so egregiously. I don't think there's another food prepared more poorly by more restaurants than a hamburger.

It's not that a hamburger has to be bad. Those at the now-defunct New Boonville Hotel had wonderful buns baked in their kitchen, and flavorful meat grilled over mesquite, probably from the cow down the street. Add some sauteed spinach fresh from their garden and melted goat cheese, and you've got a hamburger that's pure ecstasy.

Where to find a good hamburger in the Bay Area? One possibility immediately came to mind: Fatapple's in Berkeley. When you pass by this place after work at 5:30, there's a line out the door. When you pass by at 10 P.M., there's a line out the door. Something good has to be going on.

Recently Fatapple's opened a branch in El Cerrito, a much bigger place where you can actually walk in and get a table. So I rounded up some hamburger-loving friends, and we worked our way through both restaurants in one night.

While the food is the same at both, there's a big difference in atmosphere that almost makes the wait in Berkeley preferable. The El Cerrito Fatapple's, a cavernous room with high ceilings strung with vent pipes, is as depressing as some of the state-owned restaurants in China. The Berkeley branch is a total contrast: a small, cheerful room pleasantly decorated with blown-up photographs of Jack London on the walls.

In the old days, your choice at Fatapple's was limited to a hamburger or a top sirloin steak. That has changed, though, and now there are a couple of lasagnas, chili, a chicken cannelloni offered only at El Cerrito, and three dinner-sized salads.

Still, what you see on almost every table is a hamburger and french fries. And, frankly, I'm mystified.

The hamburger patty itself is decent: fairly thick and charcoal grilled. But the so-called kaiser roll is little more than a tasteless, mushy hamburger bun. The sliced tomato is cottony, the lettuce run-of-the-mill, the cheddar cheese shaved on cold instead of melted. As for the french fries, they're nothing less than a disaster, greasy and tasting primarily of overused cooking oil. I'd sneak in a bag from McDonald's.

But when you dispense with all this stuff and order the hamburger steak platter, you'll do much better. You get a half-pound slab of meat, which turns out to be much tastier all alone. With it comes a fabulous baked potato, not wrapped in foil, but baked in an oven the way it should be—until the skin turns crisp—and served with butter and sour cream.

The platter also includes a cup of soup and a hot, home-baked whole-wheat roll. The two soups I tasted, pumpkin and cream of mushroom, had a fresh home-made flavor.

The other dishes at Fatapple's are a mixed bag, distinguished by big portions of fresh ingredients, but marred by almost a total lack of seasoning. The pasta salad looked magnificent; it was a heaping platter filled with shreds of turkey, vegetables, and lots of pine nuts, virtually obliterating the cold pasta underneath. It was a lot of food, but had no taste.

Two of the three pastas, the lasagna bolognese and the chicken cannelloni, were gloppy, unseasoned messes, inundated with thick sauces. The spinach lasagna was much better; it needed more spices, but at least it had some texture from lots of chopped fresh spinach.

Two of the other offerings were much better than the pastas. The spinach salad was huge, even the small one, and covered with tasty feta cheese, walnuts, and black beans. The chili had first-rate ingredients, but it lacked the heat that could have made it spectacular.

Fatapple's makes a big show of its home-baked desserts, and both restaurants have takeout bakeries. The bran muffins, pecan pie, and a lemony, New York–style cheesecake were excellent. The apple pie, with its puffy crust, looked terrific, but the apples had been cooked to mush, and the predominant taste was sugar rather than apples.

It's possible to put together a very decent inexpensive meal at Fatapple's if you order soup, a hamburger platter with a baked potato, and cheesecake for dessert. But so many of the other things are disappointing that I'm still mystified by those ever-present long lines in front. After eating their hamburger and french fries, I'm ready to go back to the monkey meat and snake. ■

—Stan Sesser, December 20, 1985

Faz Restaurant and Bar

★ ★

132 Bush Street, San Francisco. 362-4484. Open for lunch Monday through Friday 11 A.M. to 3 P.M.; for dinner Tuesday through Friday 5 to 9 P.M. Full bar. MasterCard, Visa, American Express. Reservations accepted. Inexpensive to moderate.

A little over a year ago Faz Poursohi opened Caffe Latte, a financial district cafeteria that garnered three stars in this column for being the best of its kind. A few months ago, Mr. Poursohi opened his second restaurant, practically next door to the first, and it, too, is out of the ordinary. Eponymously named Faz, it offers a unique selection of smoked and grilled foods paired with salads—a combination that satisfies both light and serious eaters in the business district lunch market.

Mr. Poursohi appears to be one of those people who instinctively know how to cook. His good sense about food is evident in his simple and tasty dishes. The freshness of the ingredients and the method of cooking are more important to him than complicated recipes. Likewise, his restaurants are cleanly decorated and efficiently served. There's nothing extraneous or unnecessary about his plates or his service. He goes for straightforward preparation of good ingredients in his cooking and organization and helpfulness on the dining room floor. When he comes to your table, always in immaculate chef's whites, to suggest a dish or see if you like your meal, you can see that he loves what he's doing.

Faz, the restaurant, looks like it was

squeezed upward. It inhabits a long narrow building with three floors. The noisy first floor is packed with banquettes along one wall and a long counter with stools along the other. An open kitchen takes up the back of the room, and if you want to be close to the cooking action and Mr. Poursohi, there are a few tables that are intimate with the stoves. Upstairs, a more formal, carpeted dining room with tables and chairs and windows that look down to Bush Street provides a somewhat quieter ambience. A third floor is used as a private dining room. The potentially cramped space gets a basic white paint job to make it feel more spacious, along with some subtle touches like beams sponged with pastel pink and blue paint to give them a phosphorescent glow, white marble counters and floors downstairs, and comfortable upholstered chairs.

Much of the impetus behind the menu of the new restaurant comes from the cooking equipment, a smoker and a mesquite grill. Mr. Poursohi learned how to smoke foods when he was the chef at MacArthur Park in Palo Alto and his own ribs and chicken have been consistently moist, smoky, and delicious. The tart, mild barbecue sauce is reminiscent of MacArthur Park's, but with the addition of a little more catsup. Though ribs and chicken are a staple of the menu, many other items are smoked, like a three-inch-thick pork chop, which is then grilled to order and served with lukewarm red potatoes roasted with rosemary. Faz smokes all kinds of fish—mahimahi, salmon, cod, tuna, swordfish—with varying success. One day on the smoked fish platter thick slices of meltingly tender smoked salmon were draped over a pile of greens in a sour-cream dressing garnished by a half-pound slice of tomato. I liked everything about the plate and would come to Faz to lunch just for it. Some of the other smoked fish tends to be a little dry; some cod has been too fishy. No technique is trickier than smoking fish, though one day's special appetizer of paper-thin slices of smoked venison, sprinkled with grated fresh horseradish and a creamy mustard sauce, was stunning.

One of my favorite dishes here is a miraculously velvety chicken breast warmed on the mesquite grill and served with green salad and a mild sesame dressing. It is a spectacular dish. Mr. Poursohi is one of the few who understands how to cook chicken breasts! A gently smoked fillet of turkey with balsamic vinaigrette and sliced strawberries in the salad is interesting but doesn't work as well. Just a plain house salad made with crisp romaine tossed in a fine, tart tarragon vinaigrette and garnished with those improbably good tomato slices hits the spot. A gigantic artichoke, watery from overboiling, pales before the other appetizer choices.

As good as the smoked chicken and ribs are, the jumbo shrimp that come off the grill may be my favorite dish here. The large, meaty shrimp are split down the back, grilled in their shells just until they turn pink, and served with a ramekin of basil butter, which you don't even need. The grilling is so expert that all the sweetness and tenderness of the shellfish come through. They reminded me of shrimp I'd had on the beach in Mexico. Another delicious creation is Faz's lamb burger, a spicy patty smothered with sauteed onions, chopped tomato, parsley, and scallion on a soft, hollowed-out sesame-seed roll. My mouth waters just thinking about it.

For dessert there's a heavy, high, lemony New York–style cheesecake, a fudgy but not excessive chocolate torte, and a bowl of warm apples with a buttery crumb topping and sour-cream sauce that smelled like it had been kept warm over the smoker.

The restaurant gets high marks for its large selection of wines by the glass and its well-chosen wine list.

Faz is already packed at lunch but still comfortable at dinner. If you are looking for a reasonably priced, forthrightly delicious meal, you can depend on this restaurant any time. ∎

—Patricia Unterman, May 4, 1986

Ristorante Firenze

★

1421 Stockton, San Francisco. 421-5813. Open Monday through Friday for lunch 11:30 A.M. to 2 P.M., Monday through Saturday for dinner 5:30 to 11 P.M. Beer, wine. MasterCard, Visa. Reservations accepted. Moderate.

Ristorante Firenze belongs to an older style of Italian restaurant in San Francisco, though it is less than a year old. From its sleek, modern look you would expect *nuova cucina*, but a glance at the menu reassures you that this restaurant is breaking no new culinary ground.

What used to be Frank's Extra Bar, a North Beach hangout with an espresso machine, a pool table, and a pizza oven, has now become a chic little spot, with a maitre d' who is determined to pack as many people in as possible. The cramped dining room is made to feel more spacious by clean, geometrical lines, a soft peachy-pink color scheme, and indirect lighting. You sit at small, white-linen-covered tables pulled up to upholstered banquettes and soft chairs framed with blond wood. The handsome marble exterior stands out on a block where North Beach cedes into Chinatown.

The Italian waiters are old hands, able to squeeze between chairs pushed too close together and to gracefully make people get up in the middle of their meals to allow other diners to leave their tables. The waiters are good natured and pleasantly gruff. It's impossible for them to give complete service at Firenze, because there just isn't room.

The food comes out of the book written by Doro's, Orsi's, and the era of Continental/Italian dinner houses, though prices are much cheaper and ambience more informal. The food has a homogeneity about it—it's all professionally turned out: the plates look finished; the attack, on the pastas especially, is refined; but the food, to my palate, is not exciting. You can eat pleasantly and consistently at Firenze, but the dishes lack sparkle. You expect them to taste better than they do.

The dining-out public these days is sophisticated enough to hold a kitchen to the promises on its menu. Firenze falls short on this count. Their salad of golden tomatoes does not bring the bright yellow tomatoes so readily available, nor red vine-ripened tomatoes now in season, but slices of pink tomato garnished with red onion, anchovies, capers, and the bland, emulsified house vinaigrette. Hearts of romaine dressed with blue cheese is a perfectly acceptable green salad, but it's made of torn leaves of the lettuce, not the whole, small, crisp heart leaves as advertised. Grilled bay eel turns out to be smoked eel from a bay in New Zealand, and I couldn't find the promised wild mushrooms in a sauce over some quail. Sauteed veal scallops with porcini, or boletus mushrooms, simply substituted the common domestic variety. These discrepancies don't inspire confidence in the integrity of a kitchen.

While we're discussing salad, a spinach salad sprinkled with little bits of very mild goat cheese and even milder olives tastes exactly like the other salads on the menu, under its blanket of innocuous dressing.

I do like the pasta dishes at this restaurant. They're delicate and well balanced. The sauces coat the various noodles and dumplings voluptuously without being too rich. Especially good are the house-made, rosemary-scented potato gnocchi, tender dumplings about the size of the first digit of a little finger, in a combined white sauce and tomato sauce. Our waiter gets a gold star for recommending it. Some lovely manicotti were made of delicate noodle dough stuffed with ricotta and lavished in a similar duo of light tomato sauce and cream sauce, though this time they were applied separately. *Pappardelle*, wide, satiny ribbons of house-made pasta, are tossed in a meat and mushroom sauce smoothed by cream. Narrower white and green fettuccine noodles get a similar sauce without peas and mushrooms. Everything about these pastas is soft, smooth, and round, the kind of dish people wish their mothers had made for them. They are more about texture than flavor.

The best of the main courses was a special one night, a plate of fork-tender veal stew flanked by a split Italian sausage in brown gravy on a bed of buttery polenta, an endearing, home-style dish. Roast chicken had a deeply browned skin and a lemony, rosemary-seasoned gravy afloat with butter. However, two whole quail wrapped in *pancetta* never browned. Their meat tasted as if it had cooked more by its lemony marinade than heat from the stove. The ubiquitous brown sauce with domestic mushrooms didn't make them any better.

A grilled steak strangely lacked flavor, tasting like neither beef nor veal. The previously mentioned porcini-less veal scallops came in a flour-thickened brown sauce without the least bit of character. Sauteed calamari had the mealy texture of long-stewed calamari, another surprise deviation from the menu description. A seafood stew called *cacciucco* developed a delicious broth enriched with the flavors of fresh tomatoes and garlic, but the shellfish themselves were tired. Garlic toasts stuck into the broth were the best part of the dish.

Most of the main courses come with tasty vegetables, either sauteed spinach or broccoli, both fresh, buttery, and garlic-infused.

For dessert, the restaurant makes its own *tiramisu* with layers of coffee-soaked sponge cake and mascarpone, or Italian crème fraîche.

The wine list is adequate, with bottles like a 1982 Carmignano, a lighter-bodied, flavorful Italian red wine, leading the field.

Firenze has revived the San Francisco brown sauce, resurrected the creamy meat and tomato sauce and hit on a salad dressing of such dullness that it could come from a bottle. Yet, these old-fashioned San Francisco tastes still appeal to enough people to keep Firenze painfully full. They don't appeal to me. ∎

—Patricia Unterman, September 6, 1987

565 Clay Restaurant and Bar

★

565 Clay Street (at Montgomery), San Francisco. 434-2345. Open for lunch Monday through Friday 11:30 A.M. to 3 P.M.; for dinner Monday through Friday 5 to 10 P.M., Saturday 6 to 10 P.M. Full bar. MasterCard, Visa, American Express. Reservations accepted. Moderate.

The Restaurant and Bar at 565 Clay was brought to my attention by its owner, David Cohn, a former Zen priest who was the business manager of Greens. In a long self-composed press release entitled "The Zen of Dining in the Financial District," Cohn revealed the unique resources available to his new restaurant.

He has a direct pipeline to the organic produce grown at Green Gulch Farms and to the breads from Tassajara Bread Bakery. He once managed both operations. His years in the Zen community taught him how to serve others, and his experience as vice-president of the Zen Center's numerous projects gave him business savvy.

Yet his new restaurant in a former Scoma's, though very carefully thought out, is not quite at peace with its Financial District location directly across the street from the Transamerica Pyramid. In many ways, 565 Clay is a refreshing addition to the neighborhood. Here is a restaurant that offers food made with the most honest ingredients; that excels at salad and vegetable dishes, that decorates its walls with Chris Brown portraits of American presidents (on loan from Paule Anglim's gallery). This elevated approach to Financial District dining is somewhat undercut by the smoke-filled dining rooms and hard liquor bar. And the service, on the two occasions I visited this restaurant, fell somewhere between "estian" ooze and Zen outer space. 565 Clay seems to be a restaurant in search of both a name and an identity, though on both visits the food was encouraging.

For lunch, during this restaurant's first month of operation, we began with a huge plate of skillfully deep-fried calamari, tender, crisp, and clean-tasting. The crunchy rings were sprinkled with parmesan cheese and came with lively house-made tartar sauce. A salad composed of the prettiest leaves of assorted lettuces and watercress arrived damp and underdressed.

A thinly sliced grilled rib-eye steak nearly flopped off its plate, it was so big. I would have preferred a thicker, more compact piece of beef. A huge coin of zinfandel butter melted on top of it, a combination of fats I don't like. Delicious grilled red onion rings reminded me of the best of Greens, though the shoestring fries were limp and greasy—a far cry from the perfectly fried calamari.

A soupy pasta dish of fettuccine, fresh shrimp, smoked salmon, and several cups of reduced cream stayed tasty for two bites before it collapsed under its own weight. For dessert, a lemon-curd tart with a brown, buttery crust was just right with a perfect cappuccino.

At this busy lunch, both dining room staff and kitchen seemed as if they were barely keeping up. A visit about a month later at a much quieter dinner allowed both waiters and chef to concentrate mostly on us. That evening we began with airy fresh corn fritters served with a charming, vinegary/sweet tomato chutney on a bed of watercress—one of the best little dishes I've tasted.

Also fine was a lemony caesar salad scattered with croutons that melted in our mouths and a snowfall of grated parmesan. However, a warm salad of romaine, cauliflower, shiitake mushrooms, and hot and sweet peppers in a vinegary szechuan dressing was not entirely successful.

A warm scallop salad sprinkled with grapefruit zest and chives didn't come together either. Perhaps if the scallops had been chilled and marinated in the grapefruit vinaigrette the dish might have clicked.

Main courses at night are limited to three meat selections, a fresh fish, and a pasta, all prepared with slight variations from lunch. A poached chicken breast, topped with chopped mushrooms, prosciutto, and herbs, was pleasingly balanced, as was a dish of tender roast pork loin in a fruity sauce scented by ginger and accompanied by baked pippin apples.

Broiling a slab of leg of lamb like a steak, as was done here, did not show it off to advantage. All main courses came with generous portions of wonderful, crisp, buttery, garlicky sauteed vegetables. The pasta that night came with small scallops and a bland cream sauce given color by wisps of basil and red pepper. The standout dessert was a delicate crème caramel.

I wish that 565 Clay made more of a statement either one way or the other. Why not be a Greens-style vegetarian restaurant in the Financial District and really take advantage of Cohn's connections? Or, if 565 Clay wants to serve booze and beef, then pull out the thick chops, steaks, and half chickens and do it right.

The restaurant seems unfocused; the food hasn't been pulled together. Yes, you can always find something delicious to eat. But I think 565 Clay has the potential for offering something even newer and more exciting to the Financial District. ∎

—Patricia Unterman, July 28, 1985

Fleur de Lys

★★★

777 Sutter Street, San Francisco. 673-7779. Open Monday through Saturday 6 to 10 P.M. Full bar. Major credit cards. Reservations recommended. Expensive.

Hubert Keller was a three-star chef trapped in a one-star restaurant until his recent move to Fleur de Lys. Every time I visited his former dining room at Sutter 500, I was dazzled by the food but disappointed by the room. Here was a brilliant, young, incredibly well-trained French chef turning out original, elaborate, technically perfect French dishes in a venue that not only lacked personality but an aura of specialness to match the food. I'm happy to report that M. Keller's partnership with Maurice Rouas at Fleur de Lys has finally provided him a suitable dining room.

Designed by the late Michael Taylor, Fleur de Lys has never lacked for character or, indeed, drama. It's a created environment, inspired I think, by the idea of a garden tent in the French countryside, though the design is far too sophisticated to project much feeling of rustic naivete. Yards and yards of red floral fabric form an interior room. One side of this draped tent is mirrored so cleverly that it gives the illusion that you're in a room twice as large. Visible walls are made of rough wooden planks. Little wicker lamps protrude from the material, giving this soft structure an intimate glow. In the center of the room under the peak of the tent, a towering arrangement of exotic flowers rises up out of the sea of tables, giving the space a center. The setting uncannily reflects Hubert Keller's cooking, which is also highly arranged but with many references to Provencal country cooking.

Some of the most wonderful dishes from Sutter 500 have remained on the new typewritten menu—like Keller's gorgeous garden of vegetables so realistically replete with snails in a clear broth bolstered by Meursault, garlic, and fresh herbs; and a thick pureed soup of tomatoes and red peppers served at room temperature that has such a deep and unique flavor it almost becomes a new food.

Every evening a different tasting menu of four or five courses brings forth new dishes from Keller's already large repertoire. One night fresh American foie gras was set off stunningly by an imaginative stew of endive, sauterne, and fresh ginger. This was followed by a flamboyant presentation of spinach packages filled with chunks of fresh lobster and slices of salmon napped with a butter sauce delicately scented with saffron and clam liquor. Next, a lovely piece of tender veal nestled into a savory bed of artichoke hearts and wild mushrooms. For those who attempted the "menu prestige," a very strange-looking giant mushroom was delivered from the kitchen as a second main course. It was a hollowed-out and lidded baked potato standing on end with a thyme-scented squab breast inside. The potato skin served the noble purpose of sopping up a fine red wine sauce. A choice from no less than seven desserts followed by coffee and a platter of fresh, tiny cookies and chocolate-dipped fruit ends a Keller meal.

Don't fear if you want a smaller repast. Lovely a la carte dishes stud the menu. One of my favorites is an appetizer of a tender corn pancake concealing a thin slice of buttery sauteed salmon, the whole napped with chive beurre blanc and then topped with golden caviar. With each tender forkful, all the elements melt into each other in the most delectable way.

Whenever I see a dish that puts duck breast, duck *confit* (duck slowly cooked in duck fat), and cabbage on one plate, I have to order it. In this case, the duck *confit* was wrapped in the cabbage, the rare breast, a little tough and fatty, was sliced, and the rest of the plate was decked out in poufs of hubbard squash puree, sauteed peeled cherry tomatoes, and assorted baby vegetables.

Many dishes, whether they are appetizers or main courses, bring at least two separate main ingredients to the plate and Keller's trick is to bring them together. A custardlike mousseline of scallops accompanies thick medallions of roasted salmon in a ginger-butter sauce. Foie gras on spinach leaves gets thin slices of duck breast. A chunk of grilled swordfish is but one disparate element on a plate that includes a dab of a delicious Provencal relish called *creoja* sauce, five leaves of baby lettuce, croutons, and nicoise olives.

The desserts bring to life my childhood fantasies of what sugar plum fairies eat. My very favorite is a warm, airy, souffleed pancake full of warm raspberries with vanilla ice cream in a cookie flower and a little chocolate mousse mouse drinking from a pool of *crème à l'anglaise*. Bittersweet chocolate souffle cake takes on new flavor dimensions when eaten with a terrine of grapefruit sorbet and fresh mint sauce. A pastry flower with raspberry sorbet is thrown in for good measure. There are chocolate meringue swans and crème brûlée and mint-flavored nougats and all sorts of house-made sorbets and ice creams. The dessert menu certainly holds up its end of the meal. You stagger out of the floral tent, heady from your visit to Hubert Keller's brilliantly imagined world of food and wine.

Keller reminds me of Norman Mailer, not in personality, but in the depth and style of his talent. He's unstoppably prolific. Once he gets going on a tasting menu or even a dish, he pours every idea he has into it. There's always something brilliant on the plate, but there's often too much going on peripherally, too many garnishes and flourishes and comments and phrases that don't relate to the structure of the dish. This doesn't diminish the overall effect of his cooking so much as side-tracks it. Hubert Keller is so exuberant, so technically adept, so eager to please, that he doesn't edit. He kills you with kindness.

I should add, however, that the highly decorated plate is exactly what everyone is doing in France right now. When Americans go to three- and two-star restaurants they expect it, as they do right here at Masa's and Fleur de Lys. But it seems to me that an important chef has to be very thoughtful about every single thing that's put on the plate. If his style is elaborative, the elaboration should clearly relate to the main idea. That which is only decorative is not art. Perhaps as Keller settles into his new restaurant, he will feel freer to simplify, shorten, and sort out a bit, which will only expand his cooking, not lessen it. ∎

—Patricia Unterman, October 19, 1986

Flower Lounge

★★★

1671 El Camino Real, Millbrae. 878-8108. Open 11:30 A.M. to 2:30 P.M., 5 to 9:30 P.M. Wine, beer. MasterCard, Visa, American Express, Diners Club for tabs over $20. Reservations accepted except for lunch on Saturday and Sunday. Moderate.

Rumors of extraordinary Chinese meals served at the Flower Lounge, an outpost of a Hong Kong restaurant in Millbrae, followed me around. They reached me in unlikely settings—at fancy dinners prepared by visiting French chefs, at wine-tasting luncheons, at picnics with kids. Finally, I was invited to a dinner at the Flower Lounge arranged by someone who eats often at the restaurant and knows its repertoire. The banquet, served course by course, was the best Chinese meal I've had in this country.

To make sure that this was not an isolated experience, I returned to the Flower Lounge with my own group of six. My first heady experience was confirmed. We ordered a delicious and exciting meal straight off the menu. The Flower Lounge, hardly a rumor, beckons loud and clear as a temple of great dining.

Unlike many of the newer, family-oriented Chinese dining rooms, the Flower Lounge boasts a distinctive decor. Jade green ceramic tiles on the facade of the low-slung building echo inside in the coral-colored main dining room. They form an interior tile roof held up by wooden columns that rim the room. The pretend patio is meant to blur the difference between outdoors and indoors. A similar kind of illusion happens in smaller side rooms where mirrors are used to make the rooms seem bigger.

Light from recessed fixtures and wrought-iron chandeliers is bright and cheerful but not stark. Antique ceramic figures in mirrored cases built into the walls, carpeting, and white tablecloths give the Flower Lounge a slightly dressy look. Most of the customers in this ever-bustling restaurant dress up a bit, too, in casual but stylish attire. Hong Kong businessmen in three-piece suits, whole families outfitted in Versace, and lots of modern haircuts make you wonder if you really could be on the Peninsula. The Flower Lounge turns out to be an enclave of sophisticated, pan-Pacific culture tucked a wing's length away from the San Francisco airport.

The food comes as a surprise, too, because it's so tasty, carefully prepared, and stylish. Most of the dishes are Cantonese, which means that they are subtly seasoned, based on excellent stocks, and use the freshest of ingredients, but there are some dishes from other provinces as well. At the prearranged banquet, many of the dishes were handsomely garnished with intricate borders of sliced vegetables.

Of those special advance-order dishes, winter melon soup dramatically presented in a whole winter melon best represented the astounding capabilities of this kitchen. In a clear, rich broth inside the melon were tiny cubes of duck, duck cracklings, and meltingly tender giblets, straw mushrooms, and chunks of the satiny flesh of the winter melon scraped off the sides as it was served. I even liked the shreds of surimi, a processed fish product that looks like crab meat, pushed off the edge of the melon into the soup at the last minute. Another stunning presentation brought a whole braised duck with glistening skin stuffed with dried sea scallops and surrounded by baby bok choy in a delicious brown sauce. The waiter deftly split the breast open with two spoons, removed the breast bones, and scooped out the stuffing.

Two other dishes not listed on the menu are worth remembering and ordering ahead. Squab with mango involved two separate methods of cooking. The breast was sliced and stir-fried with the mango; the legs and head deep fried until crisp. The combination of tropical fruit with the dark-fleshed poultry could have inspired a French master. The Flower Lounge also prepared a superb conch dish. Thick strips of the slightly chewy shellfish were scored and stir-fried with scallops in a delicately constructed sauce seasoned with garlic and red chilies. I couldn't stop eating it.

Don't think there aren't many gorgeous dishes to be ordered straight off the menu, like the intriguing combination of crisp, juicy deep-fried shrimp and fire-roasted walnuts ever so lightly tossed in a mayonnaise-based sauce, or a simple, irresistible roast chicken with miraculously moist flesh and crackling skin.

I never think of tofu as being exciting, but at Flower Lounge it figured in two fantastic creations: in tender little dumplings of tofu and ground fish, steamed then fried, and served over mustard greens (must be ordered ahead); and as a creamy stew seasoned with salted fish and ground pork cooked and presented in a covered ceramic pot. One treatment was reminiscent of the most elegant French quenelles; the other represented a homey, accessible family-style dish. What amazes me about many Chinese kitchens, particularly the Flower Lounge, is that they can turn out both difficult and casual cuisine with equal conviction.

Some other dishes to look for on the menu are a Hunan-style lobster cooked in a ceramic pot with an explosive seasoning of ginger, garlic, black beans, and hot chilies; and the signature, magically crisp deep-fried catfish, split and filled with stir-fried scallions and Chinese parsley, a masterpiece of Chinese fish cookery. Big, meaty chunks of pork sparerib are braised in a ceramic pot with aromatic spices until the meat falls off the bone and creates a rich, greaseless pot gravy that's slightly sweet and sour. Thin, chewy slices of fresh squid get a quick stir-fry with asparagus-sized rounds of scallion and a handful of black beans. Shredded chicken gets tossed with fire-dried, sugar-glazed almonds and lettuce in the inventive "rainbow chicken salad."

And whatever you do, order *fook kin* (Fukien) fried rice, really an Asian risotto delivered in a glass dish. A copious sauce of scallops, mushrooms, and aromatics soaks into the seasoned rice making it moist and delicious. I ate bowls and bowls of it at both meals.

In an attempt to reorder the fabulous conch dish from the banquet, I got a conch dish that wasn't nearly as good—stir-fried sliced conch with vegetables. The conch was thinly sliced instead of served in those voluptuous chewy-tender strips and the mustard greens were tired. This was the one single dish out of many that I would not reorder.

For dessert there's a fruity, clean-flavored mango gelatin or a bowl of gently sweet, warm tapioca pudding that's so soothing and refreshing that it ends the meal perfectly.

You walk out of this remarkable restaurant knowing that you've only scratched the surface of what this kitchen can prepare. If you're serious about exploring Chinese food, head right down to the Peninsula with a hungry group, making sure to call ahead for reservations and a special dish or two. I asked one of the managers over the phone how people who don't speak Chinese can get some of the dishes not translated on the menu and she assured me that plenty of captains and waiters who spoke English would help. Judging from the deft, friendly treatment I received on both occasions, I have to believe her. ∎

—Patricia Unterman, June 21, 1987

Fog City Diner

★

1300 Battery Street (at the Embarcadero), San Francisco. 982-2000. Open daily 11:30 A.M. to 11 P.M., Friday and Saturday until midnight. Full bar. MasterCard, Visa. Reservations essential, often a couple weeks in advance. Moderate.

Fog City Diner opened two years ago, and the reservation books have been filled days and weeks in advance ever since. Last year, this enormously appealing restaurant took in $2.69 million.

But the restaurant is also in the middle of a labor dispute with its employees. Reading about the dispute led me to wonder what has been going on in the kitchen.

For one thing, Cyndi Pawlcyn, who made such a name for herself with her concept of innovative "small dishes," is no longer there cooking. She now divides her time as executive chef of Fog City, Mustard's in the Napa Valley, and the Rio Grill in Carmel, which are all under the same ownership. Fog City's new chef is Carroll Knapp, who comes from Kuleto's.

While opinions about restaurants are of course very subjective, I think anyone who eats at Fog City will agree on two points. First, no place has a more pleasant, more responsive staff. If you fear waiters who are surly because of the labor dispute, forget it. They're not only friendly, but so competent they don't miss a cue.

The small dish concept—much of the menu is devoted to dishes that are larger than appetizers, smaller than entrees, and cry out to be shared—means that each table orders lots of food. That could lead to chaos if everything came at once. But the waiters pace things perfectly without being asked. And if four of you order a dish that comes in threes, which happened to us with the crab cakes, the waiter tells you about it and offers to bring you a fourth.

The second irrefutable fact about Fog City is that the place is great fun. It looks like a diner, but no diner was ever so fashionable and so comfortable. The whole concept of Fog City has stood the test of time; it's just as unique and interesting as the day it opened.

In fact, eating there is so much fun it's hard to pay close attention to the food. I did so only by being a spoilsport, hunched over my note pad writing down reactions as each dish came.

What I found was a variation in quality so dramatic that I could hardly believe everything was coming from the same kitchen. Only the desserts were uniform—and unfortunately, uniformly lousy.

First, some pluses. There are two salads that are not only wonderful but great bargains. What's called "unintimidating mixed greens" turns out to be wonderfully fresh lettuces, handled and presented perfectly. And a caesar salad featured good, crisp romaine with an unusually light and delicate dressing.

Several of the small dishes were impeccable. Garlic custard is a creamy, heavenly invention, surrounded by a saute of shiitake mushrooms, walnuts, and chives. The onion rings are the best in town, flavorful and not a bit greasy. The crab cakes with spicy sherry-cayenne mayonnaise are beautifully seasoned and fried to crispness.

Buffalo chicken wings—something that's almost always a disaster—shine; they emerge from the fryer juicy and greaseless, and the accompanying gorgonzola dip is first-rate. And if you think those are a bargain, wait until you try the polenta. You get two big pieces, creamy and flavorful, topped with chopped tomatoes and parmesan cheese.

How, then, can you explain the cioppino, whose bland broth was flavored only by the reek of tuna that tasted so spoiled we couldn't eat it? Or tough, none-too-fresh steamed clams accompanied by a "sweet Italian sausage" with such a weird and unpleasant flavor that no one could swallow a bite? There was also grilled eggplant that not only exuded oil but sat in a pool of it on a plate. And spicy chicken salad featured tasteless chicken breast slices in the most gloppy, impenetrable peanut sauce I've ever experienced.

Many other dishes were between the two extremes. Wild-mushroom stew had some nice vegetables, but absolutely no mushroom flavor. Grilled poussin was too oily, but a tangy lemon marinade helped cut the grease. Sweetbread fritters had a pleasant interior, but a hard layer of breading and too many capers detracted from the taste.

If the five desserts I sampled were any indication, this is one part of the menu to avoid. Lemon sherbet was grainy and had the taste of frozen lemonade. A strawberry tart was too cold, too sweet, and had a tasteless crust. Apple pie was mushy and boring.

In view of the modest prices of many of the dishes, the wine list of primarily chardonnays and cabernet sauvignons was something of a rip-off. Fog City's food is too spicy for elegant, expensive wines; the food needs fruity Rhones and zinfandels that could be sold for much less, still maintaining a healthy markup. You're better off drinking beer.

So beneath the splendid decor, the competence of the waiters, and the interesting menu lies a very mixed culinary experience. You can find some excellent things to eat at Fog City. But if you order lots of dishes, you're inevitably going to encounter some disasters, too—enough to mar the whole experience. ∎

—Stan Sesser, May 15, 1987

Fresco

★

394 Broadway, San Francisco. 392-5571. Open Monday through Saturday 11:30 A.M. to 10 P.M., Thursday through Saturday until 10:30 P.M. Wine, beer. MasterCard, Visa, American Express, Diners Club. Reservations accepted. Moderate.

This city has a curious love-hate relationship with oyster bars and restaurants on Broadway. Only Swan Oyster Depot on Polk Street, a real old-timer, seems solidly implanted in the eating consciousness of the city. New comers like Odella's, which sprouted branches on Broadway next to Enrico's and Sacramento Street in the Financial District, closed them almost as quickly. Now we have Fresco, inhabiting a corner location on Broadway alive with vibrations from the past.

In the very spot where the Mystic Eye purveyed occult artifacts stands a clean, white, modern oyster bar. The once-adjacent tattoo parlor and the Tibetan import shop have been supplanted by a beer and wine bar and a dining room. As you slurp down your malpeques, you can't help but ponder how times have changed. One thing is certain, the opening of this casual, southern California–style restaurant adds new flavor to the cultural melting pot of Broadway.

Fresco should be considered mainly as an oyster bar. Its most attractive food and physical space center around the colorful shellfish laid out on ice behind a glass partition in the front of the restaurant. A counter with jars of horseradish and bottles of hot sauce set at each place beckon you to sit down and have a few oysters. Fresco is actually a large, multilevel restaurant with two separate whitewashed dining rooms and the oyster bar at the entryway. Appointments and decor are clean and simple. It's the oysters that glisten.

Every time I've eaten at Fresco, the malpeque oysters from the East Coast have been spectacular—ice cold, full of briny liquor, and firm. The gulf oysters taste flat and flaccid by comparison. Also terrific now is local dungeness crab. Fresco cracks them so that it's easy to pull out the best crab meat in the world. Tiny, tender clams on the half shell also get the highest marks. With a chunk of fresh San Francisco sourdough bread and a tumbler of Domaine Chandon poured by the glass, you can easily put together a satisfying shellfish bar meal.

However, when the kitchen gets involved, you must choose wisely. Those tiny clams steamed open in a *marinière* seasoned with shallots, wine, garlic, and enriched with a little butter are even more delicious hot. Mussels, steamed with chopped carrots, celery, and onions, did not have the brightness of flavor I look for in the best mussels, but even so they were competently prepared.

Bay shrimp louie took me by surprise. I expected the usual glop of a dressing on wilted frozen seafood, but here, lots of fresh-tasting bay shrimp crowned a salad of romaine lettuce dressed in a basil vinaigrette garnished with imported olives. A light, creamy louie sauce was served on the side. Another pleasant discovery was Fresco's relishy gazpacho, a thick, cold soup of pulverized cucumber, tomato, peppers, and onions seasoned here with oregano. Other soups did not have the gazpacho's spirit. New England clam chowder reminded me of the typical cream of cream soup, with its thick, flavorless broth and a paucity of clams. The gumbo wasn't much better. Though liberally studded with clams, scallops, and chunks of unidentifiable fish, its clunky broth was overthickened and short on sharp flavor. This gumbo smothered all the different qualities of the fish instead of using them.

Each day the kitchen grills two or three different fish, the best of which, one night, was a large, thick piece of moist swordfish. A slab of tuna came off the grill as dry as a bone. All of the fish come with crisp, buttery lightly sauteed vegetables and a rice pilaf.

Oysters get a number of different treatments. Big, creamy Tomales Bay oysters are panfried and served with a tart sauce that combines sour cream and mayonnaise. Oysters Rockefeller, as prepared here, simply ruin half a dozen good oysters. The green sauce baked onto them shows no resemblance to the spinach and herb mixture gently laced with anise liquor that one expects. At Fresco "Rockefeller" means lots of parmesan cheese and a characterless green liquid. Nor can I recommend the wrongheaded ravioli stuffed with salmon and inappropriately sauced with a cheesy "Alfredo."

In the midrange of this menu of fluctuating quality is a crab sandwich on sourdough bread made with salty crab meat, a little finely chopped celery, and good mayonnaise, and Fresco's green salads. Both the house salad and the caesar salad are composed of fresh greens and housemade croutons, but both dressings lack sparkle.

I sense that Fresco wants to project a casual, fun, carefree personality, but the kitchen and the oyster bar can be maddeningly slow in getting food out. This may keep the employees relaxed but it doesn't work well with the customers. I found Fresco to be especially annoying when I was sitting at the counter, hungry, watching a lackadaisical cook fumble around. The casual ambience should come from the menu, price, decor, the dress and manner of the staff, not from disorganization.

One thing I really do like about Fresco is the pricing. There isn't one item on the menu over $10 and from 5 to 7 P.M. you can get half a dozen oysters and a beer for just a few dollars. Now that's fun. ■

—Patricia Unterman, November 30, 1986

Golden Turtle

★ ★ ★

2211 Van Ness Avenue, San Francisco. 441-4419. Open Tuesday through Sunday 11:30 A.M. to 3 P.M., 5 to 11 P.M. Wine, beer. MasterCard, Visa, American Express. Reservations accepted. Moderate.

People resist going to branches of their

favorite restaurants. They're afraid that the quality at both new and old places will erode or that the personal treatment they earned over the years will disappear. They assume that the new version will lack the soul or spirit of the original restaurant. The commodious new branch of the Golden Turtle on Van Ness proves these misgivings groundless. The second Golden Turtle is as exciting and individual as any new restaurant could be.

The restaurant inhabits the ground floor of a large Van Ness Avenue house. While the entry looks a little awkward with its ramping for wheelchair access, a fish pond stocked with fat, lazy goldfish has been built between the stairway and the ramps and it is the first clue that this restaurant is a personal expression of its Vietnamese owners.

The interior of the restaurant took me by surprise. It's elaborate and luxurious and completely original. Lavish use of wood gives the dining room intimacy and warmth. The walls are covered with wood-collage landscapes; other parts of the wall bear floor-to-ceiling wood carvings. The carpeted dining area is raised and punctuated with burnished wooden columns out of which intertwining tree branches seem to grow. Rough halved tree trunks are part of the design as well as sconces made of gnarled wood with lights set into them. It turns out that wood carving is a hobby of owner-maitre d' Kham Tran, who has put his passion to practical use. He designed and executed the interior himself, with the help of friends.

His decor choices are assured. The tables are covered with gray tablecloths and waitresses wear graceful tunics with the same shade of gray in them. Patrons sit on sturdy wooden library chairs. The lighting is kept low; my one objection to the scheme is the sterno-fueled candles on each table which give off a chemical smell.

The food, prepared by Kimquy Tran, who co-owns the restaurant with her husband, is as wonderful as it ever was. I found the cooking to be even tastier than I remembered it from the Fifth Avenue restaurant, and these new elegant surroundings enhance it. Every dish that comes out of Mrs. Tran's kitchen exudes freshness. Many of the dishes come with piles of red leaf lettuce, watercress, Chinese parsley sprigs, cucumber, and raw carrots that look as if they had just been pulled from the garden. The fish and seafood always smell clean and sweet; the deep frying is greaseless; the sauces are light, well balanced but intense. It's pure pleasure to eat at Golden Turtle.

The Vietnamese custom of contrasting hot, savory tidbits with cool, leafy vegetables finds its highest expression in appetizers like *chao tom*, charcoal-broiled shrimp sticks that are served with silk-stocking-sheer rice pancakes, a plum sauce, and an array of raw vegetables, lettuces, and herbs. You pull the shrimp cake off pared sugarcane sticks and combine it with the vegetables and cold rice noodles in a pancake. Our waitress demonstrated. Small, thumb-sized *chai gio*, or imperial rolls, stuffed with a fragrant mixture of minced pork and shrimp, have astonishingly crisp wrappers that you also wrap in lettuce leaves.

If you want the wrapping done for you, a rice pancake is filled with thin slices of tender pork loin, rice noodles, and herbs and cut into colorful rounds that you dip into a sweet bean sauce in a dish called cold shrimp and pork salad roll. Though many of the same ingredients are used over and over again, the methods of preparation are so different that each dish tastes distinctive. A shrimp and pork salad, composed of the finest julienne strips of pork, cucumber, carrot, and mint, is tossed in a delicate sweet-and-sour dressing and garnished with lovely pink slices of shrimp. This delightful salad is piled on a crisply fried rice pancake shot with black sesame seeds. A similar salad is prepared with threads of beef, radish, cucumber, and carrot and topped with roasted peanuts. These salads rank high on my list of favored Golden Turtle dishes.

The kitchen knows how long to cook the trickiest items. Richly browned quail, flambeed at the table, offer succulent, herb-scented meat. The birds, after their trial by fire, are placed on a green salad laced with threads of onion and fresh mint. You eat the bird and the salad with your fingers, dipping it into a paste of lime juice, celery, salt, and pepper served on the side. The whole production is mouth-watering. A whole sea bass was perfectly steamed one evening, so that the fish remained succulent and flavorful from innermost bone to outermost tail. It was wreathed in fresh Chinese parsley sprigs and topped with chopped ginger and a simple, clear fish sauce. Not many chefs of any nationality know how to cook fish as sensitively as this.

The restaurant actually specializes in beef dishes, to the extent of offering a special meal of seven of them, which all can be ordered a la carte. One of the best of these is *bo luc lac*, quickly stir-fried chunks of fillet in a piquant oyster-saucelike dressing served on a salad. I've never tasted tenderer, more buttery beef. Minced beef wrapped in lot leaves is kind of a Vietnamese version of stuffed grape leaves. Both imperial beef and grilled beef kabob are skewered with pork fat and charcoal grilled to stunning effect.

The greatest of all Golden Turtle's barbecue dishes is five-spice roast chicken, which has the juiciness and flavor of those incredible barbecued chickens cooked outdoors everywhere in Thailand. One bite of Golden Turtle's exceptional chicken brought the taste memory right back.

I could go on describing dishes, but I don't see how you can go wrong ordering anything on the menu prepared by this meticulous kitchen. No dish is ever slighted, and if the ingredients for a not-often-prepared dish were not in perfect shape, I have no doubt that the kitchen wouldn't serve it. Golden Turtle is one of the rare restaurants that you can trust.

Two quick suggestions: Have the creamy, deep-fried, flambeed bananas and Vietnamese coffee for dessert, and order the Chablis Grand Cru, Bougros, 1984 to drink with the meal. This lovely wine goes uncannily well with the food. ∎

—Patricia Unterman, February 15, 1987

Guaymas

★

5 Main Street, Tiburon. 435-6300. Open Monday through Thursday 11:30 A.M. to 10 P.M., Friday and Saturday 11:30 A.M. to 11 P.M., Sunday 10:30 A.M. to 10 P.M. Full bar. Major credit cards. Reservations advised. Inexpensive to moderate.

After our walk through the Mission last Sunday, I thought it would be an interesting contrast to hop on the ferry to Tiburon to visit the hottest Mexican restaurant to open in the Bay Area since the Cadillac Bar.

Guaymas, the newest in the Spectrum group's upscale restaurant chain (MacArthur Park, Prego, Ciao, Harry's Bar), is conveniently located at the ferry landing, with outdoor patios right on the water and a stunning view of the city from the dining room.

The corporate treasuries must have been thrown wide open to build this one. Huge ceiling beams made of whole tree trunks poke through the walls in adobe-hut fashion, while more whole trees, held by cement pylons, form a dramatic outdoor railing. The first thing you see when you follow the railing into the restaurant is a tortilla kitchen cranking out hundreds of warm corn tortillas. Then you proceed to a busy bar dispensing hundreds of tangy margaritas made with fresh lime juice. After a fifteen- to thirty-minute wait, with reservations, you are ushered into the huge, white, adobe multilevel dining room with banquettes, blond wood chairs, and bright yellow tablecloths. The scale of Guaymas reminds me of eating halls in high-rise Mexican resorts during peak season when everyone is on the American plan—three meals a day included, and everyone has to eat at the same time. The best part of the Guaymas meal is delivered to the table right off the bat, a basket of those fresh, hot tortillas kept warm in a napkin and a tray of three fresh salsas—green tomatillo, smoky-sweet dried chili, and hot, fresh tomato.

Unlike usual Mexican restaurants, Guaymas emulates a more sophisticated, Mexico City style. There are tacos, quesadillas, and tostadas on the menu, but they've been miniaturized into appetizers. The main part of the menu concentrates on grilled items, unusual tamales, and stuffed chilies, and there's even a long list of desserts.

Guaymas gets credit for going for a more refined and varied Mexican cuisine, but some of the food seemed like blander versions of gutsy, ethnic dishes I have had in the Mission. The guacamole, one of Mexico's most brilliant contributions to gastronomy, tasted only of lemon juice one night. It worked well, though, spread on miniature fried corn tortillas and then topped with a tasty marinated shrimp to form one of Guaymas's signature mini-tortilla appetizers. My favorite of these were quesadillas, tender, deep-fried turnovers made with tortilla dough stuffed with potato, white cheese, and chilies—very different from the Tex-Mex quesadillas that remind me of Mexican grilled cheese sandwiches. *Tacos sudados*, or sweating tacos, are corn tortillas filled with chicken and then steamed in a banana leaf. Ample dipping into the excellent salsas brings them to life. *Garnachas* are tartlets made with tortilla dough. Filled with a lackluster combination of black beans, white cheese, and tomato, or as *chalupas*, piled with shredded unmarinated chicken, onions, and cheese, they were tough. *Gorditas*, small, thick tortilla rounds spread with a lively mixture of sausage and tomatillo salsa, also had a leathery texture. Perhaps from sitting too long after they were cooked?

I had just had a bowl of posole at La Victoria in the Mission so I was a little disappointed with Guaymas's version, which tasted as if it had a chicken broth base rather than the rich pork stew broth I like. Even so, the posole is such a hearty soup, full of pork, shredded vegetables, and hominy that it is one of the best main-course selections on the Guaymas menu.

Other main courses I liked were soft, airy tamales steamed in corn husks and filled with strips of cactus—in texture like peeled green peppers with a fruity flavor—and sliced sweet banana. Sour cream and a *salsa cruda* served on the side balanced out the flavors nicely. A roasted half duck smothered in a pale green sauce textured with pumpkin seeds was delicious, the best dish on the menu. A wonderfully tender filet mignon, butterflied, carefully grilled, and garnished with grilled leeks, also earns praise.

Typical, but sweet for my taste, were poblano chilies stuffed with mashed chicken and raisins and topped with a sweetened sour cream and walnut sauce sprinkled with pomegranate seeds. Diana Kennedy says that the sauce can be seasoned with salt instead of sugar; I cast my vote for salt.

The fish dishes were disappointing because the fish was not fresh enough. I feel like a broken record on this score, but all too few restaurant kitchens care enough to turn me off. Snapper sprinkled with mushrooms, onions, and chilies, wrapped in a banana leaf, and grilled gave off an aroma of stale refrigeration when it was opened. The flesh was mushy. The fish in the ceviche, mostly snapper, had the same tired and unpleasant flavor. If you're going to serve fish raw, it had better be sparkling fresh. Four butterflied shrimp came off the grill a bit dry, though appealingly marinated in lime and oregano.

Desserts are substantial. The favorite of my companions was a lemony, sugary, unctuous avocado pie topped with meringue. The fresh fruit ices were pallid. The "drunken" banana fritters are soused with unpleasantly raw liquor and the pecan cake with honey glaze is unsubtly sweet.

With all the rave advance publicity, I thought that I, too, would be turning somersaults over this restaurant. Certainly, there are lots of new dishes and good ideas on the menu. The prices are relatively cheap, the atmosphere electric, the location dreamy. But after two visits and extensive tasting, I'm not feeling acrobatic. What it boils down to is a lot of middle-of-the-road, formula cooking of a menu that could take a few more risks. The soul of the cooking got lost somewhere among the bleached tree trunks, the computerized order-taking system, and the mobs of gringos waiting for their tables. ∎

—Patricia Unterman, July 20, 1986

Gypsy Cafe

★ ★

687 McAllister Street (at Gough), San Francisco. 931-1854. Open for lunch Monday through Friday 11 A.M. to 2 P.M.; for dinner Monday through Thursday 6 to 10 P.M., Friday and Saturday 6 to 10:30 P.M. Beer, wine. No credit cards. Reservations accepted for dinner. Inexpensive.

The Gypsy Cafe is aptly named. From its makeshift appearance, the restaurant looks like it just set up camp on McAllister Street. The completely exposed kitchen is strewn with cooking equipment, cookbooks, cutting boards, and utensils—but large glass bowls of colorful salads sit on the tiled ordering counter like flowers emerging from a primeval goo.

The decor is half in place. The black rubber flooring still gives off the odor of new tires. Orange cords of temporary lighting dangle from the collaged ceiling. Despite the Gypsy Cafe's literal raw edges, the food is fully realized—as well as being cheap and very quickly turned out.

I think this wacky cafe is supposed to be a Civic Center fast-food restaurant disguised as a high-tech cafeteria at lunch and an inexpensive French restaurant at dinner. Whatever it is, the food is delicious.

When you walk in cold, you're not sure how to proceed. There's a good-sized room full of tables laid with place mats and silverware, and a second room with booths and a counter for ordering. One of the young cooks behind the counter beckons you over and tells you to look at the list of dishes posted above.

The dishes make little sense, an international hodgepodge that doesn't go together at all. There's chicken teriyaki and chicken kebab, either as a plate or a sandwich, which means the chicken is rolled in a flour tortilla. *Boeuf en daube* (marinated in wine) comes wrapped in a tortilla too, as do *tacos al carbon*—a clear case of anarchic cultural crossover. Salads come with the "plates," and there are main-course salads as well. It takes a couple of visits to straighten it all out. The reasonable way to look at the bill of fare at the Gypsy is that you can have anything you want in any combination and it won't cost you very much money.

The chicken in all the chicken preparations has been cut into small pieces, marinated, and then kept cooking on the grill, so that orders can be filled immediately. Amazingly enough, the charred bits retain lots of moisture and flavor. The pieces are paired with a portion of the salads set out in the glass bowls: a yummy potato salad made with copious amounts of good homemade mayonnaise; a green salad of torn leaves offered with many different house-made dressings; a mixture of yogurt, cucumbers, and plumped raisins; or some piquantly dressed shredded cabbage.

The *daube* and *tacos al carbon* are made with chewy flank steak, a winy marinated piece for the *boeuf en daube* and a more appropriate wine-free piece for the tacos. A fresh tomato salsa enlivens both.

One of the best creations at the Gypsy is the French burger, a large patty of ground beef and lamb exotically spiced with turmeric and onion juice, topped with a creamy kind of tartar sauce and ever-so-thinly sliced red onions. A pile of thin, crisp *pommes frites* sprinkled with chili powder catapults this dish into star status.

The Gypsy concocts the best rice salad I've ever tasted. It's offered as a vegetarian dish and it satisfies carnivores and herbivores alike. The salad brims with fresh artichokes, lima beans, tomatoes, peppers, and nutty al dente rice juicily dressed in a tart vinaigrette made with fresh herbs. A roasted chicken salad with lots of broccoli stems and flowerets was not as brightly dressed or moist, though also made with good, fresh ingredients.

For dessert the Gypsy specializes in flans, custards, and *clafoutis* (fruit baked in custard) with sauce. At lunch one day, a delightful little round of black cherries held together with baked eggs and cream sat in a pool of deep purple cherry puree.

I'm not sure if you're supposed to wait for your food at the counter or sit down and have it brought to you. Both have happened to me at the Gypsy at lunch. At dinner, when a fixed price meal goes into effect, you do sit down and a waiter/chef recites the menu and the wine list and takes your order. Why not menus at dinner? Because, I was told, the menu changes every night.

At any rate, not being able to remember the spoken wine list, I told our waiter/chef to bring me a glass of good white wine and, sure enough, the Australian fumé blanc from Canawara Vineyards fit the bill better than most California wines for the price.

Dinner began with a clear, flavorful broth with bits of bacon, carrots, and potatoes, as delicious and pretty a soup as any French person could turn out. A large green salad of torn romaine followed, with a choice of several different creative dressings: a creamy avocado dressing and a puree of fresh tomato and basil vinaigrette that turned into a "french" dressing.

For the main course, there was a good-sized piece of fresh salmon cut like a fillet, though the central bone was left in. It got a bath of thick basil sauce. The fish, which had been cooked over a fire fueled with bay leaves, would have shone had it been cooked less and sauced more sparingly, but why quibble when the fish is fresh and the prices so reasonable?

Another choice, some marinated slices of steak in a winy burgundy sauce, was tasty, if chewy. Both plates were filled with a buttery vegetable medley that included fresh cauliflower, carrots, lima beans, corn, and green beans. The green beans and the limas had that frozen vegetable texture, but the whole assortment was colorful and appealing.

You also get a dreamy dessert, the composed kind that you rarely see any more, cold crepes filled with lemon curd sauced with fresh lemon cream, or a molded pineapple ice in a raspberry-cherry sauce.

The dinners here remind me of those nicely cooked, well-seasoned, unpretentious French meals you can still get at places like Le Cyrano out on the avenues. The food is a little bit fancier than you would make at home because extra labor is used to gussie up modest ingredients. Josephine Araldo taught her students how to cook this way, to make the humblest ingredients absolutely delicious and to waste nothing.

Three young French cooks prepare this food, and the two brothers who own the Gypsy Cafe are right there in the kitchen with them, doing everything. The brothers go out of their way to be encouraging and friendly to customers. Though the Gypsy's odd unfinished decor doesn't suggest warmth, the people who work there make up for it with their eagerness. If the food at the Gypsy Cafe seems foreign and eccentrically international, that may be just the effect these gypsies are going for. ∎
—Patricia Unterman, June 14, 1987

Harbor Village

★ ★

Embarcadero Four, San Francisco. 398-8883. Open for lunch Monday through Friday 11 A.M. to 2:30 P.M., Saturday and Sunday 10:30 A.M. to 2:30 P.M.; for dinner nightly 5:30 to 9:30 P.M. Full bar. Major credit cards. Reservations accepted for dinner and for lunch Monday through Friday from 11 A.M. to noon only. Moderate.

The Pacific current is carrying a new kind of restaurant to San Francisco, direct from Hong Kong. For the first time, the city is seeing upscale, well-appointed, graciously staffed Cantonese restaurants that prepare elegant dim sum at lunch and a full menu at dinner. Certainly one of the best is the new Harbor Village on the second level of Embarcadero Four. Though I can't think of a more hidden-away spot for a major Chinese restaurant, the Harbor

Village has had full houses from the first day it opened. Its well-dressed Chinese patronage may have known about it from its branches in Hong Kong.

Besides its downtown location, which affords glimpses of the bay and Villancourt Fountain from an airy, glassed-in back room, Harbor Village's refined decor and service set it apart. The seemingly labyrinthine dining rooms are lushly carpeted, furnished with lacquered chairs and white damask-covered tables. Partially enclosed interior spaces can be used for private dining rooms. Shiny brass and oriental antiques abound. The waiters and waitresses wear formal black-and-white uniforms and serve out of covered silver platters and tureens. You eat on fragile, rice-shot porcelain. A detail that most impressed me was the velvety soft unstarched damask napkins that lay heavily on the lap. I haven't seen anything like it outside of three-star restaurants in France.

Almost in contradiction to its formality, Harbor Village is a huge operation, large enough to put on a full-scale dim sum lunch seven days a week. Women in starched white uniforms push carts offering bona fide delicacies silently over the carpeting. This is one of the few places that makes *shaolin bao*, twisted dumplings filled with shrimp, cabbage, black mushrooms, and a gush of flavorful stock which is put into the dumplings in a cold, gelatinized state. Clever. Beautiful shrimp pearl balls, opalescent with pearly rice, are filled with chopped shrimp barely held together with a little egg. Elegant slices of cured pork shank rest on a bed of orange soybeans waiting for a splash of vinegary sauce. Miraculously tender octopus slices freckled with hot red chilies come with a mild, green wasabi dipping sauce.

Harbor Village makes the best version of sticky rice wrapped in lotus leaves I've ever encountered. Each small package contains separately grained pearl rice with lots of wonderful, moist filling consisting of salt-cured duck, egg yolk, pork, and dried scallops. There are deep-fried rice dumplings stuffed with black mushrooms that leave a sweet taste in your mouth and soul-satisfying long-cooked beef meatballs that

are full of flavor and texture. They rest on a bed of bean-curd skin in a natural gravy.

Pork dumplings with rice noodle wrappers surprise you with the crunch of peanuts, dried shrimp, and Chinese celery, while pure-flavored *har gow*, shrimp dumplings, fulfill your highest shellfish expectations. At the end of the meal, there are sweet curried turnovers with flaky crusts and sandy-crusted egg custards. Most of the dim sum cost about just a few dollars a plate.

At night the dim sum carts are garaged and the complete menus are hauled out. They hold as many delicacies as the dim sum carts. For example, Harbor Village makes an intriguing chicken salad with velvety shreds of chicken breast, bits of crunchy deep-fried rice noodle, peanuts, bean sprouts, and the traditional jellyfish, as well as something pickled and something fruity, all in all, an ingenious balance of textures and flavors in a delicate dressing that brings them together. It is my favorite dish at this restaurant.

Another gorgeous appetizer, called stuffed broccoli, is inspired by the color contrast of broccoli and shrimp. Little broccoli flowerets stay crisp and bright green inside a pretty pink shrimp ball. A clear Cantonese sauce gives then a brilliant sheen. Dry-fried salt-and-pepper squid is not as fiery, crisp, or successful as the same dish prepared at Yuet Lee, but Harbor Village's approach to seafood could be an example for all restaurants. The raw ingredients are irreproachably fresh, then barely cooked and lightly sauced.

Tiny clams must have been startled into opening their shells by a fiery hot wok, because their insides tasted like they were just pulled from the sea. Though this preparation was called fresh clam saute with black bean and hot pepper sauce, not a black bean was in sight. They seasoned the refined brown sauce without their often overbearing presence, allowing the clams to come through directly.

A fresh crab braised with ginger and scallion had the same attributes. Perfectly fresh crab was barely cooked and boasted exceptionally soft and juicy flesh. Many stalks of scallion and coins of ginger were interspersed among the pieces, but there was hardly any sauce; the crab was fragranced instead. This subtle treatment worked because the crab was so fresh and sweet.

I suggest finishing off your meal with one of Harbor Village's noodle dishes, like fried vermicelli Harbor Village style, angel-hair-thin noodles dotted with surprises like little nuggets of shrimp and chicken, bits of sweetened egg, bean sprouts, and shredded carrot. Not a drop of excess oil marred this light, tasty plate of noodles.

For dessert, try the cold and refreshing fruit soup of pureed honeydew melon thickened with a little tapioca. It hits the spot.

I am very much taken by this restaurant. Most of all I was pleased by the high quality of ingredients, and then by the new dishes on the menu as well as new approaches to commonly prepared ones. Finally, I was gratified to see service and the appointments match the refinement of the cooking. Harbor Village gave me a glimpse of the loftier side of Cantonese cooking. Judging from the full dining room, I'm not the only one hungry for more sophisticated Chinese cooking. ■

—Patricia Unterman, March 23, 1986

Harry's Bar and American Grill

500 Van Ness Avenue, San Francisco. 864-2779. Open for lunch Monday through Friday 11:30 A.M. to 3 P.M., for dinner Sunday and Monday 5 to 10 P.M., Tuesday through Thursday 5 to 11 P.M., Friday and Saturday 5 to midnight. Full bar. Major credit cards. Moderate.

There's a certain snob appeal about imports, no matter where in the world you go. About half the T-shirts worn in Europe and Asia have names of American universities on them. In Amsterdam, I was once in a wonderful, high-class cheese and chocolate store that had a whole wall lined with, of all things, Libby's canned fruits.

I wonder if this feeling that "foreign is classier" has something to do with the crowds jammed into Harry's Bar and American Grill, which opened in the spring of 1986 on Van Ness near City Hall. My guess is that lots of people think they're eating in a branch of the Florence restaurant of the same name, or even the Venice restaurant, made famous by Ernest Hemingway, called Harry's Bar. (These two restaurants in Italy aren't related except that the original owners were friends.)

I'm sorry to say, the only thing that's been imported is the name. San Francisco's Harry's Bar and American Grill (along with the one in Los Angeles) is wholly owned by Marriott Corporation, the airline food and hotel people.

Here's the story: Spectrum Foods, Marriott's San Francisco–based subsidiary that also runs MacArthur Park and Ciao, acquired U.S. rights to the name "Harry's Bar and American Grill." While the California restaurants are supposedly inspired by the one in Florence, the menus are largely different and there's no financial connection. And the head chef of the San Francisco Harry's, according to the biographical blurb I was sent, left Italy after his training to cook in Los Angeles restaurants.

[Recently, Marriott sold Spectrum and their other restaurant holdings to a group of private investors.]

I think it's important to know all this when evaluating the food at the Bay Area Harry's Bar and American Grill. The name might be famous and the decor might be impressive. But to my mind, when you consider the food, the whole thing becomes an elaborate facade. What comes to your table simply bears no resemblance to the great food you can get in Italy.

By starting with the good stuff, I'll give you an example of how depressing my two dinners at Harry's were. I liked a total of four dishes, one a "black and white" pasta with scallops, the second black risotto with baby squid, the others a simple grilled chicken breast and a stuffed quail. There's nothing new about using squid ink to dye pasta or as a sauce for risotto; Wolfgang Puck was doing the former years ago in Los Angeles, and Paul Bertolli the latter at Chez Panisse. But I was still impressed with Harry's technique for both, particularly the risotto, which was one of the few versions I've had in the Bay Area that wasn't a gloppy mess. The rice kernels remained firm, just as they should be.

Yet the "baby" squid tasted old and tough, barely edible. And the scallops were so terrible we couldn't eat them all. We left a bowl with every bite of pasta gone, every drop of sauce mopped up, and the chewy, foul-tasting scallops lining the bottom of the dish.

And that was a comparatively good dish. What ruined the pasta—a seeming lack of concern with getting first-rate fresh ingredients—marred lots of other things we tried. Some of the mussels served with clams in tomato broth as an appetizer were so far gone they had to be spit out. Veal liver with onions had a mushy texture I associate with coming from the freezer. A rectangular "lamb fillet" was one of the weirdest cuts of meat I've ever seen; thick and tough, it had no lamb taste, resembling more a beef rump roast.

That wasn't all. Mozzarella with tomatoes and basil had tasteless cheese and tasteless tomatoes, and being served ice cold didn't help either. Even the bread tasted like the sort of "french roll" you get on a supermarket shelf.

Except for dense, doughy gnocchi, the kitchen seemed to know how to handle its pasta. But I can't say the same for lots of the other dishes I tried.

Veal scalloppine rolled with prosciutto and sage sounded great, but it turned out to have no taste but a heavy reek of salt and sage. It came in a brown gravy that resembled the taste of canned gravy, except that it had much more salt. A salad of smoked chicken and vegetables sounded appealing, too, but it was all smothered in gloppy dressing, and had no character other than the harsh reek of smoke.

That left the chicken breast as the definite dish of choice if you have to eat at Harry's. You get a large whole breast, lightly pounded, perfectly grilled, and tasting of its marinade of lemon, oil, and rosemary. It was one of the bargains in a menu that's very reasonably priced overall.

Along with the food, another problem at Harry's is the pacing of the service, which the word "erratic" barely describes. Our first dinner went on and on and on—you could have walked to Davies Hall and taken in a symphony between courses. For the second dinner, they had neglected to write down my reservations, which were under an assumed name, and we had to wait an hour in the bar. But when we finally got seated, everything came out so fast we had finished the appetizers, entrees, desserts, and coffee in fifty-five minutes.

It was really sad to experience all this, because the decor at Harry's is as pleasant as at any restaurant in San Francisco. With its wood-trimmed walls, thick red carpeting in the dining rooms, and parquet floors with oriental rugs in the bar and hallways, it looks like a lovely old San Francisco institution.

I don't know how much money was put into Harry's, but it must have been in the millions. Yet with all that investment, no one seems to have paid much attention to the question of getting the best ingredients and the most talented kitchen staff.

In Italy, the food comes first. At San Francisco's version of Harry's Bar, it seems to have taken a distinct back seat. ■

—Stan Sesser, August 8, 1986

Himalaya Restaurant and Sweets

★ ★

12469 San Pablo Avenue, Richmond (one block north of San Pablo Avenue exit off I-80). 236-4148. Open daily noon to 11 P.M. Beer, wine. MasterCard, Visa, American Express. Reservations accepted. Inexpensive.

A while back I reviewed a little family-run place in Berkeley called Himalaya. A few months ago, however, it proved a victim of the yuppification of University Avenue and disappeared.

Thanks to a reader who became a Himalaya devotee, I found it again, on a dreary stretch of San Pablo Avenue in Richmond. Trish St. John wrote that "the food is actually better than ever. When I ordered the mango juice, Mrs. Hundal went in the back and juiced a mango! The prices are still ridiculously low."

She's right on all counts. I can't think of a restaurant that serves higher quality food at a lower price. At Himalaya, the full dinner includes a choice of two different curries. Even adding appetizers, breads, and other side dishes, the total price will be surprisingly low.

My old favorites at the Himalaya were as good as I remembered them. The lamb biryani is one of the best—a heaping platter of aromatic saffron-coated basmati rice with little chunks of lamb scented with what must be at least fifteen spices. The chicken curry is splendid; it's not particularly hot, but it betrays a long shopping trip at a spice store.

Then there's the new stuff. Goat curry was as tender and flavorful as any goat meat I have ever tasted. (There's also a goat biryani.) Egg *sag* is a mixture of eggs with creamed spinach that tastes much better than it sounds. That mango juice really is fresh, and you can also get a banana drink blended with ice.

Despite all this wonderful food, it's still hard to get past the appetizers. The *samosas*, stuffed with potatoes and peas, are fried without a hint of greasiness. The *pakoras*—battered, deep-fried vegetables, fish, or chicken legs—are as good as any tempura in a Japanese restaurant. And the *dhal puri*, deep-fried garbanzo flour patties, are covered with a spicy sauce and tangy yogurt so outstanding that you'll fight off your dinner companions to get to the last drop.

The Himalaya is strictly a family operation. Amir Hundal, the father, who speaks little English, presides over the dining room. The daughter, Kamaljit, who's fluent in English, waits on tables. The mother, Surjit, who speaks no English at all, does the cooking. It's like having dinner at someone's home.

It's also likely to mean a wait for food if the restaurant is crowded, since Mrs. Hundal cooks to order. So call them first and let them know you're coming, and be a little patient. The fact that this restaurant can't turn itself into an assembly line will be reflected in the quality of the food. ∎
—Stan Sesser, January 3, 1985

India Garden

★★

120 Hazelwood Drive, South San Francisco (going south on 101, take the San Bruno exit, turn right on El Camino, then two stoplights to the Brentwood Shopping Mall). 952-8487. Open Tuesday through Thursday, Sunday 5 to 10 P.M., Friday and Saturday 5 to 11 P.M. Beer, wine. MasterCard, Visa, American Express, Diners Club, Discover. Reservations accepted. Moderate.

India Garden is the creation of Rajiv Gujral and his chef-brother Ashok Sahi, the two most active members of the family that opened the successful North India Restaurant on Webster Street in San Francisco. [When this review first appeared, the India Garden was called Nirvana.] Due to a falling out, Gujral and the young chef, who was favorably reviewed in this column, left to open their own restaurant in South San Francisco.

The curries, the tandoori-baked foods, the spicy appetizers here are just as wonderful as I remember them from the San Francisco kitchen. But the surroundings, a windowless, brick-walled room, oddly decorated with billowing cloth on the ceiling, wrought-iron railings, and indoor fountains, are frankly dismal. Little has been done to make the restaurant aesthetically comfortable. The cold, dark dining room should be made smaller with screens, drapes, or partitions; the ceiling lowered; the lighting, which pokes out of the draped ceiling on metal rods, changed; the dance floor once used by belly dancers in the restaurant's former incarnation as Taj Mahal, carpeted over. The setting is so incongruous that it takes a transcendental work of the imagination to keep from walking out.

However, when the food starts coming, albeit slowly, a kind of nirvana begins to materialize. Bowls of clams in their shells bathed in Indian spices, lemon, garlic, and fresh coriander take you halfway there. The broth is so aromatic, you spoon up every drop. Spinach leaves dipped in chick-pea batter and vegetable- and seafood-stuffed *samosas* wrapped in rich, flaky pastry are greaselessly deep fried and served with three lively chutneys. The vegetarian *samosas* are superior. Ground lentils, lamb, and spices formed into patties called *shammi kabab* turn out to be surprisingly light of texture and mysteriously seasoned. Spicy toasted lentil wafers, called *pappadums*, melt in your mouth.

Though India Garden does not stray far from the menu paths of most other Indian restaurants in the Bay Area, it is making an attempt to prepare more fish and seafood dishes, with varying results. A bowl of mussels garnished with strips of fresh ginger and coriander leaves in a fragrant red curry was rich and colorful in both appearance and flavor, but a seafood curry made with an indistinguishable mixture of scallops, prawns, and fish should have smelled fresher. Some of the large tandoori prawns were succulent and still translucent in the center while others had cooked a little too long and become dull.

Spicy marinated lamb and chicken emerge from the tandoor oven perfectly cooked and miraculously juicy and tender. Tiny racks of lamb chops explode with flavor. Bright red chicken breasts, thighs, and legs each get the right exposure to charcoal heat, and come out succulent.

Some of the best choices are the vegetarian curries, like the superb stew of eggplant, onions, tomatoes, and spices called *bengan bhartha*. I would drive to South City just for a plate of it with India Garden's exceptionally light and tender tandoor-baked bread. What a lovely combination!

To cool off the mouth from the heat of the spices, India Garden cultures its own thin yogurt, which is mixed with cucumber to make *raita* or lightly salted, sugared, and served over ice as a drink called *lassi*.

I tend to overorder in Indian restaurants because I can't resist the appetizers and all the little side dishes—*raita*, breads, the pilafs made with nutty basmati rice, the tangy, soft, house-made white cheese called *paneer* cooked with spinach. If you pile all this on top of tandoor-roasted meats and curries, you've eaten a holiday feast instead of a weekday dinner. What I like particularly about the food at India Garden is that it is so cleanly prepared and each dish so distinctively spiced, you can sit down to a huge meal there without feeling that you are drowning in oil or eating the same dish over and over. I like the cooking of young chef Ashok Sahi at India Garden as much as I did at North India. I wish the brothers had found a more suitable dining room for their heavenly food. ■

—Patricia Unterman, April 27, 1986

India Palace Restaurant

★★

707 Redwood Highway, Mill Valley (in the Travelodge on the frontage road along 101). 388-3350. Open for lunch Tuesday through Sunday 11:30 A.M. to 2 P.M., for dinner daily from 5:30 to 10 P.M. Beer, wine. Major credit cards. Reservations advised for dinner. Moderate.

Motel restaurants, which are not exactly my favorite places, generally come in two varieties. At a dumpy motel, you sit in a brightly lit room and gag down a frozen $15 surf 'n' turf dinner. At a fancy motel, you sit in a pitch-dark room and gag down a frozen $30 surf 'n' turf dinner, to the sound of piano music wafting in from the cocktail lounge.

It's a surefire formula for failure, usually luring only a handful of sales people too tired to walk a couple of blocks for a better meal. Yet, for some reason, almost every motel does it.

That's why I was intrigued to hear of a popular, year-old Indian restaurant located in, of all places, a Travelodge next to the freeway in Mill Valley. Indian food in Marin County, let alone in a motel, is unusual enough, so I went over to check it out.

The instant you walk into India Palace, it's clear there was a designer who tried to do everything possible to make you forget you're in a Travelodge. The main dining room is curtained, lit only by candles (except for a spotlight on the clay tandoor oven), and lined with mirrors.

It's a setting that can make your head spin. In the very dark room, all the people and candles reflect off the mirrors, making it difficult to sense where the reality ends and the reflection begins. A friend immediately dubbed it "Bombay bordello," but to me it was more like an amusement-park fun house.

To make matters worse, the tables are so small there's hardly any room in the center for all the dishes you're going to share. I asked if they'd bring our order in stages, but naturally almost everything came at once. The waiter just stood there holding the dishes waiting for us to clear a place, which meant some things had to teeter at the edge over people's laps.

Once we got through that, however, most of the food at India Palace was first-rate, and some of it spectacular. It's very elegant, northern-style cooking, much like you get at Gaylord at Ghirardelli Square. And prices are reasonable, too.

For appetizers, start out with a *lassi*, the thick yogurt drink flavored with rose water, and a mixture of vegetarian and meat *samosas*. These *samosas*, which are deep fried, won-tonlike snacks, are the best I've ever encountered. The skin is crisp and greaseless, the filling aromatic, and they're served piping hot. With them come two great sauces, one a blend of mint and yogurt, and the other combining tomatoes, tamarind, and cayenne.

For the entrees, there's a definite place to start, too, and that's with the spectacular tandoor dishes. Tandoor chicken, one of the best known Indian delicacies, is also usually a disaster. At the hands of an unskilled chef, it bakes in a clay oven called a tandoor until every drop of moisture evaporates. To make matters worse, the marinade sometimes includes a food coloring that turns the chicken a ghastly bright pink.

The India Palace's version, however, comes out as juicy as any chicken I've encountered. Besides not overcooking it, I think a key difference is that the restaurant marinates it for a full twenty-four hours, so that it has plenty of time to soak up the garlic, yogurt, oil, and spices.

Another fine tandoor dish is *seikh kabab*, which combines ground lamb with a long list of seasonings, including onions, chilies, coriander, cumin, cloves, cinnamon, ginger, and garlic. The spicy meat jumps alive with a bouquet of tastes.

The menu focuses largely on lamb and chicken. When I ordered fish *masala* for a little variation, I got an elegant sauce based on butter, cream, and tomatoes, but also a hunk of fish that tasted like it might have come from India on the slow boat.

Be sure to supplement your meal with lots of vegetables and breads, which were all superb. Particularly good was the cauliflower, which comes in a sauce very similar to that of the fish *masala*. Also be sure to get an order of the basmati rice, spiced up with coriander, bay leaves, cinnamon, and butter.

There were some losers on the menu, too. The *pakoras*, little puffballs stuffed with vegetables, were heavy and greasy. The mulligatawny soup had vegetables that tasted like they came out of a can. The lamb biryani, which is chunks of lamb cooked with fried rice and seasonings, was ruined by gloppy, greasy rice.

To my mind, 99 percent of Indian desserts are losers, too, and the India Palace's proved no exception. Fortunately, they only had two things to offer, an ice cream that tasted like it was made from condensed milk, and a deep-fried breaded cheese ball in syrup that tasted primarily of fried dough and sugar.

The story behind India Palace is one I hear frequently for Asian restaurants. An immigrant comes to the United States, starts off as a busboy, and ends up owning

a fine and flourishing restaurant. Particularly for Marin, which hardly abounds with great ethnic food, it makes an evening at the Travelodge a real treat. ∎
—Stan Sesser, September 27, 1985

Ironwood Cafe

★ ★

901 Cole Street, San Francisco. 664-0224. Open for lunch Monday through Friday 11 A.M. to 2:30 P.M., for dinner Monday through Thursday 5:30 to 10 P.M., Friday and Saturday 5:30 until 10:30 P.M. Beer, wine. MasterCard, Visa, American Express, Discover. Reservations accepted. Moderate.

The Ironwood Cafe was a real discovery for me. Though the restaurant has been in business for over six years, only recently, in my opinion, has it risen above the level of a neighborhood restaurant. My latest meals there have been wonderful, worthy of a special evening or a ride across town for lunch. Besides having one of the most pleasant dining rooms in town, the Ironwood kitchen is turning out inventive and exciting food that is consistently prepared.

The early American look of the cafe lets you settle in immediately. The commodious pine booths with cushions confer complete privacy, while a cozy row of tables along a balcony railing afford a perch for viewing the whole room. Homey print wallpaper, ceiling fans, colonial-style lanterns and chairs, hand-stenciled walls, and paintings of quilt patterns all fit naturally into the uncluttered, square dining room with windows along two sides. The tiny kitchen is tucked away in a corner of the room and takes advantage of a narrow, outdoor courtyard for its charcoal grilling.

The Ironwood has a home-kept feel about it. The tables, covered with white linen and white butcher paper, have sparkling glasses and shiny silverware. The service stations and open kitchen are neat as pins. And the food tastes homemade too, in the best, made-from-scratch way.

One evening we began with a coarse-textured house-made pâté, bursting with flavor, served with house-made red wine mustard, some of the best I've ever tasted. I've grown so tired of bland, over-processed, commercial charcuterie, but this was something you'd encounter in a French country house. Paired with Ironwood's house-baked french bread, yeasty, chewy, and full of character, and a side order of house-cured cucumber, jerusalem artichoke, onion, and hot-pepper pickles, you have reason enough to come back to this restaurant.

But the meal proceeded with more revelations. A salad of watercress with mushrooms and red onions grilled over rosemary branches had the most extraordinary aroma. The mushrooms took on another dimension. Some tiny artichokes, sweet, tender, and crisply deep fried, surrounded a ramekin of well-made garlic mayonnaise. Avocado and bright-red blood oranges shared a plate with lettuces and a tart vinaigrette.

I was not crazy about the rather large local portuguese oysters on the half shell; they were fresh and briny but a little too strong and meaty for half-shell presentation. Surprisingly, a simple green salad of torn lettuces looked and tasted flat.

As main courses, crusty, golden brown pieces of chicken were sprinkled with feta cheese, roasted onions, and grilled Japanese eggplant, and a perfectly cooked piece of halibut sauced with dill sour cream stunningly shared the plate with dark green deep-fried chard leaves.

The most delicious dish of all is Ironwood Cafe's buttery seafood stew loaded with clams, mussels, big chunks of juicy fish, new potatoes, and spinach. The broth is a dream, rich with fresh herbs, shellfish liquor, and good, clean fish stock. When you dunk Ironwood's house-made crackers into it, you're in heaven.

At lunch one day, the kitchen put out a remarkable warm spinach and baby artichoke salad with toasted walnuts, shaved parmesan, and a delicious walnut dressing that tied everything together. Here were four divergent elements brought together like a jigsaw puzzle—each piece kept its own color and shape, yet, when fitted together in just this way, the whole was much greater than the sum of its parts. Another salad that demonstrated this skill matched slices of cantaloupe and avocado with rocket, a tangy green, in a mustardy poppy-seed dressing. However, some big hunks of potato draped with anchovies and garnished with olives, parsley, and capers lacked the cooperative sparkle of the other salads. Theoretically, all the ingredients could have been great together, but their presentation didn't bring out their affinities.

A grilled chicken breast sandwich on Ironwood's incomparable house-baked rye bread brought into play grilled red onion, swiss cheese, sauteed mushrooms, and the deep, richly flavored red wine mustard. You couldn't ask for a more savory sandwich.

At both lunch and dinner the kitchen prepares a voluptuous plate of noodles swathed in lots of sweet butter, white wine, and handfuls of fresh, mild garlic. At dinner, spaetzle, tiny noodle dumplings, are offered as a pasta course, though the version with bacon, asparagus, and onions I tasted really works better as a side dish. The spaetzle dough itself doesn't hold enough interest.

Though the house-baked breads rival any I've tasted, the desserts are clunky. My favorite is a fresh strawberry pie with a thin cream-cheese layer right above a thick, hard crust. Pineapple cobbler and chocolate layer cake are just plain heavy, and unsweetened strawberry shortcake tasted flat.

When I had eaten at Ironwood years ago, I felt that the food was so homegrown that it was amateurish. Now, that made-from-scratch inspiration has turned into a starting-off point for some graceful and sophisticated dishes. I must admit that my recent visits were not inspired by the current menu, which still seems a little disorganized and far-flung, but by a slice of Ironwood's pumpernickel bread. It was fantastic. Then I remembered that John Birdsall, a fine local chef, had been cooking there awhile. He's behind the stove Monday, Tuesday, and Friday at lunch and Wednesday night at dinner, but the positive effects of an especially talented cook in a kitchen extend to all the days of the week. ■

—Patricia Unterman, May 17, 1987

Isuzu

★

1581 Webster Street, Kinokuniya Building of Japan Center, San Francisco. 922-2290. Open for lunch Monday, Wednesday, Thursday, Friday noon to 2 P.M., for dinner 5 to 9:30 P.M., Saturday noon to 10 P.M., Sunday noon to 9 P.M. Full bar. MasterCard, Visa, American Express. Reservations accepted. Inexpensive.

Americans love deep-fried foods—french fries, fried chicken, corn dogs, deep-fried fish—but the Japanese really do it better. Tempura, lacy, light, and varied in texture and flavor, makes for the most palatable and digestible deep-fried meals of them all. Isuzu, a pleasant, inexpensive Japanese restaurant in Japantown, makes one of the best tempuras in town.

Tempura was actually invented by Spanish and Portuguese missionaries living in southern Japan during the late sixteenth century, but now, of course, delicately battered and fried pieces of vegetable and seafood have become a fixture of the Japanese diet. In Japan, restaurants are devoted solely to the making of tempura. Customers sit at tempura bars, much as they do at sushi bars, and eat the tempura piece by piece.

Isuzu does not have a tempura bar and prepares many other dishes on its gigantic menu, yet this restaurant's tempura has all the characteristics of the best. The coating is delicate and irregular, with many nooks and crannies. The batter does not form a smooth carapace, but seems to defy gravity by being in the process of falling off each slice of shrimp or vegetable when it hits the hot oil. Good tempura looks ethereally light. The batter holds little oil and the ingredients underneath taste fresh and sweet. They are cut so they cook in about three minutes. Isuzu has this part of the preparation down as well. A tempura of shrimp and assorted vegetables preceded by salty cabbage and carrot pickle, miso soup, and rice makes for a delightful meal.

Isuzu also prepares every other category of Japanese dish, though *donburi*, or foods served over a bowl of rice, and *nabemono*, foods cooked and served in a pot of boiling broth, are the most successful. *Oyako don*, a large, deep bowl of hot rice topped with bits of chicken, onion, and egg and moistened with a sauce of Japanese broth, light and dark soy sauce, and a little sugar, rivals the ever-popular Japanese noodle dishes as satisfying "fast food."

Isuzu serves all the different beef, seafood, and chicken *nabemonos* in heavy cast-iron pots. They're loaded with Chinese cabbage, onions, glass noodles, soft bean curd, carrots, and, in the case of *yosenabe*, with chunks of succulent chicken, rockfish, tiny sweet clams, and big local mussels. I like an iconoclastic "spicy *yosenabe*" invented by Isuzu, which throws enough chilies into the cooking broth to make it taste like a Thai concoction.

Nigiri sushi brings the usual assortment of tuna, octopus, yellowtail, shrimp, clam, and salmon roe. The fish is cut thinly and is fresh if not of exceptional quality.

Grilled chicken teriyaki is tasty, juicy, and tender, though the same cannot be said of beef teriyaki, which is made with a thin, chewy slice of beef cut from the rib eye. Eel teriyaki is the best grilled dish of all.

The restaurant has entrances directly on Post and Webster streets and is next door to the Kabuki cinema. It has the feel of a coffee shop during the day, with bare, brown tables, sturdy wooden Western chairs, and very casual service. At night, the tables are covered with burgundy tablecloths and the soft light from rice-paper lanterns dresses up the room. A sushi bar under a brown shingled roof hung with small banners, Japanese screens, and bamboo planters adds a festive look. Isuzu is very popular during prime meal hours, so expect a short wait. ■

—Patricia Unterman, April 12, 1987

Izzy's Steak and Chop House
★

3345 Steiner Street, San Francisco. 563-0487. Open Monday through Saturday 5:30 to 11 P.M., Sunday 5 to 10 P.M. Full bar. MasterCard, Visa, American Express. Reservations accepted. Moderate.

Izzy's is the latest in a herd of new steak houses to open in San Francisco over the past few years, hard on the trail of Harris', the Palm, and the refurbished House of Prime Rib. Ruth's Chris Steak House is soon to follow. The capital of California cuisine seems to have developed an appetite for red meat.

Izzy's is a meticulously re-created period piece that serves updated chophouse food. Restaurant impresario Sam Duval (Elite Cafe, Samantha's, Cafe Royale) took a neighborhood bar called Mulcreavy's and transformed it into an elaborate stage set of a rundown, turn-of-the-century saloon. There are wooden floors, of course, and painted wood wainscoting and wooden booths and an old-looking solid wood bar. The ceilings and upper walls have been textured and painted to look like distressed leather. White tablecloths stand out pristinely against the many different shades of brown. The walls are hung with period photos and memorabilia; hundreds of bottles of steak condiments line wooden ledges that encircle Izzy's two dining areas. With mirrors and ceiling fans and hanging schoolhouse light fixtures and different floor and ceiling levels, you get the feeling that lots is going on. The place projects a history, a resonance, even though it's only a couple months old. The ambience makes you want to have a shot of whiskey and a steak.

The menu is simple, straightforward, and manageable for the kitchen. There are steaks and chops that come with a choice of potato and vegetable, a few salads and appetizers, and a small selection of nonmeat entrees. What Izzy's really has down is the classic chophouse plate—a charcoal-grilled steak or chop, lightly creamed spinach, and scalloped potatoes baked with onion, leek, and cheese. This satisfying trio brought me back to Izzy's several nights in a row.

Because this restaurant uses leaner, chewier, "certified Black Angus" beef instead of fat-marbled prime, the fillet is the best cut of steak to order here, delivering the most tenderness and flavor. The New York, even though dry-aged for twenty-one days, isn't quite as tasty—a real reversal. A chewy skirt steak in a sweet, teriyaki-style marinade does not lack for flavor. Loin lamb chops, cut nearly two inches thick here, are a wonderful buy. For those who like lighter meat, a gigantic veal T-bone chop has a more delicate, young animal flavor. All the meats come off the grill rare when you order them medium rare or even medium, so request at least one degree more of doneness than you usually do.

One thing I do like about this less fatty beef is that you don't feel ill after you eat a healthy chunk of it. It may not have the gorgeous velvety texture and buttery rich flavor you get from prime meat—as in the Palm's incomparable New York strip or prime rib—but Izzy's meat is more digestible and less expensive to boot.

Included in the price of these steaks and chops is a choice of vegetable and potato, the best being the scalloped "Izzy's own potatoes" and the bright green creamed spinach. Neither of these is heavily laden with cream or butter. The potatoes have more melted onion than butter and the spinach really tastes like fresh spinach. Delicious roasted onions with sweet carrot chunks offer a third excellent choice. You can also get a baked potato, unexceptional shoestrings, or bland, thickly battered deep-fried zucchini.

For starters I recommend a crisp house salad of butter lettuce with a punchy garlicky dressing, or a halved head of romaine, blanketed with crumbled blue cheese and doused in vinegar and oil.

While the croutons are house-made and garlicky, the caesar salad lacks conviction. Its dressing needs anchovies, dry mustard, lemon juice—brighter contrast. Gravlax, salmon cured with aquavit, salt, and sugar, was sliced too thickly and had a stale odor.

Duck and sausage gumbo was thick, dark, smoky, and artificial tasting.

Order the marvelous Cajun fried oysters with jalapeno sauce as a first course, split. Briny, fresh, sweet oysters—they tasted like Washington State willapas to me—are barely covered with cornmeal and get only the briefest of cooking before being placed on shells dabbed with a spicy green puree of jalapenos and scallions. If the presentation was a bit odd, the oysters themselves were right on the mark.

Somehow a meal of red meat always needs something sweet to end it and Izzy's doesn't let you down. A chocolate-rum pecan pie is rich without being cloying. Key lime pie has a soft, creamy filling brightened by lime zest but a soggy graham-cracker crust. English sherry trifle, served in a wine goblet, happily combines sherry-soaked cake with lots of softly whipped cream.

The wine list offers California bottles at fair prices and includes a large assortment of wines by the glass. The Rutherford Hill merlot is lovely with the beef. Both coffee and espresso are weak.

It's easy to patronize this restaurant. Ordering either food or wine doesn't call for much decision. You don't have to dress. The ambience is fun and casual and the food, uncomplicated and good. For a steak and chop house, prices are reasonable. Of all the Duval restaurants that have opened, closed, and changed hands in this town, Izzy's makes the most sense. ∎

—Patricia Unterman, March 22, 1987

Janot's

★★

44 Campton Place, San Francisco. 392-5373. Open Monday through Saturday 11:30 A.M. to 2:30 P.M., 6 to 10 P.M. Full bar. MasterCard, Visa, American Express. Reservations accepted. Moderate.

When two experienced French chefs open a little restaurant, I naturally expect a fairly high level of competence. I assume that the raw materials will be cooked correctly; the table will be nicely set; decent wines will be available. But I do not expect to be crazy about the food. Sauced dishes, fussy presentations, and nouvelle mannerisms have all become a bit tiresome for me. Recently I had lunch at Janot's, a sunny bistro opened by Jacques Janot, former owner of the Tricolor on Geary, and Pierre Morin, veteran of some of the best kitchens in Paris and San Francisco, and ended up loving every minute of it. Here was a new French kitchen putting out modern, unpretentious, delicious food with a flair and confidence rarely encountered in any new operation.

The two Frenchmen took over the former site of Vasilio's, a small brick building tucked away in an alley adjacent to the Campton Place Hotel. They reopened the skylights in the high ceiling, built three tiers of banquettes on two levels and covered them with a floral canopy, and recarpeted in bright green. The small brick room looks like a sunny garden and gives the illusion of both intimacy and space.

Mr. Morin, who does most of the cooking himself, has also been inspired by the garden. His compact menu offers a number of creative dishes that are based on vegetables or enhanced by them. For example, his three warm salads, big, beautiful plates of greens and savory warm ingredients, are knockouts. Endive and watercress, tartly dressed, form a wreath around a leg of warm duck *confit*. Buttery baguette croutons rimming the plate somehow turn the salad into a complete meal. The same addictively good croutons also work with a warm spinach and bacon salad with big strips of bacon, ample, warm vinaigrette, and a juicy, marinated grilled quail sitting on top. The spinach wilts a little in the warm dressing. Then, there is a coarse-textured seafood sausage stuffed with big chunks of fish and fresh peas, laid on a bed of warm cabbage in a vinegary butter sauce. Morin's hearty interpretation of a dish that became the signature of the haute cuisine crowd five years ago is a happy rediscovery.

Cold salads surprise here, too. Hearts of romaine have roquefort cheese sieved onto them, along with an assertive vinaigrette. Just this one little trick turns this salad into something French. An appetizer called *tourtière*, of eggplant, tomato and zucchini, turned out to be a layered vegetable mousse with a crust of roasted eggplant, a dish I normally would not order. But Morin has figured out how to make vegetable mousses come alive by seasoning them broadly with garlic and herbs. A garnish of many slices of velvety house-smoked salmon with those fabulous croutons turns this dish into a light lunch. The only salad that disappointed me was a vinaigrette of flavorless, end-of-the-season asparagus.

Some of the main courses please by being perfectly prepared and simple. A couple of tender, juicy rib lamb chops come with delicately minted fresh flageolets, which are light green pod beans, and a pile of buttered zucchini noodles. A butterflied New York steak is topped with a rosette of sharp herb-shallot butter, some good *pommes frites*, and a generous portion of sweet, french-cut green beans. Who could ask for anything more?

A special of grilled yellowtail produced a carefully cooked, sweet-smelling piece of fish in a fennel-scented butter sauce that didn't go with it, though a fine, thin sauce of butter-enriched poaching liquid went wonderfully with *paupiettes* of sole, stuffed with a cloudlike mousse of spinach and tarragon.

Whatever you do, save room for dessert. If M. Morin were not running a restaurant kitchen, he could easily work as a pastry chef. His pastries, like the rest of his cooking, show intelligence and skill. His masterpiece is a hazelnut napoleon, hundreds of crisp layers of very brown puff pastry spread with coffee buttercream and hazelnuts. It's a smashing dessert. His tarts are constructed of a crisp puff pastry crust, airy pastry cream, and fresh strawberries, delicately glazed. Not too sweet, very crisp, and generously fruity—they really are a triumph. An orange cake with many layers of genoise soaked with orange-scented syrup, filled with orange cream, and topped with poached orange slices was tart, moist, and refreshing for all its richness. There is excellent espresso to finish off the meal.

I like Janot's for many reasons. Its location, close to Union Square and near the Geary Boulevard theaters, fills a need in this city. I often find myself stumped when it comes to eating around Union Square without a reservation. Janot's welcomes the drop-in, especially in the afternoon. And I'm amazed at the reasonable prices. One of the gorgeous warm salads, a luxurious dessert and a glass of wine will get you out of Janot's, well fed, for under $15.

I eat in so many restaurants where the kitchen is grasping for ideas, where technical mistakes are made right and left, where the raw ingredients are not what they should be, that it always takes me aback to find a restaurant with a strong personal style, professionalism on the dining room floor, and an overall commitment to perfection. Janot's is such a place. Both its owners have paid their dues in the business. With this restaurant they carve out their own niche in the crowded restaurant scene by serving imaginative bistro fare with a sensibility more often found in fancier French restaurants. The combination is a winner. ■
— Patricia Unterman, June 22, 1986

Jewish Community Center Cafe and Deli

★

3200 California Street, San Francisco. 923-0696. Open Monday through Thursday 11 A.M. to 8 P.M., Friday 11 A.M. to 3 P.M. Beer, wine. No credit cards. No reservations. Inexpensive.

Eating out with young children always presents a dilemma. Even if they are good eaters, children's attention spans seem to evaporate the second they sit down in a restaurant, and if they're hungry, they want their food right away. I'm sure that's why the fast-food franchises direct so much advertising towards children and families. Gratification is immediate and the indestructible environments withstand any kind of behavior.

I'm a holdout for nonfranchised food. I try to find individually owned places that are casual enough to accept children and know how to get the food out quickly. One of the very best is the friendly cafe in the Jewish Community Center. Completely unlike drab institutional cafeterias, this tiny cafe has a tile counter with big, handsome wooden stools, a few booths, and four or five tables. Cheerful modern art and graceful hanging light fixtures add cachet to this homey operation, but it is the light, fresh food that attracts my attention.

It's hard to believe that a deeply flavorful chili bean soup aromatic with spices was made without meat, but all the soups at the cafe are vegetable based. An array of thick sandwiches come on good breads, like a chunky egg salad sandwich dressed with just the right amount of dijon mustard and mayonnaise. The Center Cafe is one of the few places in San Francisco where you can get a decent hot pastrami or corned beef sandwich piled high with paper-thin slices and served on fresh rye with a good pickle. What heaven!

Oddly enough, the cafe is more appreciated for its Middle Eastern dishes and salads than its corned beef sandwiches. A hummus platter comes with fresh pita bread, house-made chick-pea paste topped with creamy tahini, and piles of colorful, crisp raw vegetables that allow you to make your own sandwiches. The falafel, patties of spicy, deep-fried chick-pea batter cooked to order, are stuffed into pita bread along with a crisp cabbage and tomato salad.

Western green salads are nicely constructed with a variety of lettuces and a tasty vinaigrette. A fine-looking spinach salad and Greek salad are popular with the JCC's health-club members, but the foamy chocolate egg creams delight the children, as do cheese blintzes served with an eye-catching array of fresh fruit.

If you sit at the counter, you can order

and get your food almost immediately and it's still made to order by someone who cares how it tastes. ■
— Patricia Unterman, August 22, 1986

King of China

★ ★

939 Clement Street, San Francisco. 668-2618. Open daily 9 A.M. to 10 P.M. Beer, wine. MasterCard, Visa, American Express. Reservations accepted. Inexpensive.

Let's face it. The best Chinese restaurants in San Francisco are not in Chinatown. They've moved, along with their upwardly mobile, second- and third-generation Chinese clientele, to the Richmond. The two Oceans, the Fook, the Ton Kiangs, the Fountain Court, the Red Crane, San Wang II, to name just a few of the new crop, have joined ranks with the Yet Wahs, Lung Fung, Mike's, Vegi-Food, Kum Moon, and Kirin to serve an ever-growing Chinese community in the Geary–Clement Street corridor. And yet, despite city-imposed moratoriums on new restaurants in the area, more seem to shoot up each season. Recently, a gigantic two-story Chinese food hall called King of China blossomed on Clement Street and it immediately became one of the most popular restaurants in town.

King of China stands out because of its scale and its shiny metal exterior. The second-floor dining room must seat at least 300 and it's always full. A bank of floor-to-ceiling windows gives the illusion of open space, and mirrored walls expand the vista even more. A well-considered color scheme, carpeting, and recessed ceilings with bright lights all help to smooth the experience of eating in such a loud, busy place. The decor of King of China, more than any of the other giant Chinese restaurants that have been popping up in town lately, lives up to its glitzy Hong Kong prototypes.

And so does the food. The dim sum selection is one of the best in the city. Quail egg *sui mai* are the best dim sum I've ever tasted. Recognizable by their little domed tops, these savory, noodle-wrapped, meat-filled dumplings crowned with a steamed quail egg have a rich, buttery flavor.

As Bruce Cost (who writes about Asian food in the *Chronicle* and who took me to King of China) pointed out, a dim sum parlor can be judged by its shrimp dumplings alone, and the delicate shrimp *har gow* here passed the test. They have thin, opalescent noodle wrappers and a chunky, sweet shrimp-and-egg filling. A similar rice noodle dumpling to watch for is filled with peanuts, black mushrooms, ground pork, and cilantro. Other dim sum are wrapped in golden brown fried bean-curd skin, filled with peas and water chestnuts, and then juicily braised.

Cantonese roast duck is dispensed from carts at room temperature but that does not diminish its succulence. The ducks have been marinated in vinegar, sugar, Chinese five spices, and orange. They're stuffed with anise and onion and then deep fried and steamed until their skins are burnished and their flesh melts in your mouth. The pieces rest on a bed of nutty roasted soybeans. King of China really has duck technique down cold.

The pork *baos* are light, airy, and generously filled. The barely sweetened egg tarts have sandy crusts that disappear on your tongue. A crisp, flaky coating of taro flour contrasts with the creamy interiors of greaseless, deep-fried taro balls.

I've only hinted here at the variety of dim sum being wheeled out of the kitchen.

I liked the tea lunch so much I returned for dinner twice to sample the regular menu. On both occasions large wedding parties were in full operation with brides in pink dresses being feted while the restaurant continued to serve regular diners.

On the first night service was abysmal. Dishes came out of the kitchen cold. Bus bins of dirty dishes were left on chairs and tables nearby. Despite such adversity, we did get a stunningly fresh whole rockfish, called a bolina, simply and elegantly steamed with ginger, coriander, and scallions, and a delicious preparation of coarsely minced squab, water chestnuts, cured ham, and black mushrooms served on a bed of crisp rice noodles with head lettuce leaves as wrappers. Some Chinese broccoli was beautifully steamed with just ginger and garlic.

However, egg rolls were dull. A fresh conch dish arrived cold and full of canned ingredients, as did a seaweed and bean curd soup.

On a return visit, we were seated by the bus station, but this time we were waited on by an efficient woman who got the food to us in perfect condition.

Following the Ken Hom rule of ordering, we asked the waitress to choose bean curd, spinach, broccoli, and crab dishes, and ordered chicken, duck, and crispy Hong Kong–style chow mein noodles straight from the menu. With the exception of the crab, which was not fresh enough, we ate magnificently.

The deep-fried crispy chicken served with shrimp chips was moist and tasty. The spinach, aromatic with threads of fresh ginger, and the Chinese broccoli, with the lightest of oyster sauce dressings, were shining examples of vegetable cookery. Clean-flavored chow mein noodles underscored how good technique is in King of China's kitchen. Not one drop of extra oil adhered to super-fine noodles, yet they were moist, full of flavor, and crispy without being burned.

A steamed white bean-curd dish with a visually stunning presentation represented some of the best Cantonese cooking I've tasted in the United States. Each square of soft bean curd was topped with a piece of Virginia ham and a triangle of black mushroom. Spears of Chinese broccoli flanked the plate and a clear, delicate sauce based on good stock moistened it all. I also was taken by a crispy duck stuffed with mashed taro root and served with a bowl of clear brown gravy that brought all the parts together.

The most you can hope for when you go to a gigantic restaurant like King of China is that you will hit several good dishes. Yet I was striking gold with almost every choice.

I don't know how they do it. The kitchen must be a madhouse, yet the food comes out carefully cooked and strikingly presented. Even given the tendency to seat Caucasians at the worst tables, a reluctance to discuss the menu, and the noise level, I consider King of China to be one of the most serviceable restaurants in town. You can eat lavishly at this restaurant for under $10 a person and get fresh, high-quality, tasty food. And your kids can yell as loud as they want. No one can hear over the din. No wonder every seat is taken. King of China is the best family restaurant in town. ∎

—Patricia Unterman, January 19, 1986

Korean Garden Restaurant
★★

606 Bernardo Avenue (just off El Camino Real), Sunnyvale. 408-738-9141. Open Sunday through Thursday 11 A.M. to 11 P.M., Friday and Saturday until 2 A.M. Full bar. MasterCard, Visa, American Express, Diners Club. Reservations accepted. Inexpensive to moderate.

For serious eaters, it's worthwhile to pay attention to the demographic patterns of the Bay Area's mushrooming Asian population. The rule of thumb is simple: Where Asians settle in large numbers, good food can't be far behind.

Only last week did I learn that a community of 40,000 Koreans has sprung up in the Santa Clara Valley. It apparently started because many Koreans found work at electronics companies, and their extended families moved to be near them.

I found out about it after a barrage of recommendations to eat at Korean Garden Restaurant in Sunnyvale. I couldn't believe the number of people who told me about this place, including a friend who excitedly reported that Korean Garden serves the best intestines in the Bay Area. (It might be the *only* intestines in the Bay Area, since I don't believe any Jewish deli in these parts has yet dared to put kishkes on its menu.)

The only Korean food I'd eaten previously had been at little places with small menus. No one could ever accuse Korean Garden of that. It sprawls over several rooms, cubicles, and a cocktail lounge, including a big, raised central area decorated by tree branches with leaves pasted on. And its seven-page menu has a mere eighty-seven choices.

Although the menu has English translations for most items, ordering was a bit frustrating. We were the only non-Asians there, and the waitress kept walking by with heaping platters of unidentifiable things that looked great. When we asked, none of the waitresses knew enough English to figure out our question.

So we decided to order an untranslated dish with the marvelous name of *mae-woon pollack jim* — in the hopes that we'd hit the jackpot. I don't know whether "Pollack Jim" is the cook or something that comes in a can, but neither apparently was in that night; the waitress brought everything else we ordered, but *pollack jim* never showed up.

Actually, we did just fine working just from the translated stuff. In fact, I suspected when the kimchee came to the table that this wasn't going to be ordinary Korean food. Kimchee is the pickled napa cabbage that's a staple of the Korean diet. But at Korean Garden, it was accompanied with a virtual pickled vegetable store — radishes, winter melon, various greens, and things I've never seen before. They were all delicious, and the waitress was willing to bring refills.

At Korean Garden, some of the standard Korean dishes I've eaten in the past proved to be sensational. And everything lived up to the reputation of Korean food for not skimping on spiciness and heat. If you like garlic and chili peppers, you'll be in heaven.

Among the better-known dishes, *man-doo kuk*, the Korean version of won ton soup, vastly surpassed its Chinese counterpart in flavor. The delicate dumplings were stuffed with ground beef and pork, chopped onions, green onions, and garlic. Egg whites floated in the flavorful light broth.

The barbecued short ribs were a winner, too. Cooked rare, they had no fat, and came in a pungent sauce flavored with five-spice mixture, sesame oil, and garlic. Also out-

standing was a sizzling platter of tender barbecued pork in a rich marinade of bean paste and garlic.

The exotic dishes proved to be more of a mixed bag. On the plus side were three appetizers —"egg rolled fish," roasted seaweed, and what's called on the menu "lettuce for wrapping rice." The fish fillets had been dipped in egg batter and delicately panfried, with the fish emerging fresh and juicy. The lettuce dish turned out to be a platter of fish, meat, and vegetables in a fiery hot sauce that you moderate by making a sandwich with the cool lettuce leaves.

Another stab into the world of the exotic was much less successful. With "fish egg stew," we envisioned a heaping pot of the wonderful fish roe that's becoming such a rising star in the yuppie food world. But instead we got a bowl of broth with a huge hunk of membrane-encased mass floating in it. It was hard, unpleasant, and weird.

Then there were the intestines, or, more precisely, the "seasoned intestined vegetable in house special sauce." What appeared at the table was a delicious casserole of vegetables and tofu, with lots of chunks of intestine floating in it. For a little more you can get the same casserole without the intestines, which might give you an idea of what the intestines tasted like. Let's describe them as "offal" and leave it at that.

Most entrees at Korean Garden are inexpensive, so menu hopping won't strain your wallet. You might not like every dish, but the menu here has such variety that it's a golden opportunity to explore in depth an interesting and satisfying cuisine. ■

—Stan Sesser, August 15, 1986

Krung-Kao

3471 Mission Street, San Francisco. 550-8417. Open daily 5 to 10 P.M. Beer, wine. MasterCard, Visa. Reservations accepted.

This immaculate neighborhood storefront restaurant has been painted a soothing shade of pale pink and outfitted with matching tablecloths, woven Thai straw mats, and pink roses. You are brought a bowl of steaming hot Thai chicken broth with glass noodles and just a hint of hot pepper as you sit down. This is a most hospitable place.

Krung-Kao excels at noodles, and their version of *pad Thai*, a delicious preparation of soft, chewy noodles, tasty marinated bean curd, egg, shrimp, and peanuts in a delicate, slightly sweet dressing is worth coming back for. Also done well are various coconut milk curries. Eating an intense yellow curry with plump prawns over Krung-Kao's good, nutty glutinous rice is a real pleasure.

A shredded green papaya salad with tomatoes, chopped peanuts, and dried shrimp was a bit soggy, and Thai egg rolls, a dish that Thai restaurants think their Western customers want, were leaden. Barbecued chicken had lively flavor from a marinade, but wasn't juicy. Many Thai restaurants pregrill their chicken and then finish it off to order. This procedure takes all the life out of the chicken. Most customers would rather wait while the chicken cooks from scratch. The squid in a mild calamari salad was dull tasting and rubbery.

This modest little restaurant could specialize in Thai noodle dishes and curries, for which they really have a feel. The whole gamut of Thai dishes seems a bit much for them. After all, the best eating to be done in Thailand is from little carts and open-air restaurants that prepare soup and noodles, throwing in fishballs and meatballs and fresh herbs at the last minute. The best chicken I've ever had in my life came hot off the coals of a metal box perched in the sand in a small beach town on Phuket. I ate that succulent, aromatic chicken every day for ten days, with shredded-to-order green papaya salad. If a Thai restaurant in San Francisco served only that grilled to order chicken with sticky rice, it would be a success. ∎

—Patricia Unterman, March 29, 1987

La Creme de la Creme

★

5362 College Avenue (near Broadway), Oakland. 420-8822. Open for breakfast Monday through Friday 7:30 to 11 A.M., Saturday and Sunday 8 A.M. to 2 P.M.; for dinner daily 6 to 9:30 P.M. Beer, wine. American Express, Diners Club, personal checks. Reservations advised. Moderate.

Many restaurant reviewers, including me, feel an obligation to visit all the trendy well-known restaurants on the assumption that that's what people are talking about. Yet I'm often amazed how frequently my mail throws this assumption into doubt.

Two years ago, when I had critical things to say about Spenger's Fish Grotto, perhaps the least trendy restaurant in town, I was deluged with mail, accusing me of everything from intolerance to desecration of the American flag. But two months ago, when I wrote critically of the upstairs cafe at Chez Panisse, I received exactly one letter. The writer didn't even dispute my opinion; he simply asked how someone who demands perfection from a restaurant could be so imperfect as to talk about "leak soup." (The Chronicle's computer graciously accepts the blame for that one.)

Nor do letters suggesting places to review generally focus on the "hot" new restaurants. Most often, people are gratified to find little neighborhood restaurants where they can get excellent food at reasonable prices, and where they don't have to dress up.

One such place, a tiny French restaurant in an old house in the Rockridge section of Oakland, has drawn a steady stream of letters over the last two years. It's called La Creme de la Creme, and I finally got motivated to review it when they started serving breakfasts six weeks ago. The breakfast menu sounded wonderfully interesting and innovative—and nothing on it was more than a few dollars. The story behind this place is a classic for the Bay Area, where it sometimes seems that half the population dreams of starting a restaurant. David Nugent, a salesman of women's hosiery who always loved learning about and cooking French food, decided to make his dream a reality. At the age of fifty, he bought a cute old cottage on College Avenue and started remodeling it. (Inside the walls were newspapers from 1893.)

Some of the dishes at Creme de la Creme are excellent; others I was less impressed with. But virtually everything you order shows Nugent's dedication to his craft, going far beyond what you'd expect in a little restaurant like this.

Vegetables are a prime example. These days you can virtually predict when you walk in the door what sort of vegetables you'll get with your meal. At an ordinary restaurant, it will be sliced zucchini; at a trendy California cuisine place, it will be baby carrots and asparagus tips arranged in the shape of a fan.

But at Creme de la Creme, I was almost floored when I saw what came on the plate. There was the shell of a Japanese eggplant stuffed with eggplant puree, mushrooms, and shallots. There were braised celery root slices topped with diced canadian bacon, onions, carrots, and celery. There were silver-dollar-sized pancakes made from pureed spinach and crepe batter.

Moreover, this was no arty arrangement of one little bite of each on the plate—these and other vegetables were heaped on in substantial portions, an incredible act of generosity.

As for the entrees themselves, I had mixed feelings about the three I ordered. Scallops with mushrooms in a light madeira sauce were perfect, the scallops sweet and juicy. A breast of chicken stuffed with cream cheese, shallots, and herbs was tasty, but a heavy béarnaise sauce was exactly the wrong choice to combine with the heavy cream cheese. And poached salmon was a total disappointment; the fish seemed a little old and a bit overcooked, while the thick, creamy sauce was much too heavy.

There was no quarrel with the appetizers and desserts, however. Mussel soup, cooked in fish stock and white wine with lots of tomatoes, onions, and garlic, was loaded with tasty shelled mussels. The goat cheese and onion tart was remarkable, with a beautiful flaky crust, mild cheese, and lots of herbs. No less impressive was the mushroom tart made with gruyere cheese.

One of the desserts will drive chocolate lovers wild. In what's called a "chocolate climax," you get a piece of chocolate cake topped with homemade chocolate ice cream and hot chocolate sauce. To pull something like this off, you need the highest-quality chocolate; you can't overwhelm it with sweetness—and Nugent pulled it off perfectly.

For breakfast, you can again order those great mushroom or goat cheese tarts. But my first choice would be the two dishes that include soft, fluffy scrambled eggs. In one, the eggs are combined with corn, green onions, and bacon; the other has chunks of homemade shallot-herb sausage and comes with sauteed apple slices on the side.

The breakfasts are a bargain in themselves. But they also come with a basket of interesting home-baked breads and muffins, and with absolutely the best homemade preserves I've ever tasted. One was strawberry-rhubarb, another pear with lemon peel, the third tangelo with orange peel; all of them emphasized the fruit over the sugar.

As good as they sound on the menu, I'd suggest avoiding the griddle cakes and the french toast. They're both too leaden, leaving you feeling overstuffed.

If there's one flaw in Nugent's cooking, it's the heaviness of some dishes; he needs in particular to lighten his sauces. But these are quibbles compared to the problems in service. On both my visits, the restaurant was mostly empty, but the orders took an agonizingly long time to come from the kitchen. And both times the waiters mixed things up, bringing us something we hadn't ordered.

Poor service on a slow night doesn't bode well for a restaurant that's bound to become more crowded after people have read about it. I called Nugent to discuss the problem, and he vowed that things would be in shape by the time this review appears. I hope so, because Crème de la Creme is the sort of place the Bay Area needs more of: a pleasant, moderately priced neighborhood French restaurant dedicated to innovative cooking. ■

—Stan Sesser, April 18, 1986

La Imperial

See review for Los Compadres.

La Lanterna

★★

799 College Avenue, Kentfield. 258-0144. Open for lunch Tuesday through Friday 11:30 A.M. to 2:30 P.M., for dinner Tuesday through Saturday 5:30 to 9:45 P.M., Sunday 5 to 9 P.M. Beer, wine. MasterCard, Visa, American Express. Reservations accepted. Moderate.

La Lanterna, a family-operated Italian restaurant in Marin County, came to my attention through a long letter and a computer printout of a year's worth of the restaurant's dishes. Risotto, house-made pasta, fish soup, *osso buco*, braised rabbit with polenta, grilled veal loin, and fried calamari represented just a few of the dishes that perked my appetite on the six-page list. The letter talked about nearby gardens supplying the restaurant, quoted from my favorite Italian cookbook writer, Marcella Hazan, and included a biography of the chef, a fifty-three-year-old high school teacher who left teaching to pursue his passion to cook. I couldn't resist the story and made the short trip to Kentfield. I'm happy to report that La Lanterna does fulfill the promises of its correspondence. Its fresh, authentic Italian cooking shines all the way to San Francisco.

Like most Marin County restaurants, La Lanterna is part of a small shopping center. It occupies a low-ceilinged space with some interior red brick walls and lots of windows that look out to a manicured lawn rimmed with gorgeous flowers, where, at lunch, outdoor tables are set up. Though the interior is unpretentious and comfortably suburban, different floor levels and an irregular shape create separate dining areas and alcoves. Commodious blond wood, dowel-backed chairs, white linen tablecloths, and reproductions of famous Italian painters set the stage for the main attraction, the food.

You can tell that the food is prepared by someone who loves to cook from your first bite. The appetizers are shining examples of the Italian way of presenting especially fresh and interesting ingredients with ingenious simplicity.

Fresh squid, so velvety and tender now during the summer, got the merest battering and the quickest, cleanest deep frying. It's worth a trip over the bridge just for this dish. House-cured *bresaola*, thin, thin slices of aromatic air-dried beef, was drizzled with lemon juice and extra-virgin olive oil. La Lanterna puts out a basic and, I think, superlative version of carpaccio. Almost-translucent slices of raw beef are sprinkled with olive oil, shavings of parmesan, and a few spikes of fresh rosemary, a tiny original twist. A caesar salad was loaded with rough-cut croutons that soaked up a tart, garlicky, anchovy-rich dressing, just the way I like it. A pile of sliced ripe tomatoes topped with first-rate anchovies and rings of red onion crowned a bed of piquantly dressed lettuce.

In Italy now the Tuscan restaurants are serving a risotto and then a pasta after the first course and you can do that too at La Lanterna by splitting orders. The risotto one evening was studded with fresh peas and tender shrimp. The imported Italian rice had absorbed the requisite quantity of good chicken stock, butter, and olive oil to give it that creamy yet toothsome texture. What a marvelous culinary invention!

I think La Lanterna is trying to do too much with some of their pasta, like *pappardelle*. When I order this pasta, I expect wide, thick ribbons of rough-cut noodles.

Here, the fancy *pappardelle* is three-tone—white, green, and pink—all in the same length of noodle. I can't imagine how it's made, but the noodle lacked the distinctive flavor and handmade texture that I associate with this homey pasta. The big chunks of red and green peppers and albeit excellent house-made Italian sausage didn't work well with the noodles either. *Pappardelle* call for a real sauce—like a rabbit sauce or a spicy meat sauce, for example. Unfortunately, the traditional bolognese sauce we chose for house-made ravioli was dull and a little muddy tasting. Just some butter and cheese would have done them justice.

Main-course offerings are highlighted by the best veal I've tasted in any restaurant. It's the kind of veal you rarely get any more—white, butter-tender, but full of flavor—and the kitchen knows how to handle it. Scallops of it about a quarter-inch thick were sauteed quickly and sauced with a veal-stock reduction and dried porcini mushrooms. The rich, meaty flavor of the sauce jumps right out at you but stays in step with the meat—a great dish. So was an even more straightforward dish, an expertly grilled veal chop, thick, juicy, and tasty. These, as do all main courses, come with triangular chunks of sauteed zucchini of exceptional sweetness. They must come from La Lanterna's garden.

Eggplant parmigiana was every bit as satisfying as a meat dish. Big, pear-shaped slices of eggplant cut lengthwise were battered, deep fried, and sauced with a spritely tomato puree (this might be the sauce to choose for the ravioli). The eggplant melts in your mouth without a touch of oiliness or bitterness. A too-thin slice of grilled swordfish, though marinated in olive oil and garlic, lacked sparkle.

A homey *crème au caramel* with satiny, gently set custard and lots of caramelized sugar sits well after a four-course meal, though a house-made *zuppa inglese*, molded layers of liqueur-soaked cake and custard, provides a richer choice. The espresso comes with a frothy head and depth of flavor.

The computer-printed menu, which changes weekly, offers a serviceable selection of California and Italian wines on its flip side. The usual chiantis, barolos, and barbarescos were all present and accounted for. I would like to see on this list more of the good, wondrously inexpensive Italian wines and some of the interesting, less-known regional wines that are finding their way into the San Francisco area. The food side of the menu is so well formulated that I want the wine side to offer some challenges, too.

A final comment about the service: the dining room is staffed by young, fresh-faced men and women who do a job that would make any chef-owner proud. They're well informed, eager to please, and work hard on efficiency. They know how to wait on children, of which there are many in the dining room, and do not discourage complicated orders. Best of all, they really seem to enjoy working there.

La Lanterna feels like the proud work of a family dedicated to an exciting but demanding new endeavor. It's fun, as a customer, to be a part of it. ∎

—Patricia Unterman, July 26, 1987

La Victoria Restaurant

★

1205 Alabama Street (at Twenty-fourth), San Francisco. 550-9309. Open daily 11 A.M. to 10 P.M. No alcoholic beverages. No credit cards. No reservations. Inexpensive.

If someone asked me to describe my favorite dish, the food that comforted me the most, it would be my grandmother's chicken pancakes. This grandmother was not a great cook, but she prepared a few labor-intensive dishes that were wonderful. We never ate those dishes without pleasure.

There are a couple of women in the Mission who come close to providing that kind of culinary warmth. They have been cooking for years in a small open kitchen in a restaurant called La Victoria, behind the bakery of the same name. They have a special aptitude for soups, and one taste of their chicken broth takes me back to my grandmother's kitchen. The seasonings may be a little different, but the strength of the broth and the velvety texture of the chicken are exactly the same. Their colorful chicken soup is bright with chunks of fresh tomato, cilantro leaves, a quarter of a skinned chicken, rice, and mild green chili peppers. Like the broth, the big hunk of chicken is extraordinary. It was not used to make the broth, but instead simmered very, very slowly to be served for eating.

A close runner-up is La Victoria's *sopa de albondigas*, with big, light, loose-grained meatballs in a rich broth that is slightly minty with fresh epazote leaves, a Mexican herb. Rice and chunks of squashlike chayote are delicious in it. A bowl of dried oregano and hot chili flakes comes on the side.

For those who like soups that are almost stews, La Victoria's posole is marvelous. A bright red-chili-infused broth is full of rice, fat corn kernels, which are the posole, and chunks of succulent, garlicky pork. Posole is an Aztec invention, in which corn kernels are heated in a mild solution of lime until the skins come off. Corn in this form is called nixtamal. The kernels are then dried, then boiled in soup until they swell up and become soft like hominy. The plate of garnishes that come with this soup provides optional hotness, though a squeeze of lemon was all I needed.

Dishes like *chile relleno* can be a little soggy. All the *antojitos*—enchiladas, tostadas, tacos—come with saucy pureed beans, cooked with a lot of lard, and rice. It all runs together homogeneously on the plate.

The dining room reminds me of family restaurants in small Mexican towns with do-it-yourself decoration.

Since only two women run the place, service can be slow, empty tables don't get cleared immediately, and it takes awhile to get the check. Those soups, however, are worth waiting for. ■

—Patricia Unterman, October 27, 1985

Lady E's Restaurant

★

5327 East Fourteenth Street, Oakland (take the High Street exit off I-880, turn right at East Fourteenth Street). 261-2950. Open Sunday 11 A.M. to 8:45 P.M., Monday noon to 7:45 P.M., Tuesday through Thursday noon to 8:45 P.M., Friday 11 A.M. to 8:45 P.M., Saturday 8:30 A.M. to 8:45 P.M. No alcoholic beverages (you can bring in beer or wine). Cash only. No reservations. Inexpensive.

Soul Brothers Kitchen

★

5239 Telegraph Avenue (at Fifty-second Street), Oakland. 655-9367. Open daily 7:30 A.M. to 10:30 P.M. No alcoholic beverages (you can bring in beer or wine). Cash only. Reservations for five or more only. Inexpensive.

The proliferation of California cuisine and French restaurants that serve dainty little portions artfully arranged on a plate can create a crisis for those who like a little variety in their eating. On occasion an antidote is called for—and what could be a better antidote than soul food?

You say you're tired of those microscopic al dente baby vegetables? Consider, then, a can of green beans dumped into a pot and cooked with a hunk of salt pork until they cry for mercy. That's what you get at one of these restaurants. (The other is more yuppified, although your stomach might not recognize the difference.)

Lady E's

Lady E's Restaurant is not exactly in the high-rent district of Oakland. A security guard stands at the door, and if you go to a nearby liquor store to buy beer for dinner, a sign there informs you in no uncertain terms to park all narcotics at the curb.

Yet, in the middle of urban blight, Esther Clay and her daughter Deimentrius have created a pretty little restaurant that exudes warmth and friendliness. There are red tablecloths, wood-paneled walls covered with photos of famous visitors, and waiters who couldn't be nicer. There's also a regular clientele who seem to use Lady E's as a home away from home.

From the open kitchen come platters groaning with food; no one will ever accuse Lady E's of serving dainty portions. Seven or eight dollars buys you enough meat, vegetables, and corn bread to fuel about two days' activities; an additional few dollars brings you a "side order" that can substitute for an appetizer. (Soul food restaurants aren't much on appetizers; a side order consists of all five pounds of entree without the vegetables.)

A couple of things at Lady E's are so outstanding that the choice should be simple. Start with a side of deep-fried oysters or chicken wings, then go on to the smothered steak.

Although the batters are thick, the frying at Lady E's is terrific. The juiciness of the fresh Pacific oysters contrasts perfectly with the crisp cornmeal crust, and there's not a speck of grease. The chicken wings are peppery and moist, and the crusty flour coating again is greaseless.

Although beef is my least favorite meat, I found the smothered steak irresistible. The thick and tasty meat, which tastes like brisket, is made even better by a surprisingly light and flavorful gravy.

You'd do well also ordering oxtails and fried chicken as entrees. But you're likely to be less happy with the vegetables, since, in the best soul food tradition, the green beans and corn come from cans. My green beans included a big hunk of salt pork, such a delightful anachronism in today's health-conscious world that I wanted to take a picture.

Soul Brothers Kitchen

With its tablecloths, thick carpeting, and, above all, fresh vegetables, Soul Brothers Kitchen on Telegraph Avenue in Oakland can almost be termed yuppie soul food.

With the exception of canned peaches in the cobbler and frozen crab in the gumbo, owner Rip Wilson says, "I don't use nothing canned or frozen, no way." He also avoids animal fat. "You don't see no grease floating around on my gravy," Wilson brags.

Can it be soul food? Absolutely. The smothered chicken is a marvel, chicken that's floured, panfried, then smothered in a rich tan gravy that, true to Wilson's boast, is absolutely greaseless. The short ribs of beef are another winner, slowly steamed until they emerge tender and meaty, then doused in another delicious gravy. Both dishes are real bargains, particularly when you taste what comes with them.

The side dishes belong in the soul food hall of fame. The corn bread (some batches use yellow cornmeal, others white) is absolutely addictive, crusty on the outside, grainy and not at all sweet inside. We asked for more corn bread so many times that the waitress finally started giggling.

Then there were luscious black-eyed peas in a rich, peppery sauce, fresh collard greens that actually weren't overdone, and fresh turnip greens that suffered only from too much salt.

Soul Brothers's menu not only has traditional soul food, but also lots of things from Louisiana. I tried three, and two were losers. The gumbo had a thin, watery broth with virtually no heat to it, although the crab had survived freezing surprisingly well. (As soon as I phoned Wilson and told him about the gumbo, he shouted to his chef to put in more hot sauce, so you might find it in better shape.)

Blackened redfish was an absolute disaster, the inside inedibly rubbery and the outside so charred that the burned taste was totally unpleasant. But the deep-fried catfish proved to be first-rate, exquisitely freshtasting and not greasy.

While desserts at Lady E's were much too sweet, Soul Brothers was absolute Sugar City. Soggy cobbler filled with canned peaches and a ton of sugar presented a pretty pitiful picture in the middle of fresh fruit season.

Soul Brothers has its share of weaknesses, including food coming out of the kitchen at a snail's pace. But you can put together a really delicious meal here, the place is friendly, and the price is right. ∎

—Stan Sesser, August 7, 1987

Lalime's Cafe

★ ★

1410 Solano Avenue, Albany (take the Albany exit from I-80). 527-9838. Open for a la carte dinners Wednesday and Thursday 5:30 to 9:30 P.M.; for fixed-priced dinner seatings Friday and Saturday at 6 and 9 P.M. only. Beer, wine. Cash, checks only. Reservations essential. Moderate.

Why are restaurant prices going up when the prices of food, fuel, and lots of other things are going down these days?

This has been a major mystery to me. I read about deflation, then find that many French and California cuisine dinners I eat come out to at least $40 a head. With my friends, I taste dozens of excellent wines that retail for less than $5, then see restaurant wine lists where there's virtually nothing for less than $15.

To compound the mystery, I hear about so many restaurant owners who are crying the blues that I can't believe the answer is simply profiteering. The whole question would make a great term paper for a business student.

In view of this, it's a pleasure to discover a new restaurant that demonstrates it's possible to turn out good food in a pleasant atmosphere, but not run off with the entire contents of a customer's wallet. This new place is called Lalime's Cafe. It's on Solano Avenue in Albany, which is becoming the East Bay equivalent of Clement Street. There are so many new restaurants on Solano that I can't follow them any more, and it took a friend's constant nagging to get me into Lalime's. Then the problem was reversed: I liked it so much I went for four dinners before I could even consider writing a review.

To say simply that the food is French doesn't do Lalime's justice. The two owners are Armenians from Lebanon (who married sisters with the last name of Lalime). Perhaps because of their multiethnic background, they're filled with new ideas about what to do with their food.

There are some Middle Eastern touches, some California cuisine touches, some things that come from wild imagination. But whatever you order, there's one guarantee: At Lalime's, you're never going to get one of those hack dishes that 90 percent of the new non-Asian restaurants adopt because they seem to have proved popular elsewhere. No mesquite-grilled monkfish here.

At Lalime's you sit there constantly impressed by the innovation. And if an occasional dish doesn't work out, you won't mind because of the price. Each week there's a new fixed-price dinner and a new a la carte menu for weeknights. My last one included a fish course, an interesting pasta, a sorbet, duck, a fantastic salad, and a chocolate-hazelnut souffle. No one will leave one of *these* dinners hungry.

Consider that last meal as an example of the innovation that permeates Lalime's cooking. The first course was baked scallops, nothing unusual sounding. But the scallops came stuffed in orange slices with a sauce of orange juice, butter, cream, saffron, and shallots. It was delicious, and every bit of sauce got mopped up with the baguettes from Semifreddi Bakery in Kensington. (The Bay Area may be awash with great baguettes, but this place has managed to develop one, rolled in poppy and fennel seeds, that tops them all.)

Then we move to the pasta: spinach and egg noodles rolled around a stuffing of prosciutto, ricotta, goat cheese, and herbs, sprinkled with little wild-onion flowers. Interesting, but the dish was marred by a watery sauce.

Next came a very tart sorbet of fresh tangerines and limes. While the pastries at Lalime's are the weakest part of the meal, what they do with sorbets and ice creams, both as palate cleansers and for dessert, is nothing less than magnificent.

Next up was the duck, again a pleasant surprise. Alongside the slices of duck breast came a sausage made from meat of the duck legs, shallots, and herbs. Each course comes with a suggested wine, sold by the bottle or glass, and with the duck there's an unusual chance to taste a cabernet with some age (in our case, the 1977 Freemark Abbey).

Even the salad was a surprise. Baby radicchio, perfectly prepared fresh beets, and baby radishes were combined with a dressing that must be unique. It included extra-virgin olive oil, Oregon loganberry wine, and a few drops, believe it or not, of Grand Marnier.

The weeknight dishes are no less interesting. One night, for example, there was a huge bowl of an astonishing soup of pureed red peppers, cream, and at least a dozen fresh, juicy shelled mussels. The portions at Lalime's are sometimes impressively big, and, with a salad, this soup could have made a meal.

Not everything at Lalime's is a success, though. Chef Haig Krikorian can get carried away with a particular theme to the detriment of the food. One night several dishes had sauces that were too vinegary; another night Krikorian was experimenting with Oregon fruit wines and a couple of the sauces were too sweet.

But the occasional mistakes don't mar the overall excellence. Informal but tastefully decorated, Lalime's, with just ten tables, is a gem of a little restaurant. The waiter, Vahe Keushguerian, is as skilled as anyone at a $100 French restaurant. And on weekends, there's live classical guitar music.

I don't know how Lalime's does it, but I wish other restaurant owners would visit and see what kind of food can be turned out at these prices. The Bay Area desperately needs more restaurants like this. ∎
— Stan Sesser, March 21, 1986

Lan Xang

★ ★

5336 Geary Boulevard (near Eighteenth), San Francisco. 752-4310. Open daily 11 A.M. to 10 P.M. Beer, wine. Cash only. No reservations. Inexpensive to moderate.

Laos is a country that is closed to foreigners, and it's one whose food I've always been curious about. When you're surrounded by Thailand, China, Vietnam, and Burma, you've got all the influences you need to produce one of the world's greatest cuisines.

Although there are lots of Laotian refugees in the United States, I've never heard of a Laotian restaurant — until now, that is, and just as with Cambodian food, San Francisco lucks out again.

It's called Lan Xang, at Eighteenth and Geary, and since I've never seen a Laotian restaurant in Paris, Bangkok, or anywhere else, it could possibly be the world's only Laotian restaurant outside of Laos. If Lan Xang's food is any indication, it's a cuisine we could use a lot more of.

So what is Laotian food? It turns out to be almost identical to the regional cuisine of northeast Thailand, a style of cooking you rarely encounter in Thai restaurants here, or for that matter, even in Bangkok.

The cooking centers on barbecued meats in aromatic marinades, served with what's called "sticky rice." So what's unusual about another barbecue joint? You have to go to Lan Xang and see for yourself.

Let's start with the pork sausage. In Korat, the largest city in northeast Thailand, I had sausage so stunning I couldn't believe it. Lan Xang does the exact same thing — not a speck of grease, not a speck of fat, the marvelous aromas of Asian herbs and spices, and a crisp barbecued skin. American sausage, even the yuppie variety, will never taste as good again.

Then there's what the menu calls "beef jerky"— but don't go away, it really isn't. It's thick slices of tender fat-free beef, marinated and charbroiled. That is the classic dish to eat with sticky rice. First, you wash your hands in the bowls of cold tea with lemon slices that the restaurant provides. Then you mold the glutinous rice in your right hand as if you were molding clay, reach for a piece of beef, and eat it as a sort of sandwich.

There are other great dishes. Order as an appetizer number 15, a mixture of ground pork, bits of crunchy pork skin, shredded coconut, peanuts, chili peppers, mint leaves, green onions, and lime juice. It's an astonishing blend of textures and tastes.

Then move on to the mushroom salad—warm, delicate oyster mushrooms sauteed with mustard greens, sesame seeds, and fresh (yes, fresh) bamboo shoots.

Now you're ready for the barbecued chicken, as good as anything in a Thai or Cambodian restaurant and infinitely superior to the American variety. Then consider these: greaseless deep-fried frog legs, crisp on the outside and moist on the inside, served with a green chili dipping sauce; or "two lovers deep fried"—slices of squid wrapped around shrimp, fried, and served on sticks jutting out from half an orange.

If you can bear passing up the spareribs, which are like none other, it's time for a fish course, fish *laab* (number 27), which is flakes of fish mixed with green onions, toasted rice, mint leaves, and lime. I'll warn you away from a few things, too. The green papaya salad is much inferior to the versions served at Angkor Wat on Geary at Sixth or Plearn Thai Cuisine in Berkeley. The chicken leg soup is decent but boring, not worth wasting valuable stomach space on. Skip the vegetable and fish curry (number 40) and go down one on the menu to the rice noodle curry with ground fish.

And don't even think about ordering the one dessert, marvelously named "sweety fruity." It's yucky gooey.

All the food is very inexpensive, and it's so good you won't be able to stop ordering things. At my first dinner, three of us managed to demolish twelve dishes and run up a bill just over $50.

Lan Xang is run by a sweet couple who serve lunch and dinner seven days a week. Anant Sangchan, the Thai husband, runs the dining room, and Wilailuk Sangchan, his Laotian wife, does the cooking.

Anant is so solicitous that if the restaurant isn't crowded, he'll spend half the meal standing over you virtually wringing his hands for fear you might not be loving everything. "I need complaints," he kept saying, no doubt wondering what he could do to improve business in his modest, two-month-old restaurant.

The answer is "nothing." There may be some initial confusion and problems when Lan Xang goes from empty to full, even though I warned them. But food like this is worth any hassle. ■

—Stan Sesser, February 13, 1987

Las Parrillas

★

7600 Commerce Boulevard, Cotati. 707-795-7600. Open for lunch Monday through Friday from 11:30 A.M. to 4 P.M.; for dinner Monday through Friday 5 to 9:30 P.M., Friday and Saturday 5 to 10:30 P.M., Sunday 4:30 to 9 P.M.Full bar. MasterCard, Visa. Reservations for parties of six or more. Inexpensive to moderate.

Most Mexican restaurants offer the same old standbys—enchiladas with green or red sauce, tostadas, *chile relleno*, perhaps a *chile verde*, and, of course, tacos. These dishes may be what people expect when they go to a Mexican restaurant, but they no more represent Mexican cuisine than hamburgers and hot dogs do American. Whenever I see a Mexican menu with new entries, I make a point of trying it.

This time I ended up in Cotati, about forty-five minutes north of San Francisco on Highway 101. Cotati is just south of Santa Rosa, and many San Franciscans pass it by on the way to Sonoma County destinations. Friends who have a house in Sonoma brought me the menu of Las Parrillas after they had had drinks and *tacos al pastor* at the bar.

I can see why they got excited about Las Parrillas. The menu reads like a Diana Kennedy cookbook, with all sorts of mesquite-grilled meats and fish with regional sauces, but simple *tacos al pastor* turn out to be the best dish on it.

Las Parrillas, located right off the highway, has its own building with parking lot. The drab exterior looks like a typically featureless one-story suburban structure. It offers no hint that a lively restaurant might be inside. Yet the interior is surprisingly well designed. A long bar dispenses margaritas made with a tart mix of lime juice and sugar poured over, not blended with, ice. Alongside the bar, but separated by a partition, is a dining room full of old-fashioned wooden booths.

A second dining room holds larger round tables and Guadalajara-style tub chairs made of cowhide. Textured plaster walls with beamed ceilings and waist-high stripes of yellow, green, and red add to the Mexican motif. Thick pottery plates nicely set off the food, and the hexagonal glassware works with margaritas and golden brown Mexican beer. You can tell that all the details of this restaurant have been carefully thought out.

Everything is so well planned, in fact, that it's almost oppressive. You get the feeling that there are strict rules of procedure, not only for staff but for customers, and there are.

You can't make a reservation unless there are six or more in your party, and you won't be seated until your entire party has arrived. You are kept at the bar until every recalcitrant appears and the second that happens you're whisked off to the table. There's no sensitivity to the patrons; the waiters must have been told to keep the tables turning. Like robots, they reel off specials and descriptions of dishes, then expect you to know what you want. Perhaps Las Parrillas is frequented by regular customers who know what they want and want their meals served fast.

Some of the dishes do live up to the menu descriptions, like the *tacos al pastor*. They're made with soft corn tortillas and slowly roasted marinated pork. Pieces of the *achiote*-reddened meat are hacked off the roast, wrapped in small warm tortillas, and served with whole grilled scallions. Other appetizers, like *huastecos*, sound exotic but turn out to be a mundane plate of chips layered with Las Parrillas soupy red *chipotle* beans, guacamole, chicken, sour cream, japalenos, and tomatoes.

Queso fundido, described as a Oaxacan dish, brought a plate of melted Sonoma jack cheese with a lemon-onion salsa and warm tortillas, an interesting combination if you eat them all together. *Frijoles chipotle con queso* were nothing more than a bowl of unseasoned beans topped with bland melted cheese and chips.

None of the salsas served with the various appetizers had much punch. Mild red and green salsas came with the *tacos al pastor*, but their flavor and texture were so refined they tasted like bottled salsas. It was only when main courses were served that we found out about the delicious smoky, fiery-hot *chipotle* sauce, which could have awakened everything.

My favorite main course turned out to be a well-handled saute of scallops, shrimp, and snapper called *mariscos Cancun*, presented in a deep-fried flour tortilla. Crisp green peppers, tomato, and *jitomate salsa* made for a fresh-flavored seafood dish.

Not as successful was Las Parrillas's version of *huachinango a la veracruzana*, a piece of mesquite-grilled snapper topped with nearly raw diced green peppers, tomatoes, and onions. The vegetables barely had released their juices. I like the idea of pairing grilled rockfish with a saucy saute of fresh vegetables, but these vegetables never even softened.

Fajitas al mezquite were centered around some extremely aged pieces of skirt steak, grilled rare, and served with warm corn tortillas, grilled scallions, and a mild salsa. A similar dish, *filete tequile*, substituted thin pieces of beef fillet—surprisingly, not as tender as the skirt steak—and added a lemon and tequila salsa. *Pollo al mezquite*, a skillfully grilled but flat-tasting half chicken, hadn't been marinated or seasoned.

However, the treatment of chicken in *arroz con pollo* was both unusual and delicious. A breast of chicken was cut into chunks and sauteed gently with tomatoes, green peppers, and pickled jalapenos and onions, and served on rice. It's what the *huachinango a la veracruzana* should have been.

Bottles of Dos Equis were brought to the table in an ice bucket, a nice touch, and for dessert Las Parrillas makes an addictive Kahlua cheesecake.

Though the menu was a compendium of dishes from different states and cities of Mexico, there was a sameness about them. The cooking was too refined; it lacked spunk. Preparations needed more chilies, more spices, more fresh herbs, more depth of flavor. The salsas in particular were disappointing, except for the fiery *chipotle*. You can eat well at Las Parrillas, especially for being forty-five minutes out of the city, but the kitchen doesn't live up to its exotic-sounding menu. ■

—Patricia Unterman, January 27, 1985

Le Central

★

458 Bush Street (at Grant), San Francisco. 391-2233. Open for lunch Monday through Friday 11:30 A.M. to 3:30 P.M., Saturday 11:30 A.M. to 3 P.M.; for dinner Monday through Saturday 5:30 to 10:30 P.M. Full bar. MasterCard, Visa, American Express. Reservations accepted. Moderate.

Much beloved as the only authentic French brasserie in San Francisco, the food at Le Central took a dive when its energetic owners, the Cappelle brothers, sold out majority interest to a group of investors. The famous roast chicken started coming out of the kitchen soggy, as if rewarmed, and the *pommes frites* went limp. Thank goodness an original owner, Pierre Cappelle, is back, and the restaurant has returned to its former consistency.

It's so much fun to sit at the tiny crowded tables and banquettes, eating on butcher paper, perusing the mirrors for daily specials written in grease pencil, looking around at all the celebrity lunchers strategically seated at the tables in the front windows. If you hadn't walked down Bush Street to get there, you'd think you were in Paris.

What the food lacks in brilliance it makes up for in dependability and pure French ethnicity. Salads of butter lettuce, or plates of braised leeks with tasty green tops, or a plate of crisp julienned celery root get a mild emulsified vinaigrette.

The roast chicken is now juicy, but the skin is still not as crisp as I remembered it in its heyday. The half chicken comes with

the traditional sprig of watercress, grilled tomato half, and french fries that would be perfect were it not for the odorous brand of deep-frying fat Le Central continues to use.

The *boudins noirs*, or blood sausages, are still excellent and still from Marcel et Henri. They are sauteed to the bursting point with lots of onions, whose caramelized sweetness goes so well with the hint of allspice in the sausages. At lunch one day, the restaurant offered another dish rarely encountered outside of France, poached skate wing with capers. The soft white flesh of the skate wing, divided by a layer of cartilaginous bones, tastes like sea scallops and belongs with the slightly vinegary butter sauce.

With first-rate fresh fruit and nut tarts from TARTS and excellent espresso, a bottle of OK French wine, or a better bottle of Le Central's specially bottled house chardonnay from Chalone, all a diner's needs are met in a thoroughly French way—except for some shocking table etiquette that I'd never encountered here.

The maitre d' asked us to leave our table because he wanted to give it to someone else. There was no peace offering of an espresso at the bar, or indeed at any of the empty tables at less desirable locations. At a French cafe or brasserie even the suggestion of such disruption would be cause for mayhem. It transported us right back to Bush Street, instead of rue Saint Germaine, and put Le Central back in the bush leagues for the afternoon. ■

—Patricia Unterman, October 18, 1987

Le Petit Cafe

★

2164 Larkin Street (at Green), San Francisco. 776-5356. Open Tuesday through Friday 7:30 A.M. to 10 P.M., Saturday 8:30 A.M. to 10 P.M., Sunday 8:30 A.M. to 3 P.M., Monday 7:30 A.M. to 3 P.M. Beer, wine. MasterCard, Visa, with $20 minimum. No reservations. Inexpensive.

As an antidote to slick, trendy restaurants

where everything that goes on seems to have been dictated by a computer program, I like to seek out mom-and-pop places where you're served some down-to-earth food instead of the newest version of the latest fad.

Such a marvelously homey place is Le Petit Cafe, a little restaurant on Larkin Street on Russian Hill. The restaurant is a total anachronism. Instead of planning for maximum turnover, they have books along the walls in case you feel like reading. Instead of a staff spouting cliches, they employ a waitress who at one point became so excited describing a dish that she ran into the kitchen to bring out a sample. Worst of all, they even serve quiche—and it's not made with goat cheese and wild mushrooms.

Le Petit Cafe has been around for years as a coffeehouse, and it started serving dinners that were mostly frozen. Then, last September, it was bought by Robert and Maria Drake, who gave up careers as a publishing executive and a medical technician to pursue the dubious dream that seems to afflict half of all San Franciscans.

Out went the frozen stuff with a vengeance. Everything is fresh and homemade, including the muffins and croissants at breakfast and the tasty french and whole-wheat breads at dinner. You sit at wooden tables in two cozy, high-ceilinged rooms, with light streaming in from abundant windows.

Le Petit Cafe offers two real pluses. The first is very fresh vegetables; there are heaps of them, with everything and in everything. Even if you ignored the chicken and fish entrees, you'd find enough vegetable dishes to keep you busy for a week.

The second is prices. You can eat on Russian Hill for a Mission Street tab.

The wine list is a bargain too—they aren't rotgut wines either; it's a very carefully chosen list. For instance, we were able to try the 1985 Mâcon of Talmard, a white burgundy, and the 1985 Guigal Côtes du Rhône.

For dinner there's a fixed menu, much of it vegetables, and usually a pasta, chicken, and fish entree that change every night. I found a surprising disparity between the two meals I had, one that indicated a need for closer supervision of the cooks. The first dinner was uniformly excellent; the second had several dishes that tasted as if the chef had forgotten all the seasonings.

But both nights the chicken entree, using free-range chicken from Petaluma, was outstanding. Sweet-and-sour chicken, usually a sure prescription for disaster, turned out to be juicy and flavorful, with a delicate sauce that was not the least bit cloying. What was called Calcutta chicken was a spicy, boneless breast, breaded and deep fried to greaseless perfection.

As for the pasta, the noodles are made on the premises and both times were cooked al dente. But both the *fettuccine primavera*, with vegetables and a cream sauce, and the fettuccine with pesto cried out for more herbs and spices.

For starters, the stuffed mushrooms proved a lively version of a usually boring cliche, with the filling a very tasty mixture of spinach, almonds, and romano cheese. Seafood chowder was outstanding, rich and creamy, with big chunks of fish and potatoes. A vegetable pizza with a good whole-wheat crust was loaded with vegetables, none overcooked, and topped with mozzarella cheese.

Although the vegetables were bounteous, a couple of the salads had no perceptible dressing other than bland oil; the caesar salad was the best choice. Stay away from the hummus, which had not a hint of sesame or garlic flavor. Blandness also marred a very decent piece of broiled monkfish with cilantro sauce. And the broccoli quiche cried out for spices to liven it up.

Orange-almond torte and chocolate mousse are regulars on the dessert menu, and the wonderfully moist torte, permeated with the flavor of orange peel, is definitely the choice. The mousse proved intolerably sweet.

With the comfortable surroundings and a big list of first-rate coffee drinks, you might be tempted to linger at Le Petit Cafe for the evening. Since there are no reservations, that could be a problem if lots of people start showing up for dinner. I'd gladly trade slightly higher menu prices for a reservations policy; this restaurant is much too pleasant for the hassle of long lines. ■

—Stan Sesser, May 29, 1987

Le Piano Zinc

★ ★

708 Church Street (at Market), San Francisco. 431-5266. Open daily except Monday 6 P.M. to midnight; for brunch Sunday 11 A.M. to 2:30 P.M. Full bar. Major credit cards. Reservations advised weeknights, essential weekends. Moderate.

A couple of months ago I complained about the soaring prices at restaurants and wondered why they continue to increase even though food and fuel costs have actually fallen. I got in response a few anguished letters from restaurant owners, who said some of their costs are still going through the roof—particularly for insurance, rent, and the fancy foods like baby vegetables that have become so fashionable.

They certainly have a point. But it doesn't explain why there are still some restaurants around that have gone in the opposite direction. They offer a pleasant atmosphere and very good food, but charge significantly lower prices than many of their competitors.

One such place I reviewed recently was Lalime's in Albany, which has a wonderful fixed-price French dinner for under $30. Now I've come across a San Francisco equivalent. The a la carte prices are higher than Lalime's, but there's also a $29.50 fixed-price dinner, and it's absolutely splendid. Its name is Le Piano Zinc, a new and very comfortable place near the Castro. The owners are French, and they've given their restaurant a cheerful French feel. There are paper place mats over white tablecloths, plates decorated with nineteenth-century illustrations of Parisians, and waiters sporting black pants, white shirts, and pink suspenders. In fact, there's everything but a zinc-topped piano; Joel Coutre, who runs the dining room, explains that *zinc* is French slang for "bar," and his restaurant's bar is piano-shaped.

The chef, Michel Laurent, just returned from two years of cooking in Paris, sends a stream of satisfying French food from the kitchen. There are almost no corners cut on the $29.50 dinner.

At my second meal, for instance, the fixed-price dinner started with a magnificent puff pastry stuffed with oysters and a couple of baby lobster tails, resting on a bed of spinach and mushroom *duxelles*. Then came three warm quail halves in a salad of bean sprouts. The entree was a veal chop in a cream and sherry sauce. Finally came a choice of several interesting desserts.

It wasn't all perfect—the veal chop was too thin and its sauce too salty. But the portions were big, and there were lots of nice vegetable accompaniments, like turnip mousse, pureed carrots, and an artichoke heart stuffed with chestnut puree. For $29.50, it was a real feast.

There were lots of good things to choose on the a la carte menu, too. Laurent excels at interesting appetizers, like a terrine of shiitake mushrooms in a beurre blanc sauce, or another terrine of nine vegetables sandwiched between layers of ham and chicken mousse. Then there's the sole and wild mushrooms in puff pastry, a dish absolutely not to be missed.

The entrees aren't as inventive as the appetizers, but they're generally very satisfying. One of the best is the rabbit, a huge portion of tender boneless slices in a rich sauce of rabbit stock, red wine, cream, and brandy, accompanied with big portions of three different vegetables.

Venison, which came as a substitute on the fixed-price dinner (and added $5 to the cost), was well worth the surcharge. It was rare, perfectly tender, and, as a nice extra touch, the accompaniments included a little pastry shell filled with red currant jelly. Sliced duck breast is a good choice too; the sauce manages to be thick and rich without being cloying.

Not all the desserts were successful, but Laurent is clearly making an attempt to be innovative here, too. A pear poached in vinegar with green peppercorns tasted much better than it sounds. A frozen Grand Marnier souffle had a dense texture more like ice cream—but who could complain about really good ice cream?

Considering Le Piano Zinc is very new, the weaknesses aren't serious. Laurent, probably influenced by his stay in Paris, tends to use much more salt than many Americans prefer. The service has some rough edges; despite an abundance of waiters, at one meal we had to ask for menus, and no one brought the bread until we requested it after the appetizers came. The bread itself is a disgracefully mushy baguette. And although there are several French wines for just $12, the wine list inexcusably omits vintages and producers.

Le Piano Zinc is a most welcome addition to the San Francisco restaurant scene, particularly in an area not exactly known for an abundance of good food. It offers better meals than lots I've had at some expensive French restaurants—at less than half the price. ∎

—Stan Sesser, June 27, 1986

Le Trou

★ ★

1007 Guerrero Street (at Twenty-second Street), San Francisco. 550-8169. Open Monday through Friday and Sunday 6:30 to 9 P.M.; Saturday with one seating at 8 P.M. Wines included with the meal. Cash or personal checks only. Reservations required. Moderate.

When I tell people I eat out an average of six nights a week (and not all of them to review restaurants, either), they look at me as if I had just announced that I had an incurable disease or was moving to Cleveland.

This, of course, is a San Francisco reaction. In New York, where I developed my restaurant addiction, people would wonder what in the world I did my seventh night. I knew a woman who wrote for the *New York Times* who swore that in ten years of marriage she never once cooked dinner.

Eating at home does have its advantages. There's a comfortable intimacy and a pleasant feeling from knowing that the quality of your meal doesn't rest in the hands of some big profit-making institution.

It takes an unusual restaurant to create this sort of atmosphere, in effect providing the best of both worlds. But there is one place in San Francisco that does this remarkably well, so successfully you would be tempted to eat there even if you weren't thrilled with the food. And when you discover the dinners are delicious, you're totally hooked.

Its name is Le Trou, a little storefront on Guerrero and Twenty-second that you could easily walk by without noticing. It's the unique product of a man named Robert Reynolds, who teaches cooking most of the time but takes four nights a week to put his ideas about food into practice.

Eating at Le Trou is exactly like being invited as a guest into Reynolds's home. It's a charming little dining room, probably decorated on a shoestring budget, but achieving a feeling of warmth that has eluded many restaurants that have spent hundreds of thousands of dollars on decor.

When you walk in, you're greeted by a waiter who's either a student of Reynolds, a personal friend, or both. Then Reynolds himself comes out to explain what you'll be having for dinner. In a charming ritual repeated for every customer, he'll appear a second time to slice and serve your dessert.

Just as in someone's home, there's no worry about what to order or what wine to choose. It's a fixed-price dinner that changes weekly as Reynolds explores the regional cooking of France. On Thursday, Friday, and Sunday, there's a fixed-price dinner, on Saturday there's a different menu at a slightly higher price. On Wednesday, when Reynolds teaches, his assistant prepares a lower-priced dinner. Except for Wednesday, the menus are printed in advance for a six-week period.

These dinners are extraordinary bargains when you consider that they include two different French wines, one for the appetizer and one for the entree, and there's seemingly no limit on how many times the waiter fills your glass.

Reynolds clearly goes out of his way to find obscure regional French wines that, although not commanding the high price of a bordeaux or burgundy, are often quite decent.

Surprisingly, the food reminds me of the downstairs restaurant at Chez Panisse. The menu doesn't sound exciting, and dishes are not complicated by heavy sauces or fancy presentations. But there's a sophistication and integrity to the food that made much of what I ate taste spectacular.

The first dinner, with recipes from Alsace, started with an onion tart, something I would never consider ordering a la carte. But these onions were brightened with raspberry *eau de vie*, bacon, and cream, and baked into a splendid yeasty crust. The creation burst with flavor.

Then came what was simply called chicken with riesling. A boned chicken breast, lightly breaded with fennel-scented bread crumbs, was sauteed with riesling, wild mushrooms, cream, and lemon rind.

It doesn't sound like much, but both the meat and the sauce were as close to perfect as any dish could be. Julienned kohlrabi and a remarkable soufflelike creation featuring muenster cheese were the accompaniments.

The second dinner, from the southwest of France, started with an eggplant custard so astonishing I immediately asked for seconds. Blended with eggs, cream, and garlic, it somehow managed to preserve all the intensity of eggplant flavor. Alongside was a colorful heap of corn kernels, sweet peppers, and zucchini tossed in garlic butter.

The entree that night was a boned breast of duck braised slowly in its own fat, along with a host of vegetables, including tomatoes tossed with onions, chard

flavored with roquefort cheese, and sauteed chanterelles.

The only weakness in both meals was the desserts, which weren't nearly as exciting as what preceded them. At the second dinner, a *gâteau à la basquaise* was a dry and tasteless butter cake, stuffed with a blend of prunes and armagnac that was much too alcoholic.

Le Trou is so relaxed and friendly it wouldn't feel at all awkward to go alone for dinner and read a book. Or you could read the long and delightful essay by Reynolds on the back of the menu that wanders over his philosophy of cooking, ranging from when a vegetable reaches a state of perfect crunch to the "culinary absurdity" of the concept of blackened redfish.

In this era when restaurants trip over each other trying to be first with the latest fad, Reynolds has done something exactly the opposite. He presents a very personal statement of a talented chef. ∎

—Stan Sesser, October 17, 1986

Les Arcades

★★★

133 East Napa Street (one-half block from the main square), Sonoma. 707/938-3723. Open Tuesday through Sunday 5 to 10 P.M. Beer, wine. MasterCard, Visa. Reservations essential. Moderate.

Lots of French restaurants are tripping over each other these days keeping their food fashionable; I can't complain, since the current definition of "fashionable"— lighter entrees, prettier presentations, more interesting vegetables—can add up to a very satisfying meal.

But almost lost in the shuffle is one of the core elements that made French cooking so wonderful: beautiful sauces that would perfectly complement the flavors of the meat, fish, or poultry that was being served. Eating in Paris twenty years ago might have meant launching a flotilla of cream to do battle with your arteries, but it was a price worth paying.

A couple of months ago, I got a note from Annie-Mae de Bresson, who teaches French cooking in Berkeley. She said she had never recommended anything to a restaurant critic before, but a new French restaurant in Sonoma called Les Arcades demanded an exception.

I quickly made reservations. And at Les Arcades, I found a chef so skilled in the art of classic French sauces that it was like being transported across the ocean. It's not that you walk away staggering under the weight of the cream—a talented French chef also balances the meal so it doesn't end up too heavy—but here was the sort of dinner I remembered so vividly from France two decades back.

Chef Dominique Leiseing trained in France and then worked in a whole string of San Francisco French restaurants over the last fifteen years. ("I was a high-tempered chef," he explains.) Last year he set out to find his own place, and when he saw the site of Les Arcades, he says, he "fell in love."

No wonder. Just a half block from Sonoma's main square, this dollhouse of a restaurant could just as easily be in the French countryside. With its polished antique wood bar, flowered lace curtains, and pink tablecloths, it exudes comfort and charm. Outside is a delightful brick-paved courtyard where you can eat if the evening is warm.

There's nothing dramatic or trendy about Leiseing's menu; it's as classic as his sauces. But everything tasted wonderful. And prices are very reasonable for a meal of this quality.

If you're a lover of classic French food, you'll start with quenelles, the dumplings of fish mousse, done the way they never seem to be anymore. There's nothing floury; they're delicate, light as a feather, yet rich at the same time. And the sauce of fish stock, white wine, and cream, with pureed white mushrooms, is perfect.

But don't pass up the sweetbreads appetizer, either, butter-tender, delicately sauteed, and served in a sauce that includes capers and lemon. Equally good is the velvety cold salmon mousse with a tangy light herb sauce on the side.

There are lots of splendid entrees, but at the top of the list is the breast of free-range chicken. This is chicken the way it should taste, but almost never does. The meat, totally juicy and tender, has an unusual richness and the sauce is a glorious blend of mushrooms and truffles in brandy, white wine, cream, and demiglace. To provide color contrast, around the edge is a rim of demiglace, the classic French brown sauce. I've rarely found chicken like this before in the United States.

While the chicken is in a class by itself, there are other entrees worth noting. Scallops of veal are tender and delicate, served in a light cream sauce scented with calvados. Tender slices of duck breast again feature a sauce that's almost beyond belief, flavored with green peppercorns, white port, and a touch of dijon mustard.

Then there are the medallions of lamb, which can be cut with a fork. Alongside were sliced potatoes cooked in cream, nutmeg, and eggs. I could return, have nothing but a plate of these potatoes, and leave happy.

Desserts were outstanding, including a light charlotte, a sort of sponge cake, filled with fresh fruit, and also a dense chocolate mousse that for once tasted more of chocolate than sugar. But the winner was the profiteroles, little pastry balls filled with vanilla ice cream and topped with warm chocolate sauce.

The flaws in the meal could be remedied easily. The same vegetables came with each entree, giving the dishes a boring look that belied the interesting and distinctive sauces on each. The duck breast and lamb both were overcooked just beyond pink—although the meat was so flavorful it still tasted good. And that's it in the way of criticism.

All the wonderful food was made even better by the expert and efficient service. We arrived on a busy Saturday night a half hour late, a situation that can be unpleasant when people show up for the second shift. But the maitre d' handled it beautifully, telling us at the outset what time he'd need the table, then setting a table in the courtyard where we could have dessert and coffee.

Although the term has been abused by restaurant critics beyond meaning, here's a situation where I have to use it: Les Arcades is a gem. ◼

—Stan Sesser, July 31, 1987

Lipizzaner

★

1240 Fourth Street, San Rafael. 459-2202. Open Tuesday through Friday 7:30 A.M. to 10 P.M., Saturday and Sunday 10 A.M. to 10 P.M. Wine, beer. MasterCard, Visa. Reservations necessary for dinner and recommended for lunch and brunch. Moderate.

When the original Lipizzaner opened on upper Union Street four years ago, the restaurant seemed too good to be true. Here was the mythic eatery that puts out distinctive, elegant, and delicious European food at moderate prices. True, the eight or ten painfully small tables were pushed very close together in a tiny dining room that was often hot and noisy, but these ordinary drawbacks only enhanced the cachet of this restaurant. Each perfectly executed plate came as a surprise served in this modest setting.

The owners of the Lipizzaner, Josef Roettig and his wife, had a hit on their hands. He, a formally trained Viennese chef with an international hotel background, and she, an American who ran the dining room with much personal charm, put heart and soul into their restaurant. The little place became so popular that you had to reserve weeks in advance to get a table. Then, suddenly, the restaurant closed. The partnership had dissolved. People with hard-won reservations felt deprived and regulars grieved for the delicate wiener schnitzel, luxuriously sauced dover sole, and warm apple flan.

So the reopening of Lipizzaner by Mr. Roettig with a new partner in San Rafael five months ago was much anticipated. Would it live up to its original brilliance and charm? Sadly enough, it doesn't, the main reason being that Josef Roettig himself is not putting out all the plates anymore. In his new restaurant, three times the size of the original, Roettig has to rely upon a staff that seems to lack the sensibility and skill to prepare his complicated dishes. What was once rich but breathtakingly well-balanced food with nuanced sauces and stunning presentation has now become cloying, heavy, and artificial. The Lipizzaner has ended up imitating itself; the kitchen is in over its head.

In a few respects, the Lipizzaner has stayed the same. The dining room has been divided up into three small sections that are so tightly packed with tiny tables that you feel like you're in the old restaurant. Since the tables are always filled, noise and overcrowding persist. I was thankful that smoking is not allowed and that the air conditioning works. As in the old place, pictures and statues of the famous performing Lippizaner horses decorate the walls and Viennese waltzes play in the background. Tables are covered with lace tablecloths.

The dinner menu has been expanded somewhat, though many of the same dishes serve as poignant reminders of what the cooking once was. Lipizzaner's old wiener schnitzel, exceptionally thin, crisp, meltingly tender slices of breaded veal, have thickened and coarsened considerably. The formerly fresh, vinegary cucumber, potato, and beet salads served with it are now messy looking and wilted from overheated plates. Lipizzaner's current sweetbreads only suggest the extraordinary contrast of velvety interior and crisp sauteed exterior they used to have. You notice the membranes now, and the sweetbreads don't stay crisp as they sit heavily on top of three different mounds of vegetable puree. A fillet of dover sole came out of the kitchen one night with an oily meuniere sauce instead of the gorgeous wine-and-fish-stock-flavored cream sauce I remembered. A pile of bland, lukewarm, mushy angel hair pasta accompanied.

At lunch, a leg of capon stuffed with prunes and apples that came with a dark, gamy meat-stock reduction and wild rice was the first dish I had at the new Lipizzaner that made any sense—except that the wild rice was garnished with raw, wilted ovals of squash and carrot and gray green beans, all inedible. My companion's veal Cordon Bleu, stuffed with smoky westphalian ham and gruyere, was inappropriately sauced with the same dark, sharp reduction and served with the vinegary salads that belong with the wiener schnitzel.

Some of the appetizers work, some don't. A dinner salad of endive, watercress, papaya, and walnuts was tastily dressed and refreshing, but a lunch salad of an unwieldy wedge of romaine lettuce napped with mustardy vinaigrette and flanked by two slices of papaya was ridiculous. One evening I was served a tiny piece of practically raw foie gras on a bed of delicious braised cabbage surrounded by a strong, dark, sweet sauce and too many decorative orange segments. The previously striking sorrel and oyster soup came off more like nondescript cream of mushroom; the sorrel flavor had disappeared. The flavors in an appetizer of baby artichoke hearts stuffed with smoked trout on a lake of thick, creamy white wine sauce conflicted with each other. Tired, reheated, greasy broccoli strudel got a warm, vinegary tomato sauce that would have been stunning with something fresh and crisp.

Of all the cooking at Lipizzaner, the desserts work the best. They survived because they can be done in advance. Warm miniature apple tarts served with caramel ice cream are still fine, as is apple strudel. One day at lunch, three poufs of meringue served as landing points for three different sauces and fruits. Mutti's nut cake with a hardened layer of rich buttercream frosting merited two of the sauces, the delicious chocolate sauce and thick vanilla custard sauce.

Not much, in these meals, added up. All the sauces began to taste the same. The decorative garnishes—the tomato-peel roses, badly cooked carved vegetables, colorful bits of warm fruit—detracted from rather than added to the plates. Though the kitchen starts off with high-quality veal and sweetbreads, real dover sole, and foie gras, and sauces made from labor-intensive, highly reduced stocks, the final execution of the dishes lacked finesse. They needed Roettig's hands to bring them off, and this, of course, is impossible with a menu this large and a dining room so full.

Some formulas don't extrapolate and I'm afraid that the personally realized, labor-intensive French-Viennese menu that Lipizzaner put out so impressively in much smaller quarters doesn't work in this larger suburban restaurant. Mr. Roettig should be more sensitive to what those plates look and taste like when they reach the table and adjust the menu to what he and his staff can meticulously turn out. I know that this restaurant can do better. Given the choice between serving many sloppy meals at relatively moderate prices or serving half as many carefully wrought meals at higher prices, the true Lipizzaner spirit calls for greater expense and perfection. ∎

—Patricia Unterman, May 24, 1987

Los Compadres

★

944 C Street, Hayward. 582-1937. Open Tuesday through Sunday 11 A.M. to 9 P.M. Beer, wine. Cash only. Reservations accepted for parties of six or more only. Inexpensive.

La Imperial

948 C Street, Hayward. 537-6227. Open daily 9:30 A.M. to 10 P.M., Friday and Saturday until 10:30 P.M. Beer, wine. Cash only. Reservations accepted for parties of six or more only. Inexpensive.

People love to argue about restaurants, but there are few disputes to match the intensity of the one going on in Hayward between advocates of La Imperial and defenders of Los Compadres, two bustling

Mexican places that share a common wall. Each one appears to have a fanatic following, each of which dismisses the other restaurant with contempt.

Not being one to miss a good fight, I headed to Hayward for a dinner at each place. In the old days, according to one account, a member of the family that owns La Imperial used to stand in front of Los Compadres trying to steer people into his restaurant, until one day he was beaten off with a two-by-four. Things have apparently quieted down since, because I was able to walk into each place without so much as an angry stare from next door.

In these days of plastic tacos in Styrofoam boxes, it's nice to know there are two Mexican restaurants with some personality left.

In particular, La Imperial, where you can get a huge dish of chicken mole or *chile verde* very inexpensively, should be charging at least a little for the floor show. It starts at the door where, under a thicket of brightly colored pinatas hanging from the ceiling, you ask for the no-smoking section. "Just shout at them to put it out," the hostess replies.

La Imperial's waiters swagger down the aisles in black muscle shirts, truck driver caps, or whatever else will increase their aura of macho. Not even the most innocent question will get a serious answer. When I asked if they took credit cards, the waiter shot back, "I take credit cards, rings, wallets, everything. In college it was hubcaps."

Recently, an article in the *San Jose Mercury News* called La Imperial the best Mexican restaurant in the Bay Area. After eating there and at Los Compadres, I've got a very different opinion. Far from being the best Mexican restaurant in the Bay Area, La Imperial isn't even the best Mexican restaurant on the block. That honor belongs to Los Compadres. But both are distressingly uneven, mixing some excellent dishes with others that are dismal.

"Dismal" is exactly the right word for La Imperial's Tex-Mex fare. Some of the standard dishes simply couldn't be eaten. The guacamole had an off-color and an off-taste that made me wonder how long

ago the avocados had been mashed. The pork tamale was tasteless cornmeal mush in a gloppy sauce that resembled spiced up ketchup. The *chile relleno* was like a sponge—a thick, eggy pancake with the pieces of chili hard to find amid the batter.

Even the basics suffered. The tortilla chips were inedible, the flour tortillas chewy, and the refried beans a mushy puree with no texture or taste.

But when it came to the more interesting entrees, La Imperial did better. Heading the list was the *chile verde*, with butter-tender chunks of fat-free pork and a rich sauce bursting with flavor. The *machaca* was excellent, too, with shredded beef panfried to crispness and sauteed with eggs, onions, jalapenos, and tomatoes.

Both of these dishes are astonishing bargains. But skip the equally inexpensive chicken mole; the mole sauce is decent, but the chicken itself is lifeless.

Next door at Los Compadres, the sign advertises, "second in atmosphere, first in Mexican food." They're right on both counts. While La Imperial could never be accused of being palatial, Los Compadres, with its orange vinyl booths, Formica tables, and bare plaster walls, makes its neighbor look positively opulent in comparison.

Bargains abound here, too. You can get combination plates of four Tex-Mex items so large you'll be hard pressed to finish them. A chicken enchilada alone must have had about half a pound of chicken in it.

The enchiladas were fine, the *chile relleno* was nice and fluffy, but the big standout was the pork tamale. It's hard to find a decent pork tamale anywhere, but Los Compadres's version was a sensation. The cornmeal had a lively taste and a grainy texture, and it was filled with very tender chunks of pork.

Some other things fell down, however—while the guacamole was good, the chips were far too salty to consider eating. A *flauta* was drowned in mayonnaise. *Carne asada* was nothing more than a thin tough slice of flank steak.

If you want lots of good food for very little money, start at Los Compadres with a Tex-Mex combination platter, then move next door to La Imperial for plates of *chile verde*. It will be a fun evening—so long as no one sees you ducking out of one and into the other. ■

—Stan Sesser, May 30, 1986

Lychee Garden

★ ★

1416 Powell Street, San Francisco. 397-2290. Open daily 11:30 A.M. to 9:30 P.M. Beer, wine. MasterCard, Visa. Reservations accepted. Inexpensive to moderate.

Chinese restaurants allow families and large groups to eat out with an ease unmatched any place else. Not only are the kitchens in these restaurants able to put out a remarkable variety of dishes, but the price for the whole meal is so reasonable. When you go in a group large enough to order six or seven different dishes, and have them brought to the table course by course, you are getting a feast on a low budget.

The best way to handle a large meal at a Chinese restaurant is to call ahead. If you need help putting together a meal, the manager or the maitre d' can help. He can suggest dishes that may not be on the written menu that are particularly suited for larger groups, like festive preparations of whole fish, chicken, ducks, and larger cuts of pork. He can assist you in balancing the meal so that a range of different ingredients and cooking techniques will be represented. It's much more fun to have hot and cold dishes, roasts, stews, soups, and deep-fried and steamed foods than a meal of all stir-fries. Finally, by showing that you want to challenge the capabilities of the kitchen and that you're not afraid to try something new, the cooks will put out a superior meal. Chances are the head chef in the kitchen will take care of your order.

Recently I called the Flower Lounge in Millbrae, asked for the manager, a woman named Victoria, and told her I wanted a meal for ten people. She consulted with her chef and called me back in fifteen minutes with this menu: a cold plate with squab, octopus and jelly fish; partridge soup; deep-fried scallops stuffed with shrimp; a stir-fry of mango and beef; vegetables cooked in a tofu pancake; a spicy lobster dish; and fillets of flounder with bok choy, and melon soup for dessert. The actual meal, served course by course, was absolutely stunning, a veritable Chinese wedding banquet for all of $22 a person. If someone at the table didn't care for octopus, there was plenty of other food to eat, and this way the kitchen got to show off its repertoire.

The Flower Lounge is a restaurant that prides itself on turning out many elegant and exotic Hong Kong–style dishes. More common are restaurants that serve homey, simpler family- style fare. One of the best in the city for this kind of cooking is Lychee Garden, a bustling, medium-sized restaurant just on the edge of Chinatown.

Everyone brings their kids to the Lychee Garden—and their grandparents, uncle, aunts, and friends. Most of the round tables seat eight or ten people and most of the time they're full. A lazy susan in the middle of these tables makes it simple for each person to serve themselves from large platters and the kitchen is used to adjusting amounts of each dish to the number of people eating.

At a recent meal of six adults and three little children, we began with a platter of big, juicy salt-and-pepper shrimp with flavorful shells and heads intact. Quickly stir-fried with a coating of salt and white pepper, the papery shells were almost the tastiest part of the shrimp, though many at the table peeled them.

A crisp, glistening whole roast chicken gaily decorated with those melt-on-your-tongue shrimp chips had velvety, succulent flesh and authentic chicken flavor. Hacked into bite-sized pieces, this savory chicken and chips is always a hit with children.

The next dish, custardy, handmade fresh tofu cakes with slivers of filleted steelhead, scallions, and a light, clean sauce of ginger, soy, and clear fish stock appealed to more sophisticated tastes. The delicate texture and elusive flavor of the tofu found its complement in the aromatic sauce. A platter of simple snap peas, in the leanest of sauces, followed. These are the kind of peas you eat pod and all, and they couldn't have been more tender or sweet.

A dramatic deep-fried catfish, slit down the middle, sat on a pile of wilted scallions sauced with ginger and soy sauce. The catfish was wondrously crisped to a deep brown color that seemed to make its white flesh even juicier. Like many catfish, it had the slight aftertaste of mud in its meat. You either like catfish or you don't, but no catfish could have been more ably prepared.

A spectacular preparation of boned duck topped with taro paste and deep fried produced the interplay of textures at which Cantonese chefs excel. The taro duck comes in bite-sized rectangles. Each bite has a lacy tempuralike crust, a layer of creamy taro, a layer of dark duck meat, and then another ultra-crispy crust on the bottom. You dip them into a mild sauce that adds moisture as much as flavor, as does the cool bed of shredded iceberg lettuce. The whole thing works in a way you don't expect, and it takes a few bites to figure out what you are eating.

Frog legs are a rarely served treat in San Francisco with the demise of the old-style French dinner houses, but Lychee Garden does a smashing version of them, cut through the bone into nugget-sized pieces and tossed with garlic chives, fresh straw mushrooms, and carrots in a translucent sauce. It's a dish that the finest French chef would admire, full of subtle flavor and lovely colors.

For dessert, at Lychee, all the kids and my husband insist on canned fruit cocktail poured over almond curd, and I must admit that a few bites of it are most refreshing.

This meal cost $16 per person with a number of Chinese beers thrown in, downright amazing because of the reasonable price and the high quality of the meal. Every ingredient was fresh, most notably the sugar snap peas, the Chinese herbs, the straw mushrooms, the shrimp, and the catfish, and each preparation honest. Sauces supported ingredients and enhanced them. Each dish was carefully prepared. There was nothing fancy about this meal, but it shone as an example of typical Hong Kong–style home cooking.

Other strong suits at Lychee Garden are their "house special ribs," their duck dishes, their impeccable and barely sauced greens of all sorts, hairy melon soup, fresh eel, and catfish and tofu hot pots.

Cantonese cooking in San Francisco, by the way, is evolving, just the way northern California cooking is. Chinese chefs are equally inspired by the wide range of ingredients currently available here. Using garlic chives, a typically northern Chinese herb, in the frog legs instead of scallions is but one example of the growing eclecticism of Hong Kong chefs in San Francisco. The chef at the Flower Lounge in Millbrae claims that the ingredients he gets in California are better and more diverse than in Hong Kong, and the number of Hong Kong restaurants that have opened large branches in San Francisco, like the Flower Lounge, Harbor Village, and Ocean City, indicate that the action may be flowing with the current across the Pacific. So I think it's time to take advantage of the range of culinary talent here. Frankly, my most satisfying and exciting meals of late have been in Chinese restaurants. ■

—Patricia Unterman, August 30, 1987

Ma Tante Sumi

★

See review for Colette: A Restaurant.

MacArthur Park

★

607 Front Street, San Francisco. 398-5700. Open for breakfast Monday through Friday 7 to 10 A.M., for lunch Monday through Friday 11:30 A.M. to 2:30 P.M., for dinner Monday through Thursday and Sunday 5 to 10 P.M., Friday and Saturday until 11 P.M. Full bar. Master-Card, Visa, American Express, Diners Club. Reservations accepted. Moderate.

When this popular San Francisco restaurant closed for a month at the beginning of the year to refurbish, many people I know went into barbecue-rib shock. Not only did they miss MacArthur Park's baby back ribs, they were anxious about what was being done to the place, especially since the takeover of the Spectrum group of restaurants by Saga, a gigantic food service corporation. Well, the regulars did not have to worry on either account. The ribs are just as fine as ever and hardly anything noticeable has been done to the dining room. Most of the changes were internal.

Breakfast and a Sunday brunch have been added to the meal repertoire [the latter has subsequently been discontinued] and the waiters now use handheld computer terminals instead of check pads. Most apparent to me was that this large restaurant looked and smelled fresh. The bar and connecting dining rooms had sufficient time to air out and all surfaces had been thoroughly cleaned and shined. MacArthur Park's front seating area, a glassed-in porch with high ceilings and wooden floors, has always felt like an extension of the park across the street and now the interior dining areas with all their carpeting, brass railings, and brick walls seem fresher.

A visit at lunch confirmed that the standards of the kitchen had not been undermined by change of ownership. A barbecued ribs and chicken plate fulfilled every expectation. The ribs were tender but fat free and had a deep, delicious smoky flavor. The chicken, especially the thigh, melted in my mouth. MacArthur Park's sharp, clean barbecue sauce balances sweet, sour, and mildly hot flavors with precision and just the right amount is brushed on the meats as they are cooking. I still think that MacArthur Park makes the best coleslaw in town by tossing hand-cut cabbage in an oniony, creamy, minimally sweet dressing; a side dish comes with all the barbecued items.

One new addition to the menu are lobsters. A large one, well over two pounds, came off the grill tender and juicy if a bit too charred in a few places. It was fresh smelling and sweet-fleshed.

Italian-style grilled sausages surprise by being so fiery hot that you need to take bites of a mild green tomato chutney or molasses-sweetened baked beans just to cool your mouth off. Both the sausages and the barbecue combination came with tepid french fries.

"Filet mignon steak sandwich Harry's Bar" fell just short of being terrific. The medium-rare, thinly sliced fillet was buttery, but crustless toast triangles made with flavorless bread didn't hold up their end of the sandwich. The right bread, a little sauce of some kind...the idea is wonderful.

One of the most appealing parts of this menu is a lively list of first courses. Though the green salads tend to be sloppily composed, like the mound of damp, chopped head lettuce with crumbled Wisconsin blue cheese pressed on top I had one day, the warm appetizers are tasty. A grilled pasilla pepper filled with three different kinds of cheese never fails to please, and grilled escarole stuffed with Sonoma goat cheese and wrapped in ham make for a delicious combination. Hovering some place between an appetizer and a lunch plate, grilled skirt steak salad doesn't work. Slices of ice-cold meat were too fatty and chewy to be the centerpiece of a salad, especially with little piles of unrelated ingredients orbiting around it.

For dessert, I like the traditional strawberry shortcake and the peanut-topped, chocolate cookie-crusted coffee ice cream pie, but a well-intentioned apple pie filled with hard apple quarters and a heavy-handed crust failed.

The new breakfast and brunch service has not hit its stride. One Sunday, five of us could find nothing we wanted to finish from a large array of ordered dishes. The eggs didn't taste fresh; the bacon had a luscious honey-smoked aroma but a limp, fatty texture. Someone had forgotten to cook the beets in "red flannel hash with poached eggs." An unexceptional black-walnut waffle was topped with soggy nuts. Potato pancakes were not cooked all the way through, though accompanied with some good homemade applesauce. The oatmeal with dates was watery and absolutely flat tasting. A half grapefruit baked with brown sugar was so overcinnamoned it tasted medicinal, and it was not segmented properly so that it was hard to eat. Slices of smoked salmon draped over a cream cheese-filled omelet had been delicately smoked but were getting indelicately dry. I did finish a glass of tart blood-orange juice.

A return visit for weekday breakfast turned up some of the same flaws. I guess MacArthur Park is committed to soggy, greasy bacon because it was exactly the same this morning. Happily, the beets in the red flannel hash were al dente, not raw. The toast arrived halfway through the meal. Two orange juices arrived that were not ordered. French toast could have used a more thorough soaking as it was dry in the middle. Two beautiful *caffe latti* served in tall glasses capped with foamy milk hit the spot.

I think management's impulse to serve breakfast responds to a renewed interest in this traditional American meal. MacArthur Park has come up with a menu full of homey, American favorites—hash, fresh fruits, and juices, all sorts of pancakes and waffles, hand-sliced bread and house-smoked meats—but the execution of these dishes is inept. Our brunch tasted like something you would get in an airport terminal and it's just what MacArthur Park does not want at this time—the taint of impersonal, institutional feeding. ∎

—Patricia Unterman, March 30, 1986

Mamma Tina's Trattoria

★

1315 Grant Avenue (near Vallejo), San Francisco. 391-4129. Open Tuesday through Sunday 5:30 to 11 P.M. Beer, wine. American Express, Diners Club. Reservations accepted. Inexpensive to moderate.

Upper Grant Avenue in San Francisco is a difficult location for restaurants. A few are fixtures, but other places come and go so fast you could miss them if you blink.

A letter from a reader made one of these new restaurants sound so good I put it at the top of my review list for fear it would turn into a chop suey cafeteria if I didn't get there soon.

Its name is Mamma Tina's Trattoria, and the letter promised it had authentic southern Italian cooking. "Authentic" is a word I rarely hear modify "southern Italian" here. More typically, southern Italian brings to mind a pound of canned tomato sauce and cheap melted cheese hiding some piece of meat you wouldn't have wanted to see exposed anyway.

It turns out that "authentic" was the absolutely proper word to choose. Until three years ago, the chef, Rino Laneve, cooked in the three restaurants his parents own in Brindisi, which is right on the heel of Italy's boot. (His mother is Mamma Tina.) Laneve married a German woman of Mongolian ancestry, named Naran, who runs the dining room.

At Mamma Tina's you eat your authentic southern Italian food in a very pleasant room, but one whose mosaic tile walls and red tile floors speak more of southern Mexico than southern Italy.

Laneve produces a very strange mixture of food. You won't feel ripped off experimenting your way through the menu, because everything is reasonably priced. But many of the dishes I had were spectacular, and others just plain bad.

Here's an example: One frequent complaint I have at Italian restaurants is that the soups are too salty. Not so at Mamma Tina's. But one of the pastas and one of the entrees were so salty they were almost inedible.

In fact, Mamma Tina's soups are the perfect way to start your meal. The minestrone is the best I've ever eaten, a rich stock that's brimming over with vegetables and pasta cooked al dente. At less than a few dollars for a huge bowl, it's an astonishing bargain. The *stracciatella* is in the same category: delicious homemade beef stock with eggs and herbs worked in.

After that, go on to the prosciutto with melon; the prosciutto is meaty and not at all salty, the honeydew is perfectly ripe. Another good appetizer is the buffalo milk mozzarella, flown in from Italy, served in a salad with sliced tomatoes and fresh basil, and dressed simply in good olive oil.

These starters demonstrate Laneve's skill in selecting ingredients. Yet surprisingly, an appetizer of steamed clams was a big disappointment, with the clams tasting too old and the broth much too salty. And a linguine with pesto sauce was a total loser; the acrid and salty pesto had nothing in its favor.

Among the entrees, the big winner was the old hack dish that so many Italian restaurants do badly: veal scalloppine. For a welcome change, at Mamma Tina's you actually get veal that's tender and has some flavor, and it's enhanced by a nice, light marsala sauce.

I wish I could be as complimentary about the *vitello tonnato*. This time those same wonderful veal slices, in an Italian dish not often reproduced here, are served cold with a sauce of mayonnaise blended with tuna fish. This requires a very delicate hand to pull off, but at Mamma Tina's the sauce was much too thickly applied and impossibly salty.

Among other entrees, the eggplant parmigiana was quite decent, and the spinach cannelloni was marred only by a meat filling a bit on the heavy side. There are also several specials each day, some of them quite unusual.

For dessert, stick with the melon topped with brandy and English cream. The apple pie had an underdone crust, and the cheesecake was much too sweet.

There's a feeling at Mamma Tina's that's often missing in Italian restaurants—the notion that the cooking is a very personal statement of the chef. Laneve does everything to order: even the melon, the waitress told us, would take ten minutes because he had to beat the cream. Not everything is equally successful, but it's an honest and interesting meal. ∎

—Stan Sesser, October 10, 1986

Mamounia

★

441 Balboa Street (near 45th Avenue), San Francisco. 752-6566. Open Tuesday through Saturday 6 to 10 P.M., Sunday 5 to 9 P.M. Beer, wine. Major credit cards. Reservations advised. Moderate.

One reason it's fun to visit third-world countries is that there's a constant element of surprise. No matter what you've heard, what you expect, something totally different is bound to happen.

As one example, consider eating in Morocco. Every guidebook says you eat exclusively with your fingers. I remembered meals long ago in San Francisco's Mamounia restaurant, which I'm reviewing today, and there was no silverware. But when I arrived in Marrakesh, everyone—whether in fancy restaurants or at sidewalk stalls—was using forks and spoons.

It's simply the French influence, I reasoned. Moroccans who can afford to eat out are relatively wealthy, and they want to ape French culture. It's the same reason that even the lowliest restaurant in Morocco will serve horrid French baguettes for breakfast instead of the delicious thick Moroccan loaves that the less affluent buy in bakeries.

So when I was invited to a Moroccan home for couscous—a family so poor they didn't even have running water—I immediately plunged in with my fingers. Then I noticed that everyone else was using a spoon. Go ahead, they assured me; it was perfectly OK if I wanted to use my fingers, although *they* always ate with silverware. I'm convinced they thought I was performing some strange American ritual.

The moral of this story is: If you want to eat with your fingers, save the plane fare and drive out to the Richmond for a dinner at Mamounia. You can't get a fork there if you ask, as I did. (I've never quite mastered the art of taking notes while plunging my writing hand into thick sauces.)

I hadn't been to the Mamounia in at least a decade, and I remember liking the food but being put off by the prices. Amazingly, I don't think the price of the meal has changed a penny since then. While $18.50 for a huge full-course dinner may have seemed outrageous in the mid-1970s, it's an incredible bargain today.

That $18.50 buys you everything, literally from soup (the pungent Moroccan *harira*) to nuts (toasted almonds come with some dishes). It's the same menu you see in restaurants all over Morocco, often at twice that price. (Moroccan restaurants aren't much for variety. If you stay in Morocco more than a few weeks, you can go crazy being confronted every night with a choice of couscous, lemon chicken, and a couple of stews called *tagines*.)

The Mamounia is decorated in that pervasive style that can be called Moroccan plush, with knee-high brass tables and a choice of sitting on the floor or on comfortable couches piled with thick Moroccan pillows. Remarkably efficient and friendly service is provided by an international group of waiters (including one Thai), who are attired in green silk pajamas and red cylindrical hats that look like they came from a costume store rather than a *souk*.

Much of the food is quite good, but first a word of warning: Almost all of the entrees appear to have been prepared in advance and kept heated. While there's nothing intrinsically wrong with making stews beforehand, as the evening progresses the meats become extremely overcooked. If you come late, stick with the couscous and the delicious grilled-to-order brochettes of lamb.

The meal starts with a bowl of spicy *harira*, a thick and satisfying tomato-based lentil soup flavored by onions, turmeric, coriander, and ginger. Then comes the traditional Moroccan salad of tomatoes and green peppers marinated in oil, vinegar, and spices, which you scoop up with wedges of Moroccan bread. The salad is fine, but the Mamounia's homemade bread is too white and too bland—a pale, disappointing imitation of what you get in Morocco.

Next up is the *bastilla*, the hot pie of ground chicken, eggs, and almonds sandwiched between flaky layers of filo dough. The Mamounia's version is a masterpiece, absolutely greaseless, flavored with just the right amount of cinnamon and sugar. It's even better if you ask for it without the heap of powdered sugar that's scattered on top.

All this could easily make a dinner, but a big entree is yet to come. You can choose from couscous, hare, brains, several *tagines* of lamb, lemon chicken, and lamb brochettes.

The brains and hare are definitely to be avoided. The tasteless hare suffered from an acrid paprika sauce, and when I had it at 9 P.M., the meat was already overcooked to mush. As for the brains, they tasted like they had been sitting around the kitchen far too long waiting for a taker, and I was the unlucky victim.

Everything else, though, was excellent, although the *tagines* and chicken could have done with far less salt. The brochettes, high-quality tender lamb with a spicy marinade, came rare exactly as ordered. The lemon chicken exuded a host of seasonings and the tang of preserved lemons.

If you've never had couscous, the Mamounia is a good place to try it. This is the more delicate Moroccan version, not the Algerian version with fiery red sauce that you get in Paris. The fine-grained farina is scented with the juices of lamb and piled high with a variety of vegetables, plumped-up raisins, and a hunk of stewed lamb.

With a meal this big, you won't have a bit of room for dessert. That's good, because the Mamounia trots out wretched deep-fried strips of dough that reek of bad oil. Just ask for the mint tea, which is very refreshing if you order it without the sugar.

If you want a change of pace at a reasonable price, the Mamounia is just the spot. You've got to search to do much better in Morocco itself. ∎

—Stan Sesser, November 13, 1987

The Mandarin

★★

Ghirardelli Square, San Francisco. 673-8812. Open every day noon to 11P.M. Full bar. Major credit cards. Reservations recommended at night. Expensive.

When Cecilia Chiang opened her elegant Chinese restaurant in 1968, she was the first to offer many of the rich and spicy dishes of the Szechuan and Hunan provinces.

Twenty years ago, the garlicky, chili-infused sauces offered new taste sensations for westerners used to adulterated Cantonese cooking. Now many restaurants offer the dishes available at the Mandarin, and the main criticism of this landmark restaurant has been high prices. If you can get mu shu pork at other Chinese restaurants for $5 or $6, is it worth paying $14 at the Mandarin?

I visited this restaurant recently with the price issue in mind, and to see if ordering a meal ahead made a difference in quality. My experiences on both counts were surprising.

One Tuesday evening four of us arrived anonymously and were led to a table overlooking the main plaza of Ghirardelli Square. A waiter was there in a flash, and everything proceeded like clockwork, from ordering through service.

The look of the place is as stunning today as it was twenty years ago. Its rough brick walls plastered over in some places, thick wooden beams, high ceilings, and tiled floors have been the inspiration for many stylish conversions of industrial space to commercial use. (The much-written-about Rattlesnake Club in a converted Denver brewery takes its cues from the Mandarin's design.) All the charm of the raw space has been used, yet you feel engulfed in luxury—that juxtaposition of rustic and refined works.

Oriental antiques, calligraphy, and paintings seem more resonant against the background of red brick and unfinished wood; the tables are large, the chairs soft and comfortable, the lighting subtle. Though the restaurant is almost monumental, the space is divided into intimate dining areas.

We ordered from the menu, with the waiter recommending the famous minced squab, and had a near-perfect meal. Pot stickers were as deliciously filled as any I've tasted, and the noodle wrappers were thin and tender; however, they were a bit burned on their one fried side. The minced squab, which isn't on the menu, is always fun to eat. Black mushrooms, water chestnuts, and the squab are finely chopped and stir fried to be wrapped, with crunchy fried rice noodles, in cold, crisp lettuce leaves.

A soup of pureed chicken and corn with a sesame-scented broth was as notable for its silken texture as its comforting mild flavors. We drank every drop. A smoked tea duck, which no one does better than the Mandarin, distills the most poetically sensual aspects of Chinese cooking. The amazingly crisp skin is contrasted by velvety flesh infused with the perfume of smoke and the flowery aroma of jasmine tea.

Next our waiter constructed four little spring crepes with shreds of richly sauced pork, cucumber, bean sprouts, and scallions. I love dishes that combine hot and cold, cooked and raw, rich and clean ingredients. The soft white pancakes wrapped these opposites together neatly.

A whole deep-fried rockfish in a spicy brown szechuan sauce studded with incendiary dried red chili halves was expertly boned by our waiter and represented in all its hot, crisp glory. With it, he brought spinach and glass noodles in a clear sauce, a fine foil for the fish and rice.

I couldn't have hoped for a tastier, more graciously and intelligently served meal. The surroundings were lovely, the service exemplary, and the quality and carefulness of the preparations evident. The meal was delicious and interesting, clearly on the level of any of the few three-star restaurants in the city.

I returned on a Saturday night and asked that a special menu be assembled for us. We were greeted by Cecilia Chiang herself and seated in a narrow room at a table by a window overlooking the bay.

We started with the squab dish and then were brought a Peking duck, which must be ordered one day in advance. I've had the Mandarin's Peking duck a number of times and it has always been magnificent, but on this occasion it came from the kitchen cold, with inflexible white pancakes. Since Peking duck is a dish about crispy fat, in that the skin is the true delicacy, this dishes loses its charm when it cools off.

The glossy skin is carved into slices that are piled into the pancakes with a few pieces of meat, scallions, and a swatch of bean sauce. This tasted like a cold duck sandwich. Had it been prepared in advance for another table that chose not to have it? Had the kitchen lost its poise?

Smoldering-hot prawns a la Szechuan came in an edible deep-fried noodle basket, a crunchy contrast to the moist, opaque shrimp. Tangerine beef was studded with big pieces of peel, which should have been removed before it was served. The strips of steak take on a lovely, citrus scent if you don't mistakenly eat a piece of the overpowering rind. A plate of smoky fried rice accompanied these two dishes, and I felt as if too much was going on in my mouth at the same time.

The meal ended with a soothing shanghai cabbage dish, a baby bok choy braised in a delicate, clear sauce and topped with straw mushrooms in a mushroom-infused brown sauce.

What did delight me about this meal was how well the wines (suggested by manager John Wong) went with it. He has put together a complete California wine list, and a 1983 Acacia pinot noir was wonderful with the peking duck. The combination of a French sauterne and hot glazed bananas cooled off in a bowl of ice water was also a revelation.

On the whole the meal was not served as sensitively nor did it work as well as the first one. This is one Chinese restaurant set up to accommodate western eating patterns. Deviation from the usual procedure, especially on a busy Saturday night, will not bring you a superior meal. ∎

—Patricia Unterman, October 11, 1987

Manora

★ ★

3226 Mission, San Francisco. 550-0856. Open daily 5 to 10 P.M. Beer, wine. MasterCard, Visa. No reservations. Inexpensive.

Stan Sesser covers Thai and Cambodian restaurants so well in his Friday column that I usually leave them to him. But recently he took me to his favorite Thai restaurant, Plearn in Berkeley, and the food was so exciting that it whetted my appetite for the spices of Thai cooking.

Fortunately, the name of a relatively new Thai restaurant in San Francisco was on the lips of some of my most trusted scouts. It turned out to be an unusually attractive Thai restaurant on the outermost edge of the Mission that has drawn a dedicated neighborhood following, mostly from Noe Valley, Glen Park, and Potrero Hill.

There's a sense of refinement at this Thai restaurant, though it remains comfortable and unpretentious, and the added appointments are not reflected in the prices, which are low.

The menu is small enough so that the dishes are not repeated using just slight variations in the ingredients, nor is it so small as to be limiting. Each dish I sampled represented a different direction in Thai cuisine. All the dishes achieved a praiseworthy level of quality in both presentation, on blue-and-white-patterned china, and in taste.

The appetizers are the best part of the meal. They run the range of cooking techniques. A long rice noodle roll, *poh-pier-sod*, was stuffed with seafood, sausage, and vegetables, topped with a delicate sweet-and-sour tamarind sauce, and beautifully garnished with carrot flowers and fresh coriander leaves. The filling was delicious and the white noodle wrapper exceptionally tender.

A fiery hot squid salad, *plah pa muk*, featured velvety rings of squid marinated with equal amounts of chilies and lemon grass. The balance was perfect. A chopped chicken salad, *gai chom suan*, also packed a hot wallop. It might better follow one of the tamer dishes, such as Manora's *satays*, thin slices of beef and pork threaded on wooden skewers and carefully grilled. You dip them in a creamy peanut sauce and eat them with a sweet-and-sour cucumber salad.

I particularly liked Manora's unusual version of fish cakes. They're large, thick patties with a slightly gelatinous texture mitigated by a network of rice-noodle threads. They have a delicate lemon-grass scent. If you want to spice them up, you can put a hot cucumber salad on top of them.

As a main course, there are huge mounds of ground crab, shrimp, and pork stuffed in crab shells, then deep fried, called *poo-ja*, that reminded me of the spicy stuffed Creole crab I've had in the French Caribbean. Unlike the Creole version, these use aromatic Thai seasonings and come with a sweet plum sauce. Other main courses I sampled were more predictable but uniformly well prepared.

Mixed green vegetables brought a combination of green beans, napa cabbage, snow peas, and water chestnuts in a light, flavorful garlicky oyster sauce. Each vegetable was crisp and bright in color, a masterful rendition of a Chinese-influenced dish. Also exceptional was *hor mok*, a dish of steamed snapper, shrimp, and mussels moist and tender in a delicious coconut milk curry. On the other hand, yellow chicken curry with potatoes tasted a bit flat compared to the brightness of the other dishes.

The perennial favorite, Thai-style barbecued chicken, had crisp, spicy skin and comes with an interesting sweet-and-sour garlic sauce. Garlic was the main flavor of a mild, pan-fried pork dish called *moo-prik-king* that was served over shredded lettuce. Throughout the meal, hot rice is dispensed by waiters from elaborate silver tureens with covers. Singha Thai beer, freshly squeezed orange juice, and sweet, milky Thai iced tea or coffee all go with the food, though beer is my choice.

Eating at Manora proves, once again, why Thai restaurants have become so popular in the Bay Area. Sauces are always light, never oily or thickened. The cuisine uses not only hot chilies but aromatic herbs like basil, lemon grass, and mint. The flavors, textures, and temperatures, though often opposing, achieve a happy balance. For example, searing hot squid is cooled by mint and cold lettuce. A mild dish is enlivened with the spices of Thai curry. Grilled foods get relishes and dipping sauces, and the Thai methods of cooking fish and seafood are always appropriate. Manora's menu provides glowing examples of all these attributes of the cuisine. The good, steady kitchen combined with a small, pretty dining room and efficient service makes Manora's well worth a trip across town. ■

—Patricia Unterman, November 3, 1985

Mansion Hotel

★

2220 Sacramento Street (near Laguna), San Francisco. 929-9444. Open for dinner Tuesday through Saturday with entertainment starting at 7 P.M. and the meal about an hour later. Beer, wine. Major credit cards. Reservations essential, well in advance for weekends. Moderate fixed-price dinner.

If you are tired of the same old restaurant scene, consider this: You walk into a French restaurant and all the diners are gathered in the front room. On a stage is the restaurant's owner—sawing a woman in thirds. Her head and hands stick out of holes in the top third of the box, her feet protrude from the bottom third, and he moves her midsection two feet to the left, leaving a gap. While he's doing that, the sous chef, wearing a huge white toque, bangs away on the piano. Next to him is a parrot, squawking on his perch.

Welcome to the Mansion Hotel, a restaurant you simply have to see for yourself. On weekends you get a magic show and other entertainment before your escargots; on weeknights, it's merely a playerless piano that somehow performs requests from the audience. Then you move into a dining room with lace tablecloths and acres of stained glass, looking out on a veritable museum of Bufano sculptures. And, for about $30, you get a very competent full-course French dinner.

This elegantly restored Victorian hotel in Pacific Heights is the brainchild of Robert Pritikin, a San Francisco ad man. It has to be the best-kept secret in town. He says his magic show, which has been going on for several years and is first-rate, has never been reviewed.

Pritikin hired as his chef David Coyle, who for many years worked in England as the personal chef for the Duke and Duchess of Bedford. Coyle orchestrates a show that's almost as magic as Pritikin's act. Although the guests pour into the dining room at the same time, the food comes out of the kitchen perfectly paced, with never an unpleasantly long wait between courses.

There's no question about Coyle's competence, and once I would have given his food two stars. But I've fallen victim to a prejudice of the times, and I have to discuss that.

The prejudice is this: Fifteen or twenty years ago, you'd assume that when you ate a French dinner it would be so heavy that you'd feel queasy when you walked out. When you eat one of Coyle's dinners, you'll appreciate the skill displayed in the rich sauces, but maybe not on so many of the dishes, especially followed by calorie-laden desserts such as cheesecake.

The portions are huge, too, but you won't complain about the wonderful array of vegetables and wild rice practically spilling over the sides of the plate.

Perhaps reflecting his British background, Coyle really shines for such entrees as veal or roast duck. Scallops of veal with shallot and wild mushrooms featured very tender veal, heaps of mushrooms, and a thick marsala wine sauce that came close to overwhelming it. The duck was described as "roasted over a bed of root vegetables in the French manner with bee pollen and wild honey"; though I couldn't find any hint of the root vegetables or the pollen, it was a magnificent half duck.

Steamed prawns came out nicely too, although again the very heavy sauce, which included garlic mayonnaise, threatened but didn't quite manage to wipe out the prawns.

The appetizers were exemplary. A hot artichoke with aioli reflected Coyle's love of garlic, while a generous portion of sauteed shiitake mushrooms on a bed of wild rice couldn't have been more delicious. Although the snails themselves were tasteless and a little rubbery, the sauce of garlic, shallots, and butter redeemed the dish.

Given the big portions, the heavy sauces, the wonderful but dense whole-wheat rolls, a dessert like cheesecake seemed too much to handle. Yet surprisingly, it was one of the lightest, most satisfying cheesecakes I've ever tasted. The delicate chocolate mousse cake and the boysenberry sherbet were perfect, too.

There were only two real flaws. A butter lettuce salad (with canned mandarin oranges in a season when they could be bought fresh) was floating in an ocean of dressing. A very overcooked piece of salmon in a much-too-rich sauce reeked of dried herbs.

But overall, the fixed-price dinner, which offers several choices in each category, was an astonishing bargain—not to mention the magic show and fine art thrown in. For anyone who feels jaded from the usual restaurant scene, an evening at the Mansion Hotel is the perfect antidote. ■

—Stan Sesser, January 16, 1987

Marnee Thai

★ ★

2225 Irving Street (at Twenty-third Avenue), San Francisco. 665-9500. Open Wednesday through Monday 11 A.M. to 9:30 P.M. Beer, wine. Major credit cards. Reservations essential. Inexpensive.

It wasn't all that many years ago that Thai food in San Francisco was considered so exotic that going to a Thai restaurant became a culinary adventure. Now, at least in some neighborhoods, there's virtually one on every block—enough in total so that a restaurant critic could keep busy for months reviewing nothing else. As a result, many San Franciscans have become such Thai food addicts that dishes that once sounded exotic now seem commonplace.

So where to go for something different? Start your search at Marnee Thai, a small, year-old restaurant in the Sunset that offers some splendid and unusual dishes, from fresh corn cakes for an appetizer to fresh mango with sweet sticky rice for dessert.

Marnee Thai is one of those rare restaurants that makes up in little touches for anything it might lack in expensive decor. The place is virtually carpeted in fresh flowers, with bouquets on every table.

The waitresses joke with you, fuss over you, and will insist on giving you something else or not charging you if they see you didn't like a dish. The warm service more than compensates for a restaurant that can be noisy, smoky from just one cigaret (if ever a place needed to be 100 percent nonsmoking, this is it), and cramped (there's no waiting area, and only about six people can squeeze in by the door).

Chaiwatt Siriyarn, perhaps the world's only Thai chef who holds an MBA, presides in the kitchen, while his wife, Muaynee, runs the dining room with unrelenting good humor. They called their restaurant Marnee Thai, which means Thai jewels, as a play on Muaynee's name.

Chaiwatt turns out some astonishingly good and interesting dishes, perfumed by a long list of herbs and spices and commendably light on the cooking oil. Yet, inexplicably, alongside the wonderful dishes, I found about one in three things to be disappointing. It was such a sharp contrast that I made an effort to eat my way through the menu and pick out the best food; I'll refer to those dishes by number also to make it easier to order.

You don't have to go farther than the appetizers to know you're in an extraordinary restaurant. A couple are done in ways I've never seen before. Spicy angel wings (number 7) are chicken wings that are first deep fried, than sauteed in a curry paste loaded with chili and garlic. They emerge perfectly crisp with a fiery, delicious glaze, and they're inventively enhanced by a garnish of deep-fried Thai basil leaves.

Miang kum (number 5) is not unusual, but Marnee Thai puts its own touch on it. It is a variety of vegetables and spices—peanuts, chilies, garlic slivers, ginger—that you wrap in a lettuce leaf. But here they use spinach, a vast improvement over iceberg lettuce, and there's a seductive sweet but pungent sauce.

Corn cakes are a special during fresh corn season, and they're an absolute must. Patties are made from corn flour, wheat flour, fresh corn kernels, and eggs, then deep fried. They come out light and fluffy and without a speck of grease.

Even traditional appetizers shine. Fish cakes (number 2), enlivened by slices of fresh green beans, have never been better, again totally greaseless. Calamari salad (number 9) is a roaring hot presentation of the freshest, most tender squid imaginable.

After the appetizers, try the sinus-clearing soup called potak (number 15). A variety of very fresh seafood floats in a spicy chicken stock perfumed by lemon grass, galanga, and ginger. It's a great demonstration of how the heat in Thai food doesn't overwhelm the wonderful flavors.

The place to start for entrees is with the sensational hor mok (number 37), a dish that's cooked in lots of Thai and Cambodian restaurants but not as well as it's done here. Red snapper is blended with curry paste, coconut milk, and eggs, then steamed in a banana leaf to emerge as a fluffy fish mousse that rivals anything you can get in a French restaurant. It's served on a layer of half-cooked shredded cabbage and Thai basil.

The curries at Marnee Thai are excellent, too. Green pork curry (number 20), succulent with coconut milk, has the unusual touch of eggplant slices. Red chicken curry (number 19) is so subtly perfumed that the coconut milk broth tastes almost French. Another winner is the spicy duck (number 29), which is roasted first, then boned and sauteed with tomatoes, onions, garlic, and chilies. It's completely tender and fat free.

It was surprising to get several really disappointing entrees. Barbecued chicken was overcooked and underspiced. Sauteed eggplant with minced pork and eggs was loaded with oil, a defect I didn't find in a single other dish here. An intensely salty sauce and mussels and clams that tasted far from fresh marred *chao talay*, a combination seafood dish. And the rice noodles stirfried with crab meat tasted unpleasantly fishy.

Did you ever hear of an Asian restaurant with good desserts? Wait until you try the *roti*, an Indian-style fried bread sauced with a little sweetened milk. And if they've found mangoes in the market, you can have them in the traditional Thai style, accompanied with sweetened glutinous rice flavored with coconut milk.

There are some hassles at Marnee Thai; one night we had to wait despite reservations, and waiting in a noisy, cramped restaurant is no fun. But the food and caring service made the wait worthwhile. ∎
—Stan Sesser, August 14, 1987

Masa's

★★★

648 Bush Street (above Stockton), in the Vintage Court Hotel, San Francisco. 989-7154. Open Tuesday through Saturday 6 to 9:30 P.M. Full bar. MasterCard, Visa, American Express. Reservations essential, well in advance (they can be made up to three weeks before). Expensive.

There's a yardstick that's rarely considered in measuring the ability of chefs, but in some cases it can be crucial. The question is how well other people in the kitchen have been trained. If the chef quits, or is gone for even an evening, does the restaurant become a disaster area?

Never was that question more important than when Masa Kobayashi was murdered two and a half years ago. It was feared that his death would also mean the end of the road for Masa's, one of San Francisco's greatest restaurants.

But something of a miracle took place. Sous chef Bill Galloway stepped into Kobayashi's shoes and performed flawlessly. And rather than simply imitating what Kobayashi did, Galloway slowly introduced new dishes, lightened the sauces, and made the food better than it ever had been.

Now Galloway has left to spend the next couple of years interning in some restaurants in France. Again there's some happy news to report. I've had two dinners cooked by Galloway's sous chef, Julian Serrano, the thirty-six-year-old Spaniard who's now in charge. Uniformly, the food was as good or better than anything I've eaten at Masa's before.

To put it in a nutshell, Masa's is my nominee for the best French restaurant in the United States, an accolade more generally accorded Lutece in New York. But looking back at my last three meals at Lutece, the best dishes taken together weren't as satisfying or as innovative as what I could get in one meal at Masa's.

There's an extra bonus at Masa's, too, particularly if you compare it to a place like Lutece. For once, you can eat at an elegant French restaurant where no one is looking down his nose at you. No matter how you're dressed, no matter how unschooled in food and wine you might be, John Cunin, Masa's remarkably skilled maitre d', will make you feel like an honored guest.

All that does come at a considerable price. The nightly fixed-price dinner is over $60 and many entrees are over $30. With tax and tip, two people splitting a bottle of wine can spend $200. But that $200 will buy you sensational food, dishes that look magnificent and taste even better. You can throw a dart at Masa's menu and not lose. I, in effect, did that my last meal, ordering two entrees I don't usually get, lamb and sweetbreads. (What Masa's does with game birds is so outstanding I normally can't go beyond them to anything else.)

When I last had sweetbreads at Masa's, Kobayashi was cooking, and I remember them as one of the few disappointments he ever produced. This time they were a sensation. Lightly battered with semolina and stuffed with salmon mousse, the veal sweetbreads were butter-tender and exuded flavor. Underneath was a bright crayfish sauce capturing the essence of crayfish taste. On top was a light sauce made from deglazing the sweetbreads pan with veal stock, white wine, and shallots.

The grilled baby lamb, as white and tender as veal, proved equally marvelous. The lamb was sliced and served between thin layers of artichoke heart. Next to it was one of the most remarkable vegetable creations I've ever tasted: a mound of brightly colored confetti, made of seven different vegetables, each cut to the same tiny dimensions, and each sauteed to al dente perfection.

While the menu frequently changes, two consistent highlights are the foie gras and the shellfish bisque. The fresh New York State goose liver, sauteed and served in a light truffle sauce on a bed of spinach, is enough to convert the most militant liver hater. The bisque is rich not with butter and cream, but with the taste of crayfish or crab, or whatever is being used.

As good as the entrees are—quail, pheasant, and pigeon have never found a better home—what accompanies them can be equally stunning. Pigeon, for instance, came with a bone-marrow mousse and a chestnut puree. With those, as with almost everything at Masa's, the intensity of flavor bursts through.

The desserts at Masa's have had a more checkered past than the rest of the food. But at the last two dinners, the new dessert chef, Alicia Toyooka, shows she can provide a fitting end for a meal there. Consider, for example, a praline cone stuffed with Grand Marnier ice cream and spilling out a variety of berries onto a sauce made from fresh peaches.

Food this good is a work of art, and art shouldn't be exclusively the domain of the wealthy. What about one lower-priced dinner each night, perhaps containing less expensive ingredients, so that everyone can share in this San Francisco treasure? ■

—Stan Sesser, April 3, 1987

Restaurant Matisse

★★

620 Fifth Avenue, Santa Rosa. 707-527-9797. Open Monday through Friday 11:30 A.M. to 2 P.M., Monday through Saturday 6 to 9:30 P.M. Beer, wine. Major credit cards. Reservations recommended. Moderate; an extremely good buy for what you get.

An irritatingly energetic young man accosted me at the Tasting of Summer Produce at the Mondavi Winery last summer. "I'm your double," he said. "My name is Michael Hirschberg. I'm the restaurant critic for the *Santa Rosa News Herald* and I also have a restaurant," and he then proceeded to tell me *everything* about his cooking background, his travels to France, his two little children, his pastry-chef wife, the food situation in Sonoma County, and his aspirations.

Shortly afterward I got a packet of material in the mail about his restaurant in

Santa Rosa. He had told me it was a hole in the wall, but from the looks of the ten prix-fixe menus he sent, each with fifteen different choices, it seemed like his operation was more on the scale of La Coupole. Still more amazing, a dinner at his restaurant cost only $15.

"Could this guy be for real?" I wondered. I had to find out and drove up to Santa Rosa. I took 101 to the central Santa Rosa exit, drove toward downtown Santa Rosa on Third, turned left on D Street and left again on Fifth and parked right in front of Restaurant Matisse. It was, indeed, a small place, easily missed, but it was nicely done.

A large, clean-edged, rectangular window frames a dining room that somehow looks like a Matisse canvas. Though mostly bare and cream colored, an eloquent shade of burnt orange on the wainscoting and a thin strip of mirror at sitting-down-head-level gives the room form. Someone had thought hard about the lighting because it glowed warmly, softening the austere lines and making everyone look good. Two small Matisse copies hung unobtrusively near the front door. Not a lot of money had been spent, but you couldn't have asked for a more civilized dining room.

The menu, which changes daily, was just as straightforward and attractive. To begin, there were two fine winter salads. Spears of endive and slices of orange were bathed in a delicious mustard cream dressing, while small whole leaves of romaine were sprinkled with roquefort and tossed in a yummy garlic mayonnaise, thinned out.

A terrine of rabbit had a pleasantly coarse texture and was seasoned with lots of thyme and garlic. The garnish of beets, arugula, and cornichons dressed it up for winter. Nothing could have tasted better on that particularly frigid night than a soothing cream of onion soup that came out of the kitchen steaming hot.

The only appetizer that struck a wrong note was rilletes of salmon, which should have been fresher.

Some of the main courses ventured into "California" territory and forgot which way they were going. A medium-rare piece of bluefin tuna fought an orange-ginger butter and lost. A strong orange presence also conflicted with slices of succulent grilled pork tenderloin in a sauce already augmented by green peppercorns. But when the kitchen sticks to old-fashioned French dishes like sauteed veal sweetbreads with mushrooms, madeira, and cream, you wonder that they ever went out of style. The richness of the buttery sweetbreads segued into the delicately sweet sauce without a single unnecessary beat.

Breast of chicken stuffed with prosciutto and gruyere, another dish straight out of *Mastering the Art of French Cooking*, Volume I, pleased just the way it was supposed to on a cold night. The flavors of the ham and cheese melted right into the moist breast, making it savory. A couple of meaty loin lamb chops were enhanced by a simple sauce of their natural juices fortified by a little merlot.

All the main courses came with several carefully cooked vegetables, a timbale of cauliflower too enthusiastically seasoned with Indian spices, and scalloped potatoes or rice pilaf. One look at the big, colorful plates assured you that you were getting a balanced meal.

Two additional angles at Restaurant Matisse add to the picture: a wine list of the best Sonoma County wines at prices considerably below those you would find in the city, and a wonderful a la carte dessert menu.

The desserts, which cost extra, are like the best of the main menu, inspired by the traditional French idea about what a sweet should be. A chocolate and raspberry marquise, airy chocolate and raspberry mousses molded together, sliced, and served on orange *crème a l'anglaise* would have done a French pastry chef proud. An igloo of white chocolate ice cream molded over a chocolate mousse and praline core sat on a shiny floe of chocolate rum sauce. An unabashedly sweet filling of walnuts and caramel was sandwiched into a flaky crust and cut by caramel ice cream. Only the fruit sorbets failed to dazzle. Resorting to banana, even in winter, is not the best idea. As we drove back to the city after dinner, we commented that the Santa Rosans were lucky to have a Michael Hirschberg. His restaurant was an outpost of civilized dining much in the style of fine country restaurants in France. The food was not too ambitious but certainly special; the ambience friendly and informal; and the prices right in line for regular local patronage. While some may move to the country to open a first restaurant, Hirschberg, his pastry-chef wife, and probably his two little kids could mount a successful restaurant in the 6e arrondissement. He's got the touch. ∎

—Patricia Unterman, January 12, 1986

Max's Diner

★

Corner of Third and Folsom, San Francisco. 546-0168. Open Monday through Wednesday 11 A.M. to 11 P.M., Thursday 11 A.M. to midnight, Friday and Saturday 11 A.M. to 1 A.M., Sunday 11:30 A.M. to 11 P.M. Full bar. Major credit cards. No reservations. Inexpensive.

When I reviewed Max's Opera Cafe a while back, I thought I had found the height of chutzpah when I saw on the menu that they offered corned beef and brie on a croissant. But little did I know what Dennis Berkowitz, the Warner LeRoy of Jewish delicatessens, had in mind for his next restaurant. LeRoy, the flamboyant creator of Maxwell's Plum in New York and San Francisco, has clearly met his match.

Berkowitz's new place is called Max's Diner. Its block-long neon facade, for better or worse, has already become almost as much of a San Francisco landmark as Moscone Center across the street. You'll either love it or hate it, but you'll have to admit that it stretches the boundaries of chutzpah to previously unheard of dimensions. For instance:

■ In a city that rises to arms at the slightest hint of sexism, the cocktail waitresses at Max's are forced to wear buttocks-length black miniskirts—along with white basketball shoes.

■ The menu pledges in no uncertain terms that mustard and ketchup will come before your sandwiches and fries, and that no one will ask you whether everything is all right. "When we ask questions, they'll be helpful ones," the menu promises.

■ After the waitress brought us our food, she said, "I'll get the ketchup and mustard." When she returned to our table with them, she immediately asked, "Is everything all right?"

■ The house wine, a sauvignon blanc, comes in a bottle with a label that says, "Diner White—ice cubes encouraged." The wine turns out to be first-rate, one of the best house wines in town.

■ The men's room has just two urinals, and, because the restaurant is huge and always jammed, they're both constantly occupied. But the urinals are designed so that when the men's room door opens, half the patrons of the bar get a perfect side view of the activity.

Max's Diner, in short, is an insane madhouse. I totally hated it at first, then ended up conceding it was fun. It works on a formula that's becoming increasingly popular these days: devote half the space to the bar, have big portions and low food prices to draw the crowds, then make your money selling booze to people waiting for a table.

But the formula is carried to unprecedented extremes. The portions are so grotesque that one of my dinner companions pushed away his bread pudding in mock horror and said, "I never eat anything that's larger than my head." And the wait for a table is so unpleasant and frustrating that you wonder what kind of food could possibly make it worthwhile.

We arrived at 6:30 one evening and were told the wait would be over an hour—apparently a modest length of time by Max's standards. Then the "fun" begins. You're jammed into a bar area with a low acoustical ceiling, so noisy and smoky that your mind starts reeling. (The cigarette smoke is no joke; it's thick enough to be a real hazard.)

But you can't sit down; every table and bar stool is full. It takes a half hour of prowling the aisles to grab a table just as someone's name is called. Then it takes ten minutes of frantic waving to get a waitress so you can order drinks and appetizers. Then more waiting. From looking around the room, it appeared that as often as not the food and drinks would arrive just as they were about to call your name for a table.

Yes, Max's has food, too. I was determined to get to it before the end of this review.

The huge menu, arranged in categories like The Expensive Stuff, is typical of a Jewish deli. There are the usual overstuffed sandwiches, platters of lox, turkey, and shrimp, and very plain-sounding entrees like roast chicken, meat loaf, and brisket of beef.

Much to my surprise, a lot of the food turned out to be quite decent. You'll push away some things: The lox was unpleasantly fishy tasting, the onion rings all grease and breading, the pork ribs marred by a sugary sauce. Many of the desserts were abominable, with the devil's food chocolate cake unmatched in awfulness by any cafeteria I've been in.

But some other dishes were pretty good, and two of the things I tasted actually could be called splendid. The first is buffalo chicken wings. I've never seen them before even remotely edible, but Max's version wasn't greasy and it zinged with hot spices; even the blue cheese dip was enlivened by chili oil.

The second great dish was short ribs in Russian cabbage soup, the most expensive thing on the menu except for steak and prawns. A pot comes to your table so big you'll start laughing, loaded with tender ribs covered with sour cream and a host of vegetables in a thick broth with a pleasant sweet-and-sour taste. It was the perfect dish for a winter night.

You'll also do well, oddly enough, with the chicken-fried steak. Putting batter on a steak and deep frying it isn't my idea of the world's best recipe, but this one is far better than what you get in the Rocky Mountain states, where it's featured on virtually every menu. Max's comes out crispy and greaseless, doused in decent gravy.

As for the Jewish food, while you won't think you're in New York, some of it is quite passable. The pastrami is spicy and tender, the corned beef decent, the chopped chicken liver appropriately laden with schmaltz. But the cutesy bread of pumpernickel swirled into rye is just as ridiculous as at Max's Opera Cafe.

You can get loaded with food at Max's, some of it good, for very little money. Once you're seated, the meal can be fun. But there's a price to pay: the agony of the wait. To me, it's not worth it. ■

—Stan Sesser, February 14, 1986

Middle East Restaurant

★ ★

2125 University Avenue (just above Shattuck), Berkeley. 549-1926. Open Tuesday through Sunday 5 to 9 P.M., Friday and Saturday until 10:30 P.M.; Beer, wine. No credit cards. Reservations accepted. Inexpensive.

I've grown so accustomed to mediocre Middle Eastern food in California that I can hardly get myself to take this cuisine seriously any more. I think of it as something found around college campuses at places that cater to the propensity of many students to eat anything that's fast, cheap, and can be washed down with beer.

So I didn't pay much attention when the Middle East Restaurant opened on University Avenue, a block west of the UC Berkeley campus. But it turns out that this little place is a glowing exception to my rule, an attempt by a serious cook to make the standard Lebanese dishes sparkle. Everything is prepared from scratch, even the yogurt, and it's clearly done by people who care.

The Middle East looks like an ordinary neighborhood restaurant, but you know something unusual is going on almost the minute you walk in. You find yourself being treated like a guest in someone's home; the service is extraordinary, and the cooks keep peering out to see if you're enjoying the food.

This is entirely a family enterprise. Edward Samaha does the grilling, his wife Evelyn the rest of the cooking, and their sons, Bassel and Ehab, wait on the tables. The Samahas moved to the United States from Beirut in 1971.

What's absolutely extraordinary about the Middle East is its array of appetizers. Two people can start dinner by splitting a *mezza* — an assortment of all the appetizers on the menu. It reminds me of a *rijsttafel*, the Indonesian banquet, in that your table fills up with so many little dishes you hardly know where to start.

Everything in the *mezza* is superb. The dolmas — grape leaves stuffed with rice, parsley, tomatoes, onion, lemon, and spices — are warm, tangy, and delicate. The deep-fried falafel patties are fresh tasting and greaseless. The hummus — pureed garbanzos and sesame — couldn't have more flavor. Then there are delicately simmered fava beans, smoked eggplant with olive oil and sesame, and *labneh*, a rich creamy yogurt dish. With pita bread and beer, its a real feast.

The entrees are a little more of a mixed bag. There's one major problem here, and it's so silly it will probably vanish as soon as I write about it: The entrees focus more on beef than lamb, even in some of the dishes that are supposed to be made with lamb, such as moussaka or the blend of meat, onions, cracked wheat, and pine nuts called kibbeh. Because beef is not as flavorful, both dishes suffer.

When I asked about it, Bassel told me his parents had heard Americans don't like lamb. In food-obsessed Berkeley — where people would happily eat monkey meat if it made the recipe authentic — this is, of course, ridiculous.

While it would be improved with lamb, the moussaka is still excellent. The fluffy custardy topping, covered with the thinnest layer of tomato sauce, is the best I've ever had. Another fine choice is the *kafta kebab*, minced lamb blended with spices and grilled on a skewer.

For dessert you can choose from two kinds of baklava, pistachio or walnut. Don't even think about walnuts. The pistachio version, with the nuts sandwiched between layers of phyllo dough and the honey sparingly applied, is a spectacular departure from the more usual gooey mess. There's also a delicate and custardy rice pudding topped with ground nuts. ■

— Stan Sesser, November 14, 1986

Miramonte Restaurant

★ ★

1327 Railroad Avenue, St. Helena. 707-963-3970. Open Wednesday through Sunday from 6:15 to 9 P.M. Beer, wine. Cash or personal checks only. Reservations recommended, essential well in advance for weekends. Very expensive.

If you are dreaming about an eating trip to France, but aren't enthusiastic about mortgaging your house to finance the $500 a day that food and lodging for two could cost at a three-star restaurant, consider a California restaurant tour instead.

You could start by eating at the Miramonte in Napa Valley, the closest parallel we have to a restaurant in Burgundy. You drive past vineyards to dine in a French-style country inn and to sample the cooking of Udo Nechutnys, a pioneer in using French techniques with fresh California ingredients.

In a world of revolving-door chefs, Nechutnys has presided over Miramonte for so long that we all must be taking him for granted. Now that so many San Francisco chefs are cooking in the same style, it was time to revisit Miramonte and see how Nechutnys's food is holding up.

Before the first dish even arrived, one thing became clear: Miramonte's one exasperating problem has become even worse. To start with, you get a menu for the fixed-price dinner that's impossible to decipher. You can't tell which choices belong in which category.

Then the waiter compounds the confusion. A couple of the items on the mimeographed menu aren't available, he announces. Then he adds, "We have a few specials," which he begins to recite.

A few, indeed! At each of my dinners there were thirteen, divided among the three courses, where you have to make a choice. Moreover, about half carried price supplements, ranging from $2.50 to $6.50. (The recitation of nine desserts, with three carrying a $4.50 supplement, remained for later.)

Unless you laboriously write everything down, the result is total confusion. It is also likely to be a much more expensive dinner than the set price, since many of the things that sounded best also cost extra. Besides that, there's an outrageously expensive wine list, even for normally cheap wines such as a muscadet or sancerre (at Miramonte, $20), or California sauvignon blanc ($22 to $30).

The recitation of specials, which goes on at nearby tables all night like a gourmet version of a Hare Krishna chant, plus a long wait for the first course, isn't the ideal way to start a meal. But some of Nechutnys's dishes will be great enough to make you forget the hassle.

I say "some," although years ago I would have said "all." At both dinners—one on a jam-packed Saturday night, the second on a half-empty weeknight—there was a puzzling problem of quality control. While the majority of the dishes were wonderful, others—particularly several entrees with sticky, overreduced sauces—proved disappointing.

As the prime example, I fondly remembered the miracle Nechutnys used to work with chicken, making American chicken taste like you were eating it in France. (I don't know if it's the species, what they're fed, or how they're prepared, but the chicken served in France is uniformly better.)

This time, however, the chicken breast was wrecked by a cream sauce resembling glue, so heavy and sticky I felt afterward like brushing my teeth. It was so awful I ordered it again at the second dinner to see if the first was a fluke. This time the sauce was a little better, but only a little. It had a gravylike texture, was starting to

form a skin, and made it difficult to enjoy the chicken itself.

Veal medallions showed the same problem: a sticky sauce, much too concentrated, much too salty. The same with fan-shaped slices of delicious muscovy duck breast; the red currant sauce was sweet and cloying. It was the sort of thing you'd find in American imitations of French restaurants twenty years ago.

Those weren't the only disappointments. Duck terrine was much too fatty. A mussel soup scented with saffron turned out to be surprisingly thin and watery. And dinner rolls were completely flavorless.

Yet many of the other things were spectacular, showing Nechutnys at his best. All three seafood dishes I tasted were glorious: steamed salmon in a perfect beurre blanc turned bright green from pureed watercress; incredibly flavorful scallops in an herb butter sauce, and a delicately sauteed soft-shell crab.

Several appetizers were no less astonishing. A hot chicken liver mousse in a tomato *coulis* was fluffy and velvety. Buttery sliced lamb's tongue was served on a bed of lettuce with walnuts and a beautiful vinaigrette scented with fresh herbs. Gazpacho included bits of shrimp and a bright green circle of pureed bell peppers and watercress to contrast with the brilliant red soup. Delicate Japanese eggplants came with an interesting sauce that tasted like eggplant puree, and basil had been blended with olive oil.

Desserts—surprisingly, there were no tarts or cakes offered—proved a mixed bag. Profiteroles stuffed with chocolate mousse, crème fraîche, and Grand Marnier looked beautiful, but the mousse was much too sweet. Pistachio ice cream, by contrast, tasted bitter. Crème brûlée turned out to be simply a soupy bowl of milk custard, very good, but without a burnt cream topping.

Except for the entrees, portions were tiny. The scallops course included just three small scallops, a prawn dish had only two medium-sized prawns, and, for a sizable supplement, you still only got one soft-shell crab.

Different diners would have dramatically different reactions to Miramonte. Some would delight in those dishes that turned out to be wonderful. Others would focus on the confusing menu, the price supplements, and small portions, and leave feeling a bit ripped off. It's too bad something that could be fixed so easily would spoil many meals. ∎

—Stan Sesser, July 3, 1987

Mitoya

★★

1855 Post, San Francisco. 563-2156. Open daily 5:30 to midnight daily, Friday and Saturday until 12:30 A.M. Full bar. MasterCard, Visa, American Express, JCB (Japanese credit card). Limited reservations accepted, weekdays only. Inexpensive.

The oldest way to cook is over an open fire. Those benighted critics who think that grilling meats, vegetables, and fish over charcoal is "trendy" ought to remember that the gas stove and indeed the restaurant itself are relative newcomers to society. The Japanese still do not use the stove in the fuel-extravagant manner of Westerners. After raw fish, most dishes in the Japanese diet are either simmered or grilled, and it is the grilled things that Mitoya, a small counter restaurant and adjoining bar in the Japanese Cultural Center, does so well.

Mitoya is a *robata*, which means that customers sit at a bar and order from an array of fresh foods spread out before them. Their choices are then quickly marinated or salted, skewered or wrapped in tin foil, and grilled over charcoal. It's a marvelous way to eat.

Mitoya has a dark wood counter with thin cushions placed around it. You doff your shoes and sit on the pads with your feet dangling comfortably into a recession. The iced display in front of you reveals many beautiful foods, including baskets of clear-eyed fresh fish. There's a low wooden table at one end of the room where larger parties can sit flat on the floor. A stone path leads you into Mitoya from the cement halls of the Japanese Cultural Center, and if you follow it through the little *robata* room, it takes you into one of the most popular Japanese bars in San Francisco, a dark, rather elegant room that features professional singers and sing-along tapes of Japanese songs.

Whenever you go to a restaurant like Mitoya where the menu is unfamiliar, start by ordering dishes you know, and if they're good, get more daring. For example, a bowl of comforting yellow miso soup with tiny, briny clams in their shells breaks the cultural ice, and then all you have to do is look at the raw ingredients set in front of you. At Mitoya, they always end up tasting a little surprising,

Skewers of grilled beef are not soft and rare but have the cooked-through firmness of chuck sweetened with teriyaki sauce. Bundles of asparagus pieces are wrapped in bacon and grilled until the bacon crisps and the vegetables are just warmed through. They're fantastic. If you're a fan of beef tongue, as I am, slices of it are put on the grill raw, that results in a startling but pleasantly chewy texture. The tongue is then brushed with the traditional yakitori sauce, which goes nicely with the richness of the meat.

Of course grilled fish are the highest form of *robata-yaki* and the chef at Mitoya does them classically. Each fish is prepared for the grill differently. A large sardine is deeply scored and appealingly blackened around the edges, and gets a thorough cooking that works against the fish's oiliness. It reminded me of grilled sardines I've had along the Mediterranean. A whole little flounder is more gently crisped to maintain its creamy white flesh and a contrasting lightly salted skin. Don't miss it. Each bite offers a new sensation.

The grilled shellfish I've had at Mitoya is not great. Tiny grilled shrimp that you eat shell and all were mealy and dry, and scallops did not taste fresh enough. Clams, interestingly enough, are commonly served at *robatas* because they are cooked in a pan over an open fire. Mitoya does them beautifully, presenting them in a bowl of their own liquor with scallions and an enrichment of butter, which is also traditional in a somewhat modern style. The large, heavy shelled clams were plump, juicy, and sweet.

As anyone who loves to cook outdoors knows, the charcoal fire does wonders for vegetables. A small tinfoil boat of spaghettilike enoki mushrooms dressed with butter and soy sauce is placed directly over the fire to warm through. Triangles of green pepper do particularly well because they have so much moisture. Smoky, creamy eggplant presented with eerily waving bonito flakes on top of it was broiled and then peeled in cold water, which gives this eggplant its extraordinary texture. You dip the slices into soy sauce with grated ginger. Thin slices of white potato, first steamed and then finished off on the grill, are served with a pat of butter.

Mitoya also does *agemono*, or deep-fried dishes. My favorite is a delicious and satisfying creation called tofu steak, a large square of deep-fried tofu with a velvety interior presented in a gravy of thin, gingery soy sauce. The fish cakes, half-dollar coins of ground fish speckled with bits of salmon, are moist and slightly vinegary. You dip them into wasabi dissolved in soy sauce, like sushi. I could eat about a dozen of them.

I noticed that most people sitting at the bar were eating tempura, so we ordered it too. It was greaseless and crisply battered, but I would have liked a more interesting assortment of deep-fried ingredients. For those who want to stick with the most familiar of Japanese dishes, tuna sashimi is handsomely laid out on a wooden palette garnished with threads of bright green seaweed.

Finally, the restaurant makes some big, tasty rice balls, called *onigiri*, that satisfy that last bit of hunger at the end of a meal. Slightly salty rice is pressed together, filled with bits of salmon or sour plum sauce and wrapped in big sheets of seaweed. My choice will forever be a large squid stuffed with ginger and wasabi-seasoned rice, grilled and then cut into round slices.

Even though the menu can be baffling for Westerners who have never been to a *robata* before, you don't have to worry about misordering. A meal here is made up of many small dishes, so if you get something you don't like you can just write it off to experience. I have found that I've loved practically everything I've ordered at Mitoya, including some preparations I've never tasted before. The food is very fresh, sensitively seasoned, carefully cooked, and attractively presented, which makes any kind of cooking, no matter how exotic, taste good. The fact that Mitoya offers hundreds of small dishes, many of which are not seen on the repetitive menus of other San Francisco Japanese restaurants, is reason enough to rejoice. ■

—Patricia Unterman, November 23, 1986

Modesto Lanzone's

★

Opera Plaza (bounded by Van Ness and Franklin, Golden Gate and Turk), San Francisco. 928-0400. Open Monday through Saturday 5 P.M. to midnight. Full bar. Major credit cards. Reservations recommended. Moderate to expensive.

Opera Plaza has never been a cheerful place architecturally, but these days it's looking even a bit more gloomy than usual. Kundan, the elegant Indian restaurant, has closed, and at Modesto Lanzone's there is a handwritten sign on the door saying that it's no longer open for lunch.

Once inside Modesto's, however, you're in another world. Lanzone, a modern art collector of impeccable taste, has made his restaurant a museum that rivals in quality lots of more conventional modern art museums. The pieces constantly change; I saw several wonderful sculptures and paintings that weren't there on my last visit a couple of years ago.

Would that the menu kept up with the times as successfully as the art. Although Lanzone has turned over the operation of his original Ghirardelli Square restaurant to his son and is presumably now able to concentrate on Opera Plaza, he still hasn't revamped the menu to include new and exciting dishes. Being locked into the past is an affliction that Modesto's shares with much of the San Francisco Italian restaurant scene.

What has changed, however, are the prices. Salads and entrees remain fairly reasonable, but appetizers and pastas have soared into the stratosphere. Five of the eight appetizers are over $10, and the cheapest is not much less. A platter of risotto for two boggles the mind at well over $20, proving once again that the Italian word *risotto* seems to carry some magic that's lacking in its English translation, "rice." I wonder how many people would pay that much for something called "rice prepared Italian-style"?

I recently had two huge dinners at Modesto's (no one will ever complain about skimpy portions here) to see what's been happening with the food. While the menu may not be terribly innovative, Modesto's kitchen in the past has cooked many things with extraordinary skill.

What I found was a very strange mixture. There were some lovely dishes--and, oddly enough, many of them were among the cheapest ones. But others proved leaden and boring, about as boring as the supermarket-type mushrooms included in so many of the entrees.

Consider starters as an example. You can choose a fatty, flavorless slice of cold stuffed breast of veal; it was a complete disaster. Or you can order mozzarella cheese with tomatoes in olive oil, but the cheese and tomatoes had very little taste. There was also an antipasto of squid and zucchini that proved much too oily; the dish was redeemed only by a nice piece of plain poached salmon.

But you can also have a beautiful bowl of thick minestrone soup, filled with vegetables that weren't the least bit overcooked. Or there's the soup of the day; our chicken soup, with its rich broth and shreds of tender chicken and vegetables,

would have done any Jewish mother proud.

The salads, elegantly prepared at tableside, were terrific, too. The spinach salad was slightly wilted by a hot dressing, which included flambeed brandy along with olive oil, vinegar, and meaty bits of bacon. It was plenty to serve two people.

For pasta, I'd stick with my old favorite, the *guanciali ai funghi*, which I remember fondly going back at least a decade. Tender pillows of pasta are stuffed with ricotta and topped with a garlicky sauce of mushrooms and tomatoes. A few wild mushrooms would have made this dish absolute heaven.

The risotto was grandly named *ai frutti di mare*, but in this case, the fruit of the sea turned out to be nothing more than pieces of squid with a couple of really awful shrimp thrown in. But the rice itself, made with fish stock and what must have been a pound of butter, was gloriously prepared.

The entrees varied all over the map. Chicken Jerusalem and eggplant parmigiana had their points, but the former suffered from an intolerably heavy sour cream sauce, and the latter from too much cheese and a completely bland tomato sauce. No complaints can be aimed at the veal piccata, however; the meat was fork tender and the butter-lemon sauce with capers light and delicate.

Two of the nicest entrees were among the cheapest on the menu. The rabbit saute was perfection, with fresh-tasting, juicy meat and a butter sauce enlivened by red and green peppers, capers, and olives. The sweetbreads were delightfully tender, and the light wine sauce didn't intrude.

It's often said that you can do best at Modesto's by ordering specials, because the kitchen pays more attention to them. But the two specials I tried proved unmitigated disasters. Sauteed calamari was overcooked to rubber-tire oblivion and presented in a tomato sauce that had not a bit of seasoning. And a breast of capon in marsala wine sauce was dry and boring, helped not a bit by the ubiquitous mushrooms that appeared in so many of the entrees.

When the pastry cart rolls by, look in the other direction. Some are made on the premises and others come from Italian bakeries, but all the ones I tasted were overly sweet and overly gloppy. A much better choice is the hot, frothy zabaglione.

Anyone who walked into Modesto's and ordered a soup or salad, followed by the rabbit or sweetbreads, is likely to leave delighted, and with a reasonable check. And, while the wine list is generally expensive, you can do very well with the house red, a soft and fruity barbera d'Alba.

But Modesto's, with its national reputation and world-class art, should be doing better than this in the food department. It's time for some innovative new dishes that can match in excitement the paintings on the walls. ■

—Stan Sesser, July 10, 1987

Moshi Moshi

★

2092 Third Street (at Eighteenth), San Francisco. 861-8285. Open for lunch Monday through Friday 11:30 A.M. to 3 P.M., for dinner Monday through Thursday 5 to 9:30 P.M., Friday and Saturday until 10 P.M. Beer, wine. MasterCard, Visa. No reservations. Inexpensive.

Esther's Ironworks Cafe

★

657 Harrison (between Second and Third streets), San Francisco. 543-6242. Open Monday through Friday 7 A.M. to 3 P.M. Beer, wine. No credit cards. No reservations. Inexpensive.

We expect to find lots of restaurants on commercial avenues running through established residential neighborhoods. So many have opened, as a matter of fact, that there are restaurant moratoriums on Clement Street, Union Street, Fillmore Street, Polk Street, Castro Street, and Twenty-fourth Street. As a result, restaurants are beginning to pop up in new places, in locations where you would not expect a restaurant to survive.

When you stumble upon one of these out-of-the-way eateries, you realize two things — that people who live and work in any neighborhood will support a good local restaurant; and that the restaurants themselves have a unique character and spirit that comes from pioneering an area. A common element in these two restaurants is that their rents and, concomitantly, their prices, are refreshingly low.

Moshi Moshi

When a friend of mine who prides herself on discovering obscure places guided me to Moshi Moshi, I was amazed to see a pleasantly full dining room at eight o'clock one night. There wasn't much street life in this neighborhood of warehouses of various sizes. However, in one of those warehouses two blocks away is a Safeway-sized outlet for the Esprit clothing and shoe line; and a short distance up the hill is the burgeoning Potrero Hill community, which has been crying out for good family restaurants for years.

Moshi Moshi is charming, a simple renovation of an ancient corner bar. The designer used the colors of nineteenth-century Japanese prints. Big square windows cut into the walls are framed in dark green paint. Lighter, sea-green lower walls and green shades are set off by a beige ceiling and upper walls. The floors have been carpeted and a platformed dining area demarcated with handcrafted wooden railings. Boxy wooden chairs also have a handmade look. The tables are covered with white linen. A high counter with a large vase of flowers in front of a service area affords five or six extra seats. Some of the kitchen is visible from the dining room, and it is so neat and shiny it adds to the decor. A white canvas hangs outside a side door, hiding a yard of broken-down buses next door. A modest amount of money was spent, but the return is large. When you walk in, you're taken by surprise by the aesthetics of it all.

As you would expect, the food is artfully presented and arranged. Everyone is brought a deep, square porcelain bowl with marinated Japanese cucumbers at the bottom. With most meals you also get a bowl of chicken broth.

The best dish here is the buckwheat *gyoza*, dumplings with tender brown wrappers and a succulent meat filling. They're served with a Western-style green salad, a breaded potato pancake, and an addictive dipping sauce of hot pepper, soy sauce, and vinegar that you end up using on everything.

Another standout dish on the small menu is chicken teriyaki, as good a version as I've tasted. The flattened pieces of chicken were butter-tender and juicy, and the syrupy teriyaki sauce achieved a good balance of sweet and sour.

The tempura is passable. It was not crisp or light enough in texture for my taste and the traditional ginger-soy dipping sauce here was not lively enough. The most unusual item on the menu, lobster *isobe age*, turned out to be deep-fried chunks of lobster wrapped in seaweed and dipped in tempura batter, which sounded wonderful but turned out to be bland. A brown, cornstarch-thickened gravy didn't help. As fine as the chicken teriyaki was, the seafood *kushi yaki*, skewers of scallops, rockfish, squid, and vegetables were a bit dry and their teriyaki-style sauce too sweet.

The fried and breaded potato pancake comes with everything instead of rice, and it fits into the Westernized style of this restaurant.

Moshi Moshi does offer high-quality sashimi and sushi. Perhaps because it is an offshoot of the now-closed Nikko on Van Ness, which is known for its sushi bar, the tuna is exceptionally fresh, tasty, and firm and the sushi beautifully presented.

What's fun about this small Japanese restaurant is that you can get a complete meal for around $6 or $7; the surroundings are unexpectedly handsome; and if you live or work anywhere near the neighborhood, Moshi Moshi provides a much-needed oasis for eating out.

Esther's Ironworks Cafe

The neighborhood around Esther's Ironworks Cafe is changing more quickly than Moshi Moshi's because of its proximity to the Moscone Convention Center. But Esther's location is certainly a pioneering effort. With its gently punk/low-tech decor and eye-catching asymmetrical entryway, you don't expect the kitchen to serve hearty, made-from-scratch soups like a delicious beef vegetable or a rice and vegetable casserole slightly upscaled from the vegetarian era. Salads, which accompany most of the hot dishes and sandwiches, are made with fresh, crisp greens and vegetables and get a real sour-cream dressing. The kitchen doesn't hold back on the imported black olives and the pickled cherry peppers, either.

A daily special might be a simple lasagna with a high ratio of Italian sausage and ricotta cheese to pasta. Another good bet is the *muffaleta*, a vaguely New Orleans-style poor boy distinguished by pickled red and yellow peppers.

You order this bright, fresh, and inexpensive food at a counter and then wait for your name to be called in the Ironworks's attractive little dining room that looks out onto Harrison Street. I noticed that many customers picked up food to go. For those who eat lunch out every day in the area, the Ironworks Cafe's homey food and affordable prices must be a welcome respite from pricy, downtown commercial operations.

—Patricia Unterman, December 1, 1985

Mudd's

★★

10 Boardwalk, San Ramon. 837-9387. Open Monday through Friday for lunch 11:30 A.M. to 2:30 P.M.; for dinner Wednesday through Saturday 5:30 to 10 P.M., Sunday 5 to 9 P.M.; for brunch Sunday 10 A.M. to 2 P.M. Full bar. Major credit cards. Reservations accepted. Moderate.

The proximity of the garden to the kitchen makes a restaurant's food special. It certainly was the charm behind the now-closed New Boonville Hotel. I remember chef-owner Charlene Rollins going out to the garden to pick what we had just ordered. As anyone who has eaten from a garden knows, the fruits, vegetables, and herbs that have been picked minutes before they are eaten have a taste all their own. There's no duplicating the flavor even with the most careful handling, shipping, and refrigeration. This understanding of the importance of the garden, of growing techniques, of species of plants, of freshness, is the pulse behind "California" cooking and the Boonville epitomized it.

Well, another California garden restaurant has been quietly growing much of its own produce on a three-acre enclave of edible landscape and nature preserve in San Ramon. Founded by Virginia Mudd five years ago, Crow Canyon Gardens and her eponymously named restaurant are parts of an ambitious project that includes the nonprofit, educational Crow Canyon Institute. The restaurant building has won awards for its self-sufficient, energy-saving design, and recently a new young chef who apprenticed for several years at the estimable West Beach Cafe in Venice has taken over the kitchen. On my most recent visit, I felt that Mudd's had finally shifted over from amateurish, though sometimes inspired, performance to a fully realized restaurant. All the facets of the operation seem to be working well at last.

The restaurant building has always been noteworthy for its skillfully carpentered redwood construction. You don't notice the passive solar energy collectors or the circulating hot-water system or the gravitation-flow toilets or the fact that all the landscaping is edible. What you do see is a low-slung wooden building with several wings and long rooms. The arched ceilings are covered with wood slats; the windows are beautifully framed; the floors are paved with handsome terra cotta tiles. On warm days a patio right in the middle of the gardens provides glorious outdoor seating. A rainbow of flowers from the gardens always decorates the white-linened table.

The service used to be clumsy and uninformed. Now it is top-notch. The waitresses know how to serve correctly; they're well informed about the menu and the California wine list; and they're efficient without being intrusive. The serving staff certainly brings City standards of sophistication to their job.

The kitchen has improved enormously in consistency. There wasn't one lapse on the menu. The food is beautiful, wondrously fresh, colorful, and always tasty. The menu concentrates on what has come ripe in the gardens. One night the tomatoes must have been plentiful for we were served a delightful soup, really more like a chunky tomato and basil stew, topped with a dab of crème fraîche. A hot, spicy puree of red peppers, carrots, and tomatoes with a rich chicken broth base married all its divergent flavors deliciously. Salads here look like miniature gardens. Not only are they made with a variety of perfect, freshly picked lettuces, but with all sorts of edible flowers and herbs as well. I would have liked, however, a lustier vinaigrette, perhaps infused with some shallots or garlic.

Everyone seems to be doing pastas now, but few of these noodle dishes are really satisfying. This is not the case at Mudd's, which puts out a transcendent vegetarian lasagna. The noodles are layered with locally made Ferrante mozzarella and ricotta and crisp grilled vegetables finely chopped and folded into the cheese. The top gets a fresh tomato sauce and lots of parmesan. Each bite delivers the flavors and textures of many different, slightly smoky vegetables. The colorful bouquet of small garden vegetables, warmed through and dressed with rosemary and olive oil that come with it, don't seem repetitive though some of the same vegetables are used in the lasagna. The effect is different.

Another delicious pasta one night combined tender fettuccine noodles and some delicately cooked clams, scallops, and shrimp in a buttery *marinière* sauce. Entwined in the pasta were tiny green and yellow beans, thin strips of pepper, and squashes. How refreshing to get such carefully cooked seafood in a sauce other than tomato!

The main courses did not let us down as they have in the past. Skate wing came out of the saute pan crisp and traditionally sauced in a brown butter, albeit scented with ginger and green peppercorns instead of capers. A slab of roast beef, gently blackened with Cajun spices, also got a lively red wine sauce, a slathering of garlicky mushrooms, and roasted Japanese eggplant and potatoes. A crisp-skinned game hen, stuffed with a savory apple and bread dressing, stayed moist and tender during roasting. Only an overdone fillet of salmon in a disconcertingly sweet lemon and caper sauce (did the kitchen use meyer lemons?) did not live up to the rest of the meal.

All the plates are decorated with sprigs of herbs and edible flowers and mounds of marvelous vegetables from the garden—baby carrots, tiny yellow pear tomatoes, squashes the size of large marbles, rings of the sweetest red and green peppers, string-sized green beans, and juicy red tomatoes.

The pastry chef knows how to work with chocolate, but I wanted fruit desserts after this garden-inspired meal. There's a very seductive black-bottom pecan pie that melts in your mouth like a great candy bar, and one of those souffleed chocolate cakes, light textured but intensely rich. The berry sorbets have a smooth texture but not enough fruit flavor. A strawberry and pear pie boasts a good, flaky crust, but the lime zest, fresh ginger, and dearth of sugar in the filling make it taste a bit medicinal.

Discipline finally combines with exuberance in Mudd's kitchen. The plates come out looking like garden fantasies, but they're held down to earth by careful cooking and top-notch meats, poultry, and seafood. ■

—Patricia Unterman, October 26, 1986

Neiman-Marcus—The Rotunda

★

150 Stockton, San Francisco. 362-4777. Open for lunch Monday through Friday 11 A.M. to 3 P.M., Saturday 11 A.M. to 4 P.M.; for high tea Thursday through Saturday 3 to 5 P.M. Full bar. Neiman-Marcus credit cards, American Express. Reservations accepted.

The Plum at Macy's Annex

★

120 Stockton, San Francisco. 984-7463. Open Monday through Friday 11 A.M. to 8 P.M., Saturday 11 A.M. to 5 P.M. Full bar. Macy's cards, American Express. Reservations accepted.

The Orchard-In

★

75 O'Farrell Street, San Francisco. 986-5069. Open Monday through Saturday 7:30 A.M. to 4:30 P.M. Beer, wine. MasterCard, Visa. Reservations accepted. Food to go.

French Room at the Clift Hotel

Geary and Taylor streets, San Francisco. 775-4700. Open daily noon to 2 P.M., 6 to 10:30 P.M. Full bar. Major credit cards. Reservations accepted.

You've hit the wall. It's only five days until Christmas and you can't look at another sweater, think of yet another clever but affordable gift, or push your way through the crowds gazing at store windows around Union Square. You're hungry. Your back aches. You want lunch.

You're in partial luck. Every major department store has a dining room and most have a policy of reserving only a limited portion of their tables each day during the holidays, thereby leaving places for hungry, spur-of-the-moment diners to eat. Some qualifications: You will probably have to wait if you don't have a coveted reservation, but most department store dining rooms will take your name and tell you when they expect a table to open, allowing you to fit in a little chunk of shopping while anticipating lunch. Also, no maitre d' will seat you without your full party in attendance, whether you have reservations or not. So be on time if you're meeting someone.

The Rotunda at Neiman-Marcus

The Rotunda at Neiman-Marcus tries very hard to provide a festive and comfortable lunch. The maitre d's are tactful but firm in their task of matching grumpy shoppers with the first available tables and the wait staff knows how to endear themselves to their clientele, mostly of women. It really is quite wonderful to sink into the roomy upholstered booths in the glass-domed, tiered dining room that overlooks the store and be brought demitasses of lemony chicken broth while you ponder the menu. One day the broth was a shot of energy; another day it was too salty. Another Rotunda lagniappe is the warm, airy popovers brought to every table with whipped blackberry butter. They alone could get me to The Rotunda. An ample wine list and a full bar for those midday martinis can change the whole tone of frenzied holiday shopping.

Half the lunch dishes I sampled were fine, like two small tender lamb chops, grilled exactly to specification, with crisp wild-rice pancakes, a deep-flavored sauce infused with roasted garlic and sage, and some fresh, buttery green beans and carrots. However, a half chicken nicely browned was juiceless and boring in a pool of sweet cream sauce flavored with calvados and apples. At another lunch, a lobster sandwich on a grilled brioche with roasted peppers and avocado turned out to be a sophisticated and yummy tidbit, but a warm duck *confit* salad with wet stewed duck on underdressed greens missed the mark entirely.

For dessert, there's a sundae with Double Rainbow's rich, nutty pecan ice cream drizzled with a bourbon-spiked caramel sauce that I find irresistible.

For a special, albeit pricy, lunch with dishes of varying success, The Rotunda offers all the amenities.

The Plum at Macy's Annex

One of the best kept lunchtime secrets downtown is The Plum in Macy's Annex. Hidden away at the back of the basement with a cafeteria section in front of it, The Plum puts out good, straightforward lunches with all the amenities for very reasonable prices. The soothing gray dining rooms, outfitted with carpeting, soft upholstered chairs, old photos of San Francisco, and pink linen tablecloths, take you away from the bustle of shopping. The staff is pleasant and efficient, which means you can eat relatively quickly if you want.

The daily soup, like a hearty lentil with a beef broth full of finely chopped vegetables, is always a good bet here, as is the handsome salad nicoise, a glass bowl full of chunky canned tuna, potato slices, slender, crisp green beans, anchovies, capers, olives, and tomatoes in a lively vinaigrette. The star dish at The Plum is the calf's liver, three or four thin, buttery slices, sauteed perfectly to bring out their natural sweetness and creamy texture, topped with a sauteed avocado half. The combination works magically. You also get a scoop of The Plum's delicious, chunky carrot and onion melange, and some tired precooked broccoli. An open-faced crab sandwich was made with old-smelling, seemingly defrosted crab meat. Coffee is excellent; pastries, brought in from various bakeries, are on the heavy side. The carrot cake had the density of a fruit cake, but all the right carroty flavors. Cocktails as well as eight different wines are sold by the glass, a selection much appreciated at lunch when you don't want to order a whole bottle.

At The Plum you get the full restaurant treatment for bargain prices and the convenience of being right in the store.

Orchard-In

If you have ever worked downtown, you know about the Orchard-In, a tiny, cheerful cafeteria right behind Macy's Annex on O'Farrell. Eight or ten small tables with ice cream parlor chairs are crowded into this little box of a room, currently decked out with Christmas lights, wreaths, and decorations. It's a sweet, tearoomy kind of place run by kindly women in pink uniforms, but you'll see plenty of men as well as women ordering the delicious American sandwiches, the freshly made pies, and bowls of thick spinach puree topped with an hard-boiled egg, for which the place is famous. This spinach puree, called spinach soup here, is bright green, full of true spinach flavor, and soothingly bland. The hard-boiled egg and some salt really work wonders on it. As for the sandwiches, one of my favorites is a moist egg salad with a slice of Danish ham and shredded lettuce on thick, airy slices of white bread. A pickley, finely chopped potato salad is served with it. The Orchard also makes excellent "smoothies," which blend a mixture of fresh fruits with yogurt and honey in just the right proportions. The apple pie is piled high with fat slices of crisp apple and crumbly crust. The Orchard-In is the right place for a wholesome quick lunch, and is particularly useful if you have lost your mind and are shopping with children.

French Room at the Clift Hotel

We tend to eat and drink too much during the holiday season and sometimes we want the respite of lunch without loading up on calories. I thought the luxurious, Louis XV decor of the French Room of the Clift Hotel would be just the ticket. The kitchen offers "Alternative Cuisine" dishes that run less than 500 calories each at lunch and 650 at dinner and are low in cholesterol and sodium. A sampling of these dishes turned up mixed results. Very successful was an appetizer of paper-thin slices of eggplant and tomato dusted with parmesan cheese and broiled. The cooked juices of the seared vegetables provided ample flavor. Also first-rate was a moist grilled breast of chicken with a tasty mushroom compote and brightly steamed vegetables. However, dry, overcooked scallops of veal paired with doughy noodles and a vapid red pepper puree represented the worst of spa food and an open-faced sandwich of tired scallops and salmon submerged in a thick, flat-tasting sour cream dill sauce held no charms at all.

Our waitress was brusque to the point of rudeness, just what you wouldn't expect in this gracious room.

I applaud the Clift's idea of offering nicely served low-calorie dishes, but sloppiness in execution dampens my enthusiasm. If anything, the naked or hardly sauced foods in low-calorie dishes should be particularly fresh and sensitively cooked. ■

—Patricia Unterman, December 21, 1986

New Central Restaurant
★

301 South Van Ness (at Fourteenth Street), San Francisco. 431-8587. Open daily 8 A.M. to 9 P.M. Beer, wine. No credit cards. Reservations accepted, maybe—a language barrier. Inexpensive.

The New Central Cafe is a family-run operation with an open kitchen and a barebones dining room, though the service is efficient. The New Central is known for its wonderful, thick handmade corn tortillas, excellent carne asada, and aromatic Mexican stews.

My favorite dish here is carnitas, succulent deep-fried marinated chunks of pork topped with a fresh salsa of tomatoes and onions. The frying fat is clean and neutral so it seals in the silken texture of the meat without adding its own flavor.

When you eat the carnitas with New Central's warm tortillas, you get very close to perfection. Another gorgeous combination is New Central's chili colorado, a mouth-watering stew of pork, hot and sweet peppers, and a tasty red sauce. The dominant flavors are green pepper and garlic.

The other specialty, carne asada, comes in different forms, though the one I like the best is the carne asada taco that comes on the handmade tortilla. The thin grilled steak is coarsely chopped and topped with fresh tomato-and-onion salsa with chopped cilantro.

The quesadillas come on corn tortillas and are topped with a cooked tomato-and-onion sauce and shredded lettuce—halfway between a melted cheese sandwich and a salad. They're delicious.

You get an important impression of any restaurant from the first thing you eat there, whether it be bread and butter or kimchee or breadsticks. At New Central, a basket of warm, thick, crisp tortilla chips is set on the table along with a fiery, but not impossibly hot, house-made salsa. They're both so well-done that you know that whatever follows will be tasty. ∎

—Patricia Unterman, October 27, 1985

Nyala Ethiopian Restaurant

★ ★

39A Grove Street (near Polk), San Francisco. 861-0788. Open Monday through Friday 11 A.M. to 11 P.M., Saturday and Sunday 4 to 11 P.M. Full bar. MasterCard, Visa, American Express. Reservations accepted. Inexpensive.

Every time a new restaurant opens serving California cuisine, I get the same nightmare. I worry that soon there will be no other sort of restaurant left, that each week I'll be doomed to review the latest version of mesquite-grilled monkfish.

But now something has happened that's going to produce some pleasant dreams. It involves a place near San Francisco's City Hall where I had made the monkfish rounds in the past at two California cuisine restaurants that failed— first at Le Vaudeville, then at its successor, 39 Grove. In an area that seems able to support an endless number of new restaurants, some of them pretty awful, this location seemed jinxed.

However, a new restaurant has opened there that from all indications is booming. And it serves food that's as far removed from mesquite-grilled monkfish as you can get. Its name is Nyala, and the cuisine is Ethiopian.

To anyone who ever ate at Le Vaudeville, ordering Ethiopian food in such a setting can be a little jarring. The surroundings at Le Vaudeville were as trendy as you can get, with brass railings and exposed pipes in pastel colors a la the Pompidou Center in Paris. 39 Grove painted the railings black and the pipes gray, and Nyala hung some Ethiopian travel post-

ers, but you still expect at any moment to be assaulted with slices of pink duck breast.

The change in prices is jarring, too. I remember how expensive it used to be to eat at the same tables. Now the same amount will feed six people.

Ethiopian food really can be fun. Meals are built around *injera*, the cold moist bread that looks like a cross between a giant pancake and a chamois. *Injeras* are spread across the middle of the table, and on them are heaped various spicy stews that are the essence of Ethiopian cuisine. You take your own *injera*, tear off a piece, and reach into one of the stews to make an instant sandwich.

Nyala started out on the philosophy of doing a few things well, then added specials to the menu as the restaurant found its stride. At the moment there are only four meat dishes, a combination platter featuring three of them, and a vegetarian platter.

But there are also on the menu four Italian dishes, or, more precisely, Italian dishes cooked Ethiopian-style. Italian food in an Ethiopian restaurant?

Owner Fesseha Araya, who goes by the nickname "Fish," and who can speak to you in Spanish or Italian if you don't know any English or Ethiopian, says it's a logical extension of his growing up in northern Ethiopia, a land once occupied by Mussolini. "Ethiopians there eat a lot of spaghetti," he reports.

What does Italian food cooked Ethiopian style taste like? If it's lasagna, it's really good. You get the noodles, ricotta cheese, garlic and meat sauce that you'd expect. But you also get some jalapeno peppers to spice things up and a rich buttery taste. With Ethiopian-style mustard greens and summer squash on the side and a surprisingly good tossed salad, it's actually one of the better lasagnas in the city.

I was less thrilled with the spaghetti. The meat sauce was decent, although there just wasn't enough of it.

But it wasn't Italian food I came to Nyala to eat. It was, among other things, *doro wat*, the slowly simmered chicken in a spicy dark brown sauce that's Ethiopia's most famous dish. Nyala's version is first-rate, incredibly rich and buttery, scented with garlic, cardamom, and ginger, and aflame with the mixture of ground peppers called *berberé*.

Nyala shares a peculiar trait with Sheba, the excellent Ethiopian restaurant on Telegraph Avenue in Oakland. If you order the *doro wat* alone, you get a chicken leg and a hard-boiled egg. For just a little more on the combination plate, you get the same portion of chicken—minus the egg—plus two other meat dishes. I'd gladly sacrifice the egg for the beef and lamb stews the combination plate includes.

The lamb dish, called *alecha wat*, is every bit as good as the chicken. Chunks of lamb, fat free and tender, are cooked with clarified butter, ginger, turmeric, and green chilies. The beef is called *tibbs*, and it's sauteed with butter, onions, chilies, and garlic. The beef chunks themselves were excellent, but there was an unpleasant, raw peppery taste that came from too much of the Ethiopian equivalent of cayenne.

The fourth thing on the Ethiopian side of the menu is *kitfo*, which combines raw ground beef with butter and spices. Alongside, you get a sort of dried cottage cheese made from buttermilk, and you mix the two together. It's delicious, but order the beef cooked; they're happy to do it. No matter how clean the restaurant, any raw beef poses danger.

Nyala seems to have evolved into two shifts: Early on is the opera and symphony crowd, then later at night mostly Ethiopians. Both crowds should be pleased. In what was once a temple of expensive California cuisine, you can get first-rate Ethiopian food at bargain prices. ■

—Stan Sesser, September 12, 1986

Ocean City

644 Broadway, San Francisco. 982-2328. Open daily for dim sum 8 A.M. to 3 P.M., for dinner 5 to 10 P.M. Beer, wine. MasterCard, Visa, American Express. Reservations accepted. Inexpensive.

Ocean King

★

684 Broadway, San Francisco. 989-8821. Open daily 11 A.M. to 3 A.M. MasterCard, Visa. Beer, wine. Reservations accepted. Inexpensive.

One would think that after twenty years of living in San Francisco, an avid eater like me would know how to get a good meal in Chinatown. I don't. I proved that to myself last week when I invited Ken Hom to dinner. He's the reigning expert on Cantonese food in Hong Kong, the author of two best-selling books on Chinese cooking, and the star of a wildly popular British television cooking show. He also takes select groups on culinary tours of Hong Kong where they market and cook as well as eat out in Hong Kong restaurants.

Ocean City

I wanted him to come with me to Ocean City, one of the glitzy, new Hong Kong–style restaurants that are popping up on the second and third floors of renovated commercial buildings in the city. [See Yank Sing review for Ocean City dim sum service.]

Ocean City takes up the whole second floor of a new development on Broadway above the World Theater. A young woman stationed by the front door in a white rabbit fur jacket sends diners up to the restaurant in an already battered elevator. You are let out in a huge carpeted room with a sea of white-linened tables and faux-stained-glass insets in the ceiling. The most notable features of the dining room are handsome lacquered wooden chairs with curved backs and a view of Broadway from the tables by the windows. However, most of the patrons—large parties of babies and grandparents and everyone in between—sit at the opposite end of the restaurant, in back. The waiters all wear identification tags with mug shots clipped to their jackets. Hom said that was a new Hong Kong practice that allows customers to identify waiters who give them bad service.

As usual, we were handed menus with pages and pages of dishes. My heart falls when I'm confronted with one of these tomes. How can a kitchen possibly turn out hundreds of dishes well? How can you deduce the restaurant's strengths, especially if you can't read Chinese?

But this time I had Hom. He gave the menu a cursory glance, mostly looking at the specials written in Chinese. An unusually large number of squab dishes were listed. Hom, speaking Cantonese, asked our waiter, who had just come from Hong Kong, about the squab. The waiter told him it didn't have the flavor of Hong Kong squab. Hom put down the menu and asked what live seafood was available. We ended up with one crab and one lobster, both simply wok-steamed with ginger and scallions; a plate of Chinese greens barely but tastily dressed with a little soy sauce and aromatic stock; and a clay pot of taro, chicken, and black mushrooms. All of it was delicious.

Both the crab and the lobster were sweet, moist, and delicately perfumed with ginger and garlic. The amount of time they spent in the wok was accurate to the split second. The flesh was just cooked and miraculously silky and tender. Nothing masked the fine quality of the raw materials.

The clay pot dish held whole black mushrooms, pieces of tender chicken, and squares of taro, a starchy root vegetable that produces a creamy sauce as it cooks in the clay pot. The squares of taro had a little bite left in them, which I did not find unpleasant. Hom said they should have been softer.

Ocean King

We then moved up the street to less fancy quarters, Ocean King, which has tanks of crabs and fish in its front windows. Once again, the menu was cursorily consulted, though there was a lengthy talk with a personable waiter in Cantonese and English.

This time we ended up with several eel, netted from the tank, cut into disks, and braised in a thickened brown sauce with whole cloves of garlic and lots of onion. It was a marvelous dish, more thickly sauced than it would have been in Hong Kong, where, Hom said, stocks are richer and need less bolstering. We popped the circles of eel into our mouths and spit out the bones.

A classic preparation of clams in rich, musky black bean sauce had no off-flavors and you could taste the garlic, fresh coriander, and ginger clearly. The meeting of clam and salted black bean is a fortuitous one. Also wonderful at Ocean King was an appetizer recommended by the waiter called Chiu Chao egg roll, a tofu skin wrapped around a filling of water chestnut, rice, pork, and shrimp, then cut into rounds and deep fried.

To finish off the meal, we were brought a large, very fresh catfish, steamed with ginger and green onions. In addition to the carefully prepared dishes, the rice here was particularly tasty, each grain dry and separate with a nutty flavor, like basmati rice.

By this time I felt like I was getting the hang of eating out in Chinatown. The rule was to go for freshness and the simplest of preparations. Base a meal around what you like—vegetables, seafood, noodles, what have you—and rather than consulting the menu, tell the waiter what you want and how you like it prepared. ■

—Patricia Unterman, December 22, 1985

Ocean King (Dim Sum)

★

See review for Yank Sing.

Oishi/So: Too

★ ★ ★

1019 Camelia Street, Berkeley. 525-9443. Open for lunch Monday and Wednesday through Friday 11:30 to 2 P.M., for dinner Wednesday through Monday 5 to 10 P.M. Closed Tuesday. Beer, wine, sake. MasterCard, Visa, American Express. Reservations accepted. Moderate.

Kaiseki is an elevated form of Japanese cooking that evolved centuries ago as an adjunct to the ritual of the tea ceremony. Its principles are simple but rigorous: Only the freshest ingredients of the highest quality are used. Dishes must reflect the season and be appropriate to the occasion. The dishes must be presented and arranged in artful, carefully chosen containers. In a broad sense, *kaiseki* is to everyday Japanese cooking what haute cuisine is to cuisine bourgeoise. The aesthetic goes beyond competent preparation of food into a realm that delights four of the senses. The difference between Japanese *kaiseki* and French haute cuisine is the intervention of Zen sensibility that insists on perfect but everyday ingredients, beauty without ostentation, and a "less is more" approach to the amount of food being served. In either case, the quotidian experience of eating a meal is raised to a confrontation with art.

Oishi/so:too is a tiny new sushi restaurant in Berkeley that gives Westerners an exhilarating taste of *kaiseki* cooking. This restaurant is the most exciting discovery of the year. All the commonly served sushi, appetizers, and miso soups are transformed into something new and brilliant. I realize that "brilliant" suggests some kind of showiness or extravagance that is not part of this place, but the personal aesthetic expression of the three people who own and cook here come through so clearly, so individually, that I'm moved to use Western hyperbole.

The dining room of Oishi/so is as strong and subdued as a rustic piece of pottery from the Edo period. The color scheme is limited to mauve and different shades of gray. There's one red brick wall, contributed by the converted brick warehouse that Oishi/so is in, one cementlike wall, and one smoothly plastered wall. The Memphis-style tables and chairs are made of lacquered blond plywood with black, tapered, triangular legs—a Japanese turn on the usual speckles and bright colors of this furniture. Small, black Italian light fixtures hang from the high ceiling. Large, colorful wooden replicas of sushi hung behind the sushi bar and a striking sliced-off dome at one end are the only self-conscious decoration, though pottery filled with austere Japanese flower arrangements are displayed on obelisklike platforms in a couple of places. New wave licks the shores of Japanese tradition at Oishi/so:too.

The food carries the marriage of new and traditional a step further. Oishi/so means "looks tasty" in Japanese, a comment that the three partners jokingly throw off when one of them invents a new dish. Indeed, all the food looks breathtakingly beautiful at this restaurant. Each sushi, each soup, each *maki* comes on graceful pottery made by Berkeley ceramicist Ryusei Arita based on old designs. A glorious red *miso* soup, with a rich, delicious broth afloat with pine nuts, enoki mushrooms, a tiny squash with its blossom, and a barely translucent butterflied shrimp is served in an thick pottery bowl with a cover. Each sip brings a surprise. *Gohan*, a daily rice dish dotted with roasted cashews, pickled japanese eggplant in psychedelic purple, and dried papaya, comes in a small, deep bowl with a lip. Something unexpected is revealed about rice in this dish, both in flavor and appearance.

A daily appetizer called *tsu/kidashi* is served in a handsome square pottery container, glazed dark outside, light inside, with a jewellike arrangement of pickled mackerel, ripe and unripe peach slightly gingered, minced scallion, and macadamia nuts. It tasted like a transposed herring and apple salad.

Sushi is not merely rice draped with fish here, but miniature works of visual and culinary art. Seaweed-wrapped ovals of rice hold bright orange flying fish roe, pistachios, and a tiny cucumber fan. Octopus is brushed with a a sweet sauce, cinched in seaweed, and sprinkled with purple chia seeds. Grilled freshwater eel gets two tiny strips of orange peel tucked beneath its seaweed belt. The ever-popular yellowtail, or *hamachi*, is slashed with a pencil-thin spear of asparagus on one piece, a microscopic mince of scallion on the other, and a sprinkling of toasted macadamias over all.

The chefs' use of nuts in practically every dish works surprisingly well. The earthy, quiet flavor of nuts harmonizes with rice and fish and they add an interesting texture and buttery richness to everything. I never once felt they were out of place or unnecessary. In fact, what is so special about the sushi at oishi/so was that so many new ingredients are used so effectively.

A special sushi, left to the whim of the chef, was constructed of a paper-thin sheet of cucumber rolled into a cylinder and stuffed with rice, smoked salmon, macadamias, and a *shiso* leaf. The textures, the flavors, the contrasts, subtle but effervescent, showed off the depth of this sushi chef's talent. I was further impressed by a *maki*, a rolled sushi, of yellowtail, mango, nuts, pickle, and a hint of scallion that tasted so intriguing, it soared beyond California and Japanese sushi styles into some other world. A special *maki*, again left to the invention of the chef, brought six fat rolls filled with an abstract expressionist design made of shrimp, honeydew, bright orange burdock root, radicchio, and pistachios. All the *maki*, seaweed-wrapped logs sliced into six pieces, come in lovely bowls in special arrangements. Your eye is engaged first and then your palate catches up. The whole experience made me very happy.

We have many sushi bars in the Bay Area and many of them serve delicious sushi made with skillfully cooked rice and fresh-smelling fish. A few places like Kabuto on Geary Boulevard have inspired sushi chefs that use a great variety of ingredients, experiment with local fish, and are intensely creative within a strictly proscribed aesthetic. Oishi/so:too is one of these places and I'm glad it's in a hidden away in a corner of Berkeley, not of Japan. ∎

—Patricia Unterman, July 13, 1986

Orchard-In

★

See review for Neiman-Marcus—The Rotunda.

Pacific Heights Bar and Grill

★

2001 Fillmore (at Pine), San Francisco. 567-3337. Open for lunch Monday through Friday 11:30 A.M. to 2:30 P.M.; for dinner Sunday through Thursday 5 to 10 P.M., Friday 5 to 11 P.M., Saturday 3 to 11 P.M.; for brunch Sunday 10:30 A.M. to 2:30 P.M. Full bar. MasterCard, Visa, American Express. Reservations advised weekdays, essential on weekends. Moderate.

Let's face it: There are restaurants that are put on earth for the benefit of the people who eat in them and not for restaurant critics.

One such place is the Pacific Heights Bar and Grill, which was jammed, with lines out the door, almost from the day it opened on Fillmore Street at Pine. If a computer had designed this restaurant based on a survey of residents in the neighborhood, it couldn't have come up with anything that filled more needs.

First, there's a big, comfortable Victorian-style bar that takes up about a third of the premises and almost instantly became the body bar of choice for the

Pacific Heights crowd. Everyone dresses up, everyone pays a stiff tab for beer or wine—and absolutely everyone is on the prowl.

Second, there's a menu that caters beautifully to the fashion of the day. Lots of people like to pick at a piece of fish, then feel so virtuous from the calories saved that they pig out on fudge-walnut pie or pecan tart. Pacific Heights B&G offers a very light menu—the fish even comes with vegetables instead of the more usual french fries—followed by an array of calorie-laden desserts.

Third, there's the requisite place for snacks. In this case, it's an oyster bar, thank heavens, and not yet another tapas bar.

For the oyster bar, I've got nothing but praise. You can choose from more than a dozen varieties, ordering as many of each as you want. They're not cheap, but they're impeccably fresh, and there are lots of unusual varieties on the menu.

With the restaurant itself, however, I've got some real problems. The fish was fresh, but the cooking tended to be boring and lifeless. You get the feeling that the same computer that could have designed the restaurant may be overseeing the kitchen.

The problem starts when you look at the menu, which is perfectly described by the word "derivative." If it were written on a blackboard instead of mimeographed, I'd swear I was at the Hayes Street Grill. There's a list of mesquite-grilled fish and a choice of sauces. There are a few saute dishes. There's the *salade niçoise* made with fresh tuna.

Of course, there's nothing wrong with a menu that's not terribly original if the cooking itself shines. But almost all the food at Pacific Heights B&G seems to fit into two categories—decent but dull, or disappointing.

Among the latter, that *salade niçoise* had tuna that was drastically overcooked, and there wasn't even a hint of dressing on the whole thing. A platter of smoked tuna, salmon, and trout was disastrously dried out—in the case of the trout, almost like jerky. A nice piece of grilled sturgeon came with "walnut garlic sauce" that seemed much more like a congealed lump of cream.

The appetizers included corn-and-oyster fritters that tasted of neither; I could have sworn I was eating a patty of mashed potatoes. A dish called Mexican marinated squid might have been describing the origin of the main ingredient rather than the spiciness I'd anticipate, since it was bland and unpleasantly cold from the refrigerator. Overcooked red potatoes came with a rouille that reminded me more of russian dressing.

Yet other dishes were nice, if not very exciting. For the very fresh and juicy mahimahi, I chose a cucumber-dill sauce that was light and pleasant. A redfish was beautifully deep fried, without a speck of grease, but the Creole sauce on it had the taste of tomato paste. Swordfish was perfectly grilled and brushed with a mixture of good olive oil and cracked black pepper.

For the appetizers, the definite choice was fettuccine tossed with chicken, *andouille* sausage, bell peppers, tomato, and fresh thyme, served in a creamy light sauce with a smoky taste. Ironically, for a fish restaurant, this pasta was the best thing I ate during two dinners.

It's clear that for many of the patrons of Pacific Heights B&G, my criticisms will be dismissed as irrelevant quibbles. After all, the oyster bar is outstanding, the fish is fresh, and the entrees are reasonable for that neighborhood. Moreover, no one could complain about the service or the wine list, which offers excellent choices from California in the $15 range.

But the owners, who obviously put lots of money into the restaurant and clearly had good ideas about how to please their patrons, could have planned on one thing more: a kitchen that puts together original, interesting, and expertly cooked dishes. ■

—Stan Sesser, May 6, 1986

Palm

★

586 Bush, San Francisco. 981-1222. Open Monday through Friday 11:30 A.M. to 3 P.M., Monday through Saturday 5 to 10:45 P.M. Full bar. Major credit cards. Reservations accepted. Expensive.

I'm not sure why the owners of Palm think that journalists, politicians, sports figures, and entertainers like to eat brontosaur-sized steaks and five-pound lobsters, except that people of these persuasions frequented the original Palm in New York. I can tell the San Francisco branch is after a similar crowd because flattering cartoons of local media celebrities grace the shiny new walls of the bar. I asked a *Chronicle* colleague, whose face happened to be staring down at me while I was attacking dinner one night, how he got his face pasteled on the wall. He told me he sent the Palm PR person his picture as requested. He also told me he'd never been to any Palm because on the skimpy salaries the local rags pay, shelling out $60 for a lobster and $21 for a steak—without potatoes—meant that his kids might go hungry.

It remains to be seen who in San Francisco will frequent this New York-style restaurant. Palm is set up to feel like a clubhouse and everyone is waiting to see who will join.

A labyrinthine, mostly windowless set of dining rooms (195 seats) has been carved into the renovated Hotel Juliana, a new Kimpton moderate-priced-hotel venture. The decor, modeled on the original Second Avenue Palm which was built in 1926, is meant to look like a turn-of-the-century saloon, with pressed ceilings, wooden floors and wainscoting, and brass-toned light fixtures supporting glass lamps. The net effect seems awkward because all this looks recently manufactured, and cheap, at that. Someone told me that the San Francisco Fire Department wouldn't let Palm throw sawdust on the floors, a la original Palm. It wouldn't have helped anyway.

The bar room is certainly the most pleasant place to sit. It has the windows and booths for two or four. Larger parties must sit in the next room at longer booths, and an even deeper room hints at Siberian exile. It was to this cold room we were led one day at lunch, seemingly for no reason, since tables nearer air and light were open. Our waiter commiserated. He too felt lousy about getting assigned the back seats. He was very sweet but we had to hear his whole employment history with the Palm operations.

On a second visit a group of six of us got a place in middle earth where we were waited upon by a wise ass. Frankly, I would have preferred him to the first waiter if he had been smart enough to do his job right. He brought all our main courses, set them in the middle of the table where we stared at them for five minutes waiting for plates. And then, when a lesser waiting person got them to us right before the waiter brought a set, our helper got yelled at. It wasn't cute. It wasn't clubby.

So, you must be wondering about the food. Take my advice and the advice of the waiters. Don't even look at the menu. Order beef. It's the richest, tastiest, tenderest beef on the West Coast. You can tell from first bite that it is fat-marbled, aged Eastern beef. Portions are huge, easily over a pound. A pound of filet mignon is a big mouthful. The New York steak is spectacular; the roast beef with a bone, served rare, is gorgeous—a roast beef eater's dream. It melts in your mouth.

The lobsters are another story. A three-pounder, the smallest served at Palm, was well grilled, juicy, and sweet-fleshed. A five-pound lobster, the only size available another evening, was unappetizing. I have my doubts whether any five-pound crustacean, which has probably reached the ripe old age of twenty-five years, makes for suitable eating. They should be left in the sea to mate or fertilize or do what they do. This one was a little tough but, more awful, it tasted of iodine. The toughness may come from trying to grill such a large animal. The outside gets overcooked while the interior stays raw.

I suggest starting with a roquefort salad made with chopped head lettuce, radishes, scallions, and tomato in an Italian-style dressing full of crumbled cheese. Salads like quarter-pound slices of out-of-season tomato and onion are plain stupid. Clams oreganato are topped with mushy bread crumbs that taste like they came straight from a package. A small portion of asparagus arrived luke-warm, raw and limp, blanketed in a bland hollandaise that was supposed to come on the side.

Do order a combination plate of threadlike french-fried onions and paper-thin potato chips, which are called cottage fries here, to go with your beef. All but one time they were greaseless and crisp. The baked potato comes in a foil wrapper, which means the skin won't be crisp. The hashbrowns are too mushy for my taste. Everyone at my table liked the creamed spinach; I thought it tasted like unseasoned white sauce with a little spinach thrown in for color.

Three thick lamb chops aren't particularly outstanding and I can't figure out why the expensive steak a la Stone has such a good reputation. Slices of sinewy sirloin, a cut well below the other steaks, are put on soft toast and smothered with sauteed red peppers. There's no seasoning and the whole dish comes off rather dull.

The kitchen knows how to do a few things like grilling steaks and deep frying potatoes, but any dish out of this range has a good chance of tasting flat and ill-prepared.

The one plausible dessert to order is a gargantuan wedge of New York cheesecake, which felt heavy on my tongue but was much loved by everyone else.

You would think that a restaurant that specializes in red meat would have a well-formed red wine list. Wrong again. Palmians drink hard liquor, not wine. The wine list reveals no vintages but some lofty prices for wines that, I assume, are very young.

All told, I don't think the Washbag (Washington Square Bar & Grill) should worry about losing its own loyal following of politicians, journalists, and sportsmen. Even if these guys stop by the Palm for a drink, they couldn't possibly get down one of these mountainous steaks more than once a week. According to my constant dining-out companion, it takes that long to digest a Palm meal. I took most of mine home. ■

—Patricia Unterman, March 9, 1986

Pasta Bella II

★ ★

30 Fremont Street, San Francisco. 397-2786. Open Monday through Friday 7 A.M. to 10 P.M. Full bar. MasterCard, Visa, American Express. Reservations accepted. Inexpensive to moderate.

A couple of years ago, you couldn't eat anywhere without running into pasta salad. I didn't know why cold boiled dough and vinaigrette so captured the fancy of food editors, party hostesses, caterers, and restaurant chefs. Well, on second thought, I know now.

Cold pasta is cheap, easily prepared in advance, and colorful. Still, you wouldn't catch a self-respecting Italian sitting in front of a plate of it. And neither would I. So with great trepidation, I visited Pasta Bella II, a restaurant built around pasta salad.

The original opened in 1982. With limited eating, it dispensed paper plates full of pasta salads made with good-quality noodles and fresh vegetables from a spot on the podium level of Embarcadero Four.

The place was justifiably successful. Here was truly fast food that had only to be dished out, that was different, tasty, and reasonably priced. But the question in my mind was whether the concept could support a full-scale restaurant.

The new Pasta Bella still has a cafeteria section at lunch that dishes out pasta on paper plates, but there is also table service, a full bar, and resplendent, modernissimo Italian surroundings. The decor is striking, especially at night when the cafeteria service is shut down.

The Pasta Bella is on street level, part of a small complex of stores and eating places that adjoin the new Skidmore building at Mission and Fremont. The place has tall, tall windows that look out onto sidewalks and urban "gardens." Yards of thin slatted venetian blinds are let down over the windows at night; their shade of gray matches gray tile floors, gray tablecloths, and the gray skirts on the waitresses.

Yes, red and black are also represented, on chrome-legged chairs, on tables, on fabric-covered banquettes, on banks of hanging, cone-shaped light fixtures. Neon artwork, Pellegrino posters, and soft sculpture are part of the design.

Shiny cases of cheeses, salamis, desserts and strings of hanging garlic and peppers add atmosphere.

The menu is not as sophisticated as the decor. The same list of dishes applies at both lunch and dinner, but you order it differently at each meal. At dinner one evening we eschewed the pasta salads for warm pastas, appetizers, and grilled items. At lunch, green salads and pasta salads seemed more appealing. You expect a Prego restaurant-style menu. What you get is cheaper but less interesting.

The hot pastas I sampled were delicious. The noodles had texture, the sauces the right proportions. Pasta Bella's version of carbonara combined cream, *pancetta* (Italian bacon), peas, and a whisper of thyme to form a lovely sauce.

Even more delightful were noodles dressed with a julienne of vegetables and duck breast in a duck-flavored gravy. Tender green-and-white ravioli stuffed with ricotta cheese and lemon zest were splashed with tomato sauce and topped with a dollop of mascarpone, a tart Italian cream cheese. Split orders of these pastas are not overly rich as first courses.

Appetizers were also fine. The antipasto plate includes sliced-to-order prosciutto and toscano salami, a variety of imported olives, a roasted head of garlic, pickled peppers, some forgettable cheese, and a lively carrot-and-currant salad that tasted just right.

Roasted red peppers filled with mozzarella and anchovies may be the most delectable combination known to man. The warm olive oil they were dressed in was not virgin, however, and should have been; if olive oil is going to be sauce it should have flavor.

Green salads reflect this restaurant's commitment to fresh vegetables. The house salad brought an assortment of crisp greens liberally dressed in a perky Italian vinaigrette. House-made croutons garnish it, as they do a caesar salad made with crisp romaine and an abundance of lightly anchovied dressing.

Though the restaurant concept was built around the pasta salads, I liked only one of them, the Marco Polo, an oriental chicken salad, really, of bean sprouts, very thin spaghetti, julienned carrots, red onion, and peanuts in a hot, spicy sesame-scented dressing.

Corkscrews of pasta slathered in pesto with a few slivers of green pepper lacked textural interest. Rigatoni, big fat tubes of pasta tossed with soggy salami slices and a vinegary dressing made grainy with too much domestic-tasting parmesan in it, didn't work. Neither did a seafood pasta composed mostly of noodles and capers.

The items from the grill also need rethinking. Perhaps more should be charged for the veal T-bone and a skirt steak so higher-quality meat can be used. Both were dry, tough, and flavorless, as was a cardboardy grilled duck breast.

The desserts I tried satisfied my sweet tooth without being too rich or sugary, and the wine list couldn't be better suited to the menu. It's loaded with reasonably priced bottles of interesting Italian wines such as a 1978 Inferno, Valtellinese, a resonant, ready-to-drink red wine. Good wines by the glass are offered as well. The service couldn't be nicer.

Pasta Bella is a well-run operation. I like it because the food can be trusted. The menu is consistently prepared, it emphasizes produce, and many of the dishes get a new twist. You can eat lunch there for less than $10 and still be in surroundings that are fun.

The place is also appealing at night

when the streets are deserted and the new buildings loom around it like icy sculptures. Here is an undiscovered spot for drinks, appetizers, and pastas in a striking urban setting. ■

—Patricia Unterman, February 17, 1985

Patusco's

★

300 Park Street, Alameda (take the Twenty-third Street-Alameda exit off I-880, cross the bridge onto Park Street, and drive all the way to the beach). 523-2525. Open daily 7 A.M. to 10 P.M. Beer, wine. Major credit cards. Reservations accepted. Inexpensive to moderate.

I get lots of tips about restaurants, but an amazingly large proportion of them involve California cuisine and French food. These, of course, are the kind of restaurants that are trendy, and it's natural in this period of food obsession to want to keep up with every new and fashionable morsel.

But occasionally an antidote is in order, something to remind us that life isn't all expensive pieces of mesquite-grilled monkfish. And I recently heard about a candidate so perfect for this task it immediately went to the top of my review list: a Portuguese restaurant in a bowling alley in Alameda.

No one, absolutely no one, could accuse Patusco's of being trendy. The decor can best de described as Midwestern cocktail-lounge plush. At the far end, you can hear the boom of pins. The bowling alley's female employees are nattily attired in polyester evening dresses.

What is a Portuguese restaurant doing in Alameda? Patusco's chef, Nathaniel Lee Patrick, told me that the owner, Fernando Patusco, grew up in Portugal, but Patrick admits to coming from Louisiana. "Portuguese and Creole cooking are basically the same," he explains.

Patrick says that Alameda has a large Portuguese community, and sometimes 200 people will come to Patusco's en masse for a banquet. Bowlers, he adds, are another story: "We don't get too many because they think our prices are too high." (Patusco's entrees, big enough to feed a family of six, are under $11, including soup or salad.)

Before I describe the joys of pigging out at Patusco's, a word of warning is in order. Service can be excruciatingly slow and confused. At both dinners, the waitresses were sweet and appealingly shy, but they acted as if they had never seen the inside of a restaurant before. Patrick promises things will be in better shape when this review appears, but nevertheless I wouldn't count on making an eight o'clock movie.

The service contrasts sharply with the professionalism of the open kitchen, where cooks in big white toques man a grill and saute line of leaping flames, just like at Vanessi's. The comparison is appropriate, since Patusco's menu has more Italian items than Portuguese; my guess is lasagna and fettuccine provide comforting alternatives to patrons unused to ordering items such as *bacalhau (tras-os-montes)*.

Much of the food was first-rate, although there was more than one clunker. Whether it's the heritage of Portugal or Louisiana, Patrick has a way with spicy red sauces exuding the flavors of garlic, onions, and chili.

On the Portuguese side, I had three terrific dishes, although the origins of one of them were clearly more southern Louisiana than southern Portugal. *Galinha guizada* was a beautiful saute of boneless chunks of dark meat of chicken with garlic, onions, tomatoes, mushrooms, fresh chilies, and a fiery red sauce. *Porco com amêijoas* was a tasty breaded panfried pork loin, served in a thick, spicy red wine sauce along with four clams in their shells. Like everything else, these dishes came with a whole array of al dente vegetables and about a pound of sliced roast potatoes.

Best of all was "Portuguese rice," not on the menu but a permanent fixture on the blackboard list of specials as you walk in. I'd call it Cajun paella, but whatever the name, you get a huge platter of chicken, pork, squid, fish, green peppers, onions, and mushrooms in very tasty saffron-scented rice, all of it swimming in an irresistible red sauce filled with herbs and spices.

As for the *bacalhau*, the reconstituted dried salt cod that's probably Portugal's most famous dish, there's a serious question of whether to eat it or use it for a tennis game. I chewed and I chewed and I chewed and absolutely nothing happened.

The Italian side of the menu offers several surprises. One is perhaps the best eggplant parmigiana I've ever eaten, a gigantic portion. The deep-fried eggplant is tender, not the least bit oily, and crisp from its breading. The cheese is pillowy, the sauce very tasty. In a dish that more often than not comes out a gloppy mess, everything here retains its texture.

I tried three of the fettuccine dishes, and each of the sauces proved excellent. The Portuguese variety, called *com luluas*, was loaded with tender squid and mushrooms in a white wine sauce. The pesto turned out to be blended with some cream, a pleasant if not authentic combination. The Alfredo had a delicious cheese-laden cream sauce with lots of nutmeg, but the noodles were overcooked. The portions were huge.

There were a few things on the menu that definitely should be avoided. Veal saltimbocca, with tough slices of veal floating in a heavily floured sauce, didn't tempt me to order any of the other four veal dishes. Grilled sea bass was chewy and salty. The salad that comes with dinner isn't great, but it's a far better choice than the lackluster cups of soup.

And if you have to order dessert, stick with the flan. Both the rice pudding and chocolate mousses were leaden and dreadful, exactly what you don't want given the size of the entrees.

The bowlers might not be impressed with Patusco's, but I was. It's the old-fashioned sort of ethnic restaurant where you can roll up your sleeves, let out your belt, and plunge in. ∎

—Stan Sesser, September 18, 1987

The Peacock

★

2800 Van Ness Avenue, San Francisco. 928-7001. Open Sunday through Friday for lunch buffet 11:30 A.M. to 2 P.M., for dinner nightly 5:30 to 10 P.M., Friday and Saturday until 10:30 P.M. Full bar. Major credit cards. Reservations accepted. Moderate.

A person's taste in food can change over the years but his taste memory doesn't. A memory is formed from the moment of the experience and reflects the values held at that instant. So, let's say you return to a favorite restaurant, one you haven't been to for a while. The menu and indeed the food seem exactly the same, but you don't like it as well as you have in the past. You've changed if the restaurant and your memory haven't.

Some recent dinners at the Peacock, a rather formal Indian restaurant in a Victorian mansion on Van Ness Avenue, conjured up these sorts of issues. I last visited the Peacock six years ago and hardly an item had changed on the menu since then, except, of course, for the prices.

The surroundings are the same also. Three intimate upstairs dining rooms are still decorated in pink, white, and burgundy. The lighting is still dramatically low; the upholstered chairs commodious; the linen fresh and pink to match the walls. However, service by a staff of waistcoated waiters was genial, gentle, and much improved. I remember vividly the battle of wills I waged with a waiter six years ago who didn't like taking a complicated order from a woman.

I did not like the food at the Peacock during my first recent visit. Too much of it was tepid, texturally similar, and a little muddied in flavor. What I had remembered, and indeed written about, as food of "deep, rich spiciness" tasted dull now. On a second visit, the food had the same spirit I remembered from the past. The difference, I think, was in the ordering.

On the first visit, we let the kitchen and wait staff do it their way. After the appetizers, all the food came out of the kitchen at once and the waiter painstakingly distributed it all on our four plates. By the time we started eating, everything was cold. Also, the seasoning was conservative. The pale green yogurt and fresh cilantro chutney had no bite at all and use of chilies in the curries was niggardly. It was as if the Peacock was cooking for a timid bunch that was trying Indian food for the first time.

On my return visit, I asked for a hot chutney, which the kitchen actually had to make to order, and for dishes to be cooked extra hot. The maitre d', who happened to take our order, rose to the occasion immediately. He pointed out which dishes could appropriately be made hotter and suggested menu items. I also requested that the tandoor-baked foods come out first and separately, with the curries to follow. When the curries arrived, I asked that only a small portion be spooned onto the plates with the remaining to stay in their warm ramekins on the table.

The difference between the two meals was astounding. The second meal was exciting and delicious, just the way I remembered it, while the first was pedestrian. The increased level of hotness amplified the spices and seemed to lighten the richness of the curries. The tandoor dishes were much more succulent when eaten sizzling hot from the clay ovens. Don't think that the chili level was impossible; you could feel the heat, but it wasn't numbing. The kitchen had carefully balanced the chilies with the rest of the spices in each dish.

Given this scenario, I can recommend practically everything we had at the second diner except for the appetizers, which tended to be heavy on both evenings. Deep-fried appetizers like potato-filled pyramids of pastry called *samosas*, *pakoras*, cauliflower or strips of chicken breast dipped in chick-pea batter, tasted of tired oil. Much tastier were panfried, heart-shaped patties of potatoes and spiced lentils perfumed with whole roasted coriander seeds. *Pappadums*, the giant, crisp lentil wafers that melt in your mouth, are delicate here and taste wonderful with cold Indian beer.

When the tandoor items arrive straight from the oven on a bed of onions sizzling on a cast-iron platter, you can't ask for tastier roasted foods. Everything has been strongly marinated before it goes into the oven, so flavors bake into the foods. Lamb comes out particularly well. A rack of tiny, rare lamb chops practically melt in your mouth, while big chunks of leg of lamb emerge spicier, chewier, and cooked all the way through. A sausagelike mixture of minced lamb molded on skewers tastes best of all with its assertive seasoning of fresh cilantro leaves, cumin, and hot chilies. The tandoor chicken served on my first visit lacked that wonderful juiciness I expect from yogurt-marinated chicken.

The most arresting curry was one recommended by the maitre d', *murgh tikka masala*, big chunks of charcoal-baked chicken in a hot-and-sour red curry sauce. The interesting crunchy textures in *navrattan korma*, a haunting, delicate vegetable curry of potatoes, peas, almonds, and dried fruits set it apart. You must order this one. The Peacock's dhal, a stew of kidney beans as well as lentils with cubes of white cheese, was larded with plenty of hot green chilies.

The eggplant curry here, practically a puree, doesn't hold a candle to the smoky, explosive dish prepared at India Garden, in South San Francisco. Fragrant spinach with cubed farmer cheese is what you wish you would get in an American steak house when you order creamed spinach. Of all the lamb curries, *rogan josh kashmiri* has the most extraordinary sauce, velvety, garlic rich, cardamom-scented.

The lovely Indian breads, leavened *nan* baked on the side of the tandoor, scallion-layered *masala kulcha*, and delicately layered whole-wheat *paratha*, are all skillfully done.

Times have changed. Practically everyone who eats out has dined in Indian restaurants, yet the Peacock seems to have retreated from its more sophisticated audience. They seem to be cooking down to the largest common denominator in the service of some kind of misplaced culinary refinement. You have to prod the kitchen into turning out distinctive food, which it obviously is capable of doing. If the regular preparations taste flat and re-warmed, the dishes you ask to be seasoned come alive. The Peacock should stop in-effectually strutting back and forth and spread that gorgeous culinary tail. ∎

— Patricia Unterman, April 5, 1987

Phnom Penh House

★ ★

251 Eighth Street (between Harrison and Alice), Oakland. 893-3825. Open Tuesday through Fri-day and Sunday 11 A.M. to 10 P.M., Saturday 5 P.M. to 10 P.M. Beer, wine. MasterCard, Visa. Reservations accepted. Inexpensive.

It's exciting to review Bay Area restaurants because new kinds of food are accepted here, which means recent immigrants who cook their native cuisines can attract flocks of customers.

If you're from Thailand or Vietnam, you don't have to disguise your own coun-try's food, as you still do in many cities, by sticking a couple of dishes on an other-wise standard Chinese menu. In fact, I re-cently got calls from two New York–based restaurant critics who had heard Bay Area restaurant goers were happily wolfing down dishes from Cambodia, Burma, and Laos, and they had no idea what those cui-sines were like.

It's no wonder the Bay Area is now sup-porting at least eight Cambodian restau-rants. Because it's more flavorful and in-teresting than Chinese food, but less oily and hot than Thai food, Cambodian cui-sine is proving very appealing to lots of people.

At the recently opened Phnom Penh in Oakland's Chinatown, there are a couple of bonuses, too. The food not only is deli-cious, but prices are so low that people can eat out for little more than it costs to cook at home. Moreover, you don't have to sacrifice comfort and civility, as you would at many Chinese restaurants of this price. The dishes you order aren't slapped in front of you; they're brought out one at a time by a waiter who's conscious that you're enjoying everything and is de-lighted to explain what's in the food. Phnom Penh House is a bright, cheerful place, with cloth napkins, Cambodian decorations on the wall, and very atten-tive service.

As you enter, you'll pass a photo of colorful, beautiful-looking dishes spread out on a table. A sign informs you: "This's your table going to look like with all these foods."

And, indeed, it's not false advertising. Using very fresh vegetables and an array of herbs, spices, and chilies, the restaurant seems to go out of its way to offer a bou-quet of colors and tastes in each dish.

A prime example—one of the most splendid dishes I've had anywhere—is a double-cooked, deep-fried pompano, which appears on the menu as 38a. The whole, fresh fish is first deep fried, then poached in chicken stock. It emerges really juicy, with the skin crisp and grease-less. Then it gets a sauce that includes ground pork, ginger, green onions, red bell peppers, and green chilies. It's noth-ing less than seafood heaven.

Close seconds are two barbecued dishes, the pork and the chicken. The thick strips of pork are moist, tender, and beautifully spiced. The chicken, served in boneless strips, is unlike any other Asian barbecued chicken I've had. It's mari-nated overnight in a long list of sauces, herbs, and spices until the flesh turns brown. So the strips end up looking like pork but tasting like flavorful chicken.

You should also try the *hamok*, one of the nicest inventions of Cambodian cui-sine. Pureed halibut is folded in with coconut milk and spices: Phnom Penh House's version is like a very delicate and aromatic fish mousse.

There are several good choices to start. In the spicy squid salad, fresh, tender squid is mixed with baby ginger, mint leaves, carrots, lemon grass, green onions, red bell peppers, and shredded red cab-bage, and it forms a dazzling array of col-ors. The very tasty Cambodian version of an egg roll, delicate and greaseless, is stuffed with ground pork, bean threads, and mushrooms.

The one soup that I sampled, beef soup with lemon grass, proved a great choice. Slices of beef and little green Asian eggplants are cooked in chicken broth with lemon grass, fish sauce, Cambodian preserved fish, and tamarind powder to produce an aromatic, flavorful broth.

A few dishes were too subtle for my taste; I wanted more heat and more pronounced spicing. Those include the chicken salad appetizer, the eggplant stuffed with shrimp and pork, and the duck curry. If you don't share my desire for being set on fire by Asian food, try them; they were very pleasant and fresh tasting.

But a couple of things should be avoided. The beef with spinach in peanut sauce features tasteless beef and thick gloppy sauce. The vegetarian duck sounds good—marinated tofu substitutes for duck meat and shiitake mushrooms for duck skin—but the weird, sweetish sauce tastes as if it comes out of a can.

Phnom Penh House was recommended to me by Eric Crystal, a Cambodian food freak who's coordinator of Southeast Asian studies at the University of California, Berkeley. He thinks it's the best Cambodian restaurant in the Bay Area. I'd place it a notch below Cambodia House and Angkor Wat, both on Geary in the Richmond. But all three rank among the best Asian restaurants in the Bay Area.

One problem exists with all three, though, and now that Cambodian food is well established here, it's time to bring it up. Cambodians, and many Thais, think westerners only want to eat beef, pork, chicken, and shrimp, so their menus tend to be confined to those areas and to repeat each other. We miss out on tripe and other innards, and on wild game, frog legs, snails, and all the other things popular in Asia. It's time for some unusual dishes on Southeast Asia menus. ■

—Stan Sesser, May 1, 1987

Pho 84

★★

354 Seventeenth Street (between Fourteenth and Fifteenth avenues, one block east of Harrison), Oakland. 832-1429. Open Monday 11 A.M. to 3 P.M., Tuesday through Friday 11 A.M. to 8:30 P.M., Saturday 9 A.M. to 9 P.M., Sunday 9 A.M. to 3 P.M. Cash only. No alcoholic beverages. No reservations. Inexpensive.

Pho Hoa

★

431 Jones Street (between O'Farrell and Ellis), San Francisco. 673-3163. Open daily 8 A.M. to 8 P.M. No alcoholic beverages. Cash only. No reservations. Inexpensive.

Since I'm hopelessly addicted to the food of Southeast Asia, I thought I knew a thing or two about the various regional cuisines of the area. Then one day my colleague on these pages, Joseph Mallia, called and asked me what I thought about a particular *pho* restaurant.

Normally I could maintain my credibility as a restaurant critic by responding "too greasy," and leave it at that. But in this case my curiosity was overwhelming my credibility, and I had to admit I had absolutely no idea what a *pho* restaurant is.

Well, for those of us who are trying to keep up with the Thai restaurant explosion (three of them opened within five minutes of my home during one recent month alone), and for those of us who are trying to visit every Cambodian restaurant (four) and every Burmese restaurant (three) before they hopelessly mushroom, too, now we have to deal with *pho*.

It's pronounced "faw," and much to my amazement I'm suddenly noticing the restaurants all over the place. They represent one delight of Asia I never thought I'd find here—an indoor version of the sidewalk soup stand.

If there's one unifying thread among different Asian cuisines, be they Chinese,

Thai, or whatever, it's curbside soup. The little stands are everywhere, from early morning till past midnight, with a bubbling vat of broth and a selection of various noodles, meats, and vegetables. You point to what you want, and about two minutes later you get a wonderful steaming bowl of soup.

Pho is a particular type of Vietnamese soup, the beef soup that's popular in the north of that country. The basis is beef stock and rice noodles. When the waiter comes, you tell him what types of beef you want in it, then you add condiments at the table.

The menu of a *pho* restaurant is hilarious. It lists separately every possible combination of soup that includes one to five types of beef. You can have any or all of rare beef (thinly sliced raw beef cooked by the heat of the broth), cooked beef, tripe, tendon (skip it unless you're a fan of chewy beef fat), and beef balls (slices of beef sausage).

Pho 84

So what's the big deal about a bowl of beef soup? Consider what you get at Pho 84, a little place in downtown Oakland. Pho 84 (the year it opened) looks like it was started on a shoestring budget, yet it manages a sense of style and elegance in its food that's completely missing in many million-dollar French restaurants I've been to. It's run by Vo Trieu Ba, the talented chef, his wife, her sister, and their niece and nephew.

When you taste the beef broth here, you could swear they used bones from a whole herd of cows just for your bowl. Never has a broth been so rich with the essence of beef taste. The rice noodles are thin, delicious, and not the least bit overcooked; the beef is butter-tender.

But that's not all. A plate of garnishes for the soup, arranged like a work of art, comes to your table. There are bean sprouts, Thai basil, cilantro, slices of lemon and chili peppers. On top is a piece of red pepper cut like a flower.

You also get a variety of sauces, including hot chili sauces and the intensely salty Vietnamese fish sauce. With the sauces and garnishes, you can add your own touch to the bowl of soup. But the broth is so perfect you might be tempted to leave it as is.

There are two other soups here besides the *pho*, and they're both wonderful also. A soup of crab, shrimp, and pork has an interesting fish stock with a peanutty flavor, while a chicken soup has a broth of such marvelous intensity that it could win a competition at a convention of Jewish grandmothers.

Besides soup, there were two special dishes the day I ate at Pho 84. A Vietnamese chicken salad has a wonderful variety of marinated shredded vegetables and a pungent vinegary sauce. The chicken, though, like the meat in the chicken soup, was chewy enough to make me suspect it came from a retirement home for fowl. The other dish—rice, mushrooms, vegetables, and shellfish baked in an earthen pot, sounded wonderful, but it badly needed some of those special sauces to season it while it was cooking.

Pho Hoa

Pho 84 proved so good that a couple of days later I tried Pho Hoa, one of the new restaurants that is rapidly turning the Tenderloin into a little Southeast Asia. Pho Hoa is as plain as Pho 84 is decorative; it's a huge room filled with tables and loud American canned music.

But the *pho*—the only thing offered on the menu—proved excellent also. The broth was rich, the beef tender, and the noodles cooked perfectly. The defect came in the condiments; there was simply a plate of old-tasting bean sprouts with a few coriander leaves. Also, the service was brusque, while at Pho 84 a wonderful waitress had patiently explained everything to us.

If you're willing to forego the atmosphere and the condiments, Pho Hoa is a convenient place to try your first bowl of *pho*. But I'd prefer the trip to downtown Oakland, particularly for weekend brunch when you don't have to fight traffic. Most Vietnamese eat their *pho* in the morning, and I found it a delightful change from the usual Sunday brunches. ■

—Stan Sesser, January 10, 1986

Ping Yuen

★

650 Jackson Street (below Grant Avenue), San Francisco. 986-6830. Open daily 7 A.M. to 7 P.M. No alcoholic beverages (you can bring beer or wine). Cash only. No reservations. Very inexpensive.

My track record for French restaurants serving meals for less than $5 isn't such a good one. The last such place I wrote about was the grandly named Le Cafe de l'Ambassade, a lunch counter on the sleaziest block of Market Street. It was so small the name would hardly fit across the window and you had to dine in the company of locals sleeping it off, but the food was splendid.

After the review appeared, I got calls from people who were not exactly amused. They found hour-long waits to get in and a staff so overwhelmed you were lucky to get your lunch by dinner time. Then, as mysteriously as it had begun, the cafe closed.

Being a resilient sort, I'm going to try again. This time it's a big, pleasant place, a veritable cathedral compared to l'Ambassade. It has a lovely French name— Ping Yuen. Believe it or not, it's a place in Chinatown where Chinese go when they want foreign food for a change.

Now listen to the entrees you get for Ping Yuen's rock-bottom prices: pork chops lyonnaise, or braised oxtail jardinniere, with home-baked rolls, vegetables, and very good french fries; or stuffed veal florentine. And if you really want to splurge, for just a little more you can get soup, dessert, and coffee.

This restaurant, whose discovery I owe to Sharon Silva, is run by an irrepressibly cheerful man named Kelly Choy, who learned European cooking in Hong Kong, Japan, and on cruise ships, and who is executive sous chef for the restaurants in the Fairmont Hotel.

Choy works hours that the rest of us would find staggering. He comes to Ping Yuen in the morning, does preparation work and makes the sauces. Then at 12:30 P.M. he leaves for the Fairmont, and his wife takes over.

At Ping Yuen, Choy has created a menu that's virtually a world tour. Besides French food, there are dishes from Germany, Italy, Hungary, Syria, and even America. If customers want Chinese food, there's that too. For "big spenders," there's prime rib of beef or beef medallions rossini.

The remarkable thing about Ping Yuen is that a lot of these dishes are actually good. This is not exactly trendy cooking; there's jello on the menu, and iceberg lettuce salads with canned peaches. But for a hearty meal at a rock-bottom price, this restaurant is a terrific bargain.

The place to start is with the prime rib. I challenge anyone else to come up with a piece of beef that tasty elsewhere for three or four times the price. It's an inch thick, perfectly tender, and cooked either rare or medium rare. It's marred only by oversalted pan juices.

Another winner was the beef medallions rossini. Despite the low price, this is a delicious filet mignon, wrapped in bacon and served in what the menu calls a "truffle sauce." While you won't see thick slices of truffle, the sauce is really pleasant.

There's an excellent juicy barbecued chicken, with a thick smoky, spicy sauce that would do credit to a ribs place. The pork chops lyonnaise, pan fried with sauteed onions, were decent too, although the chops suffered from being too thin.

Not everything was as good as these dishes. The mixed grill, with pork chop, calf's liver, sausage, bacon, and steak, was salty and tough. The fisherman's platter was overbattered and overfried, although the fish tasted fresh and free of grease.

The small additional charge for soup, dessert, and coffee brought me a cup of good hearty split-pea soup, orange sherbet, and better coffee than at many American restaurants. For dessert, you can get pies and cakes that might be far removed from today's yuppie desserts, but everyone would have raved about them thirty years ago.

There are no tablecloths or candles, and the Chinese waitresses don't ask whether everything is satisfactory, monsieur. But you'll find the service prompt and pleasant, with the waitresses constantly giggling at the strange ways of western patrons. While there's no alcohol, they don't mind you bringing in wine, but don't forget corkscrew and glasses.

Beware of one problem: Ping Yuen closes at 7 P.M. I hope this review will persuade them to extend their hours.

Eating French food at a Chinese restaurant is great fun. And when much of it is good, and when prices are insanely low, Ping Yuen becomes one of the nicest offbeat discoveries in San Francisco. ■

—Stan Sesser, November 7, 1986

Ping's Vietnamese Restaurant

★★

820 Franklin Street (in Chinatown, between Eighth and Ninth streets), Oakland. 444-1142. Open Monday through Thursday 11 A.M. to 9 P.M., Friday 11 A.M. to 10 P.M., Saturday 10 A.M. to 10 P.M.; Sunday 10 A.M. to 9 P.M. Beer, wine. MasterCard, Visa. Reservations accepted. Inexpensive to moderate.

Recently Herb Caen has taken a couple of digs at an unnamed restaurant critic who is so "obsessed" with Thai and Cambodian food that he keeps reviewing out-of-the-way, hole-in-the-wall Thai and Cambodian restaurants.

Since I'm (a) somewhat paranoid and (b) definitely obsessed with Thai and Cambodian food, I have a sneaking suspicion that I might be the object of the barbs. I could respond that in these days of food fixation, a restaurant critic is hardly needed to talk about all the new trendy French and California cuisine places. Sometimes it seems that by the end of their first week of business, everyone but me has eaten there and already formed an opinion.

But small ethnic restaurants like most Thai and Cambodian ones—often owned by recent immigrants who have neither the command of English nor the resources to make their places known—are another story. If they're serving great food at low prices, it should be the job of a restaurant critic to seek them out. In addition, it's a nice feeling to recognize people who have no other way to make a living.

That's my defense, but I'd also like to keep everyone happy. So this week I'm going to do a radical shifting of gears. I'm going to review an out-of-the-way, hole-in-the-wall *Vietnamese* restaurant.

I normally have mixed feelings about Vietnamese food, as I do also about Japanese cuisine. They can both be beautiful to look at and pleasant to eat, but too often they're characterized by blandness and sameness. What can you say when you're writing about chicken teriyaki for the seventeenth time?

But Ping's, a bustling Vietnamese restaurant in Oakland's Chinatown, has no such problem. The dishes encompass a broad variety of flavors and tastes of Southeast Asia. There are fiery-hot stir-fried dishes, intensely aromatic soups and remarkably good noodle dishes. I've never before seen so much variety come from a Vietnamese chef.

Ping's is unusual in another way, too. It seems to be designed primarily for Chinese customers who want "foreign" food for a change. Although the cooks are Vietnamese, it's owned by a Chinese family that also has two Chinese restaurants. The signs on the wall advertising daily specials are in Chinese, not Vietnamese.

When you walk into Ping's, the first thing you'll notice are the tempting-looking firepot dishes that almost everyone seems to order. These are big metal pots, with a flame in the middle to keep them warm, brimming over with meats and vegetables bubbling away in rich stocks.

My first dinner, I had a great catfish firepot, filled with boneless chunks of fish, a host of vegetables, including bean sprouts, celery, bitter melon, and tomatoes, and lots of herbs, all floating in a rich aromatic broth. My second dinner I went all-out and ordered the seafood deluxe firepot, which would have been excellent without the crab and shrimp, which tasted canned and frozen, respectively.

But neither of these, nor any of the others listed on the menu, seemed to resemble the ingredients of the firepots that the Asian customers were eating. These latter firepots were literally brimming over with unusual looking meats and seafood. It's the old mysterious "Chinese writing on the wall" game that leads non-Asians to fear they're not getting the most interesting stuff. Next time I'm simply going to point to a firepot on another table.

Perhaps the single best thing at Ping's is mysteriously called "barbecue pork with salad and crepes." This turns out to be the best "roll your own" Asian dish I've ever eaten. You get cold, thin rice-flour crepes, and inside you combine slices of pork with a variety of vegetables, mint, super-thin rice noodles, and a sauce. It's all fabulous, particularly the tender, sesame-flavored pork.

Another great dish is the spicy frog legs; for once, there's a restaurant serving frog legs that taste like they haven't been frozen. They're very tender, coated with ground peanuts, served in a nice hot black bean sauce.

All the noodle dishes I ordered turned out to be perfect. The duck noodle soup had a powerful broth tasting of five-spice powder, tender fat-free chunks of duck meat, and fresh crunchy broccoli. The beef with *satay* sauce noodle soup not only had great noodles and seasoning, but also remarkably high-quality beef for such an inexpensive dish.

Stay away from the fried dishes, though. The Vietnamese egg rolls were oozing grease and tasted of old oil. Also to be skipped are the curries, which simply aren't as delicate or as interesting as the other things.

While the restaurant is nothing fancy, service at Ping's is unusually friendly, and as helpful as the language barrier will allow.

I would hardly expect a Vietnamese restaurant to discover the best American beer I've ever tasted, but that's exactly what happened at Ping's. It's called Chau Tien ale, and only when you read the fine print do you see that it comes from the Sierra Nevada Brewing Company in Chico. Vietnamese beer in Chico? I called up Steve Harrison, Sierra Nevada's sales manager, to find out what's going on. It turns out that a young Vietnamese named Nguyen Twan approached Sierra to brew the beer under contract, and he distributes it. Chau Tien is made differently from Sierra Nevada's own ale, by going through fermentation only in the tank and not in the bottle. It's a massive, powerful ale, dark gold in color. Yet it manages to be remarkably smooth and rich, without a hint of bitterness.

The problem is that Twan is seeking new financing, and production might be suspended for a couple of months. Get your wine store to knock down the doors of Sierra Nevada with orders. ■

—Stan Sesser, April 4, 1986

Pinyo
★ ★

4036 Balboa Street, San Francisco. 221-2161. Open daily 5 to 10 P.M. Beer, wine. Master-Card, Visa. Reservations accepted. Inexpensive.

Pinyo is a completely pleasant little neighborhood restaurant on Balboa near the ocean. It's so cheap you wonder how they can stay in business. The menu offers the standard Thai dishes you can get almost anywhere, but Pinyo prepares them with unusual skill. Heading the list are the char-broiled calamari and the barbecued chicken. The squid were perfect: pounded out, marinated, and just barely grilled. They were wonderfully tender and flavorful. As for the juicy chicken, it was beautifully treated, not kept on the grill a minute too long.

The *potak*, mixed seafood in a hot and sour broth, also was a winner. There were great green-lipped New Zealand mussels, calamari, scallops, and fish in a fine, flavorful soup brimming over with herbs.

Although one of the most expensive things on the menu, it was a huge bargain.

We also had vegetables in a wonderfully complex red curry sauce. It exuded heat, but at the same time was sweet with coconut milk. Ginger beef had a great sauce too, but the beef was a little tough—not surprising considering the low price.

A new Thai restaurant in San Francisco used to be a major event. Now, there's one on virtually every block. But with nothing fancy and nothing particularly inventive, Pinyo still manages to do more than hold its own against the competition. In these days of soaring restaurant prices, it's hard to believe that so much value can be delivered for so little money. ∎

—Stan Sesser, April 25, 1986

The Plum at Macy's Annex

★

See review for Neiman-Marcus — The Rotunda.

Post Street Bar and Cafe

★★

632 Post Street, San Francisco. 928-2080. Open for lunch Monday through Friday 11:30 A.M. to 2:30 P.M., for dinner Tuesday through Saturday 6 to 10 P.M. Full bar. MasterCard, Visa, American Express. Reservations accepted.

Kitchens form and burst apart like star systems in the heavens. The latest big bang sent the staff of the renowned Union Hotel in Benicia scattering through the restaurant firmament. Judy Rodgers, the head chef of the kitchen that turned out such delicacies as squash blossoms stuffed with sweet corn, sweet cream biscuits, and the ultimate fried chicken, left for a much-needed rest in a villa outside Florence.

Two of her best cooks, Kathy Riley and Jacquelyn Jacobs, landed at the kitchen of the Post Street Cafe in the Andrews Hotel. They have put together a small, simple, ever-changing menu of dishes that are a joy to eat. What was previously a neighborhood bar-restaurant that specialized in nachos has been redecorated, restaffed, and rethought.

The odd-shaped ground floor space, stretching between Post Street and Cosmo Alley in front of Trader Vic's, has a very high ceiling and some unwieldy corners, a challenge to the designers.

They painted the whole space white and hung schoolhouse lamps, added some carpeting for warmth, and furnished the small dining room with curve-backed wooden windsor chairs and oak-trimmed laminated tables, which are bare at lunch and covered with white linen at dinner. A comfortable bar and lounge area at the entryway still gets a lot of use from hotel guests, diners waiting for tables, and patrons in the neighborhood.

The Post Street Cafe is close enough to theaters on Geary to be the best choice for pretheater dining and near enough to Union Square to accommodate shoppers. But its convenient location is just an added advantage. Like the Union Hotel in Benicia, you would seek out this cafe no matter where it was. Post Street is one of the rare restaurants in the city that you can trust to serve only the freshest, highest-quality foods.

Because the raw ingredients are so fine, they get and need no more than a straightforward presentation, which, in turn, means they must be perfectly prepared. Everything from a green salad to poached salmon comes to the table in its finest form. That salad of beautiful mixed lettuces in a sherry vinaigrette looks like a flower garden on the plate.

The same young greens are sprinkled with blue cheese or very lightly coated in a creamy blue-cheese dressing. Small whole leaves from the hearts of romaine are dressed with a delicious mixture of anchovies, olive oil, reggiano parmesan, and egg, in just the right proportions for a change, in a stellar version of a caesar salad.

Asparagus season is over now, but a

bright green asparagus soup and a plate of warm asparagus in vinaigrette tossed with *pancetta*, toasted hazelnuts, and sieved hard-boiled eggs are evidence that the kitchen puts seasonal ingredients to creative use. Other first courses that have appeared on lunch or dinner menus have been a delicate pureed potato and leek soup and a striking wilted spinach salad tossed with Oregon pepper bacon and tissue-thin slices of dry jack cheese.

Three wonderful sandwiches are served at lunch and the one I can't stay away from is layered with Molinari salami, roasted red peppers, and garlic mayonnaise on crusty light-brown bread from the Acme bakery in Berkeley. A sandwich of thin slices of rare roast leg of lamb with red onions, watercress, and garlic mayonnaise comes in a close second. Both are served with a potato salad made with tiny, sweet red potatoes that have absorbed a lively vinaigrette. Smoked salmon sandwich comes with cucumber salad. The Acme bread and sweet butter, by the way, is served with nonsandwich meals—reason alone to eat here.

I have my quibble with the pastas offered each day. My notes on a dinner pasta and one I had at lunch several weeks later are almost identical: "Too many unrelated ingredients, no sauce to bind them together, not cohesive, too many things going on." In one case, fresh fettuccine was tossed with pearl onions, cherry tomatoes, shiitake mushrooms, and parmesan; in another green fettuccine was partnered with red onions, red peppers, cherry tomatoes, hot *andouille* sausage, and spinach *chiffonnade*. Some bites were good, others were bland. The California pasta makers need a visit to Italy.

The Californians do know how to handle fish. A generous fillet of local salmon was sensitively poached, swathed in an aromatic herb-shallot butter, and accompanied by a large portion of buttery julienned zucchini. Sea scallops, one evening, were gently sauteed and perhaps a little too strongly sauced with sun-dried tomatoes, vinegar, and basil. I remember some of the most delicious main courses on the dinner menu from the Union

Hotel, like a juicy roasted chicken breast on a bed of spring leeks with cream, and rare roast leg of lamb with layers of swiss chard and cream with new potatoes. A roasted marinated fillet of beef with a cornucopia of baby spring artichokes, potatoes, carrots the size of my little finger, and tiny green beans all at room temperature with aioli (a garlic-mayonnaise sauce) for dipping looks like a *Gourmet* centerfold.

The wine list matches the menu. It's relatively small, fairly priced, and full of interesting bottles of California varietals. An example is a sauvignon blanc from the Chalk Hill Winery in Sonoma, a crisp, character-filled wine that took us through two courses.

The desserts are elegant versions of homey American favorites, such as warm, spicy gingerbread draped with whipped cream or buttery lemon pound cake with a slash of raspberry puree. Nut tarts, such as pecan caramel on a buttery crust, so consciously depart from the syrupy, cloyingly sweet pecan pie tradition that they actually could use more sugar. A pecan cake with meringue frosting was a little dry the one time I sampled it.

I'm sad about the breakup of the Union Hotel kitchen, but I'm glad that two of its best cooks ended up in San Francisco where I can visit them frequently. ■
—Patricia Unterman, July 1, 1984

RAF Centrogriglia

★ ★

478 Green Street, San Francisco. 362-1999. Open Monday through Friday 11:30 A.M. to 2:30 P.M., daily 6 to 10:30 P.M. Full bar. Major credit cards. Reservations accepted. Expensive.

The Old Spaghetti Factory, which became Cars several years ago, has now turned into RAF, a high-fashion Italian restaurant with a mystifying name. With each transformation, the place has gone more upscale. What started out as a funky North

Beach warehouse serving cheap spaghetti and bulk wine is now a society watering hole dishing out risotto with truffles and carpaccio. I hate to admit it, because I was one of those impoverished college kids who used to go to the Spaghetti Factory, but the food in its newest incarnation is the best.

The physical space has always been appealing no matter what different owners have done to it. It's current look combines minimalism with rococo. The barnlike wood-raftered ceiling has remained untouched, as has the vista at one end out to an interior garden. The floors are now tiled with terra cotta, the walls roughly textured with plaster and sponged with muted color, the space softly lit with brass candelabra. Where the patrol car crashed through the wall at Cars, an ornate cement shelf has been built, dripping with leaves and flowers molded out of grainy gray plaster, on top of which sits a gigantic terra cotta urn arranged with dried vegetation. The bar is a fantasy of fancy plasterwork work, mirrors, and candelabra juxtaposed against a dropped ceiling of painted sheet metal and a barn door. Unlike Rosalie's, which I find uncomfortably contrived, RAF has more coherence and it somehow reminds me of Italy. I felt at ease at table there. The heavy, rustic wooden chairs with straw seats, the large, white-linen-covered tables, the raw materials used for the mock elaborate decor, all somehow suggest what it feels like to be inside an ancient stone villa in Tuscany, in a drafty, high-ceilinged room with a Renaissance tapestry hung on a cracked stone wall. Though it's pure set design at RAF, the magic works.

One reason that it does is because the food and wines are so good and taste so genuine. The executive chef is a woman named Rick O'Connell, who grounded the wildly eclectic menu and inconsistent kitchen at Rosalie's and has created an Italian menu at RAF. Italian cooking must be her true love because many of the dishes have that deep, rich, heartfelt quality that comes from understanding what the preparations mean. Her risottos, Italian rice stirred with boiling stock until it achieves a creamy but al dente texture, ex-plode with flavor. One night she produced one with tiny bits of aromatic vegetables and slivers of unaromatic Oregon white truffles that tasted as complete and satisfying as any I've eaten.

Another RAF specialty is carpaccio, tissue-thin slices of raw beef garnished in different ways. One version with a pungent *salsa verde* of parsley, olive oil, and capers was superfluously garnished with mustardy pickled fruits that didn't add anything to the plate. Another version brought large raw leaves of radicchio that were supposed to be grilled laid on top of the beef. Neither elaboration was quite right, though the meat in both cases was handled beautifully; the slices were translucently thin and fresh.

The menu is top-heavy with small dishes and a fine meal could be made of them. Butter-tender veal sweetbreads are wrapped in *pancetta*, skewered, and grilled just right. Risotto is formed into little balls around lumps of mozzarella, breaded, and deep fried. When you break them open, the cheese pulls into delicate strings. A rich-brothed, subtly flavored pumpkin minestrone that included rice, diced pumpkin, and chard leaves had balance and depth.

An antipasto plate for two looked colorful but so many of these melanges of marinated vegetables and meats fail for lack of conviction. Each element has to be interesting. I could have eaten a whole plate of the warm, white Tuscan beans, but undressed peeled peppers, vinegary eggplant, slices of bland white meat that might have been rabbit loin, and some insipid marinated artichokes did not add up to anything special. Every waiter in town brandishes a pepper mill. For this dish they could use a bottle of good olive oil.

Two main courses one evening rang true and delicious, a hunter's stew of rabbit, guinea hen, and venison in a light, fresh tomato sauce that picked up the flavors of the meats cooked with it; and a plate of rib lamb chops, pounded thin, breaded, and fried. The stew came with soft, buttery polenta; the chops with a stew of potatoes and artichokes. I liked the uncloying marsala sauce on polenta that accompanied a well-grilled rabbit, but the rabbit itself was boring, in need of a marinade.

Eggplant parmigiana never fused into a dish. Three breaded disks of eggplant arrived lukewarm topped with half-melted cheese and some flat-tasting tomato sauce. Macaroni-shaped pasta tossed with vegetables tasted like something you'd get at Little Joe's—a lot of raw garlic and hot black pepper predominated. Another evening, velvet-textured *osso buco*, gently simmered with finely chopped carrot, celery, onions, and good stock wasn't quite hot enough, but who could quarrel with a plate that also contained chard cooked with olive oil and a spoonful of buttery risotto milanese.

Desserts are wonderful, if simple. A pear pie with a rich, light, melt-in-your-mouth cornmeal crust had a restrained Californian, not Italian, level of sweetness. Two lavish sundaes, one with zabaglione ice cream, chestnuts, and fudge sauce, the other with intense chocolate and espresso ice creams and more fudge sauce, come in dramatic goblets and tasted refreshing at the end of these RAF meals.

Kudos to the person who gathered the wines for the concise list. It offers some real beauties, from a rare and miraculous, still young 1971 Conterno barolo to the berryish and lively Lilliano Riserva chianti 1981.

Also exceptional about RAF is the way food is presented. Glazed terra cotta dishes, glass platters, blue-and-white-speckled tin plates, and pewter bowls set the stage for dishes prepared with their final appearance in mind, as well as flavor. Prices are high at RAF for a casual restaurant, but it has a kind of formality that distinguishes it from cafes. A meal here is a production. The experience has been designed from top to bottom, with an eye towards gracious and luxurious, if eccentric, dining. I think RAF fulfills the promise of the scattered Rosalie's. Though there are disappointments on the menu, it offers enough unusual, rarely attempted Italian dishes that succeed to make it one of the best Italian restaurants in town. ∎

—Patricia Unterman, January 18, 1987

Rapallo

★

See review for Allegro.

Eddie Rickenbacker's

★ ★

133 Second Street, San Francisco. 543-3498.
Open Monday through Friday 11 A.M. to 3 P.M.
Full bar. MasterCard, Visa, American Express.
Reservations accepted. Moderate.

Can't get into Taxi, the hottest ticket south of Market? Well, Chuck Phifer, Taxi's owner-chef, has opened a second restaurant with Norman Hobday, the founder of the now-defunct Henry Africa's. Though the collaboration may seem odd because the personalities of the two principals are so different, the resulting bar and restaurant belong together. Eddie Rickenbacker's is one of the best new eating places to open in San Francisco.

Eddie Rickenbacker's can be seen as two separate operations though they occupy the same room. There's the long Victorian bar, staffed with the best professional bartenders in the city and frequented by an old-fashioned, hard-drinking crowd. Running next to it is the restaurant, which may or may not be used by the customers who frequent the bar. The spirit of Eddie Rickenbacker's is whole, however. The generous portions and straightforward presentations of classic American dishes put out by the kitchen suit the saloon quite well. You can eat and drink with conviction here.

Located in a renovated building just south of where downtown and the Financial District meet, between Mission and Howard, Eddie Rickenbacker's draws an eclectic lunch crowd. The small restaurant is a short walk from the Montgomery Street corridor or one can park easily at metered spaces south of Howard.

The decor is both ingenious and personal to Hobday, built around a collection of authentic World War I photos, guns, and memorabilia as a theme. A real World War I biplane is suspended over the bar. One marvels at its fragility. Mannequins dressed in period soldier's uniforms stand in a group on a ledge above the room. Some fine Tiffany lamps and windows hang in the front of the house. The period look continues with white tile floors, walls paneled with dark-stained wood, bentwood chairs, and tables covered with white tablecloths and white paper place mats.

The food is a continuation of what Mr. Phifer did when he was chef at the Balboa Cafe, elaborated on at his own place Taxi, and perfected at Eddie Rickenbacker's. He has a real grill here, with a grate instead of the flat metal surface he installed at Taxi. The items cooked on it, like fish, steak, and chicken breasts, come out much better than they do on the flat iron griddle. Also, perhaps because the pace is slower at Rickenbacker's, the dishes are more carefully prepared. They taste as appealing as they look. Mr. Phifer's cooking style exemplifies good sense. He keeps things simple and savory. The menu at Rickenbacker's is particularly manageable and it shows in the high quality of the dishes that reach the table.

The menu changes each day, though the salads remain a constant. The leaves are arranged like the petals on a flower. In a mixed green salad with blue cheese, many different kinds of lettuce leaves are used, scattered with peeled, diced tomato and crumbled blue cheese. The basic vinaigrette is made with good olive oil and vinegar in harmonious balance. A caesar salad is composed of graduating leaves of romaine, and every one of them is tasty with coarsely grated parmesan, soft-baked croutons, and a fine, assertive dressing. The anchovies crisscross in the center of the salad.

A chicken salad could be a model for a glossy food-magazine picture, but in this one case, appearance seems to be sacrificed to flavor. A generous mound of chicken breast and celery napped in tarragon mayonnaise is flanked by fanned but undressed avocado, topped with strips of crisp bacon, garnished with peeled tomato in vinaigrette, and supported by a flower of lettuce leaves. You want to mix it all together to make it taste as good as it looks.

Soups are a high point of the menu. They're served in large bowls and the kitchen doesn't stint on ingredients in them. A cream of mushroom soup was so thick with coarsely chopped Italian field mushrooms, shiitakes, and domestic mushrooms that it resembled a porridge. You could practically chew on the wonderful, earthy flavors of the mushrooms. A black bean soup turns out to be a black bean chili. If these are not going to be your whole meal, I recommend sharing them, as you can do with the salads.

Main courses will not let you down. Rickenbacker's puts out the perfect hamburger. An inch thick, full of flavor and juice, cooked exactly to specification, it sits on a buttered toasted bun that's just a little bit crusty. Skinny fries melt in your mouth. A rib-eye steak seems more like a New York. It's gigantic, grilled to a turn, and capped with a pouf of garlic butter, hardly a necessary enrichment.

A butterflied slice of swordfish, one day, came off the grill juicy, pristinely fresh, perfectly cooked. It's tomato beurre blanc had broken, but tasted fine anyway with a summery medley of vegetables. A moist grilled chicken breast was dressed up with cheesy, soft polenta and a colorful fresh tomato salsa. A plate of smoky black forest ham, topped with little red potatoes marinated in vinegar, all napped in melted fontina, reminded me of the delicious raclette served at the Balboa. This version using Italian cheese worked just as well. A bacon, lettuce, and tomato sandwich was particularly delightful now, during tomato season.

Phifer goes completely American when it comes to desserts. His fresh fruit crisps and cobblers, currently of apples or peaches and raspberries, come warm from the oven, achieve the right degree of sweetness and have truly crisp, buttery tops. I adore them. The hearty shot of liquor in bourbon-pecan pie works to cut its richness in a way I haven't tasted before. It, too, is fine.

Two comments about Eddie Rickenbacker's: On Fridays the bar can get rowdy in a way I haven't seen for a long time — with hefty, middle-aged cowboys in hats making out with their girl friends and kids getting a little too drunk and putting their fists into the pictures on the wall. I was showered with broken glass one afternoon, waiting for a table. It's all handled well so you don't feel like it's out of control. And the bar serves martinis in Irish coffee glasses, something martini drinkers hate — it violates the image of the drink. If you stay in the free zone of the dining room, where you can order excellent wines by the glass, like 1983 Carmenet sauvignon blanc or 1983 Ridge zinfandel, you can watch the battles in the bar unscathed. ■

—Patricia Unterman, September 20, 1987

The Rotunda at Neiman-Marcus

See Neiman-Marcus—The Rotunda.

Route 66

★ ★

373 Broadway, San Francisco. 391-7524. Open for lunch Monday through Friday 11:30 A.M. to 2:30 P.M.; for dinner Monday through Thursday 5 to 9:45 P.M., Friday and Saturday 6 to 10:30 P.M. Beer, wine. MasterCard, Visa. Reservations accepted. Moderate.

It's a pleasure to report the opening of an interesting, reasonably priced, casual restaurant where the chef, not the decorator, is the owner. Route 66 is such a place. It has taken over the site of the former Cafe Lido, done very little to it, and basically just started cooking. The results range from spectacular to competent, but with

affordable prices and many mouthwatering choices each day, Route 66 always sends people on their way happy.

Its name would imply that some kind of American roadside food is being served here, but the menu is a hundred times more sophisticated. The chef/co-owner, Stefen Reilly, worked with fiercely American chef Larry Forgione at Morgan's and American Place in New York, and has remained a disciple in his own restaurant. This means that all ingredients are fresh; that unusual native American foods like blue cornmeal or samp (a hominylike preparation) or catfish will pop up on the menu; and that the conception behind the dishes is thoroughly original and uncategorizable. The best Route 66 dishes take off from American ideas, but end up like nothing else you've ever tasted before.

The primary example is a creation called Larry Forgione's grilled peanut sauce shrimp, inarguably the best dish on the menu. Forgione really worked something out with this one and Mr. Reilly faithfully re-creates it at Route 66. Juicy pink grilled shrimp are arranged in a semicircle on a background of sweet and piquant peanut sauce that seems to melt into thick, creamy slices of deep-fried sweet potato. A mound of spicy coleslaw galvanizes the dish. The combination of flavors is stunning — Georgia by way of Indonesia with the panache of New York.

Another tour de force features sweet, small deep-fried oysters that top a salad of crisp bacon and assorted greens dressed with a made-from-scratch russian dressing. A similarly bright-flavored red dressing enlivens a very rare and delicious slab of grilled tuna set on top of lots of different lettuces. The eloquence of this simple grilled tuna salad resulted from a fine specimen of fish, cooked just right, and the excellent and varied salad greens.

The kitchen clearly has a feeling for fish. A creamy Creole mustard sauce seemed to melt into a velvety fillet of grilled salmon that was accompanied by nutty basmati rice and carrots.

Other more complicated dishes were intriguing, if not 100 percent successful.

One evening a large, leaden, lukewarm square of panfried corn pudding, which tasted like textureless polenta, was crowned by a bouquet of the freshest oysters and shrimp, seasoned with a handful of fresh chervil and chives, and sauced with a little cream and oyster liquor. The herbs, the expertly cooked shellfish, the sauce could have come out of the best French kitchen in town. The clunky corn pudding, which was not a bad idea, would have made a northern Italian weep. Lavish use of fresh herbs also helped pull together a beautiful-looking appetizer of big chunks of succulent barbecued duck leg, arranged around a beehive of *cappellini*, moistened with a sweet cream sauce. Some potato pancakes with smoked salmon incorporated into them arrived at the table tepid and heavy.

The restaurant, which has just opened, could use a little bit of focus. The dining rooms look like they were decorated by a man who had never designed anything before and decided to do it himself. Route 66 sports a new multicolor paint job that doesn't quite make sense and a mishmash of upholstered and black vinyl furniture. Dressy white tablecloths and carpeting in one room don't go with blue-and-black-speckled linoleum and a jukebox in another, though the classic fifties tunes emanating from the jukebox have been assuredly chosen. The bar looks like it was pulled out of someone's basement "rec room" and repainted.

The menu, too, has a bit of an identity crisis and some of the dishes seem a little confused. A grilled skirt steak sandwich had coleslaw on top of it as well as on the side, and the meat itself tasted a little high. A grilled skirt steak, not in a sandwich, accompanied by crisp-cooked beets, creamed hashbrowns, and a sweet garlic jam made from old garlic, was put on the plate dull side up. A grilled vegetable salad with a creative array of winter produce on it was marred by residual meat flavor from the grill. The fennel and endive and radicchio tasted like hamburger. It seems to me that a number of the dishes were too complicated to get out perfectly under the pressures of a full house, which

Route 66 is already getting. Many of the appetizers arrived barely warm.

However, no one could argue with tasty deep-fried crab cakes with tomato-mustard mayonnaise, or winter lettuce salad in homey buttermilk dressing, or big, juicy house-ground hamburgers with skinny shoestring fries. A half chicken comes off the grill tender and juicy but could use more seasoning. A kind of dry salsa of finely chopped onion, peppers, and tomatoes sprinkled on top adds only superficial flavor, though some light and rich blue corn pudding served with it is special.

Desserts like apple-crumb pie or pecan-caramel pie have buttery, flaky crusts and don't stint on the sugar. American dessert lovers are happy here. An ice cream sandwich made of delicious toasted pound cake stuffed with vanilla and chocolate ice creams is ruined by a medicinal chocolate-raspberry sauce that brings out the worst qualities in each.

Service is a high point here. The waitresses are smart and efficient and sensitive. If the decor is slapdash, the organization of the dining room floor is not. All three meals ran as smoothly as a newly paved black top. With a little more restraint in menu conception and more meticulousness in the kitchen, Route 66 could become a main highway to exciting eating. ■

—Patricia Unterman, February 1, 1987

Royal India Cuisine
★★

1400 Franklin, Oakland. 268-9000. Open Monday through Friday 11 A.M. to 2:30 P.M., 5:30 to 9:30 P.M., Saturday and Sunday 5:30 to 9:30 P.M. Beer, wine. Major credit cards and personal checks. Reservations accepted. Inexpensive to moderate.

Eating dinner in downtown Oakland might not be fashionable, but it makes a lot of sense. There's no half-hour search for a parking space like in San Francisco, and the low rents translate into lower menu prices.

The low rents also mean a multitude of ethnic restaurants. Normally they're decorated in the fluorescent-and-Formica genre, and you wouldn't be tempted to try one without a recommendation. But a couple of weeks ago I passed a new Indian restaurant so striking I had to stop in.

While walking in off the street on a hunch can be a disastrous way of searching for a new restaurant, this time I got lucky. Royal India not only looks good but also produces some spectacular dishes. It turns out the chef, Ravi Brotia, cooked for seventeen years in several countries for the Gaylord chain, including long stints in India and London. His cooking displays the sophistication I associate with Gaylord at its best.

Two important tests for an Indian restaurant are the tandoor dishes and the breads, and Brotia passes both with flying colors. In less-skilled hands, meats can come out of the clay oven, called a tandoor, dried out and tasteless, and Indian breads too often are a greasy, leaden disaster.

But Royal India's tandoor produces juicy meats exuding a bouquet of spices. For a modest price, you can get half a tandoor chicken that's unusually succulent. The chicken *tikka*—boneless chunks of chicken marinated in yogurt, vinegar, and spices and cooked in the tandoor on skewers—is an interesting alternative. And for just a little more you can get a combination platter of the two chickens plus two tandoor lamb dishes, including *seekh kabab*, a lamb sausage that's a repository of cardamom and coriander.

As for the long lists of breads, the five I sampled were impeccable. The white-flour *nan* and the whole-wheat chapati and *paratha* were tasty and greaseless. More elaborate are the onion-stuffed *kulcha* and the *kabuli nan*, with its unusual filling of ground coconut and raisins.

Some other first-rate dishes are on the menu. I've never had a better *sag gosht*, which is chunks of lamb cooked in a creamed spinach sauce. The lamb was good quality and tender, the spinach for once fresh and not overcooked, and the sauce included fresh ginger, garlic, and a veritable supermarket of spices. Another interesting dish is the chicken *kahari*, with boneless chicken, bell peppers, chilies, chopped fresh tomatoes, and onions all tossed with spices in a big bowl.

For appetizers, the lamb-stuffed *samosas* and the deep-fried chicken *pakoras* were on the heavy side. I'd order instead the two soups, dhal with spicy pureed lentils and the thick lemony mulligatawny.

Royal India's menu harbored two disappointments. Lamb biriyani had bland, unpleasantly greasy rice. And mixed vegetables with cream sauce, called *navrattan korma*, included a couple of vegetables that tasted suspiciously like they came from a freezer. On the other hand, if you're turned off by cloying Indian desserts, you should try the *rasmallai*, a patty of homemade cheese in an unusually light cream and pistachio sauce.

In addition to the regular menu, on Saturday there's a fixed-price buffet dinner, but the menu entrees, with big portions, are so reasonable I'd recommend skipping the buffet, since steam tables and Indian food usually don't mix well.

Despite the low prices, Royal India is a beautiful place, with pleasant table settings, Indian art on the walls, and service that's almost elegant. The owner, Pushpinder Sendhu, formerly managed a Denny's and a restaurant in the Oakland Hyatt. Now that he finally has a chance at Indian food, he's brightened up an otherwise drab section of downtown Oakland. ∎

—Stan Sesser, April 10, 1987

Royal Thai

★★★

610 Third Street, San Rafael (take central San Rafael exit from Highway 101). 485-1074. Open Monday through Friday 11 A.M. to 2:30 P.M., Sunday through Thursday 5 to 9:30 P.M., Friday and Saturday 5 to 10 P.M. Beer, wine. Major credit cards. Reservations essential. Inexpensive.

What restaurants do chefs patronize on their nights off?

This is a question that always can produce a funny newspaper article. You find great French chefs pigging out at hamburger joints, or creators of the most delicate California cuisine eating heaps of barbecued spareribs.

But for one particular chef, the answer to this question has to be taken very seriously. I heard that Bruce LeFavour, the owner of the now-defunct three-star Rose et LeFavour Cafe Oriental in the Napa Valley, eats repeatedly at a place in San Rafael called Royal Thai. When I called and asked him about it, he described the food in a way that made me want to jump in my car.

LeFavour's verdict on Thai food is not to be taken lightly. Last spring, he closed his French restaurant, spent a couple of months in Thailand, and returned to create a new menu that brilliantly blended both the techniques and ingredients of the two cuisines.

So off I went to San Rafael to one of the most unlikely settings imaginable for a Thai restaurant. Royal Thai is housed in one of the cutely restored Victorians that comprise a little shopping development called the French Quarter. No one from New Orleans—and certainly no one from Bangkok—would feel that they had been transported to their native city.

Royal Thai was started a little over two years ago by a man whose story is a familiar one for so many Asians who move to the Bay Area. No matter what their profession, they feel that at the end of a rainbow lies their own restaurant.

In this case, Pat Disyamonthon was a banker in Bangkok who came here to get his MBA. But he decided he was too old and too poor to be a student, so he took the first of what turned out to be seventeen different jobs at restaurants. One night he was working at a French restaurant when a friend, who owned San Francisco's Khan Toke Thai House, asked him to help out for an evening. He took only one look at the dancer who was performing that night and fell in love.

Disyamonthon married the dancer and discovered he had also married a great cook. It's his wife, who goes by the name of Jamie, who runs the kitchen at Royal Thai.

While most of the dishes on Royal Thai's extensive menu are familiar ones, Jamie's cooking is really unique. There's less oil, less salt, and a cleaner feeling to the food. Thai food normally speaks of complexity, but at Royal Thai you get a sense of the ingredients—all of them impeccably fresh—standing out individually. It's equally satisfying, but in a different sort of way.

Of the twelve dishes I tasted, there was only one I could criticize. The green papaya salad, while fresh and delicious, had too much shredded carrot and not enough papaya. Beyond this tiny quibble, everything else was near flawless.

The service was excellent, with dishes coming out one at a time in a steady progression. And we learned from the very first dish, the squid salad, that when the menu says something is going to be hot, it's not fooling. Tender, fresh squid—mixed with lime juice, onions, lemon grass, and lots of fresh mint—was roaring and raging, setting palates on fire. There are plenty of mild things on the menu, but this is a place where hot-food fanatics will have a field day.

Less fiery but equally good as a starter is the Thai crepe. A rice flour wrapping, cooked to crispness and without a speck of grease, encloses a tasty blend of shrimp, pork, shredded coconut, tofu, and peanuts. There's a wonderful contrast of textures and tastes.

When you look down the list of entrees, you discover an amazing thing. Even though the restaurant is very pleasant, with tablecloths and fine service, the prices are less than you'd expect at the dumpiest Thai restaurant in San Francisco. The most expensive thing on the menu is the pompano. This fish is wonderful. It's very fresh, deep fried without a hint of grease, and not the least bit overcooked.

There are three other great entrees. Roast duck curry presents a big bowl of tender, fat-free chunks of duck with tomatoes and green peppers in a light, aromatic sauce. Sliced pork stir-fried with eggplant and lots of Thai basil in a black bean sauce features eggplant that retains its texture and isn't a bit oily. And the barbecued chicken once again demonstrates that the Thais can do this dish better than any American restaurant.

You should also try the stir-fried vegetables with garlic and yellow curry. All the vegetables at Royal Thai are impeccable, nothing is ever overcooked.

For once, there's an Asian restaurant that distinguishes itself with dessert. Instead of the usual ice creams from a supermarket freezer, Royal Thai has a homemade ice cream that's the essence of coconuts. You can get it plain or heaped over a fried banana.

If you were seeking a great Thai dining experience, a cutesy "New Orleans" development under the freeway in San Rafael would hardly be the first place you'd look. But in that unlikely location, Royal Thai manages to turn out some of the best Asian food in the Bay Area at real bargain prices. ∎

—Stan Sesser, October 24, 1986

Ruth's Chris Steak House

★

1700 California Street, San Francisco. 673-0557. Open Monday through Friday for lunch 11:30 A.M. to 3 P.M., for dinner nightly 5 to 10 P.M., Friday and Saturday until 10:30 P.M. Full bar. MasterCard, Visa, American Express. Reservations accepted. Expensive.

When it comes right down to it, most people love meat. I do, though I want less of it than I used to. I watched my son devour huge portions of lamb chops and steak before he even had enough teeth to chew it. And of course, my husband rejoices when the call of duty takes him to a steak house. Though people are eating more fish, chicken, and salads these days, I'd venture that deep in their hearts they yearn for a steak.

The market analysts at Ruth's Chris Steak Houses, a fifteen-unit franchise that originated in New Orleans twenty-two years ago, obviously believe that people want to eat beef and lots of it. Franchisees are opening new branches all over the country and San Francisco is the newest beneficiary. The Ruth's Chris here is gigantic, with four separate dining rooms stretching halfway down the block of California between Van Ness and Franklin. Not only is Ruth's Chris's location central, its food and ambience define middle-of-the-road, American heartland taste. None of the spiciness from its birthplace has rubbed off on any of the dishes. It turns out that the food at Ruth's Chris Steak House is prepared just the way my three year old likes it.

Salads are made of torn iceberg with bland dressings. An innocuous Italian salad gets chopped egg, canned olives, and canned marinated artichokes. A dinner salad sprinkled with croutons made from the airy french bread brought to the tables, is not enhanced by the recommended house dressing, a remoulade, a faintly garlicky, mustardy mayonnaise that doesn't have enough intensity to transform a plate of basically flavorless lettuce. A wedge of same constitutes heart of lettuce salad. A pitcher of inoffensive blue-cheese dressing is served on the side.

Crisp, sweet, greaseless onion rings are as competent as any I've encountered. The large shrimp used in shrimp remoulade, served cold with the sauce on the side, and in barbecued shrimp, awash in a spiceless pool of butter, are plump and fresh smelling.

Really, none of this presteak stuff matters all that much at a steak house. What you want most is marbled, tender, juicy aged beef that is cooked exactly the way you want it, and Ruth's Chris has some problems in this crucial area. The New York strip and the rib-eye fit the flavor and texture bill, but the petite filet is mealy and juiceless and the chopped prime steak served at lunch had the unpleasant aftertaste of meat that was too old. Unfailingly, when meat was ordered medium rare, it came medium or medium well, with centers that were barely pink. Rare orders came with cold, raw centers, just as described on the menu. Given Ruth's Chris radical interpretation of rare, the kitchen's inability to cook meat with warm red centers represents a serious flaw in the system.

Perhaps some of the problem comes from serving the steaks on searing hot, small oval plates sizzling with butter. Woe to anyone who touches them inadvertently when they are brought to the table. The meat undoubtedly keeps on cooking after they're pulled from the broiler, making timing even trickier.

However, lamb chops ordered medium came out pink and juicy and a generous fillet of halibut was nicely cooked but not fresh enough.

Some of the accompaniments to the a la carte steaks are quite good, like crusty lyonnaise potatoes with sauteed onions. Cottage fries taste like crunchy, thick potato chips, though pale shoestring potatoes seem to wilt seconds after reaching the table. Potatoes au gratin remind me of macaroni and cheese, with their copious white sauce and melted cheddar topping. Cauliflower au gratin gets identical treatment but doesn't taste as good. Creamed spinach shows little spinach character in a sea of unseasoned white sauce.

The small wine list is top heavy with pricy young cabernets. This shouldn't happen in California where so many drinkable, relatively inexpensive zinfandels, merlots, and interesting table wines abound. The Ruth's Chris house red, 1983 Domaine St. George, drinks well with dinner, though I felt that we squandered an elegant 1984 Kendall-Jackson Cardinale cabernet sauvignon by opening it too soon.

For dessert, I liked a tender bread pudding in a warm custard sauce spiked with whiskey. A very sweet, soft, cinnamony apple pie had a lard crust and a crumble top. Pecan pie, which wasn't as sweet as the apple, is also served warm with a soggy crust. Espresso and cappuccino are available and good, the one concession to cosmopolitan taste.

The color white, on walls and ceilings and in the form of snowy linen on all the tables, represents the predominant decor idea. Gray carpeting and gray upholstered booths, banquettes, and wooden chairs with gray vinyl seats blend into the rooms inconspicuously. The design is going for something a bit clubby, clean lined, and understated, but the result is oddly faceless. The front rooms with windows at sidewalk level are the most fun to be in.

The dining room is so well managed that you feel like you're being waited on by a cadre of smiling robots. Dishes were cleared too soon; wineglasses were poured too full; waiters were too aggressive soliciting drink and wine orders; coffee came too soon. The timing of the two meals I ate at Ruth's Chris was just off enough to be annoying.

San Franciscans have never taken to franchise restaurant operations and though this one is very professional and competent—except for the timing on the steaks—Ruth's Chris is ultimately too boring to make much of a fuss about either way. ■

—Patricia Unterman, May 31, 1987

A. Sabella's Restaurant

★

2766 Taylor Street, San Francisco. 771-6775. Open daily 10:30 A.M. to 10:30 P.M. Full bar. Major credit cards. Reservations accepted. Expensive.

A. Sabella, owner of A. Sabella's on Fisherman's Wharf, read my diatribe about wharf restaurants and wrote:

"My family has run Sabella's since 1920 and yes, old ideas and ways are hard to change. Many wharf restaurants are in a time warp. I do have a degree from the Cornell Hotel-Restaurant program and my brother from New York's Culinary Academy at Hyde Park. We have changed A. Sabella's. We haven't gone to mesquite yet and sometimes certain shellfish items are still purchased frozen, but we're honest with our customers and we seek out top quality. Please don't think you'll have to ask what has never been frozen. We have a fresh board in the kitchen and train our waiters to tell the truth. You may not like our food or style of cooking, but we do run an honest kitchen and really work hard to be the best we can be."

So of course I had to try it and headed down to the wharf. The restaurant inhabits its own three-story building, but only half the third floor is used for public dining. A sidewalk elevator lets you off between a large barroom and the dining room. You wait in the bar until your name is called over the public-address system, but we didn't need to wait on either visit.

Floor-to-ceiling arched windows surround the bilevel dining room, affording views of the bay, the ferry pier, and the Golden Gate Bridge. The dining room is immaculate, the windows sparkling, the carpets vacuumed, the chandeliers dusted. Large tables are covered with two contrasting colors of fabric. Impressive arrangements of fresh flowers and baskets of potted chrysanthemums add brightness.

Sabella was right about his waiters. They are honest, informative, and helpful—to the point of being paternal. They enthuse about certain items on the menu. They explain that "grilling" means panfrying, not broiling. The "fresh list" is indeed a reality, and the waiters recite it to every table. They don't want you to order too much. They clarify your wine order by checking the number on the menu. Timing between the kitchen and the waiters and busboys is flawless.

As for the food, I didn't like most of it. I am a fish lover. I like it very fresh, cooked very little, and with sauce, if any, on the side. A. Sabella's kitchen must have thought I was nuts!

At dinner we began promisingly with crisp batons of deep-fried zucchini breaded with grated parmesan as well as bread crumbs, and six juicy clams oreganato with a crunchy bread crumb-parmesan topping. However, some of the breaded deep-fried items on the chef's platter, the most popular dish at the restaurant, I was told, had cooked too long for my tastes. Scallops and prawns were dry and juiceless. The clam strips held up better and the oyster must have been added at the last minute, because it was fine. The overall effect was leaden. Shelled crab legs, sauteed in bordelaise, swam in a ramekin of butter, garlic, and white wine that had an off-flavor. Fresh Hawaiian prawns, shelled and sauteed in butter, were cooked too long to retain delicacy and moisture. Crab cioppino brought a deep bowl of a salty, garlicky tomato sauce with shrimp, clams, and crab in their shells, all cooked past the point of tenderness. The tomato sauce had that same odd flavor as the crab leg sauce, possibly caused by a low-quality cooking wine.

I was looking forward to fresh abalone, but the slices were so thin and heavily breaded that I could have been eating veal. I couldn't detect the faintest flavor of abalone. Fresh sand dabs had been nicely filleted by the waiter, but lost character to the heat of the frying pan. All main courses came with pastry tubes of rigatoni tossed in butter and garlic, and eggplant cooked with tomato sauce.

For dessert, Sabella's makes a cheesecake from a recipe that Antone Sabella learned at Cornell, a rich cream-cheese cake that isn't too heavy. Double Rainbow ice cream affords the other satisfying choice. Regular coffee and espresso are strong and aromatic without being bitter.

At another lunch we ate cooked-to-order linguine and large fresh mussels served in their shells with a tomato, onion, and garlic sauce. Though it was the most appealing dish I sampled at Sabella's, it was marred by the off-flavor (cooking wine again?) that afflicted the crab legs and the cioppino. A house salad with mixed greens and tired-looking cucumber and tomato was tossed in italian dressing.

Thick fillets of broiled salmon and halibut, ordered rare, arrived a little overdone, but still moist and flavorful.

Sabella's is an honest restaurant, but I think it could be a little more generous. The corners being cut in kitchen labor and in ingredients may not be so much a matter of style as of inertia. ∎

—Patricia Unterman, May 5, 1985

Sally's

★ ★

320 DeHaro (at Sixteenth Street), San Francisco. 626-6006. Open for breakfast Monday through Friday 7:30 to 10:30 A.M., Saturday 8:30 A.M. to 2:30 P.M.; for lunch Monday through Friday 11 A.M. to 3 P.M.; for brunch Sunday 9:30 A.M. to 2:30 P.M. Beer, wine. Cash only. No reservations. Inexpensive.

After a long, frustrating search for a good San Francisco breakfast, I've finally hit some pay dirt.

When last heard on the subject, I had gotten sixty-two nominations from readers, and I reviewed the big winner, Doidge's on Union Street. I was distinctly underwhelmed. A couple of other nominees proved equally disappointing.

By this time, I was getting pretty depressed, wondering whether you had to leave San Francisco to encounter a glass of orange juice that hadn't gone sour or a piece of bread or a muffin that couldn't be bought at a supermarket. Then I found Sally's.

There's no way that anyone could be depressed about anything at Sally's. With blond wood tables and light streaming in through a glass wall and skylights, the place exudes cheer. Then there's Sally herself—an irrepressibly cheerful woman named Sally Seymour who stands at the cash register and takes your order.

Seymour, who describes herself as "an ex-Orange County housewife who was married to a three-piece suit for seventeen years," is hardly your typical restaurant owner. When I asked her why, as was until recently the case, she wasn't open on weekends, the most profitable days for a good breakfast-and-lunch place, she said she was worried that her employees would get worn out by having to work too much. "I want everyone to have a really good time," she said.

For eight years, Seymour ran a little lunch place with no stove and only "a turbo oven bought at Macy's" at the foot of Telegraph Hill. She moved into her shining new quarters at the bottom of Potrero Hill near the design warehouses last June. Her son,

Richard Sears, did the carpentry; her daughter, Katharine Arrow, works in the restaurant as a "junior partner."

In a city where $10 omelets are not unheard of, the breakfasts at Sally's are an incredible bargain. They include good coffee with one free refill. I had three cups, and went up to the register after breakfast to pay for a third; Seymour wouldn't take a penny because a friend and I had already wolfed down well over $10 worth of food—more money, she said, than any two people had ever spent there for breakfast before.

We bought several splendid dishes. The whole-grain pancakes had a nice, nutty flavor and a pleasingly light texture. The spinach and sour cream omelet had fresh spinach that was still bright green.

Best of all was the "Potrero pocket," a pita sandwich I found irresistible. Stuffed into the pocket of a toasted pita bread were two eggs scrambled with cheddar cheese and bits of tomato and onion. It was a light, flavorful dish, perfect for breakfast.

Sally's met all my other breakfast criteria. Orange juice was squeezed close enough to consumption to be sweet and pulpy. The coffee drinks were perfect, the *caffe latte* wonderfully creamy. The muffins were homemade, and unlike most muffins, didn't taste like cakes. With both the banana-walnut-bran muffin and the blueberry muffin, you actually sensed the presence of grains and flavors instead of just sugar.

In short, Sally's served the breakfast I had virtually given up hope of finding in San Francisco. ■

—Stan Sesser, March 27, 1987

Saul's

★

1475 Shattuck Avenue (near Vine), Berkeley. 848-DELI. Open Sunday through Thursday 8 A.M. to 9 P.M., Friday and Saturday until 10 P.M. Beer, wine. Cash or personal checks only. Reservations accepted for six or more. Inexpensive.

For years I've been woldering why there

isn't a single good Jewish delicatessen north of Brothers in Burlingame. And for years I've been hearing of plans to open the definitive one in Berkeley—a deli that would compare with the best of New York and Los Angeles.

Last September, that long-awaited delicatessen finally opened. It is called Saul's, and it's in Berkeley's gourmet ghetto just a block from Chez Panisse.

At Saul's, when you walk in the door, a warm motherly woman named Andra Lichtenstein literally envelops you. She darts around the restaurant all night making sure her brood is being well fed.

At Saul's you don't need a menu to tell you're in a Jewish deli. There's the deli case and cash register in front, the de rigueur red vinyl banquettes, and pictures of such gastronomic landmarks as New York's Russ & Daughters smoked fish shop. It even smells like a typical New York deli, with that instantly recognizable aroma of pickle juice, lox, and who knows what else.

It might look like a classic deli, but what about the food? Saul's perceptibly improved in the six weeks between my first and third review dinners, but it's still plagued by teething problems.

The number one problem is coordination, that combination of alert service and an efficient, well-paced kitchen that allows you to relax and concentrate on what you're eating. All three meals at Saul's were exercises in frustration: beer that was ordered but never appeared; silverware taken away between courses and not replaced; bagels at two meals that were supposed to be toasted but weren't. At one dinner, the combination appetizer plate didn't arrive until we had finished our soups and entrees and were ready for dessert.

As for the food, some things are terrific, others weak. I think Lichtenstein senses the weaknesses and is steadily rooting them out. When I called her for an interview after my last meal, I didn't have to tell her that the corned beef was dry and tasteless; she said they were switching to the company that supplies the exemplary corned beef at Brothers.

So here's a guide to what's already good. When you sit down you get a bowl of pickled cucumbers and green tomatoes imported from New York that are second to none. You could close your eyes and believe you were at Gus's Pickle Shop on the Lower East Side.

Then have a platter of blintzes and potato latkes as appetizers. The blintzes are perfect—tender skin outside, stuffed with a delicious light cheese filling that's not too sweet, and served with sour cream and strawberry preserves. The potato pancakes, coarsely grated and very fresh tasting, are marred by excessive oiliness, but no one I ate with seemed to mind it as much as I did.

After the appetizers, at least one person should have the lox, either as a platter or in a bagel-and-cream-cheese sandwich. Saul's has two kinds of smoked salmon, and they're both fabulous.

Tongue, on wonderful rye bread from San Francisco's House of Bagels, is another good sandwich choice. The pastrami is decent, although you wouldn't think you were in New York.

A real winner as an entree—one that's almost never done that well—is the sliced brisket of beef. It's a huge portion with tasty brown gravy, a potato pancake, and—in a welcome departure from the typical Jewish deli—fresh vegetables that are cooked al dente.

Stuffed cabbage (for once the ground beef filling isn't overcooked) is another fine choice. If you like the sweet-and-sour Jewish version of the eastern European dish.

But the chopped liver is much too intensely livery; it cries out for eggs and onions. While the matzo balls are fluffy, the chicken broth tastes primarily of salt. The beets in the borscht are overcooked and tasteless. The potato knish is a sorry soggy heap.

The creamed herring is actually inferior to the supermarket version in a jar. The kishke is a greasy loser, enough to give intestines a bad name. And avoid the rice pudding at all costs; have a piece of cheesecake if your stomach can handle it.

If you stick to the recommended

dishes, you can do really well at Saul's. I've got even higher hopes for the future, but today's Saul's is still no match for Brothers. ∎

—Stan Sesser, January 30, 1987

Savannah Grill

★★

55 Tamal Vista Blvd., Corte Madera. 924-6774. Open for brunch Sunday 11 A.M. to 3 P.M.; for lunch daily from 11:30 A.M. to 4:30 P.M.; for dinner Monday through Saturday 5:30 to 10:30 P.M., Sunday 5 to 10:30 P.M. Full bar. MasterCard, Visa, American Express. Reservations accepted. Moderate.

Let Rome have McDonald's. Northern California has created its own kind of formula restaurant that outshines them all. The prototype is Spectrum/Saga's MacArthur Park, a big, casual restaurant with a bustling central bar and a state-of-the-art menu that specializes in barbecued ribs and chicken, mesquite-grilled meats, and "California" salads and appetizers. It was this operation that produced the personnel behind such success stories as Mustard's in Yountville, Fog City Diner and Caffe Latte in San Francisco, Rio Grill near Carmel, and the Savannah Grill in Marin.

All these restaurants smoke and grill foods over mesquite. Their kitchens come up with inventive small dishes and salads and combine them with hearty main courses. For a moderate price, these restaurants throw a party for their customers. They serve out-of-the-ordinary, tasty food and treat everyone nicely despite the noise and the crowds. The former Spectrum employees who left to open their own restaurants learned their management lessons well. They all balance professionalism and creativity in a likable way.

The Savannah Grill is Marin County's outpost of this family of restaurants. It's conveniently located right in the center of southern Marin in a new shopping center that also houses one of the best food markets in the Bay Area. Typical of suburban Marin real-estate development, Savannah's building is a large, sprawling single-story affair with a view that takes in a parking lot as well as Mount Tamalpais. Untypical is the clubby interior with acres of dark wood, a marble entryway, a long polished bar, an equally long open kitchen with counter seating in front of it, and gorgeous original light fixtures that seem to float on the ceiling. The designer, Pat Kuleto, had just put together the Fog City Diner when he started work on Savannah.

The menu reminds me most of Mustard's with MacArthur Park overtones. It offers eight to ten appetizers and salads, barbecued ribs, smoked duck, rabbit and meats, grilled foods, a few sandwiches, and onion rings. The same menu is prepared at both lunch and dinner with equal skill, judging from my visits.

One of the triumphs of the salad section is Savannah's chicken salad with Thai vinaigrette, a meal of moist chicken breast, baby leaves of Napa cabbage and bok choy, and clouds of crisp white rice noodles in a spicy-hot, gingery, peanutty dressing infused with fresh cilantro. The salad tastes best when it's all tossed together, and if you get the right waiter, he'll do it for you.

Nuts go into practically every salad, like sugar-glazed pecans with mixed greens and strong asiago cheese or roasted walnuts in a lunch salad of romaine lettuce decorated with fresh raspberries and topped with at least a quarter pound of blue cheese. I would have chosen apples or pears to the raspberries, but a tart raspberry vinaigrette on the lettuce somehow makes it all work. A saucy caesar salad made with lots of anchovy, shredded parmesan, and freshly baked croutons is the best salad of the lot.

Grilled eggplant with bermuda onion and red pepper pesto is one of those dishes that brings people back to the restaurant. Slices of smoky, creamy Japanese eggplant are cleverly off set by a smoky red pepper puree. Equally skillful, one night, was a very spicy, richly shellfish-flavored crayfish bisque. Some other dishes, like warm Sonoma goat cheese served with two kinds of chutney and sun-dried tomatoes, just don't add up to any-thing at all. The tendency in California cooking to bring eclectic flavors together in the hopes of some serendipitous bond-ing often backfires. Sometimes the ingre-dients fight; sometimes they ignore each other. This forced matchmaking can be a tricky business. Savannah Grill puts out its share incoherent dishes.

Main courses tend to be big, interest-ing, and satisfying. One day the kitchen paired two perfectly grilled marinated pork chops with a warm saute of pickled yellow peppers, pears, and pecans and a polenta-potato pancake. Another lus-cious combination slathered a moist pounded and grilled chicken breast with avocado butter and roasted red peppers. A smoked, then grilled, rib-eye steak turned out to be juicy and tender despite all the cooking. It was garnished with a whole head of roasted garlic waiting to be squeezed out onto the meat. However, a skirt steak marinated in beer and black bean sauce turned out too be too tough and sinewy.

I liked the plump, carefully simmered red and black beans topped with fresh salsa and sour cream that came with three grilled smoked sausages, but the sausages themselves were too fatty and processed tasting. A smoked Petaluma duck breast came off the grill so charred one evening it should never have left the kitchen.

Fish is often a problem in restaurants that don't specialize in it. Kitchens don't know how to select it well and then they don't know how to store it. Something the restaurant called sea bass smelled old and tasted like no sea bass I'd ever eaten. To make matters worse it was accompanied with a raw vegetable saute. This under-cooking of vegetables seems to be a chronic problem for Savannah's kitchen. They turned up with other grilled meats, as did some crunchy red potatoes with a marinated skirt steak.

A half slab of baby back ribs, tender, sweet, and succulent, served with pep-pery peanut coleslaw and hashed brown potatoes, can always be depended upon at Savannah Grill. They are a real drawing card.

All the savory grilled and smoked foods make you want something sweet af-terwards, and Savannah Grill makes three homey desserts each day, including the owner's Mississippi grandmother's lemon icebox pie.

Savannah Grill is not a flawless restau-rant but it offers so many choices and works so hard at being generous and lively that it has won me over. The fact that the same kind of menu has been done before by three or four other restau-rants does not diminish Savannah Grill's appeal, especially to people who do not have one in their community. ∎

—Patricia Unterman, April 6, 1986

Silks at the Mandarin Hotel
★★

222 Sansome Street, San Francisco. 986-2020. Open daily for breakfast 7 to 10:30 A.M.; for brunch Sunday 8 A.M. to 2 P.M.; for lunch Mon-day through Friday 11:30 A.M. to 2 P.M.; for din-ner daily 6 to 10:30 P.M. Full bar. Major credit cards. Reservations encouraged. Moderate at lunch and in the Mandarin Lounge; expensive at dinner.

Unlike most fancy hotel restaurants, there's something spontaneous, unman-nered, and fresh about Silks, the small, elegant restaurant in the new Mandarin Oriental Hotel. You'll find awkwardness too, but the high spirit of the staff, in both the dining room and the kitchen, ir-repressibly comes through the formulaic layers of luxury. The food tastes like it's prepared by cooks who have lots of energy and good ideas, but are a little short on the sophistication to bring the dishes off. Even with this qualification, Silks is a happy development for the Financial Dis-trict. The operation combines the ser-vices and appointments of a world class hotel with the personality of a local San Francisco restaurant.

I had hoped that the restaurant and bar would be high above the city along with the hotel rooms, which are all blessed with fabulous views. Alas, this did not happen. Midstream, the developer switched his plan from residential condominiums to offices (floors two through thirty-seven) and a hotel (floors thirty-eight through forty-eight). I gather that installing a major kitchen thirty-eight floors into the air is not easily accomplished at the last minute. Yet, the intimacy of the dining rooms and intelligence of service in both the lounge and the restaurant do provide a special, albeit ground floor, experience. I felt immediately comfortable in both places.

Silks, the main restaurant upstairs, is plush, of course, with living-room-sized upholstered armchairs pulled up to expansive tables covered with multiple layers of linen. The visual effect of a sea of gray-green carpeting, creamy enameled walls detailed in gold, pastel murals of Chinese landscapes, and a centerpiece table holding a vast flower arrangement, pastries, and fruit is somewhat offset by a low ceiling with unattractive ventilation slits and too many holes for lighting. The decor is faceless but the first-rate wait staff, selected and trained by the Mandarin Oriental Hotel management team (Hong Kong, Bangkok, Macao, Djakarta, Manila, Singapore), go far in transforming the room into something genuinely silky. Gosh, they were good!

When you read the menu, you find lots of tempting dishes to order, though they always seem to have one odd or extra ingredient in them—in fact, most of them do, but not catastrophically.

I liked spicy Caribbean shrimp-and-potato fritters at lunch one day, but a jam-sweet peach relish didn't sit right with them at all. A smoked salmon mousse had an attractive creamy texture, but the corn salad that came with it was beset by slimy okra. No complaints about the tasty sesame chicken wings in red sesame mole sauce, or about a multifaceted main course of smoky slices of grilled pork tenderloin with curried onions and poached pear on a backdrop of calvados-cream sauce. However, a big dollop of strong calamata olive butter detracted from a slice of grilled swordfish and I'm not sure that the oriental pasta served with it belonged on the plate either. A fillet of sea bass tasted delicious smothered in gently sauteed onion and mushrooms.

Crisp sesame cookies and melt-in-your-mouth, sandy pecan cookies that come as a treat when you order the excellent espresso sent us happily on our way.

At dinner, the extra-ingredient malaise lingered on but couldn't defeat the exuberance of the meal. The good idea of a grilled vegetable terrine instead of the typical, drab pureed vegetable terrine, was somewhat undermined by a layer of aggressive herbed goat cheese. Served next to the terrine, a little salad of whole leaves of fresh herbs, dressed only in lemon juice, packed a wallop too. It was hard to get a handle on this dish. A wilted spinach salad topped with cornmeal-coated oysters went astray by decorating the oysters with salmon and golden caviars. Some crisp bacon would have worked much better.

A stunning ragout of scallops, leeks, and carrots in a broth infused with slivers of mild Chinese sausage, garnished with tiny mounds of black seaweed, went wrong only with toasted pine nuts, which added a discordant flavor. A corn and shrimp chowder, unabashedly rich with cream, cleverly featured a whole grilled shrimp at its center.

A roasted poussin stuffed under the skin with ricotta and more goat cheese was surrounded by a luxuriant melange of cabbage, roasted garlic, whole leaves of Italian parsley, and a marvelous pan gravy. Curried Maine lobster was a downright disaster, with rubbery meat, tough coconut shavings, and flaccid toasted almonds, all on a bed of unpleasant-tasting spinach.

For dessert, don't pass up the warm passion-fruit souffle, a creation that well could become the signature dish of this restaurant. The essence of the fruit is suspended in warm, thin air.

The small menu downstairs in the Mandarin Lounge is the most appealing of all and you get to try it in the handsomest of tearooms for affordable prices. The multilevel dining area in the lobby is decorated like a club, with wood-paneled walls and tables set far, far apart on acres of celadon carpeting cradling commodious armchairs and sofas. At one end of the room is a buffet table laid with appetizing plates of food, like white bean vinaigrette that comes with paper-thin slices of dried sausages, or roasted red peppers served with rounds of marinated goat cheese. The red peppers needed a dressing.

Excellent are tomato, basil, and four-cheese *pizzetta* and spicy *don don* noodles with warm Chinese barbecued pork. A curried egg salad sandwich with cashews, sprouts, carrots, and cucumbers can't pull itself out of the vegetable bin. The hummus with tahini is yummy, but the pita bread chips served with it don't work.

Though all the food at both restaurants is fresh and nicely presented, the kitchen doesn't quite know how to finish its cooking. Sometimes just a vinaigrette or salt and pepper are needed; sometimes the wrong ingredients are added gratuitously to a dish. But the attempts are so earnest, you don't care too much about the mistakes. The dishes are close enough to being right to be satisfying. After all, the restaurant is only three months old and it takes time to turn raw silk into the finest material. ■

—Patricia Unterman, August 2, 1987

Soul Brothers Kitchen

★

See review for Lady E's.

South Park Cafe

★

108 South Park (between Second and Third streets and Bryant and Brannan), San Francisco. 495-7275. Open Monday through Friday 8 A.M. to 10 P.M., Saturday 6 to 10 P.M. Closed Sunday. Beer, wine. MasterCard, Visa. Reservations for dinner only. Inexpensive.

Imagine strolling in Paris on the Left Bank. You happen upon a charming square away from traffic. Children play on the swings at the center while adults sit on benches in the sun. The square is surrounded by resonant old buildings, one of which houses a small cafe; the front of the cafe opens to the square. Inside, tiny paper-covered tables are lined up against a long wooden banquette. At a well-worn bar, a man in a long apron pours aperitifs and wine. The menu is written on blackboards in small, even script. How good you feel to be in a place like this!

I felt the same way when I stumbled into the South Park Cafe. Tucked away in an industrial section of the city, South Park is a long oval of lawn and trees with playground equipment in the center and wooden benches surrounding it. The park used to be full of men standing around burning garbage cans, but the neighborhood offers such charming potential that it was not long before some of the dilapidated two-story buildings ringing the park were refurbished by designers and architects. They reside, equably it seems, with their scruffy predecessors, who still use the park at off hours. While the original inhabitants partake of Thunderbird and street drugs outside, artists and designers drink glasses of their own inexpensive wine inside their new cafe. The urban ecology works because the newcomers are not gentrifying so much as figuring out how to live well and cheaply in one of the few affordable areas left in the city.

The cafe is a direct result of what's going on in this tiny neighborhood. It looks like it's been there for years, though it has only been open since August. There's something timeless about it, European rather than American. I suppose it is the materials—red tile floor, wooden chairs, that comfortable dark wood bar, school-room lamps, small painted wooden tables covered with butcher paper, brass wall sconces with tiny silk lamps, pots of palms, and a subtle paint job that uses many muted colors. Someone figured out a smart, evocative design without spending much money or making you notice it.

The food is just what you'd get in an inexpensive Parisian cafe—broad, tasty, quickly assembled dishes that are generous and filling. There's nothing effete or arranged about the food. It seems as natural as the surroundings.

Lunch is the big meal at South Park because people who work in nearby offices walk over. I liked the big, floppy, main course salads like *salade d'Avignon*, a plate of apple slices, beets, raisins, and walnuts on a bed of romaine and endive drizzled with a bright orange, curried vinaigrette. A similarly arranged *salade à la Valencay* brings together avocado slices, walnuts and little cubes of mild French goat cheese in a creamy vinaigrette. Amazingly enough, avocado and goat cheese work together quite well. The kitchen uses tough California curly endive as the main ingredient for *salade frisée*, but tosses perfectly sauteed slices of chicken liver, bacon and garlicky croutons into it.

French-style sandwiches are also good, like the crisp, fried *croque madame* I had one day, filled with ham and gruyere and topped with an egg. Other sandwiches come on fresh, dense baguettes from La Seine and are stuffed with thinly sliced westphalian ham, or anchovies and egg salad.

Main courses can be tricky here. A grilled chicken breast was surprisingly tender and juicy, but South Park's interpretation of a *ravigotte* sauce came off like a medicinal béarnaise with armies of strong-dried and fresh herbs fighting with each other. Steamed mussels with cream were fresh but their cooking liquid too winy, a problem with other dishes I had here.

The desserts, however, are so good they taste like they come from another kitchen. They're made by the owner, I was told. Her lemon tart has a buttery, flaky, crisp crust that most cooks only dream about and a tart, delicious pure-lemon filling. The apple tart topped with crème fraîche has the same exceptional crust covered with tender apples and a caramelized glaze. As a coconut lover, I was transported by South Park's *gateau des îles*, a big wedge of moist, chewy coconut-laced cake with buttery, crunchy top and sides.

Dinner service, instituted only a couple weeks ago, offers a menu similar to the one at lunch, but South Park serves tapas from five to seven when a lot of people drop in after work. The scene is so lively and interesting that I wish the tapas were better.

Shrimp sauteed in their shells and sprinkled with rock salt are flavorful, though you have to be careful not to get a mouthful of salt. Thinly sliced sauteed mushrooms finished off in sherry and mussels marinated in a winy broth would both have been better if the alcohol in their cooking liquids had been burned off. *Anchoiade*, a coarse paste made from salt-cured anchovies, garlic, and olive oil, would have been delicious if the bread it was spread on had been toasted. The traditional Spanish tortilla, a thick potato and onion omelet served too cold here, tasted flat despite being laced, untraditionally, with hot jalapeno peppers. Octopus cut into little pieces was tough and impervious to its marinade. The one tapa that worked without any qualification was the simplest—sliced baby red potatoes with a ramekin of excellent garlic mayonnaise.

It's a pleasure to find a place of enlightened sensibility that encourages Parisian cafe behavior. The service at South Park may be disorganized and a little too informal; the cooking may be rough in spots; but I can't think of a place I'd rather be on a sunny afternoon. ∎

—Patricia Unterman, April 13, 1986

Stars

★

750 Redwood Alley (between Polk and Van Ness, just north of City Hall), San Francisco. 861-7827. Open for lunch Monday through Friday 11:30 A.M. to 2:30 P.M.; for dinner Tuesday through Saturday 5:30 to 10:30 P.M., Sunday 5 to 9:30 P.M., Monday 5:30 to 9:30 P.M. Full bar. Major credit cards. Reservations essential at lunch and dinner. Expensive.

When I first reviewed the now-famous restaurant of Jeremiah Tower, I found much of the food excellent, but my meals were plagued by inconsistency. It was a problem I had hoped would work out with time.

Since more than two years have passed, I decided to pay another visit to see what's been happening. Although Tower has achieved a national reputation and has elevated himself on the menu to "executive chef," his restaurant looks exactly the same—huge, sparsely decorated, and mobbed with people. Much to my surprise, my reaction to the food was also unchanged.

If anything, the inconsistency of what is served at Stars has been magnified and institutionalized. It's as if the restaurant deliberately set out to bedevil restaurant critics who like to paint things in either black or white. Never have I seen, in one place, blacker blacks, whiter whites, and more shades of gray.

Consider these statistics: In the course of two dinners, not including desserts, I got to taste fifteen dishes. Two were superb, absolute heaven. Five were good. Six were disappointing, and two were inedible.

So you pay the price and you do take your chances. And do you ever pay! Dinners for two, each ordering an appetizer, salad, entree, dessert, and coffee, including tax, tip, and $15 for wine, came out to almost $120. That's $60 a head, about what it would cost to eat in many of the Bay Area's great French restaurants.

That $60 buys you not only San Fran-

cisco's most unpredictable food but as much noise as a rock concert. Except for the Hard Rock Cafe, I can't remember another restaurant as noisy as Stars. A steady clamor of diners shouting to be heard echoes off the walls and fills every corner. In a trendy restaurant jammed with trendy people, "What did you say?" becomes the line of the evening.

But just like the food, I can't categorize the ambience with a broad stroke, either. Amidst this din is service that is about as pleasant as you can have—friendly, caring, informal, and informed.

The wine list, although anything but cheap, is another big plus. From a $15 bottle of Gallo cabernet to a $900 bottle of 1945 Chateau Latour, you can choose from a couple hundred wines that include what seem like very good California wines and lots of first-rate imports. But at two times the retail price or more, there are no bargains.

If there is one hallmark of a Jeremiah Tower restaurant, it's that the menu entices you with dishes that combine many ingredients that you have never seen put together before. It always sounds innovative. But as often as not, these combinations don't work.

On the positive side, consider a plate of very fresh raw tuna, pounded thin in a clever imitation of beef carpaccio. Painted onto the red tuna are stripes of ginger-scented cream. On the left are two raw oysters, on the right a heap of golden caviar. The tuna rests in a vinaigrette flavored with cilantro and chili. It all looks magnificent and tastes even better.

Or take another appetizer on the same menu. Slices of cold smoked veal loin were topped with a frothy cream into which cepe mushrooms had been blended. In the center of the plate was an elaborate construction of thin roasted eggplant slices, rosemary, and mascarpone, a rich Italian cream cheese.

Yet the same meal had a pasta dish so weirdly thrown together no one could believe it. It contained smoked duck and shelled prawns—which to my mind don't belong on the same plate, particularly without a sauce to bind them, only a broth that appeared to be a fish stock. And a very delicate poached salmon was wiped out by a gloppy sauce that contained red onions and sage.

There were surprising lapses in preparation. A warm cabbage salad with walnuts and smoked duck was just a boring heap of bland cabbage; we had to send it back to get the duck, which didn't help any. Pheasant came with a slice of overcooked breast and a virtually raw leg. A chicken breast was tough and flavorless. For a chef tied so closely to California cuisine, too many dishes were too buttery or too oily.

And imagine this at the same restaurant: One night a thick and creamy Italian white bean soup, smoky with bits of prosciutto. Another night an inedibly salty bowl of thin broth with fat globules and bits of vegetables floating in it, called on the menu "minestrone."

How do you summarize a meal at Stars? One night one of my dinner companions, an accomplished cook, was confronted with a couple of the dishes that just didn't work. "What would be interesting," she said, "would be to take all these ideas and see if you could make something edible out of them."

I love innovative cooking, and I can forgive occasional failures. But when I'm paying $20 or more for an entree, and putting up with frantic noise, I want more than a hit-or-miss meal. Stars fails to deliver. ∎

—Stan Sesser, November 12, 1986

Stoyanof's Restaurant

★

The Village at Corte Madera, 1736 Redwood Highway, Corte Madera. 924-8981. Open daily from 11 A.M. to 11 P.M. Beer and wine. MasterCard, Visa, American Express. Reservations accepted. Moderate.

A Marin County shopping center seemed like an odd place for a Greek Easter feast, but soon after we were seated at Stoyanof's in the Village at Corte Madera, we were swept up by the ethos of a real Greek party. The Stoyanof family, in collaboration with Sotiris Kitrilakis, importer of high-quality Greek foodstuffs, put on a grand food event starting with Greek olives, okra, and peppers, continuing with whole spit-roasted baby lamb and goat with all parts of the animals used for such delicacies as tripe soup and brochettes of heart and kidney, and ending with custard-filled phyllo pastry in honey syrup. The meal and the setting so intrigued me that I soon returned in search of more of this authentic Greek food.

Newly built and unabashedly current, Stoyanof's clever, neomodernist decor takes a witty look back at classic Greek architecture. Tall Greek columns soar up to the high ceilings. A decorated canopy, supported by more columns, juts out from the open kitchen. Stunning granite tables, tile floors, and the greenery of tall palms look like scenery in the airy, light-filled space. Slashes of bright turquoise paint suggest the intense blue of the Aegean Sea, while small vases of yellow lilies appear to grow out of the shiny stone tables. Stoyanof's represents a creative leap for shopping-center restaurant design.

The partially ethnic menu, too, is unusual for a shopping center. The best parts of it are prepared by Georgi Stoyanof, a Macedonian who has been baking here and in Greece for fifty years. He opened Stoyanof's on Ninth Avenue with his son five years ago, where he continues to work. His son, Angel, runs the Marin branch.

The elder Stoyanof understands phyllo dough. His buttery pastry melts in your mouth, leaving the earthier flavors of cheese, spinach, feta, or spiced ground-lamb fillings to linger on. His baklava, phyllo pastry soaked in honey syrup and filled with nuts, is as light and rich as the baklava made by my Greek landlady of nine years ago. His western pastries are first-rate too, like a perfect baba au rhum with a crumbly, rum-soaked brioche or a beautiful raspberry cake roll. All of these are made at Ninth Street and sent over to Marin.

Perhaps he is responsible for the other

spirited Greek appetizers on the menu. One could easily make a meal of rice-stuffed grape leaves marinated in just the right balance of lemon and olive oil; or little scoops of *tarama*, red caviar beaten with olive oil, and a spread made of pungent black olives; or Stoyanof's smoky eggplant salad, juicy with melted tomato, sweet peppers, and lots of lemon. Many of the savory pastries and these appetizers come together on a *mezedes plate*, which sums up some of the best in Greek eating.

The kitchen also handles salads well. The Greek salad here is made with lots of greens sprinkled with feta cheese and pickled red onions, a few calamata olives on the side. A tart vinaigrette brings them all together. A lot of different ingredients were juggled successfully one day in a special curried chicken salad made with bits of cold grilled chicken, raisins, carrots, apple, and celery on a bed of greens. However, the shredded rockfish presented on top of greens in "fresh fish salad" did not live up to its title.

The kitchen runs into trouble with its entrees. House-made pork sausages were not only cardboard-dry but unpleasantly seasoned with excessive amounts of grated orange peel and cumin. Even a tasty yogurt sauce, a ramekin of sauteed raisins and onions, and a lentil and red pepper stew could not help these sausages out. Though the restaurant uses grain-fed, chemical-free chickens, you could never tell from a dry, overcooked chicken leg topped with a pale saute of peppers and tomatoes and accompanied by bland white rice. A swordfish brochette strung with bay leaves and paper-thin slices of lemon looked promising until I tasted it. The fish smelled none too fresh and had a texture akin to wadded paper.

Stoyanof reheats its moussaka to order in ramekins and something gets lost the second time under the broiler. The eggplant disintegrates and the whole preparation loses definition, especially under a thick blanket of white sauce and browned cheese. The lamb-filled moussaka is certainly superior to the cheese-filled moussaka, which tastes like a plate of cheese sauce. I prefer a more traditional layered presentation.

Most of the entrees on both regular meal visits came with fresh asparagus, raw on one visit, barely cooked enough on another.

At one lunch, a cream of mushroom soup, thick with pureed mushrooms, was lightened by a *chiffonnade* of fresh spinach. For those of you who like lamb, Stoyanof's offers a half pound of it, ground and patted into a burger with all the usual hamburger trimmings. A fine red potato salad in a creamy, garlicky dressing comes with it.

To fulfill its role as a rest stop for shoppers, the restaurant pours a number of good California wines by the glass and makes espresso and Turkish coffee. After sampling the baklava there, I'd be hard pressed to visit the Village shopping center without stopping for a piece.

Though as far away from a Greek village as you can get, the hot Marin sun — which you can take in on Stoyanof's patio — and the olives and grape leaves and phyllo pastries make me start thinking of Greek islands. I would like to see the restaurant kitchen think more about them too, and make the food reflect the fresh, straightforward flavors of the Greek countryside. ∎

—Patricia Unterman, June 8, 1986

Sugar's
★★

1785 Union Street (at Octavia), San Francisco. 776-2920. Open daily 6 to 10 P.M., Friday and Saturday until 11 P.M. Beer, wine. MasterCard, Visa. Reservations accepted. Moderate.

The ultimate in new age restaurants has finally happened. At the former site of a string of failed Union Street eateries, a combination California grill and sushi bar is succeeding.

Called Sugar's, it's a collaboration of owner Koetsu Akasaka, sushi master Naono Sato, and a young Western chef, Dan Harvey. Akasaka used to own the tiny Sushi Kinta in Embarcadero Four, and Harvey worked the grill at Hayes Street Grill and the cafe at Chez Panisse.

Though from diverse culinary backgrounds, everyone here seems to be on the same wavelength. What I like about Sugar's is that the two cuisines are kept distinct. There's none of that awkward mixing of opposing traditions. What does tie the two together is an insistence on freshness and simplicity. You get the feeling at Sugar's that everyone really cares about the food.

In many ways, Sugar's represents the best of what's going on in California restaurants. It's comfortable, small, unpretentious, and with moderate prices. You can go in blue jeans or a tie. You can order sushi for dinner or have it as a first course. The white, high-ceilinged, tracklighted dining room looks like a canvas waiting to be filled.

The food, too, is uncluttered. On an initial visit, a huge green salad, a little too exuberantly dressed in herby italian vinaigrette, and a cup of delicious white-bean soup, full of meaty, dried porcini mushrooms, segued nicely into a perfectly grilled, moist fillet of halibut and a fiery Indian-style brochette of tender lamb with fruit chutney. Piles of vegetables landscaped each plate.

An anticipated return visit unearthed many other treats, foremost of which were appetizers from the sushi bar. Halibut *usuzukuri* sashimi with *ponzu* sauce — translucently thin slices of raw halibut fanned out on a white plate — looked like the most fragile of flowers. These wondrously thin slices smelled sea fresh and, delicately enhanced by the *ponzu*, a lemony dipping sauce, they melted in my mouth.

The sushi department also turned out a stunning array of *nigiri* sushi. It included unusual pieces like mustardy asparagus tips strapped onto the rice with a strip of seaweed, and ever-so-slightly-grilled fillet of beef sushi.

A different kind of Asian cooking inspired a spicy sesame chicken salad, with enough hot peppers to make a dragon cry. It was delicious though, and pretty with a confetti of red and green peppers and cooling cucumbers. The soup this day was a baby food-thick puree of vegetables with a Chinese parsley seasoning.

The main courses brought a moist, lean grilled hamburger with cheese and bacon on a terrific hamburger roll. A steak cut from the fillet, also on the regular menu, was perfectly grilled, tender, tasty, and attractively priced for its generous size.

Yellowtail in the guise of *hamachi* is a favorite sushi. Its buttery, meaty white flesh makes this member of the jack family superb raw. At Sugar's, yellowtail is also grilled, and it is just as delicious. You may choose your sauce here for any of the grilled items, and a lemon and herb butter goes well with it. A roast-pepper sauce recommended with it tasted better with the fillet. The chefs here are interested in cooking with new and unusual ingredients. One night, buffalo sausage with polenta and ratatouille was on the menu, but I couldn't pass up a grilled half partridge with juicy, marinated, slightly gamy meat served with a plateful of nutty moist wild rice and chestnuts. The fresh homy breads come from the Tassajara Bread Bakery, and the wine list offers many California wines by the glass. Given its size, I'd say the kitchen made an intelligent decision to bring in pastries from the nearby Nouvelle Patisserie.

The quality and price of Sugar's is unbeatable, and I like being able to choose which way to eat. The food is not confused here as it is at so many other "California" restaurants. Sugar's may reflect sensibilities and styles garnered from older places, but it has developed a character of its own. What its chefs and owner learned, they learned well. ■

—Patricia Unterman, February 9, 1986

Taxi

★★

374 Eleventh Street, San Francisco. 558-TAXI. Open for lunch Monday through Saturday 11 A.M. to 4 P.M.; for dinner Sunday through Wednesday 5 to 11 P.M., Thursday through Saturday 5 P.M. to midnight. Beer, wine. American Express, Diners Club, Carte Blanche. Reservations accepted. Moderate.

You don't expect a brand-new restaurant

to be as good as Taxi, but then, its owners know what they are doing. The forty-seat restaurant in a warehouse in the heart of the South of Market hub has been deservedly packed from the day it opened, less than a month ago.

The difference between Taxi and most other new restaurants is that the food is so uncontrived, generous, fresh, and consistently prepared.

The stage for this hearty eating is a small high-ceilinged room with exposed beams, a bank of windows that looks out onto Eleventh Street and the DNA Lounge across the street, white walls, and cheerful lighting. The tables, covered with white linen and white butcher paper, huddle close together.

A coat of shiny varnish painted over the original flooring celebrates the different qualities of wood and cement. A compact open kitchen, about the size of a large pantry, staffed with three very neat, fast-moving cooks, turns out the concise daily menu. This unadorned room of tables and wooden chairs has a clean, inviting, airy feel to it. No artifice diverts from the main activity, the raison d'etre of a restaurant—eating and drinking.

Instead of taking the popular path of "little dishes," Taxi opts for bigness. Portions are gigantic. Salads spill over the plate. They're beautiful and fresh, but they're absurdly large as first courses. You might want to split them, but then you miss out on getting to taste something else.

A caesar salad, made with whole, light-green romaine leaves, gets an assertive and very garlicky dressing, great croutons, and a snowfall of freshly grated parmesan on top. The house green salad must take two whole heads of red leaf lettuce to compose. Larger leaves are arranged along the outside rim, then gradually smaller leaves fill up the plate in a concentric circle. Who wants to eat so much lettuce by itself, albeit so tastily dressed with vinaigrette? Too much of a good thing.

Some salads really work best as main courses, like a lovely smoked chicken salad full of colorful vegetables and roasted peppers, nestled into greens dressed in a mild black-bean vinaigrette. A traditional cobb salad, with big chunks of chicken breast, hard-boiled egg, bacon, and avocado and rocks of blue cheese, gets a handsome presentation in a deep glass bowl. All these dishes are available at both lunch and dinner.

Two starters that might actually be considered appetizers include a clever and sprightly sea scallop ceviche with mildly pickled pearl onions and a fresh tomato salsa, resplendent in a wine goblet; and a puree of seven different members of the onion family in a satisfying "seven lily soup."

Some of the main courses are bigger than life—like a brontosaurus-sized slab of prime rib with the bone, as juicy and pink and marbled with fat as any you would find in the best steak houses. A plate of pink tomato fettuccine bathed in garlic-infused cream with sweet white shrimp, peppers, and spinach brings enough of this rich pasta for three, though after the first bite you're loath to give any of it away.

Taxi uses a flat metal griddle instead of a wood- or charcoal-burning grill, and the foods cooked on it are not flavored by smoke. I think the unmarinated fish that come off it need more flavor, as exemplified by a bland piece of halibut offered one night, dabbed with a little basil-tomato sauce. At lunch, the meatier mahimahi was given the treatment that the halibut needed: it was served with a piquant orange-onion relish on a bed of buttery snow peas. Still, all the fish I've tasted at Taxi have been pristinely fresh.

A chicken breast fared better on the grill by developing a golden brown skin onto which a spoonful of snappy anaheim chili butter slowly melted. What really made this dish take off was the plateful of fresh sweet corn dotted with red and green peppers served under the chicken breast.

There are always sandwiches on the menu for those who want to eat quickly and robustly. Taxi treats chicken breasts and rockfish like hamburgers. They come on soft buns with tomato, lettuce, and onion—but they also get ramekins of house-made tartar sauce or tarragon mayonnaise.

The desserts, often just emerging from the oven when you order them, are just like the rest of the food at Taxi—big and satisfying and stylishly prepared. The temptation of warm rhubarb cobblers with rich, crumbly top crusts, tall apple pies, and hot fudge and hot caramel sundaes leads diners into higher levels of gluttony. You think you can't eat one more bite and then you find yourself dipping into a large piece of chocolate cake with custard sauce. The Taxi kitchen knows how to bake, too.

Taxi strikes me as just the kind of operation that deserves success. Its owners put their time into learning how to cook professionally and run a dining room. Chuck Phifer graduated from the California Culinary Academy, where Jeremiah Tower was his teacher. He then went on to work at the Balboa Cafe for five years during the Tower regime. His partner and dining room manager, John Crucianelli, spent two and a half years waiting on tables and managing at the Santa Fe Bar and Grill in Berkeley. They learned from their mentors well.

They found a location in an area of town that's still developing, and they opened their place on a small manageable scale, avoiding the fatal consequences of undercapitalization. They built their restaurant from the kitchen outward, with their vision of what kind of food they wanted to serve determining what their place would be.

Because Taxi is so clearly dedicated to the food side of their operation, customers feel like beneficiaries behind their towering salads and bowls of hot cobbler. Hop in a cab! ∎

—Patricia Unterman, June 7, 1987

Tommaso's

★ ★

1042 Kearny Street, San Francisco. 398-9696. Open Tuesday through Saturday from 5 to 10:45 P.M., Sunday 5 P.M. to 9:45 P.M. Beer, wine. MasterCard, Visa. No reservations. Inexpensive to moderate.

No one knows better than I how difficult it is to keep a restaurant vital over the years. Tommaso's, a North Beach landmark, has succeeded in keeping their food absolutely consistent and irresistible since opening fifty years ago.

It's as if time has stopped when you walk down into the poorly lit, cavelike dining room, with partitioned-off tables along the walls and a long communal table stretched down the middle. You can barely see the murals of the Naples coast from the poor light of ancient fixtures— and perhaps it's just as well. Decor is not the reason anyone goes to Tommaso's. It's the luscious smell of pizza baking in a wood-burning oven that makes you endure the long waits inside the drafty, chairless front vestibule. The restaurant takes no reservations and Tommaso's is as popular as ever.

If there's one universally loved item that Tommaso's makes, it's their pizza. Way before pizza baked in a wood-burning oven was a glimmer in Alice Waters's eye, Tommaso's was turning them out with perfect crisp, sweet, chewy crusts scented with smoke and copious amounts of whole-milk mozzarella, among other ingredients. The aroma of a vegetarian pizza blanketed with green pepper, onions, fresh mushrooms, and olives has driven me to ask for a small piece from the guy next to me at the long central table shared by many different parties. I never do that. The pizza super deluxe with mushrooms, peppers, ham, Tommaso's allspice-scented Italian sausage, and anchovies is spectacular—without the anchovies, which are too strong for this particular blend of ingredients. Frankly, the "pizza a la Neapolitan" with just the usual generous amount of cheese and Tommaso's tasty tomato sauce is a delight. The superlative crust, so elastic, so full of character, so beautifully browned underneath as well as on the puffy edges, so enticingly smoky, needs very little elaboration.

Tommaso's also puts out a massive calzone stuffed with a skillful blend of ricotta and mozzarella, prosciutto, and Tommaso's special spice mixture that tastes greater than the sum of its parts. All the elements seem to melt together in a happy way inside the impeccably crisp, folded-over crust. A second calzone is stuffed with slices of the aromatically spicy Italian sausage, mushrooms, and a little tomato sauce, all of which seem to melt into the ricotta and mozzarella in a special way. The calzone withstand time. I eat them cold the next day.

Of course, Tommaso's still offers their famous starters, plates of peeled peppers, crisp whole string beans, and trees of bright green broccoli, all lightly dressed in lemon juice and olive oil. They're tasty and refreshing and just what you want before the rich pizzas and calzone. The zucchini, however, is sauteed in thick rounds before it's chilled and tends to be a little soggy, and the mundane dinner salad, innocuously dressed and full of mushy cooked carrot, is something to avoid.

What surprised me about Tommaso's on my recent visits was the quality of the pastas. A daily lasagna special, layered with tender fresh noodles and that winning combination of ricotta, mozzarella, and pleasant tomato sauce, was put together in such a way that putting your fork to it felt like cutting into a pillow. A similar cheese filling was rolled into house-made manicotti smothered in tomato sauce; and basically the same mixture of cheeses augmented by ground veal filled delicate house-made ravioli. You can get either of these dishes flanked with a sausage or delicate meatballs.

Some of the kitchen staff is Chinese. This explains why calamari were so tender and sensitively fried and a bowl of steamed clams, in an odd but not unpleasant broth seasoned with vinegar and oil, were so plump and juicy. The sea-food bespoke of the freshness that results from wise Chinatown buying.

For dessert, a custardy spumoni frozen into individual bowls comes as a happy departure from the artificial-tasting spumoni served all over North Beach.

The original recipes must have been carved in stone and executed with unending attention, because this beloved North Beach joint really is as satisfying today as it was when I first ate there—and I won't tell you how long ago that was. ∎
—Patricia Unterman, September 27, 1987

Tommy Toy's
★

655 Montgomery Street, San Francisco. 397-4888. Open for lunch Monday through Friday 11:30 A.M. to 3 P.M., for dinner Monday through Saturday 6 to 10 P.M. Full bar. Major credit cards. Reservations accepted. Expensive.

Proudly printed across the top of the dinner menu at Tommy Toy's in the Montgomery-Washington Tower is this phrase: "The Chef's Specialties for the Season of Spring." Matters of syntax aside, the season is late summer, but at Tommy Toy's, time does seem to have stopped.

The elegant and mysterious dining room has the exoticism of a forties film noir set. Not a ray of natural sunlight sullies the created environment. Any number of plots could be hatched at the classy bar, or more intimately in a tiny draped tentlike room at one end of it. A major collection of chinoiserie, including a display of small pieces of ancient pottery along the wall on the way to the dining room, screens, vases, furniture, exquisite porcelain table lamps, and ornate wall moldings are set off against textured walls of celadon. It's not hard to imagine a trench-coated leading man walking into this richly furnished Asian room with a weapon concealed by the shadowy light from hundreds of tiny lamps. In the case of Tommy Toy's, he'd be better off going after the captain than the spy who had abducted the heroine.

Formally suited to match the splendor of the room, the waiters, straight from central casting, balked and complained. One night in a half-full house, we were ignored for thirty minutes after we declined cocktails. I was literally waving my arms for attention. It seemed as if the inscrutable captain, fawning over a nearby table of business men, might have noticed us out of the corner of his eye, but he chose not to. At last I flagged a bus person, who relayed the message to a waiter, who finally got to a captain. We ordered many courses to share. Much grumbling and grumpiness ensued. We asked for chopsticks and relations improved.

I expected a disastrous meal after all this, but it didn't happen that way. Beautifully arranged platters were trotted out of the kitchen and presented for approval before they were divided up. Many of the preparations had a sweet component that was balanced off by other strong flavors, much in the Shanghai style but with less oil. Ingredients were of high quality, most notably veal and pork. I think the restaurant is going after a Trader Vic's, middle-of-the-road cuisine, but, thankfully, the food turns out to be more Chinese than Western.

An unusual chicken salad with pieces of preserved ginger, tender chicken breast, black mushrooms, and fried won ton strips came off too sweet for my taste, though others at table liked it. Minced squab in lettuce leaves could have been minced anything, but I'm a pushover for this savory preparation full of black mushroom and water chestnuts. Honey and garlic spareribs were so velvety of texture, rich, and garlicky that their cloying sweetness could not stop me from nibbling every morsel off the bones.

Tommy Toy's veal tenderloin sauteed with roasted pecans is a genuine invention. The tender veal, cut into thick pieces, gets tossed with whole black mushrooms, tree ears, crisp baby carrots, and pecans. The combination was irresistible. Not so with deep-fried pork in garlic sauce, which drags you to heaven,

kicking. The pork is so crisply fried, pungent, and tender that your palate submits to the very sweet honey coating on the meat.

An insipid fillet of chicken in black bean and hot pepper sauce did not live up to its billing. Though chunks of chicken were tender and plentiful, the sauce amounted to very little. Duck braised in sweet rice vinegar had dry, sweet, tough flesh and a startling jet black color. Thin slices of grilled salmon with ginger sauce were overdone. A gray-green sauce seasoned mostly with Chinese parsley didn't enhance them.

Tommy Toy's is obviously not a noodle house, as evidenced by mushy, sweet, gutless "spicy meat sauce noodles." "Four flavors fried rice," pushed by the waiters, is innocuous and not worth the price.

At lunch, the distinguished service crew wheeled out a cart fitted with cans of burning sterno and a tasty preparation called Szechuan spicy lamb with marinated spinach. They painstakingly spooned half the lamb from the hot platter to a warm plate that they gave to me. The rest was spooned onto a cold plate and set at the table, after much conferring. Pot stickers, also served from the flaming cart, were tough of skin and cold inside.

As for the lamb dish, the meat had been "velvetized" and had the resulting soft and slippery texture. The sauce was indeed spicy and wonderful over a huge pile of delicious wilted spinach with braised shallots. A lobster and mushroom dumpling with spinach in bouillon read more enticingly than it tasted. The bouillon turned out to be pale chicken broth with a little chili oil floating on top, the dumplings thick skinned, and the chopped lobster and black mushroom stuffing muddled in flavor. I liked a preparation of diced scallops with fresh water chestnuts served on cold lettuce leaves, reminiscent of the minced squab dish.

It's fashionable now in the restaurant world to mix Chinese and Western cooking techniques and ingredients. A number of restaurants like Chinois on Main in Santa Monica and China Moon [q.v.] on

Post Street in San Francisco are doing it; many others are attempting. The best of them are forging a new style which takes creativity, trial and error, risk, and dedication, but at Tommy Toy's, ennui seems to be the order of the day. The restaurant may have jumped onto the crest of a new culinary wave but it doesn't belong there. ∎

—Patricia Unterman, September 14, 1986

Tortola

★

3640 Sacramento, San Francisco. 929-8181. Open Tuesday through Saturday 11:30 A.M. to 10 P.M., Sunday 5 to 9 P.M. Beer, wine. Master-Card, Visa. Reservations accepted for five or more. Inexpensive to moderate.

The notion of a restaurant dedicated to early California food is intriguing. How far back do you go? To the cooking of North American Indians? To native Mexican and Spanish settlers? To the immigrants brought into the state by the gold rush? Tortola, which calls itself an early California restaurant, has chosen a predominantly Mexican motif for its menu. My regret is that the menu does not begin to explore the possibilities of early Californian cooking, or, for that matter, Mexican cooking either.

What Tortola does do well is provide a striking but casual neighborhood restaurant with prices that allow families to dine out without spending a fortune. I've rarely been in a more stylish restaurant where you can eat heartily for under $10.

Tortola, which opened on Polk Street years ago, now inhabits a long, narrow space in what looks like a renovated brick garage. You enter from an airy, skylit, tiled corridor into an high-ceilinged sandy pink room furnished with blond wood benches and tables and squared-off red wooden chairs. The long, austere lines of the restaurant are softened by rectangles of loosely mounted canvas dyed the same color as the walls. This device works uncannily well at adding texture to the hard

surfaces and absorbing sound. Color comes from some brightly painted canvases and a green-stained wooden wall, about chest high, that runs lengthwise down the center of the dining room, separating counter seats from the tables. A few terra cotta pots of cacti are de rigueur.

In contrast to the stunning dining room, too many of the "Early California Specialties" are monochromatic. For some reason, the restaurant makes a single filling, combining chicken and beef, that is used throughout the menu. You might first encounter it in miniature appetizer tamales called tortolettes and as a filling in four miniature tacos. Then it's used on a tostada; a thick, flaky, deep-fried cornmeal pancake drowned in iceberg lettuce; in normal-sized tacos and refritos; and in *chalupas*, cornmeal cups stuffed with the mixture. The filling turns out to be in most of the items on the menu, especially if you order combination plates. Though it is moist, cumin scented, and tasty in the little tacos or tamales, you tire of it, just as you do of the ubiquitous brown ranchero sauce poured over every one of the Early California Specialties.

Probably the best way to order is to start with an unadorned bowl of simply made guacamole, just avocado mashed with garlic and hot chilies and some mildly hot fresh tomato salsa, which you have to order on the side. These are to be scooped up with Tortola's thick, fried-to-order tortilla chips. Then look to the daily specials printed on a separate menu. The cleanest and tastiest of this restaurant's dishes are to be found there.

One evening, a thin flank steak became the filling for a quesadilla along with jack cheese and roasted chilies. The garnish of julienned jicama and avocado slices, green tomatillo salsa, and sour cream lent the flour tortilla sandwich textural interest. Each flavor element was distinct, in contrast to the muddy Early California plates. However, a special of grilled chicken breast tostada reverted to form. The grilled chicken disappeared in a sea of lettuce and brown ranchero sauce. A simple grilled rib-eye steak with sauteed strips of green pasilla peppers, red bells, and onions came with a cup of piquant, soupy black beans garnished with sour cream and some bright carrots and asparagus. If you wanted the flavors to merge, you could wrap some of the steak and beans in a warm corn tortilla and season it with hot pickled green peppers or fresh salsa brought to the table with the entrees.

Another evening the quesadilla was stuffed with Pyrenees ham along with the cheese and roasted chilies, and garnished with sour cream and fresh tomato salsa. It reminded me of a Mexican grilled ham and cheese sandwich. Even better was a spring lamb stew served in a flat bowl over herbed rice. Hardly spring lamb, the meat had a muttony flavor and was cooked to the point of falling apart with green and red peppers, fennel, and onion.

The short wine list offers some excellent wines by the glass, including a Ridge zinfandel and Sandeman Founder's Reserve port. The port makes a fine dessert if you don't feel like an inappropriately heavy if tasty bread pudding seasoned with cinnamon, raisins, and walnuts, or a puddinglike sour cream apple pie with a crumble top. The flan is rubbery.

Despite some of the monotonous menu items, I think Tortola shows promise. Short of revamping the regular menu, the daily specials allow for lighter, more interesting fare, and the fresh tomato salsa and pure guacamole with warm chips show that Tortola is heading in the right direction. To that end they have hired Kathy Riley, formerly of the Zuni Cafe, to help them develop some new dishes. With a culinary point of view to match their sleek, modern dining room, Tortola could find new identity as a contemporary early California restaurant. ■

—Patricia Unterman, May 10, 1987

Tourelle Cafe and Restaurant

★

3565 Mount Diablo Boulevard, Lafayette. 284-3565. Restaurant open Tuesday through Friday 11:30 A.M. to 2:30 P.M.; Tuesday through Sunday 5 to 10 P.M. Cafe open Tuesday through Saturday 11 A.M. to 11 P.M., Sunday 10 A.M. to 2:30 P.M. and 5 to 10 P.M. Full bar. Major credit cards. Reservations necessary for restaurant; no reservations in cafe. Restaurant expensive; cafe moderate.

If there's any kind of restaurant I love to avoid, it's an expensive French restaurant in the suburbs. These places seem to compete with each other over who has the plushest vinyl banquettes, and how many times during a meal their waiters will ask you whether everything is satisfactory, monsieur.

Then there's the food. Were their menus not reprinted frequently to raise prices, they'd be yellowed with age. Many of the dishes offered are those cliches that you somehow never see in France, but only in American shopping centers.

To anyone accustomed to this sort of scenario, Tourelle in Lafayette will come as a shock. Never has a restaurant been put together with more taste, both inside and out. The building is of old brick and wood, built around a courtyard with tables and a fountain. The high-backed fabric chairs are both elegant and comfortable; the soft lighting comes from the most stylish chandeliers I've ever laid eyes on.

And the staff really knows its stuff. Instead of robots who tell you their names and spout all the standard lines, you get friendly, knowledgeable people who are genuinely concerned about whether everything's going well.

You can add to this some very interesting menus, even though the format is practically a carbon copy of Chez Panisse. Like Panisse, there's a formal restaurant with reservations and a fixed-price dinner and an informal pasta/pizza/salads/grilled meats cafe. (The fixed-price dinner does not include coffee and dessert.)

In short Tourelle would be the perfect

place for suburban dining—were it not for one maddening problem. I've encountered lots of restaurants with good food and lots with bad food, but few where you can get such an inconsistent mixture of both in one meal. In two dinners in the restaurant and one in the cafe, I had several fabulous dishes, several that couldn't be eaten, and lots in between.

Here's the most extreme example: My first meal in the restaurant, I ordered a roast saddle of venison stuffed with currants in a sauce with fresh juniper berries. It sounded wonderful, but it came from the kitchen so overcooked that the meat was dry and gray. I told the waitress I couldn't eat it—and then she confided that the chef had wondered whether he should have sent that piece out. The replacement was perfect, but what a shabby performance.

That same dinner brought a smoked fish chowder sent from heaven—an array of house-smoked fish in a rich creamy soup lightly scented with the smoke flavor. But then there were tiny rubbery snails in a bland cream sauce accompanied by a burned piece of puff pastry. And three kinds of caviar on dollops of crème fraîche resting on endive leaves, with the caviar applied so sparingly and the whole dish so cold from the refrigerator that your taste buds couldn't even detect the caviar.

The second dinner continued the pattern. Lobster served in the shell, sauteed with leeks, shallots, ginger, and apple, couldn't have been better. But truffle flan had absolutely no taste or smell of truffles, smoked salmon was oily and fishy, and a duck pot pie with wild mushrooms—a really interesting variation on a boring American dish—had virtually no mushrooms and a bland gravy that lacked even a hint of seasoning.

The cafe, where prices are lower and ordering is a la carte, came out notches below the restaurant in quality. In fact, it would have been a total loser had not the meal been redeemed by a first-rate fettuccine with tiny fresh peas, *pancetta*, and cream. The pasta was so expertly prepared that it was clear some people in the kitchen knew what they were doing. But you couldn't have told it from the other dishes.

The calzone was a mess—a thick doughy crust and thick gloppy cheese that overwhelmed the wild mushrooms in the stuffing. A pate featured pork that was much too fat, and a carrot curry soup with sauteed apples was too sweet and had too much heavy cream—there was simply no carrot flavor.

For the entrees, a mixed grill was dry and bland, with no taste of the advertised herbs. The top sirloin in it was ordered rare, but one piece came out raw and another medium. Veal stew—which oddly enough included some snow peas that were raw and others hugely overcooked—was ruined by a tomato-based sauce so overreduced it was actually sticky.

Desserts in the cafe were mediocre, with a pear and strawberry crisp made with scandalously underripe pears. The restaurant had much better desserts, including an outstanding homemade hazelnut ice cream served in chocolate shells with *crème anglaise*.

I had enough good dishes at Tourelle—at least in the restaurant part—to realize that a person lucky enough in ordering could come out with a fine meal. But there's clearly a total absence of quality control. Everything was done correctly in building the restaurant and hiring and staff. The ingredients are all fresh—everything from bread to ice cream to smoked fish is made on the premises. But if my meals were any guide, someone needs to watch much more carefully what comes out of the kitchen. ■

—Stan Sesser, October 31, 1986

Tra Vigne

★ ★

1050 Charter Oak Avenue, St. Helena. 707-963-4444. Open Sunday through Thursday noon to 9 P.M., Friday and Saturday until 10 P.M. Full bar. MasterCard, Visa. Reservations accepted. Moderate.

Scientists say that being near a body of water makes you a calmer and happier person. Though I've lived for many years close to the Bay, nothing makes me happier than being in the middle of vineyards.

Many people feel the same—the wine country has grown a lot in fifteen years. What was once a sleepy countryside dotted with small towns of people who stayed home and tended their land and families has become glamorous, like the wine areas of Bordeaux and Burgundy. The development of restaurants in the valley is a case in point.

Just ten years ago, restaurants in the Napa Valley depended on seasonal visitors and weekend tourists. Their menus were limited, their dining rooms charming and small, their prices relatively high. But so many people were pouring into the valley, not just as visitors but as wine makers, vineyard owners, weekend-home owners, wine sellers, and winery public relations personnel, that the need for a different kind of restaurant grew. Cindi Pawlcyn, a young woman who was then chef at Meadowood, and some partners decided to fill that need and opened Mustard's, a smokehouse and cafe that hasn't had an empty table since construction was completed five years ago. At the time, no one thought that a large, trendy, California restaurant could succeed in the still isolated, conservative valley, but everyone was dead wrong.

Now Pawlcyn and her partners have opened a second major place right off Highway 29, called Tra Vigne, which translates "among vines." It is one of the most beautiful restaurants in California, and a delightful place to stop in the Napa Valley.

Located in the former St. George building, a gorgeous stone house with tiled patios and high ceilings, Tra Vigne's designers have created a strikingly austere but romantic ambience. The small rooms and bar from the old venture have been opened up, so now Tra Vigne is one gigantic room with a long bar serving drinks and food along one side, and an open kitchen along the other. Dan Friedlander, head designer at Limn Studios, created the neo-medieval look, which captures the feeling of ancient Italian villas but is completely modern. The plastered walls look like old stone, while the marble work on the bar suggests Florentine opulence.

The menu goes off in its own direction. I'm sure the Spectrum people who opened Tutto Bene in San Francisco soon afterward took a close look, because their menu is very similar. Lots of *antipasti* and small portions of pasta are listed, as well as pizzas from a wood-fired oven, Italian sandwiches, and some grilled meats and fish. You make a meal by ordering lots of different things. Practically everything is colorful, tasty, and fun. It's not exactly Italian food, but Italian-inspired food. The dishes are witty takeoffs rather than replicas of any regional Italian dishes I've ever tasted.

From the *antipasti* section you won't want to miss mozzarella and prosciutto wrapped in romaine lettuce and grilled over a fire. It's sauced in a sharp sun-dried tomato vinaigrette and surrounded by a wreath of arugula and baby greens. Also delicious are heads of radicchio grilled until they wilt a little, sauced with a warm vinaigrette enriched with black olives and *pancetta*.

Another terrific first course called *fusilli Michelangelo* comes from the pasta section, a warm pasta salad, really, of corkscrew noodles tossed with still-crunchy radicchio, shiitakes, and a fresh tomato sauce. The small pizzas are nice too, like the *pizza Margherita* with fresh tomatoes, mozzarella, and basil, though with the end of the tomato season here, this pizza will have to be changed. The crust on the pizza needed a little more elasticity and flavor.

A salad of marinated white beans, parmesan, and lots of nutty-flavored arugula was simple and pleasant if a little bland. Another composed salad of grilled, then chilled, rare tuna dressed in smoked tomato salsa really hit the mark. The smoky tuna and tomatoes made a colorful presentation with sweet, skinny green beans dusted with parmesan and a mustardy potato salad.

The foods cooked on the grill have had

their ups and downs. Successful one afternoon were prawns wrapped in crispy *pancetta* with a mild nutmeg flavor. The succulent shrimp got a savory roasted garlic vinaigrette and was accompanied with a batch of bright vegetables. But from the same grill came a sliced chicken breast with slices of grilled eggplant and shiitake mushrooms. It would have been a fine dish had it not been for an odd petroleum smell—from burned California olive oil? Or, perhaps, from being grilled over coals that were just beginning to ignite? It was a flavor I detected one evening in some grilled sausages covered in a soapy sauce seasoned with too much rosemary. The two crisp triangles of deep-fried polenta served with them were fun.

The desserts were delightful. Crisp chocolate *cannoli* shells were filled with lightened and sweetened fresh ricotta, golden raisins, and pistachios, and a barely poached pear came in a merlot custard with crisp chocolate bread sticks. Some mildly orange-scented vanilla ice cream was sprinkled with bits of crisp *biscotti* and toasted almonds. Only a generic berry *sorbet* lacked character.

As one would expect from a Napa Valley restaurant, there's a good selection of local wines at reasonable prices, as well as an interesting Italian list. In the current fashion, the restaurant bakes its own breads and serves them with olive oil instead of butter.

Between my two visits several months apart, the menu had been changed quite a bit—some raw quail I had been served was no longer on the menu, but a delicious, very rich wild mushroom lasagna was new. Also new were sandwiches and the terrific tuna salad.

The main difference was in the level of confidence in the kitchen. Unmonitored seasoning and shaky cooking technique had all but vanished by my second visit. There are still problems to be worked out in executing the long, detailed menu, like the chemical flavor on some of the grilled foods, but the lunch I had on the patio one afternoon was pure pleasure. One bit of advice: If you're ordering lots of dishes, be sure to tell the waiter exactly how you want them served or everything will come out of the kitchen at the same time. ■
—Patricia Unterman, November 22, 1987

Triple Rock Brewery

★ ★

1920 Shattuck Avenue (near Hearst), Berkeley. 843-2739. Open daily from 11:30 A.M. until after midnight. Beer, wine. Cash only. No reservations. Inexpensive.

It's very fashionable to write about the matching of wine and food. But I'm going to talk about a somewhat less elegant subject—beer and food. Pull up a garbage can and listen.

Czechoslovakia, which has the best beer in the world, also has what is probably the worst food. Germany is a close second for best and worst in each category. In England, you can sample some wonderful beers in pubs—accompanied by indigestible steak and kidney pie.

Are beer drinkers masochists? I'm not sure, but it was with extreme trepidation that I set out to explore one of the newest and most interesting phenomena in the California food-and-drink scene: the brew pub. These bars have mercifully decided to free us from the embarrassment of American mass-produced dishwater by brewing their own beer.

I stopped at the Triple Rock Brewery in Berkeley, near the UC campus. Triple Rock is owned by John and Reid Martin, ages twenty-six and twenty-nine, who decided to branch out from their Berkeley cookie store and yogurt stand.

"We wanted to do something that wasn't being done on the next corner," John Martin explains.

You wouldn't want to go to Triple Rock with the intention of concentrating on a volume of poetry. It's a big, high-ceilinged, sparsely furnished room, with rock music and loud conversations. But it's also a friendly place with a nice feeling to it.

Food is sold at a window that opens onto the kitchen, and the menu of nachos, chili, hot dogs, sandwiches, and the like doesn't offer much hope. But with my first bite of nachos, I knew that this place was going to be something special.

I had never tasted nachos I didn't gag on. But instead of a leaden heap of mush, Triple Rock serves a remarkable version—fresh spicy salsa, delicate cheese, good crispy chips, and guacamole and sour cream topping.

The hot dog, believe it or not, is equally good. It's steamed in beer, topped with chili and cheese, served on a sesame bun, and accompanied by lots of corn chips and yellow chili peppers. And if you order a bowl of black bean chili, you're going to get something fresh tasting and flavorful (fresh chili in a bar?); it would be perfect with a little more spiciness.

As for the sandwiches, head right for the "Bro Martin"—good rare roast beef, swiss cheese, and blue-cheese dressing, served on a baguette studded with anise and poppy seeds from Kensington's Semifreddi Bakery. It is one of the world's great baguettes, and it doesn't surprise me that the few restaurants I've been in that care enough to serve it have good food.

Good nachos, hot dogs, and sandwiches are a rare treat, but when you can wash them down with home-brewed beer, it becomes a perfect light meal.

The Triple Rock generally has two ales and a porter, and if you're lucky, it also may have a special ale that's stronger and tastes more of hops. Of the two regular ales, the Pinnacle Pale Ale had a satisfying clean body with a bit of sweetness, but the Red Rock Ale was disappointingly flat and weak. The porter, a gutsy black beer, was smooth and clean with a roasted taste. ▪

—Stan Sesser, January 23, 1987

Tutto Bene

★

2080 Van Ness Avenue (at Pacific), San Francisco. 673-3500. Open Monday through Thursday 11:30 A.M. to 11 P.M., Friday 11:30 A.M. to midnight, Saturday 5 P.M. to midnight, Sunday 5 to 11 P.M. Full bar. Major credit cards. Reservations accepted at lunch and for parties of six or more after 5 P.M. Moderate.

All seems to be going very well at Tutto Bene, the newest restaurant in the upscale Spectrum chain. The crowds waiting at the bar are thick, the food coming out of the kitchen is colorful, and the look of the place is fun and stylish. But all these things could have been said of its predecessor, Sam Duval's Cafe Royale, in its opening months.

Tutto Bene is a little different. Once a piano showroom, it still has a long rectangular double bar at front center, on display through massive windows that look out onto Van Ness Avenue. Shelves of Italian groceries are suspended above it, and near the entry are refrigerated cases of Italian hams, cheeses, and vegetables, the makings of *antipasti*.

The back wall is covered with a huge dreamlike mural of filled plates and glasses, a facsimile of which brightens the front of the menu. At Cafe Royale, the seating was arranged on gradually elevated tiers, all looking down to the bar. The new owners have elevated the dining room floor but leveled it out. To break up the large open expanse of the room, they've erected bulky, free-standing, squared-off arches. The new design works much better.

Watching other people is a primary draw at this restaurant. When Cafe Royale opened several years ago, it pulled a very young crowd, which has since emigrated South of Market. The Tutto Bene diners look older and are there, most of all, to be part of a scene. The mandatory 45-minute wait for a table in the evening, whether you have actually gathered six people for a reservation or not, is considered part of the fun. However, I was put off by the maitre d's arrogance one evening when he kept us waiting well over 45 minutes and then was unable to seat us in a non-smoking section. With no apologies, he acted as if he were doing us a favor by seating us at all.

The large menu is top-heavy with appetizers and small portions of pasta, all reasonably priced. We started one evening with a handsome plate of prosciutto, *speck* (Italian smoked ham), and *bresaola* (air-dried beef) with figs.

Other appetizers weren't as successful. The raw tuna in *tonno alla giapponese* wasn't fresh enough, and bundles of raw beef held an unpalatably salty filling of parmesan, capers, and celery. A tossed salad of varied lettuces and bland smoked duck needed a stronger dressing, while some soggy marinated eggplant was beset by too much dressing of conflicting flavors.

A strange appetizer of skewered browned ravioli filled with potatoes and mozzarella developed tough edges. Everyone at my table liked a dish of soft polenta, rich with tart *stracchino* cheese, flanked by a head of roasted garlic, but I didn't care for all the biting raw garlic in the sauteed mushrooms on top of it.

The pastas offered intriguing combinations such as little pasta shells with shrimp, tiny white beans, and parmesan, which might have been fun if the shrimp had been fresher. Tulip-shaped pasta with tomatoes, olives, and capers, among other rich and salty ingredients, withered under big chunks of black olive. Amid all this mediocre food, along came a delightful pasta of thin black noodles, tender fresh squid, and bright-red tomatoes.

Among the main courses, I liked a platter of braised veal shanks and duck legs, served with soft polenta and garlicky spinach; and a skewer of grilled veal tenderloin seasoned with sage on top of a slab of irresistible deep-fried polenta. A dried-out quail on an inedible hard-fried noodle pancake and a soapy-tasting, over-herbed roast rabbit with an undercooked half eggplant next to it, was charmless. A whole small braised rock fish, flanked by grilled tomatoes and fennel, looked mouthwatering, but a heavy hand with fennel seeds and some anisey liqueur, combined with overcooking, brought me down to earth.

With a menu packed with so many good ideas, it seemed a shame that the kitchen couldn't come close to getting them out that busy night. I returned for lunch, when the place was quiet, and had a better meal.

An antipasto platter looked as colorful as the wall mural. The marinated eggplant this time was fresher, firmer, and more balanced in seasoning. A juicy toast covered with fresh tomatoes and mozzarella was echoed in a rolled cheese pinwheel with swirls of pureed sun-dried tomato, olives, and basil and pine nuts. The beef packets this time were carefully filled with capers, parmesan, and celery, and were tasty.

Then the pastas came and once again I had to wonder if anyone was home in the kitchen. *Cappellini* with tomato, blanched garlic, olive oil, and basil had a heavenly smell, but it was so highly peppered and so undersalted it seemed as if the cooks had confused the two condiments. Some doughy potato *gnocchi* had a rabbit sauce with the same soapy, too-much-rosemary flavor of the rabbit I'd tasted before.

Just when I was about to throw up my hands, an ethereal pasta materialized, tender thin-skinned ravioli filled with a delicate mixture of smoked salmon and ricotta in a basil-infused cream sauce.

Grilled halibut, part of a seafood platter of the day, was juicy and fresh, but some whole shrimp with heads and shells were grilled into oblivion. A heap of fruity-flavored glossy black Chinese rice, whose brilliant color comes from the lava soil in which it grows, looked spectacular next to the fish, as did colorful strips of sauteed peppers. A grilled chicken breast sported a savory sauce of sun-dried tomatoes, olives, and garlic, in much better balance than the sauce on the pasta from the other evening.

I recommend a wine-soaked, pine-nut-studded cornmeal pound cake for dessert, fresh and wonderful at lunch though dry at dinner.

Though there are some high points at Tutto Bene, my experiences so far have been chancy. The overall problems seem to be freshness, strong herb and raw garlic abuse, and quality control. ■

—Patricia Unterman, October 25, 1987

231 Ellsworth

★ ★

231 Ellsworth Street, San Mateo (take the Third Avenue West exist off 101, turn right on South Ellsworth). 347-7231. Open Monday through Friday 11:30 A.M. to 2 P.M. Monday through Saturday 5:30 P.M. to 10 P.M. Beer, wine. Major credit cards. Reservations essential. Moderate to expensive.

Is the Bay Area restaurant scene getting dull and predictable? You could argue that the burst of creative energy spurred by the development of California cuisine has faded, that new trends such as Cajun food have fizzled out, and that little interesting is going on beyond the explosion of restaurants from Southeast Asia. Or you could get in your car, drive to San Mateo, and have your hopes raised again.

What's happening in San Mateo, at a restaurant named 231 Ellsworth, is demonstrating that young, innovative, idealistic chefs are still making their mark. The kitchen isn't perfect yet—you're likely to encounter an occasional flawed dish—but I'd already rank the year-old 231 Ellsworth among the top French restaurants in the Bay Area. On the Peninsula, it's perhaps the single best restaurant of any sort.

231 Ellsworth represents the partnership of Kurt Grasing, who runs the kitchen, and Ken Ottoboni, the maitre d' and wine buyer. Grasing, an Oregonian who is all of thirty-one, has a long list of restaurant kitchens to his credit, including a couple of the best French restaurants of France and England. Ottoboni comes from Le Castel, a San Francisco restaurant that for years has made good service into a fine art.

Naming a restaurant after its address might be mundane, but there's nothing mundane about the way 231 Ellsworth was designed. What could have been a large barnlike room was instead gracefully divided into intimate dining spaces, with the tables luxuriously far apart. With soft lighting, a raised floor area along one side of the room, and a series of panels protruding from the pink and gray walls, there's a degree of elegance and comfort that's rarely encountered in a restaurant.

Even before the food arrives, you'll notice the skilled, professional service and the first-rate wine list. Ottoboni has put together a collection of 134 wines that could serve as a model for French restaurants, where wine lists are too often little more than a haphazard attempt to part the customer from the maximum amount of money. There are lots of good choices for about $15, some interesting and affordable older wines (such as the 1976 Guigal Côtes du Rhône) and even four 1970 bordeaux for little more than they'd cost in a wine store.

But the food was definitely at the top of the list of attractions. Grasing is a classic French cook who sautes lots of meats in duck fat and uses butter and cream in many sauces. Yet he has such a deft hand that nothing, absolutely nothing, comes out heavy.

Take the breast of duck with rhubarb as an example. The duck breast has been sauteed in duck fat; the rhubarb has been cooked with port and then pureed; the sauce includes not only port, but butter blended with foie gras. Yet when you eat it, there's not a hint of anything sweet, greasy, or leaden.

The tender rare slices of duck breast melt in your mouth; the rhubarb is perfect, not a bit astringent, and the beautiful sauce has been lightened with duck stock and raspberry vinegar. Duck breast might be on everyone's menu these days, but you won't find a better preparation.

Or take halibut fillets, rolled in bread crumbs and sauteed in butter. Who needs the batter and the butter when you could simply grill it? In this case, though, it turned out to be one of the nicest fish dishes I can remember. The very fresh halibut wasn't at all buttery, and the bread crumbs, instead of making it mushy, added a pleasant crunchy texture. Underneath was a finely chopped saute of shallots, wild mushrooms, sweetbreads, and bay shrimp in a bit of cream. Just a touch of butter sauce was spread around the edge. Absolute heaven.

The menu is very reasonably priced considering the elegant and innovative French food. And Monday through Thursday there's a fantastic bargain of a fixed-price dinner that includes a choice from three appetizers, a salad, a choice from one fish and two meat entrees, and dessert. The dinner cuts no corners; the halibut was on the fixed-price menu, and so was a magnificent roast baby chicken resting on a flan of pureed leeks.

Many other dishes stood out. Sweetbreads, coated with almonds and bread crumbs and served on a bed of spinach, couldn't have been more juicy and delicious. Agnolotti, raviolilike pasta stuffed with a puree of mushrooms, were served with gloriously sweet bay scallops in a sauce of cream and brie that somehow managed to be not the least bit heavy. Smoked salmon and new potatoes on a bed of boutique lettuces lightly dressed with vinaigrette proved an ideal appetizer.

Yet in the midst of all this wonderful food, the kitchen fell down on an occasional dish. Mignons of beef with wild mushrooms came well done, although they had been ordered medium rare. Outrageously wonderful slices of venison were wrecked by a sauce so sweet it should have gone on pancakes. Shredded warm cabbage with bacon and roquefort was overwhelmed by too much cheese. And linguine with duck and wild mushrooms was dull and underseasoned the first time; at the second dinner it was considerably better.

I can utter no complaints about the eight desserts I tasted. Dessert chef Phil Ogiela is creating some of the most interesting and successful treats in the Bay Area. A lemon tart lover will shed tears of joy at his version, with its absolutely in-

tense lemon flavor that's neither sweet nor sour, and a white chocolate hater (like myself) will have second thoughts after tasting Ogiela's white chocolate ice cream with fresh fruit compote.

The Bay Area already has wonderful French food of every conceivable style. Yet 231 Ellsworth has managed in just a year to emerge as one of the best of the lot. ∎
—Stan Sesser, September 11, 1987

Umberto

141 Steuart Street, San Francisco. 543-8021. Open for lunch Monday through Friday 11:30 A.M. to 2:30 P.M., for dinner Monday through Saturday 5:30 to 11 P.M. Closed Sundays. Full bar. Major credit cards. Reservations accepted. Moderate.

When I moved to San Francisco seventeen years ago, innovation in cooking went little further than serving a fresh vegetable instead of a frozen one. Great bread was supermarket sourdough; great French cooking was daring to prepare something out of Julia Child Volume I.

Times have changed, but if you ate nothing but Italian food, you'd never know it. Excepting perhaps Vivande, and Chez Panisse when Paul Bertolli cooks Italian dishes, Italian menus, styles and tastes remain constant.

But being an eternal optimist, I keep looking, and for Italian food, my latest try was Umberto, a large, handsome basement-level restaurant behind the old Rincon Annex post office.

Umberto, which opened in 1984, is an offshoot of a successful chain of restaurants in Vancouver, British Columbia. The San Francisco branch initially got very mixed reports; many people said you could have dishes ranging from mediocre to fantastic at the same meal.

What lured me to Umberto was a friend's description of their seafood lasagna with the noodles dyed black from squid ink. Using squid ink as a pasta dye isn't new; I first had it at Spago in Los Angeles several years ago. But innovation in San Francisco Italian food has to be measured in small steps, and I quickly headed off to Umberto for two dinners.

It's an attractive place, on a block of brick buildings that makes you think you're in Georgetown in Washington, D.C. The red tile floor and the low ceilings don't help the noise level any, but they create a cavelike ambience that you find much more frequently in the East than out here.

As for the food, there's now a fairly uniform level of quality, but that level is distressingly low.

If you're lucky at Umberto, you'll get a good piece of meat that has been left fairly unscathed by the cooking process. That describes the *osso buco*, a nice meaty veal shank that's tender and delicious. The meat and the bland tomato sauce on top betrayed not a hint of herbs or seasoning, but the meat itself was enjoyable.

That wasn't the case with the veal scaloppine. Some decent pieces of veal—although again dramatically underseasoned—were sandwiched between rubbery cheese and spinach so overcooked it looked black. On the side were snow peas that had turned gray and some greasy potatoes.

As for the lasagna, a heavy, heavy lobster cream sauce had turned the dish to lead. Those wonderful black noodles were drowned by a thick brown sauce. The whole dish was so heavy-handed that I couldn't even distinguish what sort of seafood I was eating.

From the listless Italian bread to the stale-tasting cannoli and the gluey cheesecake, other dishes were equally bad. Minestrone tasted sour and featured overcooked vegetables. Grilled radicchio had an aroma vaguely reminiscent of lighter fluid. A salmon and tuna special suffered from having been far too long on the grill, and the advertised bell pepper sauce hadn't a hint of the peppers.

A couple of dishes, though, were decent. The best was a cold fish salad, a pleasant assortment of shellfish accompanied by dill mayonnaise on a bed of butter lettuce. Prosciutto and melon was also fine, and fresh-tasting fried calamari

suffered only slightly from a too doughy batter.

The dinners at Umberto left me wondering why so many San Franciscans eat so happily at Italian restaurants that are mediocre. Maybe that's the problem: We all like Italian food so much there's little incentive for the restaurants to change. ∎

—Stan Sesser, May 22, 1987

Vanessi's on Nob Hill

★

1177 California Street, San Francisco. 771-2422. Open Monday through Thursday 11:30 A.M. to 10 P.M., Friday 11:30 A.M. to midnight, Saturday and Sunday 4:30 P.M. to midnight. Full bar. MasterCard, Visa, American Express, Diners Club. Reservations accepted. Moderate.

I found it hard to believe that Vanessi's on Broadway would find its second wind on Nob Hill, but I guess I underestimated the endurance of Vanessi's customers. The Nob Hill restaurant opened to immediate success, and the Broadway location is beginning to regain its North Beach clientele.

I myself numbered as one of the Broadway regulars for a period of about three years in the early eighties when Giovanni Leoni, now owner of Buca Giovanni, was still cooking and Vanessi's was packed every single night until one in the morning. What a fabulous scene it was! The crowd pulled from every social strata, every profession, every age group. You had to pay the maitre d' to get into the place, even with a reservation. The tourists stood by and watched the regulars privateer their tables.

How fondly I remember the countless plates of linguine with clams, spaghetti carbonara, charcoal-grilled marinated T-bone steak, and sliced tomatoes with anchovies and onions I ate at the counter, watching the cooks preparing the food. It amazed me how a seemingly chaotic system of ordering could work so well.

But the system stopped working. The pressure of the crowds affected the kitchen and items like pasta started being cooked sloppily. Mr. Leoni left to open his own place and the restaurant workers' strike hit Vanessi's with a vengeance. The restaurant barely recovered. The food went straight downhill and so did patronage.

So how could a famous North Beach restaurant in this beleaguered condition open a large branch on Nob Hill, of all places? Owner Bart Shea knew who and what he was after. He transformed the former Mama's site in Gramercy Towers, across the street from Grace Cathedral, into a spacious, comfortable, slightly formal dining room that feels just like the original Vanessi's. He installed his trademark open kitchen with counter seating and lots of burgundy vinyl booths, mirrors, and chandeliers. Even the bar, which is full again, feels the same. Mr. Shea claims that his customers stopped coming to the Broadway restaurant because they couldn't park. At the Nob Hill location he arranged for subsidized parking right in the building and the crowds are back, the majority of them older.

As for the menu, it's the same as the original, though somewhat edited. Unfortunately, the food has not returned to its former dependability; carelessness still has a grip on the kitchen. At both of my visits to the new Vanessi's, the kitchen got backed up and the food that finally arrived was wrong. Both times the waiter did not rise to the occasion.

I was served a petite culotte steak, ordered rare, that was so burned and tough I couldn't eat it. The kitchen had obviously held it on the broiler while the rest of the food at our table was being prepared; the steak never should have left the kitchen. Given that it did, and that the waiter saw me cut into it and not eat it, he offered no redress. Frankly, no one either time, including the management, seemed to care that bad food was being served.

On another occasion, forty-five minutes into a wait between courses, the waiter handled the delay by disappearing. We were ready for another bottle of wine, some more bread, a slight acknowledgment that something had gone wrong, but everyone walked by our table besides our waiter. Our waiters both times were older, middle-aged men, who had the moves of professionals but none of the substance. This kind of dumb service doesn't wash in San Francisco any more.

I watched one of these waiters make my caesar salad at tableside. He poured in about a cup of vinegar and spooned out about half a cup of dijon mustard, which produced a dressing so abundant it formed a deep acidic puddle at the bottom of the plate. The romaine and house-baked croutons were ruined. Luckily, the pantry put together Vanessi's tasty spinach salad sprinkled with lots of real bacon and sliced mushrooms. Also dependably good because of a lively house vinaigrette were hearts of romaine and tomato slices with anchovies. Minestrone soup was as ever—mushy and tired.

The spaghetti carbonara brought back memories of the old Vanessi's. The al dente pasta stood up to the rich sauce of *pancetta*, shallot, cream, and egg, but linguine with clams lacked all character. The pasta was soggy, the sauce winy with no flavor of clams. Vanessi's version of noodles Alfredo started out promisingly with thick ribbons of tender fresh pasta, but instead of the traditional tossing with butter, cream, and cheese, Vanessi's used unseasoned white sauce and the result was bland.

Chicken saute Vanessi arrived done to a turn, pieces of nicely browned chicken tossed with peppers and onions, parsley and garlic with a deglaze of a little white wine. Perfect. Veal piccata, however, was awash in a floury sauce, and the veal was not as tender as I would have hoped. Fillet of sole meunière comes as a spongy egg-battered fillet. Crisp shoestring potatoes and big portions of precooked vegetable melange accompany various entrees.

For dessert, Vanessi's warm, frothy zabaglione, overflowing its dish onto two lady fingers, remains a lovely constant.

An order-by-number wine list with a cellar that produces about 50 percent of its listed bottles makes you consider sticking with martinis throughout the meal. After the two experiences I had there, I needed a couple. ∎

—Patricia Unterman, September 7, 1986

Ristorante Venezia

★★

1902 University Avenue (at Martin Luther King, Jr. Boulevard), Berkeley. 644-3093. Open Tuesday through Thursday 6 to 10:30 P.M., Friday and Saturday 5:30 to 10:30 P.M., Sunday 5:30 to 9:30 P.M. Beer, wine. No smoking. MasterCard, Visa. Reservations essential. Moderate.

There's a wonderful doctoral thesis to be done on the significance of what's happened to the Vietnam protest generation in Berkeley. To a remarkable extent, so many of the people who demonstrated against the war are still out on the streets—but this time scouring the menus of the latest restaurants. The search for the perfect society has been supplanted by the search for the perfect goat cheese tart.

I was thinking about this when I spoke with John Solomon, the owner of a first-rate Italian restaurant in Berkeley called Ristorante Venezia. His food obsession started early, in the days of People's Park. As a "poor hippie" in 1970, he opened a food cart at the University of California, Berkeley's Sather Gate selling health foods.

Ristorante Venezia is a much more formal undertaking, if you can describe as "formal" a restaurant decorated with clothes hanging from wash lines. Venezia takes its Italian food seriously—so seriously that Solomon and his chefs just returned from Italy and a search for new dishes.

Ristorante Venezia (not to be confused with Caffe Venezia, Solomon's pasta place across the street) not only has some of the nicest Italian food in the Bay Area, but it's also great fun. On Tuesdays, you get an opera singer, the other nights the manic bustle of waiters, cooks, and a crowded room of customers, all of them seemingly having a great time.

The food is inventive, but sometimes the emphasis on trendy California cuisine gets overdone. I could imagine someone happily going through life eating Italian food without ever seeing what appeared one night on Venezia's list of specials: a sliced duck breast salad with nectarines and quail eggs.

No criticism, however, can be directed at the wine list. This is one of those rare restaurants that cares enough to get good wines that also are good values. The largely Italian list has several reds and ten whites for a reasonable price; we had the 1985 Santa Cristina chianti classico, a soft, fruity example of what's being rated as one of the best years ever for Tuscan reds.

The food is as reasonably priced as the wine—even New Zealand venison, usually insanely expensive; no one will complain about the portion size, either.

Almost every appetizer and pasta I tasted was superb. If it's your first visit, a good place to start is with the *antipasti misti* for two. It's a colorful and bounteous platter that includes roasted peppers, the highest-quality mozzarella cheese, marinated eggplant, toast spread with homemade pesto, sliced tomatoes, and anchovies. Antipasto plates like this too often are floating in oil, but Venezia's version had nothing oily or heavy.

The pastas were nothing less than sensational. *Spaghetti alla puttanesca* is the spaghetti dish for those of us who haven't ordered the stuff in years because anything on a restaurant menu called "spaghetti" is usually so terrible. In this case, the noodles were perfectly al dente and the sauce a magnificent blend of oil, capers, hot peppers, hunks of fresh tomato, and chunks of mild blanched garlic. On top were big swirls of goat cheese, which sounds superfluous but in practice works well.

Then there's the seafood risotto, about ten times as good as the same dish that Modesto's sells for twice the price. This is risotto exactly as it's supposed to be done, with the moist rice retaining its texture and taking on the flavors of the sea. Scallops, mussels, and squid were all tender and absolutely fresh.

With the entrees, you have to be a little more picky. Saltimbocca is a good choice, an unusual preparation in which the veal slices, stuffed with prosciutto and fontina cheese, are rolled tight as a sausage. Grilled pork tenderloin, a special both nights I had dinner, also was excellent, with very flavorful meat enhanced by a pear sauce that wasn't the least bit heavy or sweet.

The venison and lamb dishes presented excellent meats marred by what came with them. The tender venison had no need for a heavy-handed béarnaise sauce, and the accompanying polenta was totally dry and flavorless. As for the lamb, it was overdosed with rosemary. Both dishes featured a variety of al dente vegetables, but they were largely flavorless.

Two of the entrees proved absolute disasters. A piece of grilled salmon was strangely dried out although it came undercooked, and it was so tasteless that if you had your eyes closed you wouldn't have known what fish you were eating. And duck breast was tough, gristly, and overdone.

The waiters are wonderful, and it's not their fault that they're so overworked; service can deteriorate drastically when the restaurant is full. There are just two cooks doing all the orders, and I've never seen cooks and waiters work so hard.

Despite these flaws, Venezia is already one of the best Italian restaurants in the Bay Area. With a larger staff, and with more attention paid to the uniform quality of the entrees, it could easily be at the top of the pack. ∎

—Stan Sesser, September 25, 1987

Wallaby's

★

Pier 33 (where Bay Street runs into the Embarcadero), San Francisco. 788-4329. Open for lunch Monday through Friday 11:30 A.M. to 3 P.M., for dinner Monday through Saturday 5 to 10 P.M., for brunch Saturday and Sunday 11 A.M. to 3 P.M. Full bar. MasterCard, Visa, Diners Club. Reservations essential. Moderate.

Until a month ago, my only contact with Australian food was what has been described as the signature dish of that country's cuisine: Vegemite on toast. Don't ask me what Vegemite is, just head rapidly for the nearest exit if you ever find yourself in the same room with a jar of it.

Because of my experience with Vegemite, plus the stories of friends who visited Australia, I wasn't very hopeful when I went to dinner at Wallaby's, San Francisco's first Australian restaurant.

Wallaby's opened in March with a suspicious amount of hype, leading me to suspect it was more an attempt to capitalize on America's new-found infatuation with Australia than to unearth a worthy but neglected cuisine. In fact, the principal owner of Wallaby's, Terry MacRae, transformed City Yacht Club, his previous restaurant on Pier 33. He got the idea for Wallaby's when he honeymooned in Australia.

Once again, it turns out that restaurants can be full of surprises. Whatever hype surrounded Wallaby's, the owners hired a chef, Dennis Clews, who is clearly making a serious attempt to do interesting things with Australian ingredients and culinary traditions. Wallaby's ends up being far more than Trader Vic's with a barbie. While not everything is successful, much of the food is worth trying, and the restaurant itself is great fun.

It's the fun part that becomes evident the moment you enter. Almost all the employees are transplanted Australians. The waiters, with their khaki bush uniforms and in some cases short pants, are clearly having a good time, and you end up having one, too.

Nor are the Australian touches in the decor overdone. Wallaby's is basically a comfortable restaurant looking out over the bay, with a pleasant bar offering lots of good Australian beers and modestly priced wines. Australian wines can be a real discovery.

In fact, the only false note is on the menu, which is written in Australian jargon and ludicrously fails to provide translations. How many Americans should be expected to know what they'll get when they order "yabbie timbale" or "chook with billy tea" or "jumbuck loin"?

Presiding over the kitchen is Clews, an Australian whose California credits include working under Masa Kobayashi at Auberge du Soleil. You suspect Masa's influence in a few of the sauces, which turn out to be as heavy as Masa's, but unfortunately also heavy-handed.

There's one major problem with the cooking: Wallaby's is trying to bring in as many products as possible from Australia and New Zealand, and their origin seems to be of more concern than the shape in which they arrive. Much of the shellfish and the venison is frozen, and in some cases they suffer for it.

Take shrimp-on-the-barbie as an example. I'd be much happier eating good fresh Louisiana shrimp than Wallaby's tasteless Australian shrimp, whose bout with a freezer leaves them with a mushy texture. Clews's "Queensland tropical marinade," an enticing sweet-and-tart combination that includes plums, pineapple, and dill, provides all the Australian touch I'd want for that dish.

Nor did the New Zealand venison make the journey in any better shape. A scallopine of venison was mushy, flavorless meat in a boring, heavy red wine sauce. Foul-tasting New Zealand mussels might not have been frozen, but they wrecked a pasta dish; they should never have gotten past the kitchen.

Other imports survived much better. A fish brought in fresh from Australia, called John Dory, sparkled in a crisp coating of macadamia nuts, accompanied on the side by a tropical fruit sauce that wasn't at all cloyingly sweet. Moreton Bay bug tail—a prehistoric-looking creature that's a cousin to a lobster—survived freezing much more successfully than the shrimp. And charcoal-grilled lamb chops from Australia, presented with beautiful scalloped potatoes and an array of al dente vegetables, had a rich muttony taste.

Clews also was very successful with some Australian recipes containing California ingredients. That chook with billy tea turned out to be a poussin marinated in tea and herbs, giving the chicken meat a nice smoky flavor. The appetizer called "brawn" was a tasty and spicy potted beef pâté. Yabbie timbale was a pleasant seafood mousse topped with crayfish tails and a fennel butter sauce.

Save room for a Pavlova roll for dessert, a cream-laden pastry loaded with kiwis and berries. If they had a little less sugar, the brandy lace snaps would have been excellent also—a mousselike creation of chocolate and orange served in a cookie dough crust.

Although Wallaby's is only a couple of months old, it's already so crowded that reservations are no guarantee of getting your table on time, even on a weeknight. And once you do order, dishes can be agonizingly slow coming out of the kitchen.

Despite the uneven food, Wallaby's proves to be a very pleasant surprise. There are already lots of good dishes, and I would expect more if the chef is allowed to concern himself with the quality, rather than the novelty, of the ingredients. ∎

—Stan Sesser, June 19, 1987

Wolfdale's

★★★

640 North Lake Boulevard, Tahoe City. 916-583-5700. Open for lunch (June through Labor Day only) Wednesday through Monday 11:30 A.M. to 2 P.M., for dinner Wednesday through Sunday from 6 P.M. to 10 P.M. Full bar. No smoking. Major credit cards. Reservations essential, well in advance through Labor Day. Moderate to expensive.

It seems California cuisine restaurants these days must spend a lot of time looking over each other's shoulders. When one introduces a successful new dish or concept, you quickly see the same thing on menus all over the place.

One of the pleasures I found in discovering Wolfdale's two years ago was that its food, by contrast, has developed in something of a culinary vacuum. In the relative gastronomic isolation of Lake Tahoe, chef Douglas Dale drew on his years in Japan and on his own strong sense of aesthetics to create a light and beautiful cuisine, but one that followed none of the usual rules for trendiness. Wolfdale's distinctly funky quarters were a perfect match for the food.

So it was with trepidation I discovered last winter that Wolfdale's had moved from tiny Homewood to bustling Tahoe City, where hordes of vacationers descend on restaurants like locusts on a cornfield. Moreover, the new quarters were not only much bigger, but almost plush.

I shouldn't have worried. The new Wolfdale's, amazingly enough, has improved distinctly. What do you do when you give a restaurant the maximum rating of three stars, and find out it has gotten even better? It's a quandary I wish I faced more often, one I thought about during three fantastic Wolfdale meals on July Fourth weekend.

Today, the entrees are more consistently wonderful than ever before, the desserts have improved dramatically, and a source has been found for beautiful baby vegetables. And, for the warm weather, the new location offers glorious lunches outside on a big deck overlooking Lake Tahoe.

Wolfdale's food can be described as California cuisine with a Japanese accent, but that doesn't really do it justice. With just three cooks—Dale, sous chef Craig Thomas, and dessert chef Tammy Clarey—the food is not only delicious and innovative, but as much attention is paid to presentation, textures, and colors as is to taste. Even the plates and bowls—some of which Dale made himself when he studied pottery making in Japan—are visually exciting.

The small menu, which changes frequently, sounds simple, but there's a great complexity to most of the dishes. Take, for instance, a spinach salad appetizer that incorporates cubes of steak in hoisin sauce. Normally, you'd expect a bed of spinach topped by meat in the usual thick, sweet hoisin sauce that Asian restaurants get from a can. But Dale marinates filet mignon in hoisin that he himself has made from miso and tomato sauce. After the meat is grilled, he pours a cilantro-mint vinaigrette on top, which blends with the hoisin to give it a light, intriguing character. The spinach is deep fried, emerging crisp and paper-thin. Then the dish is garnished with fried Japanese noodles.

Much of the menu features fish, and at Wolfdale's you needn't fear ordering seafood so far from the ocean. Occasionally, but just occasionally, a piece of fish will taste less than sparkling fresh, but generally Dale has developed such a broad network of suppliers that sometimes the Reno airport must seem like a fish market.

At lunch one day there was a perfect grilled trout, topped with a fresh mint vinaigrette and accompanied by fluffy scrambled eggs enlivened by fontina cheese, scallions, and fresh dill. For dinner, crispy oyster fritters came in a bowl of creamy corn chowder spiced with a red pepper aioli. The fresh white corn tasted so sweet you'd suspect it was grown in Wolfdale's backyard.

Best of all was the deep-fried soft-shell crab flown in from Maryland. Dale does his frying in a tempura batter that uses three different flours and no eggs. I've yet to find a Japanese restaurant in San Francisco that can match it.

Meats and poultry are equally good. Two boneless quail came stuffed with couscous and homemade sausage; they had been marinated in juniper berries and white wine, and were served with a version of red pepper beurre blanc. An appetizer of duck sausage, made in Wolfdale's kitchen and scented with fennel, parmesan cheese, red wine, cracked pepper, and shallots, couldn't have been more meaty and delicate; there wasn't a hint of fat or grease. And for lunch, a grilled breast of chicken was perfection itself, topped with pesto sauce and pine nuts and accompanied by a succulent couscous salad with bits of fresh vegetables.

Wolfdale's has always had irresistible homemade ice cream that somehow captures the absolute essence of the fresh fruit or whatever else is being used. Now, however, the pastries no longer take a back seat. A peach tart arrived with peach slices barely cooked, a baked custard filling, and a flaky crust that was absolute heaven. An intense, flourless chocolate torte came in a puree of fresh raspberries.

The fancy new restaurant, with windows looking out onto the lake, hasn't meant an end to the delightfully informal service. Head waiter Graham Rock sets a style of service I've only seen duplicated at Masa's in San Francisco. It's completely expert, yet no one is ever looking down their noses at you.

From the home-baked bread flavored with fresh herbs that starts your meal to the espresso that finishes it, Wolfdale's is virtually faultless. In San Francisco, a restaurant like this would stand out above its competition. For Tahoe, where there is little culinary tradition and where good fresh ingredients are hard to come by, Wolfdale's is nothing less than miraculous. ■

—Stan Sesser, July 17, 1987

Yank Sing

★ ★

427 Battery, San Francisco. 362-1640. Open Monday through Friday 11 A.M. to 3 P.M., Saturday 10 A.M. to 4 P.M. Full bar. MasterCard, Visa. Reservations accepted. Inexpensive.

Ocean City

★

644 Broadway, San Francisco. 982-2328. Open for dim sum daily from 9 A.M. to 3 P.M. Full bar. MasterCard, Visa, American Express. Reservations accepted. Inexpensive.

Post-revolution Chinese tea lunchers used to have to travel to Hong Kong for the ultimate dim sum, but many aficionados now consider tea lunch a San Francisco experience. We have dim sum parlors of every dimension here, from the gigantic multifloor dining halls of Ocean City and Canton Tea House to the medium-sized and more refined operations of Yank Sing and Harbor Village, to tiny tea parlors like Tung Fong. And they all seem to be packed. Dim sum is taking this city by storm.

On weekends you have to steel yourself for a mob scene, but of course that's when the variety and freshness of the dim sum is at its highest. Slightly off-hours and weekdays are the best, but you should find a group of at least three or four to go with you in order to sample a respectable number of different tidbits.

One aspect of tea lunch that Westerners overlook is the selection of tea to go with the meal. In Hong Kong, the choice of tea is almost more important than the food and certainly as interesting as the California exercise of pairing wines with food. The dim sum houses here offer a wine list-sized, though unprinted, variety of teas and your choice can add a new dimension to your lunch.

There are three major classifications of tea: mild green tea, made of tea leaves that are simply dried; strong fermented black tea; and semifermented oolong tea, in which the fermentation of the leaves is stopped when the leaves are brownish green. Different kinds of tea from different areas of China fall into one of these three categories. For example, dragonwell tea produced in Hangchow is light, elegant green tea. The strongest tea, called *po nay*, is black tea, a full-bodied, dark red brew that many Chinese order with dim sum and deep-fried foods. *Look on*, slightly more fermented than oolong but less strong than *po nay*, is also often drunk with dim sum.

My dim sum group orders scented teas, the favorite being chrysanthemum, a combination of black tea and slightly astringent, fragrant dried chrysanthemum flowers. A popular tea with Westerners is lightly fermented oolong perfumed with jasmine, which I find a little cloying with food. Another choice is litchi tea, oolong or black tea, sweetened by fruity dried litchi nuts.

Your meal at either of the following dim sum parlors will be enhanced by the tea you choose. When you need a fresh pot, turn over the lid.

Yank Sing

The surroundings at Yank Sing are so modern and well appointed that you feel like you're in a upscale Financial District restaurant until the carts laden with exotic Chinese delicacies come around. The dim sum here is beautifully made with the freshest shrimp and crab, tender noodles, and oft-changed deep frying. The overall meal comes off clean and delicate. Flavors are explicit.

The kitchen shows particular strength and invention in my favorite part of the dim sum repertoire, the dumplings. The translucent, shrimp-stuffed *har gow* boast the freshest and sweetest of shrimp. Liberal use of black mushrooms add a wild, meaty flavor to rice-noodle-wrapped items, such as an addictive vegetarian dumpling seasoned with pickled turnip or a chicken-stuffed dumpling with bamboo shoots. The pork-filled *sui mai* are brightly decorated wih carrots and fresh peas. There are perhaps eight different variations of wrappers and stuffing, all excellent.

Other dim sum items to look for are succulent, foil-wrapped chicken bits in a sweetly caramelized sauce; heavenly deep-fried crab balls with a crab claw leg stuck into it; rich, cleanly fried shrimp toasts; delicious spicy chicken feet, first deep fried, than braised in a Hunan-style sauce; a magically crisp, lacy taro ball filled with a tasty pork stuffing; a lotus leaf wrapped around sticky sweet rice stuffed with pork; and those noodle dumplings I like so much, crisply deep fried and stuffed with shrimp.

Yank Sing also prepares dishes from heated carts, and if you want something as familiar as won ton soup, theirs is excellent. The won ton are stuffed with smoky barbecued pork and the chicken broth has good flavor. A bowl of tiny, tender fish balls in a lively brown gravy also comes from the cart. They're made from a paste of many different fish and lack distinctive character.

For dessert, try to nab a saucer of flaky-crusted egg custard tarts when they're still warm. Yank Sing does them better than any other dim sum house.

Ocean City

Ocean City at its busier times reminds me of Grand Central Station at rush hour. The dining rooms roar. People sit at tables covered with sheets of thin plastic placed over the linen. When they get messy, they're just rolled right up and thrown out. Over all the din, there are periodic announcements on a public-address system about the band that will be playing that night, including snatches of the music, and advertisements about dinner.

Some of the items to watch for on the carts as they ply the sea of tables are succulent roast pork with crackling crisp skin, velvety dark meat, and some rib bones, and a meaty roast duck, also with crisp, glossy skin and juicy flesh served on a bed of marinated soy beans. A large dumpling of seasoned sticky rice tastes great with them, if it comes to you at the same time.

Among hundreds of interesting dim sum are hot, spicy orange-scented beef balls, typically gelatinous in texture; shrimp-stuffed *har gow*, not so fresh one time; sweet clams in a garlicky but well-balanced black bean sauce; thick rice noodles stuffed with black mushrooms; crispy taro balls a bit too heavy with oil; and egg custard tarts that only suggest the wonders of the ones at Yank Sing.

There are scrawny, saucy ducks' feet, bowls of tender tripe, bean skin wrapped around braised pork and gelatinous fish belly, little bowls of characterless sharks-fin soup, and cups of egg and tapioca custard with bean paste that's sweet, soft, and comforting.

The dim sum at Ocean City are not quite as brightly flavored or texturally distinct as those at Yank Sing, though many enticing and exotic tidbits are to be found. Ocean City is going for volume rather than the highest quality. The relatively new complex which includes the World Theater, a boutique, a take-out food shop, as well as two gigantic floors of dining rooms serving dim sum every day and a regular menu every night [see review for Ocean City], plus a bandstand and dance floor, really is its own Pacific village. ■

—Patricia Unterman, September 13, 1987

Yuet Lee (Chinatown)

★ ★

1300 Stockton Street at Broadway, San Francisco. 982-6020. Open Wednesday through Monday 11 A.M. to 3 A.M. No alcoholic beverages (bring your own beer or wine). Cash only. No reservations. Inexpensive to moderate.

A brilliant chef of Asian background, presiding over one of San Francisco's best restaurants, is murdered. Can the restaurant keep up its culinary standards without him?

Surprisingly enough, I'm not asking this question about Masa's. In the uncanny way that tragedy has of repeating itself, there was also a murder of a second great San Francisco chef, a death that received far less publicity than that of Masa Kobayashi.

I'm talking about Michael Yu, who ran the kitchen at Yuet Lee, the Cantonese seafood restaurant on the corner of Stockton and Broadway. With its rickety tables, blinding fluorescent lighting, and big Coca-Cola sign out front, no restaurant could be more physically different from Masa's. But like Masa, Yu also turned out magnificent dishes, taking the freshest seafood and making it sparkle.

Since Yu's death, I've heard claims that Yuet Lee has slipped. So I decided to join the ever-present lines out front and try it out for a couple of dinners. Amazingly, my verdict is the same as it was at Masa's; if anything, the food has actually gotten better.

But here the parallel with Masa's ends, because before we get to the food, we've got to deal with a much less happy subject. Yuet Lee has made itself one of the most unpleasant restaurants in town. Some of the food is of three-star quality, but to enjoy it you've practically got to put yourself into a trance that filters out everything else that's happening. Consider:

■ There's no waiting area, so you have to hover over people who are eating. A sign invites you to skip the wait by eating downstairs. But when you check it out, you run into a grotesque stench of mildew and who knows what else that immediately makes it apparent why tables there are empty.

■ To call the service "abrupt" is being kind. We placed a big order, and asked for the dishes one at a time. The waiter then proceeded to bring everything within ten minutes. Since there was no room at the table, he wanted to take away things we hadn't yet finished.

■ While there are still good inexpensive dishes on the menu, the prices of others have soared. So your bill can be relatively high, but you can't pay for it with anything but cash. Not even personal checks are accepted. Add this to the list: noise, bustle, no beer unless you bring it in, tiny paper napkins, and no change of plate unless you ask. No one even thinks of bringing you an extra bowl so you can dump your crab and clam shells. In short, it's an experience I've never had before—spectacular food that practically goes to waste because you're too hassled to enjoy it.

And "spectacular" is an apt description for many of the dishes. Yuet Lee is that rare Cantonese restaurant that prepares seafood in a way that enhances it rather than messes it up. No gloppy cornstarchy sauces. Nothing oversalted or swimming in grease. And everything perfectly cooked, just on the slightly underdone side.

Salt-and-pepper squid is a prime example: Without a hint of grease, with a crunchy batter that's not too salty and not too peppery, it puts to shame the fried squid anywhere else. A huge bowl of this and a couple of beers would satisfy me for the evening.

All the shellfish I tasted were impeccable. Sauteed clams in black bean sauce were about as delicious and fresh tasting as clams can get.

Another winner is the clay pot casserole of oysters and roast pork. Juicy Pacific oysters, chunks of pork, green onions, and a mountain of fresh ginger are stewed in a rich brown sauce flavored by drippings of the pork fat; it's one of the great bargains on the menu.

But perhaps best of all is the curried crab. This is one of my key test dishes for a Chinese restaurant, because practically no one does it right this side of Singapore. More often than not, you get crab that has been dramatically overcooked in a sauce reeking with the harshness of curry powder. But at Yuet Lee, the crab was fresh and firm, a remarkable specimen in what has been a bad crab year. And we mopped up every drop of the sauce. It was complex, with a nice bite, and filled with ginger, onions, and green pepper.

Even if you're a vegetarian, you can be equally impressed with Yuet Lee's food. Vegetables here are treated as carefully as the seafood. Asparagus in oyster sauce featured crunchy green spears in a sauce that was light and not at all salty. Bright green spinach came in an interesting sauce thickened with preserved bean curd. Steamed stuffed bean cake was like a delicate custard. And the chow mein noodles, which can be ordered with various meat or vegetable combinations, were absolutely succulent.

I had only two quarrels with any of the dishes I tasted. The whole steamed flounder, while delicately cooked, came out tasteless, and it was drowned in a puddle of oil and soy sauce. Stick with the shellfish. And otherwise fine won ton soup was marred by gristly, fatty filling in the won tons.

Is it possible to eat at Yuet Lee's and actually be able to enjoy the food? A couple of things might help. First, don't go during the peak dinner hours, when you'll have to wait and when everyone is frantic. Second, order just a couple of dishes, then order more later. You'll get glares from the waiters, but that seems to come

with the service anyway. It's a shame a restaurant with food so good can make everything else so unpleasant. ∎

—Stan Sesser, April 11, 1986

Yuet Lee (Mission District)
★ ★

3601 Twenty-sixth Street (near Valencia), San Francisco. 550-8998. Open Wednesday through Monday 11 A.M. to 10 P.M. Beer, wine. MasterCard, Visa. Reservations accepted. Inexpensive to moderate.

Yuet Lee, a Hong Kong–style noodle and seafood house on Broadway and Stockton, started out not much bigger than an Asian food stand. The miniscule kitchen, really a galley lined with ferociously hot woks, was barely partitioned off from a narrow dining area. The room was fashioned out of worn vinyl, linoleum, and plastic, but tanks of fish, crabs, and lobster belied the subsistence appearance of the place. You could get a stew in a clay pot or a bowl of noodles for $3 or $4, but the freshest delicacies from the sea were available as well, always wonderfully prepared.

The place became so popular that it expanded by annexing a small space next door. At first, you didn't even notice that Yuet Lee was bigger because the new part had exactly the same vintage look as the original space. There were a few more plastic tables set with metal napkin holders and somehow a coat of Yuet Lee's signature and remarkable shade of green paint was extended seamlessly into the new section. But the food was often not quite as good as it had been in smaller quarters.

Recently Yuet Lee opened a second store way across town on the edge of the Mission. The interior, brand new and sparkling clean, has a completely separate kitchen, large fish tanks and two sets of bathrooms, but you know immediately that this could only be Yuet Lee. That singular lime green color has been lavished on the exterior of the whole building this time, and all the same materials have been used. Red-speckled linoleum tile floors, plastic tables in a fake wood veneer, acoustic-tile ceilings, arched insets in tall windows covered with venetian blinds, and a glowing green line painted around the circumference of the room are all present and accounted for under the glow of fluorescent light.

What's exciting is that the food is even better than at the original Yuet Lee. Dishes are prepared more carefully and consistently, and look more attractive. That sloppy, street-food edge is gone. I thought, at first, that this offhandedness was part of Yuet Lee's charm. It's not. I prefer drinking my tea hot, in china cups, poured from a warm tea pot instead of tepid in plastic tumblers. I like the food to be arranged on the plates just a little bit and for the chopping and cutting to be neat and perfect. A meal at the new Yuet Lee looks and tastes more appealing.

Also, ordering is easier. A pink sheet of specials will steer you to the restaurant's best dishes. Two of them, pepper-and-salt-roasted fresh squid and pepper-and-salt-roasted shrimp turned out to be the best I've ever eaten at this restaurant. The squid, so crunchy and spicy outside, were contrastingly tender and rich beneath their thin crust. The same balance of flavors and textures worked on the shrimp as well, especially when eaten shell and all.

Spicy black bean sauce seasoned with minced pork, fresh chilies, onion, scallions and loads of fresh Chinese parsley work magic on crab. You have to extract the crab meat from cut up shells with your fingers, but it's worth the mess for the pleasure of the fabulous, thick, dusky sauce. Fresh, large, briny, clean-tasting clams released their liquor into this same black bean sauce, giving it a different dimension.

The restaurant keeps catfish in tanks, but also produces spectacularly fresh flounder and rockfish from the kitchen. The flounder we were served recently, steamed with ginger and scallions, soy sauce, and stock, garnished with bright green Chinese parsley, was just about the best fish dish you could hope for. The meat of the flounder was firm but delicate and

ever so moist. The steaming with aromatics seemed to bring out all its finest qualities.

I love the way Yuet Lee treats vegetables. They're either sauteed with a little garlic and practically no sauce or steamed with oyster sauce. Chinese broccoli, *ong choy* or Chinese watercress, and asparagus always look intensely green and fresh. You get a big plate of just the vegetable you order with no distractions and they go nicely with the fish.

You should go to Yuet Lee for fish and seafood, but if there's a young child in your party, order crispy chicken, a glistening, brown-skinned bird with succulent flesh that comes garnished with festive pink, white, and yellow shrimp chips and sprigs of parsley. It looks like a child's fantasy.

Yuet Lee's noodles, another area of specialty, bring me back almost as often as the straightforward preparations of the fish and seafood. A dish as humble as barbecued pork chow mein gets a meticulous execution here. Carrots, cured pork, and scallions are all julienned to the exact width of fat, round noodles. Thin noodles braised with ginger and onions and crispy panfried chow mein noodles offer texture variations on the same theme. The wonton in soup have tender wrappers and tasty meat fillings.

One soup that I always order for its clean and refreshing flavors has a clear stock and beautiful white cubes of bean curd, shiny white, gelatinous fish balls, and pearly gray straw mushrooms. The tastes are subtle, but always distinct.

I see the cooking at Yuet Lee as an extension of the way I like to eat Western food. High standards of freshness for both fish and vegetables, quick cooking with skillful technique, and tasty, simple sauces make the food at this restaurant appealing, visit after visit. At the Twenty-sixth Street branch, you can be sure that the food will be perfect every time. Also, they'll be glad to see you, a point of view sometimes missing at the bustling Stockton Street location. ∎

—Patricia Unterman, April 26, 1987

Yujean's Modern Cuisine of China

★ ★

843 San Pablo Avenue (near Solano), Albany. 525-8557. Open Tuesday through Sunday 11 A.M. to 2:30 P.M., 4 to 10 P.M. Beer, wine. Major credit cards. Reservations accepted. Inexpensive.

With the fierce competition among restaurants these days leading to all sorts of innovations, I'm normally not surprised to find something unusual. But when I walked into a nondescript place in Albany grandly named Yujean's Modern Cuisine of China, I was really thrown for a loop.

There, alongside the Chinese menu, was perhaps the single best wine list in northern California. The thirty-four wines, including several from France, represented such a fine selection that I could envision a tasting panel of wine critics having picked them. And, in a world of rip-off restaurant wine lists, the prices were remarkable—in some cases no more than the retail price in a wine store.

In this instance, the "tasting panel" was one man, Yujean Kang, the proprietor. He turns out to be a wine nut determined to have a Chinese restaurant unmarred by the usual selection of rotgut California jug wines. If you're a wine nut yourself, Kang will excitedly pump you for recommendations.

While I was reading the menu on my first visit, a friend, who happens to be a wine writer, was perusing the wine list. He looked up and said, "You know, this would be a great restaurant even if the food were lousy."

He needn't have worried. After my first taste of the pot stickers and smoked tea duck, I was hooked.

The pot stickers, which come in both meat and vegetarian versions, are nothing less than miraculous. I must have eaten pot stickers in hundreds of Chinese restaurants, but it was the first time I could bite into them and not have grease squirt out. The wrappers are crisp and delicate,

the filling of minced pork, napa cabbage, and bok choy (black mushrooms replace the pork in the vegetarian kind) light and aromatic.

As for the smoked tea duck, it absolutely puts the Mandarin's famous version to shame. The duck has crisp skin and pungently smoky meat betraying not a hint of fat or grease. Instead of serving it with buns, the usual way, the waiters roll the meat and skin into thin delicate pancakes with plum sauce and scallions, just like Peking duck. I could eat it six nights a week, and it's got to represent the biggest bargain in the Bay Area.

Yujean's mother, Yufong Kang, who has a been a chef in Taiwan, gets credit for these two spectacular dishes. In general, her cooking is basically Mandarin in style, but more inventive than that at most northern Chinese restaurants. It lacks the excessive oiliness, saltiness, and cornstarched sauces that mar so much Chinese food. She also uses no MSG.

But there's a problem with some of her dishes, too: Certain items lack assertiveness; her hand is too light with ginger, garlic, chili peppers, and other flavorings. That is partially due to a deliberate effort to tone down the food so that it will go better with wine, Kang said.

During my first dinner, I found *kung pao* squid, a normally fiery dish that includes chili peppers and peanuts, to be disappointingly bland. On a later visit, I ordered *kung pao* chicken, but specifically asked for it very hot. That time it was perfect.

There are three outstanding dishes. Beef with broccoli is very tender flank steak marinated and sauteed with garlic in sweet wine vinegar. The broccoli is flavorful and crisp. Pork with garlic and cilantro sauce is a perfect demonstration of what good quality meat and a sauce without cornstarch can do for Chinese food. The third winner is "chicken in the nest," a julienned chicken breast sauteed in red pepper sauce and served inside an elaborately woven nest of crispy noodles.

There are some other good dishes. "Ants climbing a tree," a blend of minced pork, black mushrooms, and bamboo shoots served on a bed of crispy rice noodles, is first-rate. Instead of serving it as an entree, Yujean's wraps it in a lettuce leaf and offers it as an individual appetizer, a nice idea.

While every entree was decent, some other things I tried, such as the mu shu pork and the prawns in orange sauce, were on the bland side—a problem I suspect would vanish if you requested lots of garlic and whatever else.

The soups, which in a pleasant departure from Chinese tradition can be ordered in individual bowls, suffered from blandness also.

Service is so elegant—at least when the restaurant isn't crowded—you might think you were in France. Dishes are brought out one at a time, and everyone gets served from a cart. Yet prices are no more than at those Chinese restaurants that slap everything in front of you.

I'd become a little suspicious of the new breed of innovative Chinese restaurants sprouting up, since a main innovation seems to be high menu prices. But Yujean's, where you can eat magnificently and drink great wines, represents value second to none. ■

—Stan Sesser, February 27, 1987

Zuni Cafe and Grill

★ ★

1658 Market Street, San Francisco. 552-2522. Open Tuesday through Friday 7:30 A.M. to midnight, Saturday 9 A.M. to midnight, Sunday 9 A.M. to 11 P.M. Full bar. MasterCard, Visa, American Express. Reservations accepted. Moderate.

There are some restaurants that encourage you to linger. It doesn't much matter exactly what's on the menu or how efficient the service is or what time of day it is, because the place always feels so good. The Zuni Cafe, with its new physical expansion complete, is now one of those places. With a long, copper bar and French-style oyster stand in place and early morning till midnight hours, you can practically live there, much the way Parisians live in their neighborhood cafes.

Billy West, Zuni's founder and guiding spirit, has spent time in Paris and he knows the value of a good cafe. If you live in a city in a small apartment or shared quarters, cafes improve the quality of your life. You use them all the time, as places to drink your morning coffee, to write letters, run into people, or watch your fellow man—and the crowd at the Zuni is particularly suited for this activity.

West's goal, I think, was to create a truly European-style cafe in San Francisco. He started out eight years ago with a storefront serving lentil salad and sandwiches; then he put in a hot kitchen and a mezzanine and began serving dinner. Then he acquired the triangular space next door and built the bar. Zuni's growth didn't happen overnight, but developed because both West and his customers wanted it. Now there's something for everyone, no matter when you walk through the door—espresso, oysters, cocktails, snacks, sandwiches, full meals, sidewalk seating on nice days, even Berkeley's incomparable Acme bread for sale.

One Saturday we ate just oysters served in the traditional French way on a metal platter of shaved ice set on a wire stand. Underneath was a plate of chewy Acme *levain* bread and butter. You buy the oysters by the piece. Lately the kumamotos from Eureka and Tomales Bay oysters have been clean and briny, and the tiny Washington olympias have been superb. The Eastern oysters, like the Cape Cod blue points we were served one day, had no flavor at all, tasting as if they had been washed in water. Some of the oysters were carefully opened with their flesh and juice glistening in the shell; others were hacked up in the process of opening.

One evening when I was alone with my little boy, I was served one of the most delicious dishes I've ever had in a restaurant—two perfectly grilled quail on a bed of bitter wilted greens with two toasts spread with buttery squab liver. At another dinner when four of us were seated in the mezzanine above the piano and yelling to make ourselves heard, we ate a fine, simple lamb stew with sweet carrots and turnips, an extraordinary *fritto misto* of crunchy deep-fried catfish fingers, deep-fried fennel, and deep-fried lemon slices, a grilled quail on a bed of tasty braised white beans with wilted radicchio, and a clever antipasto of shredded raw artichokes tossed with slivers of parmesan cheese and pine nuts served with tissue-thin slices of coppa and salami.

That same night, big slabs of cold, raw tuna, barely grilled around the edges, were paired with tiny leaves of *tat-soi*, a cabbagy Chinese green in a vinaigrette. This rather unsavory main course, misconceived from the outset, might not have been served if someone in the kitchen actually had sat down to a plate of it. A thin veal chop came off the grill tough, though airy cubes of deep-fried polenta and sauteed greens made the plate more interesting.

Some fruity house-made strawberry ice cream, refreshing grapefruit-Campari sorbet, and a satisfying hot fudge sundae sent us on our way.

At lunch one day, we ate thick, garlicky lamb sandwiches moistened by baked onions and a wonderful warm spinach salad with handfuls of diced, peppery bacon, hard-boiled eggs, and delicious croutons. The barely set eggs turned the salad into a full meal. A succulent grilled coho salmon was appealingly draped with vinegary red peppers and came with tender baby mustard greens and those winsome deep-fried polenta cubes. The Zuni kitchen also put out a stunning, thin mushroom soup of intense flavor, swirled with crème fraîche, and their hallmark, made-to-order guacamole with warm chips. The caesar salad, as usual, didn't have enough oomph for my taste.

Dessert brought some kicky bourbon-pecan ice cream and a mouth-awakening lemon tart with a buttery crust.

Before and after main meal hours, Zuni serves a cafe menu with the likes of grilled cheese sandwiches, guacamole, caesar salads, special sandwiches, and oysters.

There's a competent wine and beer list, offering many reasonable bottles as well as six wines by the glass. Two wines particularly suited the eclectic menu one night—a 1985 Rully, premier cru, "Les Margotey" from Umberto Pagnotta, a crisp, structured burgundy with lots of flavor, and a lovely, flowery 1983 Bourgogne pinot noir, "Cuvee Joseph Faiveley." Here were two relatively obscure, gorgeous burgundies that didn't cost an arm and a leg. I wish more wine lists had the likes of these on their cards.

Sometimes both the Zuni kitchen and the service can be erratic, but you can always depend on every ingredient and raw material being of the highest quality and the service never being grudging or unpleasant. If the concept or execution of certain dishes falters now and then, or if the dining room staff seem vague, the odds are greatly in your favor of having a terrific, well-served meal.

The truth is that Zuni is possessed of a marvelous spirit. It's one of those eccentric, very personal establishments that runs on ideological energy rather than businesslike procedure. Just the look of the place, with its many odd shaped rooms, its unmatched chairs, its romantic flower arrangements, its little paintings and prints hung here and there, its asymmetrical tables and garretlike stairs, reveals a singular nature. But, the tall, handsome, rather formal but unfinished wooden doors that let you into the place show where the cafe wants to go, and that, by hook or by crook, they're going to get there. ∎

—Patricia Unterman, May 3, 1987

Critics' Choice
Capsule Reviews

Adriana's

★ ★

999 Andersen Drive, San Rafael. 454-8000. Open for lunch Monday through Friday 11:30 A.M. to 2:30 P.M., for dinner Monday through Saturday 5 to 10 P.M. Beer, wine. MasterCard, Visa, American Express. Reservations recommended. Moderate.

The expansive personality of Adriana Giramonte makes this large, cheerful pink dining room an extension of her open kitchen. Her confident cooking exemplifies what it means to be a fully developed cook, and it's a joy to eat her food. With her light touch and keen palate, she makes simple Italian dishes taste terrific. Cold seafood salads sparkle with freshness; a molded cake of marinated eggplant is one of the best dishes around. The pastas all burst with flavor, and her Italian fish stews redefine North Beach cioppinos. At lunch, the menu offers a number of delicious, colorful salads that are worth a trip across the Golden Gate to eat. This is definitely a family restaurant with a dinner menu that includes salad and pasta in the price of the meal. ■

—Patricia Unterman

Angkor Wat

★ ★

4217 Geary Boulevard (near Sixth Avenue), San Francisco. 221-7887. Open Tuesday through Sunday 5 to 10 P.M. Full bar. MasterCard, Visa, American Express. Reservations recommended weeknights and essential weekends. Moderate.

When Angkor Wat first opened, Cambodian food in the Bay Area was a novelty. Now there are almost a dozen Cambodian restaurants, but this remains one of the best. In fact, it's one of the best Asian restaurants of any sort in San Francisco. Try the green papaya salad as an appetizer, the chicken curry soup flavored with coconut, the marinated, panfried catfish, and their sensational charcoal-broiled chicken, which has been marinated overnight in a variety of Cambodian seasonings. Angkor Wat is a magnificently decorated restaurant with an elegance of service that comes from the French tradition brought to Cambodia. It's a place to spend a long and pleasant evening eating an unusual and very satisfying cuisine. ■

—Stan Sesser

Bay Wolf Cafe and Restaurant

★ ★

3853 Piedmont Avenue, Oakland. 655-6004. Open for lunch Monday through Friday 11:30 A.M. to 2 P.M.; for dinner Monday through Friday 6 to 9:30 P.M., Saturday and Sunday 5:30 to 9:30 P.M. Beer, wine. MasterCard, Visa. Reservations recomended. Moderate.

Michael Wild, the executive chef and owner of this charming, long-established East Bay restaurant, understands what it means to serve his customers in a European tradition yet give them new and interesting dishes that reflect current California and international cooking trends. The wood-frame Victorian house with several cozy dining rooms and a deck improves with age, as does an extensive, well-priced, and carefully compiled wine list. There's more emphasis now on cuisines from other countries like Spain and Portugal, but whenever duck shows up on the biweekly-changing menu, order it, or the sensitively cooked mixed grills, or the delicious lamb dishes. The Bay Wolf stands tall as a philosophical leader in that first generation of restaurants spawned by the Berkeley food revolution. Now it's an institution along with Chez Panisse and the Fourth Street Grill. ■

—Patricia Unterman

Brothers Delicatessen and Restaurant

★★

1351 Howard Avenue, Burlingame. (Take the Broadway/Burlingame exit from Highway 101; from Broadway, turn left onto California and right on Howard.) 343-2311. Open Sunday through Tuesday 8 A.M. to 7:45 P.M., Wednesday through Saturday 8 A.M. to 9 P.M. Beer, wine. MasterCard, Visa, American Express. Reservations for dinner only. Inexpensive.

It took a Chinese couple, Cathy and Sam Hou, to bring the Bay Area a first-rate Jewish deli. I can say with certainty that Sam Hou is the only former Taiwanese fighter pilot in the world who cooks better matzo ball soup than my grandmother did. The corned beef and pastrami sandwiches are fabulous, and the potato pancakes miraculously crisp, without a speck of grease. You might be waited on by a blond surfer, but the food is authentically Jewish and authentically good. ■

— Stan Sesser

Buca Giovanni

★★

800 Greenwich Street (at Columbus), San Francisco. 776-7766. Open Monday through Thursday 5:30 to 10:30 P.M., Friday and Saturday until 11 P.M. Beer, wine, MasterCard, Visa. Reservations essential. Moderate.

This bustling North Beach Italian restaurant is presided over by Giovanni Leoni, formerly chef at Vanessi's. The enthusiasm here is infectious; everyone is clearly having a good time. The restaurant excels at salads and pastas. *Panzerotti*, which are veal-stuffed ravioli in walnut-cream sauce, are as good as any pasta in town. Some of the entrees don't live up to the standard of the pasta, but any rabbit dish is a good choice. ■

— Stan Sesser

Cafe Beaujolais

★★★

961 Ukiah Street, Mendocino. 707-937-5614. Open daily for breakfast and lunch 8 A.M. to 2:30 P.M.; for dinner Thursday through Saturday 6:15 to 9:30 P.M. Closed for part of the winter. Beer, wine. No smoking. Cash or personal checks only. Reservations advised. Moderate.

The breakfasts and lunches of Margaret Fox have over the years become almost legendary, and you can see her influence in some Bay Area restaurants. But no imitator comes close to Beaujolais: fluffy omelets with unusual fillings, waffles with wild rice and pecans in the batter, and a lunch menu so tempting you wish you hadn't stuffed yourself for breakfast. For dinner, chef Chris Kump combines his French training with a desire to search out the best and freshest local ingredients. Fishermen bring in their salmon, local kids pick wild berries, and Kump picks herbs and lettuces from his garden to use in his often experimental dishes. Cafe Beaujolais is a required stop on any trip to Mendocino. ■

— Stan Sesser

Cafe Fanny

★★

1603 San Pablo, Berkeley, 524-5447. Open for breakfast Monday through Saturday 7:30 to 11 A.M., for lunch 11 A.M. to 5 P.M., for brunch Sunday 9:30 A.M. to 2:30 P.M. Beer, wine. No credit cards. No reservations. Inexpensive.

This charming little stand-up cafe was conceived by Alice Waters in the tradition of French tabacs and Italian espresso bars. In addition to first-rate coffee, Cafe Fanny puts out lacy buckwheat crepes with house-made jams and soft-boiled eggs fresh from a local farm for breakfast, and an array of small prebaked pizzas, interesting open-faced sandwiches, and lacy green salads for lunch. Warm muffins and fruit crisps are augmented by the neighboring Acme bakery's excellent bread used for all the sandwiches. Wines by the glass come from Kermit Lynch next door. San Franciscans regularly make the journey across the Bay Bridge to pick up bread, wine, and a quick bite at this Chez Panisse enclave. ■

—Patricia Unterman

Caffe Sport

★

574 Green Street, San Francisco. 981-1251. Open Tuesday through Saturday noon to 2 P.M., dinner seatings at 6:30, 8:30, and 10:30 P.M. Beer, wine. No credit cards. Reservations essential. Moderate.

Caffe Sport is not a restaurant for everyone. The interior is made out of layer upon layer of dusty glued-on trinkets. It would be kind to call the service informal. Most often the waiters tell you what you're going to get and how much of it. You're herded into the claustrophobic dining rooms at three separate seatings regardless of reservation times. Indeed, it's almost impossible to get a reservation over the phone—you have to stop by. But the inconvenience can be forgotten when your steaming plate of expertly cooked clams, prawns, and calamari arrives, glistening with olive oil, redolent of garlic, and absolutely irresistible. Prawns and scallops also get a careful saute with handfuls of garlic and fresh tomato. Al dente pasta with creamy fried eggplant is terrific, as is Caffe Sport's unctuous pesto. The restaurant is known for its garlicky mayonnaise sauce and perfectly fresh shellfish. Don't go here unless you adore garlic. ■

—Patricia Unterman

Cambodia House

★ ★

5625 Geary Boulevard (near Twentieth Avenue), San Francisco. 668-5888. Open daily for lunch 11 A.M. to 3 P.M., daily for dinner Sunday through Thursday 5 to 10 P.M., Friday and Saturday until 10:30 P.M. Beer, wine. MasterCard, Visa, American Express. Reservations accepted. Inexpensive.

Cambodia House offers a wonderful alternative for Asian dining out on the Avenues. While it's as cheap as any of the neighborhood Chinese restaurants, you eat in style, with tablecloths and very pleasant, attentive service. The Cambodian food is excellent—lighter and more delicate than Chinese cooking, and far less oily. Try the Cambodian crepe appetizer, the chicken curry (the best anywhere), and the charbroiled pork. ■

—Stan Sesser

Chez Panisse—The Cafe

★ ★ ★

1517 Shattuck Avenue, Berkeley. 548-5525. Open Monday through Saturday 11:30 A.M. to 11:30 P.M. Beer, wine. major credit cards. Lunch reservations accepted the day of the meal only. Moderate.

If you prefer some choice about what you eat and want to spend a moderate amount of money, you can get Chez Panisse-quality food upstairs at the cafe, and a more casual ambience. The menu features individual pizzas from the wood-burning pizza oven, a couple of savory pastas, salads made from greens from the Chez Panisse gardens, and a few delightful appetizers and main-course dishes. The fabulous desserts duplicate those served downstairs. One problem with the cafe is that reservations are not taken for dinner, so you must prepare yourself for an hour wait during prime evening hours. Lunch, however, is a good bet, since you can reserve. The cafe is relaxed and sunny then, and though the menu is a bit smaller, you'll also be able to visit the fabulous Cheese Board across the street, the best cheese store in the United States. ■

—Patricia Unterman

Chez Panisse—The Restaurant

★★★

1517 Shattuck Avenue, Berkeley. 548-5525. Open Tuesday through Saturday with seatings at 6, 6:30, 8:30, and 9:15 P.M. Beer, wine. Major credit cards. Reservations essential. Expensive.

With Paul Bertolli at the helm of this citadel of American cooking, the restaurant has taken on a gentle Italian point of view. The prix-fixe menus are as unfussy and as sumptuous as ever. Whenever he gets the chance, Bertolli sneaks in a risotto or a braised meat or an Italian seafood dish. The prix-fixe menu, the only meal available each night, exemplifies the philosophy of cooking and eating that Alice Waters has proselytized throughout the country: find the best and most seasonal, heathfully raised ingredients—and if they aren't available, raise them yourself; prepare them in ways that reveal their flavors rather than mask them; and always present them beautifully if simply. Like a French three-star restaurant, every detail of food and service has been rigorously thought out, but the style that Chez Panisse has cultivated is more like a one-star in the countryside. The experience of eating there is so unique and subtle that first-timers have to think about it awhile to get it. Dining there is not the formal or showy experience that people expect from such a famous restaurant. However, you will find that whatever the restaurant decides to put on your table that day, from bread to coffee, will be the best you can find any place in the world. ■

—Patricia Unterman

Downtown Bakery and Creamery

★★★

308A Center Street (on the plaza opposite the bandstand), Healdsburg. 707-431-2719. Open Wednesday through Monday 9:30 A.M. to 6:30 P.M., Sunday to 3:30 P.M. Inexpensive.

Lindsey Shere, the pastry chef at Chez Panisse and author of the best-selling *Chez Panisse Desserts*, has opened a wonderful country bakery with her two daughters on the main plaza of Healdsburg. Called the Downtown Bakery and Creamery, the Shere women turn out breads, pastries, and ice creams on a level that can only be found at the mother ship in Berkeley. The ice creams are a dream, made with farm eggs that have so much flavor that you can taste them in the finished product. Like an old-fashioned creamery, they put out milk shakes and sundaes as well as cappuccino and espresso, to go along with baked goods like buttery cookies, caramel-glazed pecan rolls, and yeasty croissants. Nothing is fancy but everything is special. If the Downtown Bakery and Creamery were in San Francisco instead of Healdsburg, there would be lines stretching out the front door. As it is, you should call ahead for special orders or to reserve items currently being baked. People in Santa Rosa, Sebastopol, and Sonoma have cause to rejoice. ■

—Patricia Unterman

Flint's

★ ★

6609 Shattuck Avenue (near Alcatraz Avenue), 653-0593; 3114 San Pablo Avenue (at Thirty-first Street), 658-9912; 6672 East Fourteenth Street (take the Sixty-sixth Avenue exit off I-880), 559-1312; Oakland. Shattuck and San Pablo open Sunday through Thursday 11 A.M. to 2 A.M., Friday and Saturday 11 A.M. to 4 A.M. East Fourteenth Street open Sunday through Tuesday 11 A.M. to midnight, Friday and Saturday 11 A.M. to 3 A.M. No alcoholic beverages. Cash only. Inexpensive.

After I wrote a glowing review of Doug's Barbecue, I got a letter from a man who thanked me profusely, explaining that all the idiots were now at Doug's and therefore the lines were shorter at Flint's. That's typical of the Oakland barbecue scene—people have their favorite place and dismiss everything else. It's easy to see why Flint's has such a following: The pork ribs are excellent, the links the best anywhere, and the hot sauce can take the bark off a tree. If you don't want to splatter your car in the frenzy of starting on the irresistible ribs before you get home, the East Fourteenth Street branch has an upstairs dining room. ■

—Stan Sesser

Fourth Street Grill

★ ★

1820 Fourth Street, Berkeley. 849-0526. Open for lunch Monday through Friday 11:30 A.M. to 2:30 P.M.; for dinner Monday through Thursday 6 to 10 P.M., Friday 5:30 to 10:30 P.M., Saturday 5 to 11 P.M., Sunday 5 to 9:30 P.M. Beer, wine. MasterCard, Visa. Reservations accepted for dinner. Moderate.

Though founding chef Mark Miller left to open the Coyote Cafe in Santa Fe, New Mexico, his former partner Susan Nelson and new chef Amey Shaw have kept the Southwest chili fires burning with an eclectic and whimsical menu of spicy, international dishes. Many of the old favorites remain, however, like the exemplary caesar salad, the canadian bacon, lettuce, and tomato sandwich, the terrific shoestring potatoes, and many nicely grilled fish. Also look for Shaw's addictive garlic grits souffle, which usually accompanies a steak or chop. The refreshing chicken tostadas make a satisfying lunch. The restaurant has expanded its seating by roofing over the patio, which means less of a wait at peak meal times. ■

—Patricia Unterman

Gaylord India Restaurant

★ ★

900 North Point (Ghirardelli Square), San Francisco. 771-8822. Open for lunch Monday through Saturday 11:45 A.M. to 1:45 P.M., Sunday noon to 3 P.M.; for dinner daily 5 to 10:45 P.M. Full bar. Major credit cards. Reservations necessary. Moderate to expensive.

This is one of the most elegant and nicest Indian restaurants in San Francisco, and a great place to eat if you want to visit Ghirardelli Square. Gaylord is a chain that started in Bombay and has since spread around the world, but each restaurant retains its individual stamp. The Ghirardelli Gaylord does wonderful tandoori cooking, where meat is marinated in a host of spices and then hung to bake in a tandoor, an oven with clay-lined sides. Try the tandoori chicken and tandoori fish, and accompany it with onion *kulcha*, a puffy round bread stuffed with onions and slapped on the side of the tandoor to bake. Some of the curries are excellent too, particularly the *sag gosht*, with chunks of boneless lamb cooked with spiced creamed spinach. ■

—Stan Sesser

Gertie's Chesapeake Bay Cafe

★ ★

1919 Addison Street (near Milvia), Berkeley. 841-2722. Open for lunch Monday through Saturday 11:30 A.M. to 2:30 P.M., for brunch Sunday 10:30 A.M. to 2:30 P.M.; for dinner Monday through Thursday 5:30 to 9:30 P.M., Friday and Saturday 5:30 to 10:30 P.M., Sunday 4:30 to 9:30 P.M. Beer, wine. Major credit cards. Reservations recommended. Moderate.

Gertie's specializes in Maryland and Louisiana seafood dishes, and crab lovers can find things here rarely seen on Bay Area menus. The crab cakes are extraordinary, as is the spicy Maryland crab soup, heaped with crab meat. Recently, the kitchen has been doing a different special each night, ranging from Vietnamese curried duck to *lasagne verde*. Every Monday is all-you-can-eat Maryland panfried chicken night. It's delicious, and portions are too huge for seconds. The Sunday brunch is outstanding; try the seafood hash with poached eggs on top. ■

— Stan Sesser

Greens

★ ★ ★

Building A, Fort Mason, San Francisco. 771-6222. Open for lunch Tuesday through Saturday 11:30 A.M. to 2:15 P.M.; for a la carte dinner Tuesday through Thursday 6 to 9:30 P.M.; for Friday and Saturday prix-fixe dinner at seatings every 15 minutes beginning at 6 P.M. until 9:30 P.M.; for brunch Sunday 10 A.M. to 2 P.M. Beer, wine. MasterCard, Visa, American Express. Reservations required for dinner, recommended for lunch. Moderate.

Recent meals at Greens underscore once again that this vegetarian restaurant run by the Zen Center is one of the best eating places in the city. At lunch you'll encounter an open-faced sandwich on grilled country bread spread with delicious mixtures of cheese and fresh herbs. This might be paired with an orange, *frisée*, and olive salad. There might be a rich square of papery phyllo pastry filled with artichokes, leeks, and mozzarella with a crunchy salad of marinated fennel and radicchio. Sunday brunch brings lively omelets and the best crusty red potatoes with roasted cloves of garlic. All breads, muffins, and pastries are made by the Tassajara Bakery. The cafe dinners and weekend prix-fixe dinners focus on more substantial dishes, though rich pastas and wonderful individual pizzas are featured, too. The wines are well chosen, the view of the bay and Golden Gate Bridge spectacular, the space airy and cheerful, and the service newly efficient. The philosophy of the restaurant is to use ingredients of the highest quality and extremely fresh organic produce in the tastiest and most imaginative ways. ■

— Patricia Unterman

Ristorante Grifone

★ ★

1609 Powell Street, San Francisco. 397-8458. Open Monday through Thursday 5 to 11 P.M., Friday and Saturday 5 P.M. to midnight, Sunday 5 to 11 P.M. Beer, wine. Major credit cards. Reservations accepted. Moderate.

In North Beach, there are probably eighty Italian restaurants within a ten-minute walk, but very few are worth recommending. Grifone, a marvelously comfortable little place, stands out. It's one of those restaurants that seem entirely the product of their ever-present proprietors, in this instance a delightful man named Bruno Pella. The linguine in tomato sauce laden with seafood and the gnocchi in pesto sauce are about as good as San Francisco pasta gets. For a main course, try one of the veal dishes or the *medallioni filetto*, a butter-tender steak with a reduced red wine glaze. The atmosphere is pleasant, the service attentive, and the prices modest for such well-prepared food. ■

— Stan Sesser

Gulf Coast Oyster Bar and Restaurant

★★

763 Washington Street (at Eighth), Oakland. 839-6950. Open for lunch Monday through Friday 11:30 A.M. to 2:30 P.M.; for dinner Monday through Saturday 5:30 to 10 P.M. Beer, wine. MasterCard, Visa. Reservations accepted. Moderate.

Located in an area of Oakland that has been targeted for major redevelopment, with Alice Waters's proposed open market and nearby hotels and restaurants to be built in refurbished Victorians, Gulf Coast was ahead of them all. For six years the restaurant has been putting out sumptuous gumbos, oysters rockefeller, oyster stews, and other Cajun and Creole specialties using authentic ingredients from Louisiana. The smoky hot *andouille* sausage that permeates the gumbos is put on a plane by one of the owner's mothers, who lives in La Place, Louisiana. However, California respect for vegetables lightens and brightens some of the richer dishes, making them more palatable on a daily basis. The dining room has sandblasted red brick walls, and sunlight pours in through massive plate glass windows. This is one of the best spots to eat in downtown Oakland. ■
— Patricia Unterman

Harris'

★

2100 Van Ness Avenue, San Francisco. 673-1888. Open for lunch Monday through Friday 11:30 A.M. to 2 P.M.; for dinner Monday through Saturday 5 to 11 P.M.; Sunday 4 to 10 P.M. Full bar. MasterCard, Visa, American Express. Reservations recommended. Moderate at lunch, expensive at dinner.

This grande luxe steak house reflects the personality of gracious but iron-willed Ann Harris, whose goal was to create a San Fran-

cisco institution the moment she opened the doors of her restaurant three years ago. She insists that men wear jackets at night; that her wait staff be uniformed; that her clubby, booth-filled, thickly carpeted dining room runs like clockwork. Steaks and chops arrive perfectly grilled. A favorite is the bone-in New York called the Harris steak, which I order along with the tasty spinach salad. Actually, many love Harris' at lunch when the kitchen serves up more casual dishes like deeply seasoned chili, thick with tiny beef cubes and just a few beans. Brains and scrambled eggs with house baked sunflower-seed toast is a brilliant Harris creation, and the hamburgers reach a new level on the restaurant's own freshly baked buns. All the presentations carry Ann Harris's signature. Even the martinis come in little glass pitchers sunk into a miniature ice bucket so they stay icy cold as you drink them. If the food seems a little old-fashioned, it's because Ann Harris wants it exactly that way. ■
— Patricia Unterman

Hayes Street Grill

★★

320 Hayes Street (near Franklin), San Francisco. 863-5545. Open Monday through Thursday 11:30 A.M. to 10 P.M., Friday 11:30 A.M. to 11 P.M., Saturday 6 to 11 P.M. Beer, wine. MasterCard, Visa. Reservations necessary. Moderate.

I'd feel very virtuous if I could be critical of Hayes Street Grill, since it's owned by Patty Unterman, the co-author of this book, and some negative comments would mean no one could accuse me of conflict of interest. But I can't; to my mind, it's nothing less than the best fish restaurant in San Francisco. It's the only place you can be sure of getting the freshest fish; it's the only place with service so well synchronized that you can eat before the opera or symphony and be certain of getting out in time. Moreover, lately they've gone beyond fish to do some marvelous salads as appetizers and some great meat dishes as daily specials, including rabbit and veal liver. Desserts are splendid; the crème brûlée has actually won a national reputation. ■

—Stan Sesser

House of Prime Rib

★

1906 Van Ness Avenue (at Pacific), San Francisco. 885-4605. Open Monday through Friday 5:30 to 10 P.M., Saturday 5 to 10 P.M., Sunday 4 to 10 P.M. Full bar. Major credit cards. Reservations accepted.

The decor of the House of Prime Rib, an old and beloved San Francisco institution, has been gently rejuvenated by its new owners, Heide and Joe Betz, but the gorgeous roast beef has not changed, thank goodness, nor has the "spinning salad bowl," the rich creamed spinach, or the mashed potatoes. That's about all the restaurant prepares, except for an occasional well-handled very fresh piece of salmon. We're happy to report one innovation. The predominantly California wine list now records vintages. ■

—Patricia Unterman

Il Pollaio

★

555 Columbus Avenue, San Francisco. 362-7727. Open Monday through Saturday 11 A.M. to 9 P.M. Beer, wine. No credit cards. No reservations. Inexpensive.

Il Pollaio, which means the chicken coop, is a tiny, friendly North Beach grill that specializes in juicy grilled chicken, fresh, crunchy salads dressed in oil and vinegar, and house-made Italian sausages. The couple that runs it may be the nicest people in town. They go out of their way to welcome children, though their clientele is mostly comprised of older North Beach regulars. Much Italian is spoken over

glasses of good inexpensive Italian red wine and plates of the tasty marinated chicken. Though Il Pollaio is relatively new to the neighborhood, already it has become a neighborhood institution. ■

—Patricia Unterman

Joann's

★ ★

1131 El Camino Real (on an access road across the street from and just south of Kaiser Hospital), South San Francisco (take the Hickey Boulevard exit off 280). 872-2810. Open Tuesday through Friday 7 A.M. to 2:30 P.M., Saturday and Sunday 8 A.M. to 2:30 P.M. Beer, wine. Cash or personal checks. No reservations. Inexpensive.

JoAnn's is nothing less than the Bay Area's greatest hash house. I don't want to be intimidated at breakfast by a restaurant putting on airs; I want to feel comfortable in blue jeans and a T-shirt—but also to get great food. JoAnn's fits the bill completely. The omelets are superb, the muffins are sold all over the city, and if you eat there in the fall, you can have fantastic pumpkin pancakes. Presiding over your breakfast feast is one of the sweetest restaurateurs anywhere, JoAnn DiLorenzo. Lunches are great too, but nothing could get me to pass up an omelet. ■

—Stan Sesser

Kabuto

★ ★ ★

5116 Geary, San Francisco. 752-5652. Open Tuesday through Saturday 5 P.M. to 1 A.M., Sunday 5 to 11 P.M. Closed first Tuesday of each month. Beer, wine, sake. Major credit cards. No reservations accepted for sushi bar, accepted for restaurant. Moderate.

Sachio, the intense young chef-owner of this extremely popular sushi bar, channels his manic energy into creating gorgeous dishes. He wields his knives like a new wave robot warrior, shouting in Japanese as customers walk through the traditional entry curtain. Not only is the usual sushi and sashimi impeccably fresh and generously cut, but Sachio's invented pieces are spectacular. Once he gets to know you, there's no telling what he'll come up with. Every day a list of small cooked dishes is written on a blackboard behind the sushi bar to augment the raw foods. The variety of ingredients and the artistry of the presentations rank Kabuto as the best and most innovative sushi bar in the city. ■

—Patricia Unterman

Khan Toke Thai House

★ ★

5937 Geary Boulevard, San Francisco. 668-6654. Open daily 5 to 11 P.M.Beer, wine. MasterCard, Visa, American Express. Reservations accepted. Moderate.

Khan Toke was one of the first Thai restaurants in the Bay Area. More precisely, it's the granddaddy of our Thai restaurants, since waiters, cooks, and even dancers have left to start places of their own. What's happened to Khan Toke with all the new competition? It has doubled in size, and if anything, the crowds at the front door are greater than ever. They're coming for splendid dishes like an appetizer of pork balls that you roll with condiments into a won ton skin, a fiery squid salad, a soothing chicken curry in coconut milk, and a delicate Thai omelet stuffed with ground pork and vegetables. In a beautifully decorated room, you can sit at low tables and watch Thai dancing while you eat. ■

—Stan Sesser

La Cheminee

★ ★

8504 North Lake Boulevard, Kings Beach (take Highway 257 from Truckee to the north shore of Lake Tahoe, turn left; the restaurant is about .5 mile on the right). 916-546-4322. Open Thursday through Monday with seatings on the half hour from 6 to 7:30, 8:45 to 9:30 P.M. Beer, wine. Major credit cards. Reservations only. Expensive.

Lake Tahoe might not be the first place that comes to mind when you're wondering where to eat good French food. But in Kings Beach on the north shore is a very French and very excellent restaurant called La Cheminee. I was put off on my visits by a lengthy explanation of each dish on the menu that went on like a chant from table to table to the detriment of conversation. But once the food started coming, things brightened considerably. It's classic French cooking, with lots of butter and cream, and sauces of reduced stocks and red wine. But the cooking is skillful, the presentation lovely to look at, and the ingredients impeccable—no small feat, particularly in midwinter, when you're transporting everything to Tahoe. The fish in particular is outstanding. ■

—Stan Sesser

La Cumbre

★

515 Valencia Street, San Francisco. 863-8205. Open Monday through Saturday 11 A.M. to 10 P.M., Sunday noon to 8 P.M. Beer. No credit cards. No reservations. Inexpensive.

If you've never eaten a great burrito, you owe it to yourself to wait in line at La Cumbre for one stuffed with *carne asada*. The thin slices of beef are charred over coals to order, then cleaved into strips and put into a warm flour tortilla covered with melted jack cheese. Whole soft red beans and a spoonful of fresh salsa are layered in. This one-pound tortilla then gets rolled and wrapped in foil to stay warm as you eat it, either in La Cumbre's cheerful dining area covered with bright folk murals and furnished with hand-carved wooden picnic tables or taken to go. Other favorites are the cheese burrito with green chili and a barbecued pork burrito that gets rice as well as beans. ■

—Patricia Unterman

La Mexicana

★ ★

3940 East Fourteenth Street, Oakland (take the High Street exit of I-880 and turn left on East Fourteenth). 436-8388. Open Wednesday through Sunday noon to 8 P.M. Beer. Master-Card, Visa. No reservations. Inexpensive.

La Mexicana is nothing fancy, to put it mildly, but it probably has the best Tex-Mex food in the Bay Area. It's hard to believe that enchiladas, tacos, and the like can be so light, so delicate, and so flavorful. A Mexican-American family has owned this place for three decades, and what the restaurant lacks in atmosphere is more than made up for by the food. The tortillas, thick and fluffy and served steaming hot, are handmade there in the kitchen. The chorizo, spicy Mexican sausage, is incomparable. The *chiles rellenos* use fresh chilies, not canned, and the batter is superbly delicate. Everything in La Mexicana is prepared from scratch using fresh ingredients and served by a family that really cares. ■

—Stan Sesser

La Traviata

★ ★

2854 Mission Street (between Twenty-fourth and Twenty-fifth Streets), San Francisco. 282-0500. Open Tuesday through Sunday 4 to 10:30 P.M. Beer, wine. MasterCard, Visa. Reservations necessary. Moderate.

In San Francisco, lots of Italian restaurants are long on atmosphere but short on food. La Traviata is one of the friendliest of all, and the good news is that the food is excellent. In particular, they do a great job preparing veal and calamari, dishes that in many San Francisco Italian restaurants leave you longing for a meal in New York's Little Italy. Try the veal Traviata, topped with thin layers of prosciutto and melted parmesan cheese. The tortellini in cream sauce makes a wonderful pasta appetizer, and the chicken Beverly Sills is worthy of being named after a great singer. It's a strange concept to drive to the Hispanic Mission district for Italian food, but La Traviata is definitely worth the trip. ■

—Stan Sesser

Little Joe's

★

523 Broadway, San Francisco. 433-4343. Open Monday through Thursday 11 A.M. to 10:30 P.M., Friday and Saturday 11 A.M. to 11 P.M., Sunday 2 P.M. to 10 P.M. Beer, wine. No credit cards. No reservationns. Inexpensive.

This bustling dining hall is where San Franciscans head for big portions of hearty, saucy North Beach-style Italian food. There are no pretensions about anything at Little Joe's. The completely open kitchen bares the organized frenzy of the cooking line to the whole dining room. In fact, the most coveted seats are at the counter, practically in the kitchen. The waitresses are gruff but efficient, and the food is just plain good — the best of its much-imitated kind in San Francisco. Try the boiled tongue or a brisket with piquant green sauce; the cheese-blanketed veal saltimbocca; the creamy sauteed chicken livers; and gigantic plates of al dente spaghetti with aromatic pesto. No one ever walks out of Little Joe's hungry, and its prices and crusty North Beach atmosphere even make the older generation of bohemians happy. ■

—Patricia Unterman

Madrona Manor

★ ★

1001 Westside Road, Healdsburg. 707-433-4231. Open daily 6 to 9 P.M.; for brunch Sunday 10:30 A.M. to 2 P.M. Beer, wine. Major credit cards. Reservations accepted. Expensive.

This country inn and restaurant in a romantic Victorian mansion amidst tall trees merits a special trip to Sonoma County. Founded and run by two generations of the Muir family, the kitchen is outfitted with a wood-burning oven for bread, a mesquite grill, and a smokehouse. The family has cultivated a garden and put in an orchard. The dinners served in the inn's two high-ceilinged, parlorlike dining rooms are inspired by homegrown and local products. A recent five-course prix fixe meal made use of specially raised Sonoma lamb, figs and peaches from the orchard, seasonal salmon, and house-made basil tagliatelle with a sauce of yellow and red tomatoes from the garden. An a la carte menu also emphasizes Sonoma products. The Madrona Manor has developed considerably since it opened three years ago. The lush, rustic grounds now include a swimming pool, and the food served in the graceful dining room has become more formal, realizing the Muir family goal of turning their country inn into a first-class destination. ■

— Patricia Unterman

Mandarin House

★ ★

817 Francisco Boulevard, San Rafael. 492-1638. Open for lunch Monday through Sunday 11:30 A.M. to 3 P.M.; for dinner Monday through Thursday 5 to 9 P.M., Friday and Saturday 5 to 10 P.M., Sunday 4 to 10 P.M. Full bar. MasterCard, Visa, American Express. Reservations accepted. Inexpensive.

Though inauspiciously located in a cement block shopping center by the freeway, this popular northern Chinese restaurant distinguishes itself with its rich, spicy dishes and co-owner Lillian Tien's personal ministrations. She personalizes the warehouse-like dining room with vases and vases of fresh flowers and her own challenging advice on what to order. Her guidance has helped many regulars establish their favorite dishes, like captivating deep-fried eggplant coins, bowls of won ton in hot and spicy Szechuan sauce, richly sauced braised prawns, and rice-coated "pearl balls." Every bit emerges from the kitchen meticulously prepared in a manner that must pass Mrs. Tien's ever-vigilant eye. As you might imagine, her restaurant has attracted a large and loyal following, so call ahead. ■

— Patricia Unterman

Ristorante Milano

★ ★

1448 Pacific Street (at Larkin), San Francisco. 673-2961. Open Tuesday through Saturday 5:30 to 10:30 P.M. Beer, wine. MasterCard, Visa. No reservations. Moderate.

This wildly popular neighborhood trattoria has a tiny dining room and won't accept reservations, which means you may have to wait out on the street to get in. However, parking, which is impossible anywhere on Russian Hill, has been provided at the gas station across the street. The family-run kitchen puts out delicious al dente pastas with authentic Italian meat sauces; spicy mixtures of hot peppers, anchovies, and olives; and lovely combinations of fresh vegetables unified by freshly grated parmesan cheese. The meat dishes are lightly done and the *antipasti* and carpaccio excellent. Everything is prepared with the restraint and balance that comes from using excellent ingredients. After a meal at Ristorante Milano you feel well fed without being weighed down by too much cream or olive oil—just like eating in Italy. ■

— Patricia Unterman

Nan Yang

★ ★

301 Eighth Street (at Harrison), Oakland. 465-6924. Open Tuesday through Sunday 10:30 A.M. to 9 P.M. Beer, wine. MasterCard, Visa. Reservations accepted. Inexpensive.

Nan Yang, a Burmese restaurant in Oakland's Chinatown, is one of the most interesting and extraordinarily wonderful Asian restaurants in the Bay Area. It's the creation of Philip Chu, a Burmese architect who takes his task as seriously as any French three-star chef. He has created a Burmese menu filled with unusual dishes that are a joy to eat. Come with lots of people and try the ginger salad, the "eight precious bean curd" (which is actually milk, ham, and seafood formed into a paste and deep fried), the curried fish noodle soup, and the chicken curry. The restaurant is nothing fancy, but it's extremely pleasant and the service is excellent. ■

— Stan Sesser

Narai

★ ★

2229 Clement Street, San Francisco 751-6363. Open Tuesday through Saturday 11:30 A.M. to 10 P.M., Sunday until 9:30 P.M. Beer, wine. MasterCard, Visa, American Express. Reservations accepted for six or more. Inexpensive to moderate.

This bright, cheerful neighborhood restaurant features both regional Chinese Chiu Chow and Thai dishes on its long and interesting menu. A warm salad of silver noodles with pork and shrimp has put Narai on the local culinary map along with deep-fried quail, a seafood hot pot with a light Thai sauce, and long-simmered ham knuckle in an anise-scented gravy. The food here is clean flavored and emphasizes textural contrasts. While the dishes are intriguingly unusual, the main ingredients are not inaccessible to Western palates. ■

— Patricia Unterman

New Asia

★ ★

772 Pacific Avenue (near Stockton Street), San Francisco. 391-6666. Open for dim sum daily from 9 A.M. to 3 P.M., for dinner 5 to 10 P.M. Beer and wine only with dinner. Visa, American Express (for dinner only). Reservations accepted. Inexpensive.

It's the size of a football field, and the noise level will make you think that someone has just scored a touchdown. But New Asia [formerly Asia Garden] is one of the most authentic places in San Francisco to eat dim sum, the wonderful Chinese tea pastries that are so popular in Hong Kong. Just as in Hong Kong, waitresses push carts down the aisles singing out their wares in Chinese. They'll take the covers off the steaming pots for you to have a glance, and you point to what you want. The deep frying is exceptionally good here (theirs is the ultimate egg roll), and some of the steamed dumplings are magnificent. After the meal, again in Hong Kong style, they'll count the plates on your table, and that determines the bill. ■

— Stan Sesser

Pat O'Shea's Mad Hatter

★ ★

3848 Geary Boulevard (at Third Avenue), San Francisco. 752-3148. Open Monday through Saturday 11:30 A.M. to 9 P.M., Sunday 11 A.M. to 3 P.M. Full bar. No credit cards. Reservations for six or more only. Inexpensive to moderate.

Known as a sports bar with a satellite dish and six televisions, the Mad Hatter also serves unexpectedly delicious and inventive food at astoundingly reasonable prices. You might think that you've walked into a corny Irish pub until you get your sensitively grilled veal sweetbreads or roasted anglerfish with briny mussels that melt in your mouth. My mother doesn't make a better beef pot roast and the hamburgers are great. The young woman who runs the kitchen goes out of her way to buy organic produce from Green Gulch gardens, truly fresh fish, and the highest quality meats. For every barroom classic she turns out, she also creates original dishes that expand the culinary horizon of her typical patrons. Many who used to go to the Mad Hatter to drink and watch the games now go there to eat. Sports fans have never had it so good. ∎

—Patricia Unterman

Pier 23

★

Pier 23 on the Embarcadero (near Lombard), San Francisco. 362-5125. Open Monday through Saturday 11:30 A.M. to 2:30 P.M., 6 to 10 P.M.; Sunday brunch 11 A.M. to 3 P.M. Full bar. MasterCard, Visa. Reservations accepted. Moderate.

Two bona fide San Francisco characters, Peggy Knickerbocker and Flicka McGurrin, own this bayside restaurant, really a shack on a pier, with wonderful views of Treasure Island from the small copper bar and an outdoor eating area by the water. The place exudes gritty San Francisco charm. There's absolutely nothing chic or touristy about it, yet everyone from society matrons to longshoremen can be spotted there lunching on superlative meat loaf with a smoky Cajun barbecue sauce and mashed potatoes, juicy half-pound hamburgers, and green salads sprinkled with pine nuts. Sunday brunch brings an old-fashioned corned beef hash topped with two perfect poached eggs, one of the best dishes anywhere. Flicka and Peggy seem to know everyone in town and like everyone equally. ∎

—Patricia Unterman

Pierre at the Meridien Hotel

★ ★

50 Third Street, San Francisco. 974-6400. Open Monday through Saturday 6 to 10 P.M. Full bar. Major credit cards. Reservations recommended. Expensive.

This restaurant on the ground floor of the San Francisco outpost of the Meridien Hotel chain sets itself apart by being so totally French that diners feel like they're eating in Paris. The restaurant got off to an auspicious start by hiring three-star French chef Alain Chapel as a consultant, but soon realized that someone on the day-to-day scene was important. So they enlisted Jean-Pierre Moule, a seven-year alumnus of Chez Panisse, to oversee the food service. With an ambitious program of visiting chefs, Pierre became a destination in the city's culinary galaxy. Moulle has left, but the kitchen hierarchy has remained in place, along with the Pierre's philosophy of preparing au courant French dishes using excellent local ingredients. ∎

—Patricia Unterman

Plearn Thai Cuisine

★ ★ ★

2050 University Avenue, Berkeley. 841-2148. Open Monday through Saturday 11:30 A.M. to 3 P.M., 5 to 10 P.M. Beer, wine. Cash or personal check only. Reservations accepted for five or more. Inexpensive.

Thailand is one of the greatest countries on earth for restaurants. But in moving across the ocean, Thai food often loses something in the translation. Not at Plearn Thai Cuisine, however, which is the most authentic reproduction of eating in Bangkok that I've encountered in the Bay Area. Other people must think so too, because the crowds waiting for tables at Plearn seem to grow year after year despite a huge increase in the number of new Thai restau rants. They come for the sparkling fresh seafood, the fiery beef and calamari salads, the complex flavors of the curries, the aromatic and sinus-clearing chicken soup with lemon grass and coconut milk—and even for an unusually good wine list. Plearn is nothing less than my favorite Asian restaurant in the Bay Area. ■

—Stan Sesser

Rice Table

★★

1617 Fourth Street, San Rafael. 456-1808. Open Thursday through Saturday 5:30 to 10 P.M., Sunday 5 to 9 P.M. Beer, wine. Major credit cards. Reservations advised. Inexpensive.

A dynamic Indonesian woman, Leonie Hool, has presided over this exciting little restaurant for nearly two decades. She and her family prepare a stunning rijsttafel, a feast of Indonesian dishes, each night in their tiny immaculate kitchen. She uses old family recipes from west Java, which she has compiled into a cookbook available at the restaurant. Her curries and satays are lush with fresh spices and deep flavors. If you don't want to sample the whole range of Indonesian cooking at one sitting, the succulent chicken satay, Indonesian fried rice noodles, and stir-fried shrimp perfumed with tamarind and lemon are extraordinary. ■

—Patricia Unterman

Rosalie's

★★

1415 Van Ness, San Francisco. 928-7188. Open for lunch Monday through Friday 11:30 A.M. to 2:30 P.M., for dinnery daily 5:30 to 10:30 P.M. Full bar. Major credit cards. Reservations advised for lunch, essential for dinner. Expensive.

One ponders the reason behind the wacky decor at this style-obsessed restaurant—the sheet-metal tables, the wash-pail wine buckets, the knotted-dish-towel napkins, the terra cotta plate liners, the plaster curtains, the aluminum palm trees. Is it supposed to be Southwest? Or is it simply the fantasy of the owner and former model Bill Belloli? The kitchen, headed by Rick O'Connell, a woman who rose from the amateur cooking ranks to run not one, but two kitchens (RAF), comes up with its own interesting fantasies, like saucy duck burritos, sweetbread tacos, or shellfish pan roasts and fried chicken with mashed potatoes, all redone in Rosalie's very elaborate style. The food can be a revelation—like O'Connell's deep-fried parsnip chips—or so complex that it's impossible for the kitchen to execute it well, but a visit to Rosalie's will always be intriguing. ■

—Patricia Unterman

Sanppo

★★

1702 Post Street, San Francisco. 346-3486. Open Tuesday through Saturday 11:45 A.M. to 10 P.M., Sunday 3 to 10 P.M. Beer, wine. No credit cards. No reservations. Inexpensive.

This was one of the first Japanese restaurants I visited many years ago and I still think it's one of the best. Unpretentious, always busy, relatively small, Sanppo turns out a whole range of Japanese dishes with consistent high quality. *Gyoza*, or Japanese pot stickers, with delicate skins and savory stuffings, grilled eel over rice, pretty Japanese soups with an array of fresh vegetables and seafood, lacy tempura, delicious fried oysters, and cold spinach and cucumber salads in perfectly balanced dressings never fail to please. You might have to wait for or share a table, but this amazingly inexpensive little restaurant is worth the inconvenience. ■

—Patricia Unterman

Sear's Fine Foods

★

439 Powell, San Francisco. 986-1160. Open Wednesday through Sunday 7 A.M. to 2:30 P.M. No alcoholic beverages. No credit cards. No reservations. Inexpensive.

Sear's is an old-fashioned American breakfast restaurant famous for its huge bowls of excellent California strawberries, raspberries, and melons and gigantic baked Rome Beauty apples served with thick cream. For those who can't decide on one fruit, the fresh fruit bowl, a goblet brimming over with a gorgeous assortment of ripe cantaloupe, honeydew, pineapple, and berries splashed with lemon-scented fresh orange juice is just the ticket. Juices are all freshly squeezed. While the omelets are mundane, other breakfast classics are done to perfection, like Sear's famous Swedish pancakes, crisp egg waffles, and sourdough french toast. The Canadian bacon and smoked country sausage made especially for Sear's are excellent. If you have room for dessert, you won't find a better strawberry shortcake in anyone's home. ■

—Patricia Unterman

Sheba

★★

3109 Telegraph Avenue (at Thirty-first Street), Oakland. 654-3741. Open Tuesday through Thursday 11:30 A.M. to 10 P.M., Friday 11:30 A.M. to 11 P.M., Saturday 1 to 11 P.M., Sunday 5 to 10 P.M. Beer, wine. MasterCard, Visa. Reservations accepted. Inexpensive.

Ethiopian food is unlike any other cuisine in the world. It's a series of spicy stews, spread out over a flat spongy bread called *injera.* You eat with your fingers, wrapping the *injera* around the pieces of stew. It's messy and it's delicious. The Bay Area's best Ethiopian restaurant is Sheba, near downtown Oakland. Sheba offers a host of wonderful things, which you can sample as combination plates, or, on Fridays, in a buffet dinner. Vegetarians will have a particularly wonderful time here; from lentils to collard greens to bulgur wheat, the vegetarian dishes are a joy. ■

—Stan Sesser

Siam Cuisine

★★

181 University Avenue (between San Pablo and Curtis), Berkeley. 548-3278. Open for lunch Monday through Saturday 11 A.M. to 3 P.M.; for dinner Sunday through Thursday 5 to 11 P.M., Friday and Saturday to midnight. Beer, wine. MasterCard, Visa. Reservations for four or more. Inexpensive to moderate.

One of the first Thai restaurants in the Bay Area, Siam Cuisine continues to turn out perfect renditions of what have now become Thai restaurant classics. Their incendiary squid salad has meltingly tender rings of warm squid tossed with a perfectly balanced dressing of lime, chili oil, and ginger. Grilled rare beef is substituted to make another delicious but searing hot salad. The crisp Thai-style shrimp toasts, piquant hot and sour shrimp soup, and opulent coconut milk curries seasoned with fresh basil leaves or complex red spice pastes are excellent. Of course, there are many unusual items on the menu, like a paper-thin egg pancake stuffed with peanuts and ground pork, and called an omelet. A whole generation of Berkeley residents learned about Thai food from Siam Cuisine, and everyone still goes back for more. ■

—Patricia Unterman

Square One

★★

190 Pacific at Front, San Francisco. 788-1110. Open Monday through Friday 11:30 A.M. to 2:30 P.M., Monday through Thursday 5:30 to 10 P.M., Friday and Saturday 5:30 to 10:30 P.M., Sunday 5 to 9:30 P.M. Full bar. MasterCard, Visa, American Express. Reservations advised. Moderate to expensive.

When Joyce Goldstein opened Square One a few years back, she took a tremendous gamble. The menu changed completely every night and almost everything, including the breads, was made on the premises. Can you successfully feed a large number of people and still be this innovative? The verdict is in, and the answer is clearly yes. The prices aren't cheap, the noise level can be uncomfortably high, but people jam into Square One day after day because the food is so interesting. It's a multiethnic menu, and the Italian and Moroccan dishes tend to be particularly wonderful. From soup to dessert to a big and very well-chosen wine list, every element of Square One makes for an exciting meal. ■

—Stan Sesser

Tadich Grill

★

240 California Street, San Francisco. 391-2373. Open Monday through Friday 11 A.M. to 9 P.M. Full bar. No credit cards. No reservations. Moderate.

Tadich Grill, a San Francisco fish restaurant that dates back to the gold rush days, feels like a piece of the city's history. The ancient dark wood paneling, the booths that enclose white-linen-covered tables, bentwood chairs, the cracked plaster ceilings, and the veteran waiters all give Tadich its splendid ambience. As at Sam's, the other traditional fish house in the Financial District, the owners are Yugoslavian and were the first to cook fish over mesquite charcoal. Ask your waiter what's fresh that day, and if it's the generously cut salmon or swordfish, order it rare if you want it moist in the middle. Tadich is justly famous for its buttery grilled sand dabs, rex sole, and petrale sole, all local fish. The fancier preparations don't hold up to today's standards, but the rice custard pudding and baked apples certainly do. A line forms at eleven o'clock which doesn't disappear until two P.M. or so, but you can usually grab a single seat at the long counter. ■

—Patricia Unterman

Taqueria Morelia

★★

4481 East Fourteenth Street, Oakland. 261-6360. Open daily 10 A.M. to 11 P.M. Full bar connected, next door. No credit cards. No reservations. Inexpensive.

When a food-loving friend of mine from Washington, D.C., comes to the Bay Area, his first order of business isn't one of the trendy, well-known restaurants; it's instead a scruffy fast-food operation in Oakland called Taqueria Morelia. No wonder. This is Tex-Mex food at its finest, things that are so beautifully prepared you never tire of them. Start with the quesadillas, tortillas topped with melted jack cheese and stuffed with tomatoes and onions. Then move on to one of the fantastic burritos; my favorite is the *chile verde*, lean pork simmered with hot green chilies. Prices are amazingly low, and the meal is both satisfying and filling. ■

—Stan Sesser

Taqueria San Jose

★★

No. 1, 2830 Mission Street, 282-0203; No. 2, 2282 Mission Street, 558-8549; No. 3, 3274 Twenty-fourth Street, 282-7018; San Francisco. No. 1 open Monday through Friday 8 A.M. to 1 A.M., Friday and Saturday until 4 A.M., Sunday until 3 A.M. No. 2 open daily 8 A.M. to 2:30 A.M. No. 3 open daily 8 A.M. to midnight. Beer. No credit cards. No reservations. Inexpensive.

These popular Mission district taquerias represent the best of the genre, and obviously the best item to order is the double-layered soft tacos, filled with spit-roasted pork, beef tongue, head meat, or grilled steak. Spicy freshly chopped tomato salsa with lots of fresh cilantro is spooned on and you have the best taco in town. They're so good because they're so fresh and the structure is so simple: the freshest corn tortillas, savory meat, and salsa. The chopping never stops in the taquerias' open kitchens, and neither does the flow of customers. Watch out, McDonald's! ■

— Patricia Unterman

Trio Cafe

★

1870 Fillmore Street (at Bush), San Francisco. Open Tuesday through Saturday 8 a.m to 6 P.M., Sunday 10 A.M. to 4 P.M. Beer, wine. No credit cards. No reservations. Inexpensive.

This Fillmore Street cafe, inspired by Cafe Fanny in Berkeley, nearly doubled in size this year to accommodate all the neighborhood folks who like to drop in for their morning cafe au lait, or a delicious open-faced sandwich accompanied with a trio of little salads, or buttery spice cookies with tea. The whitewashed light-filled rooms still feel intimate. The three women who run the cafe are as friendly and accommodating as ever, except now you can find a place to sit down. Their formula of quickly assembled small dishes using interesting in-

gredients, inexpensive prices, and good coffee has justly brought them success. ■

— Patricia Unterman

Tung Fong

★★

808 Pacific Avenue, San Francisco. 362-7115. Open Thursday through Tuesday 9 A.M. to 3 P.M. Beer. No credit cards. Reservations accepted weekdays only. Inexpensive.

Dim sum places in San Francisco that serve the delicate Chinese tea pastries so popular in Hong Kong are often big and noisy. A combination of good dim sum and a relaxed atmosphere is a rarity, but Tung Fong offers both. Try the superlative foil-wrapped chicken, the green pepper squares spread with a paste of shrimp and egg, and the sensational pork bao, a fluffy bun stuffed with barbecued pork. Almost all the steamed dishes are excellent, too. This is a place to take friends from out of town for an "only in San Francisco" meal. ■

— Stan Sesser

Vicolo Pizzeria

★★

201 Ivy Street, 863-2382; and Ghirardelli Square, 776-1331; San Francisco. Ivy Street open Monday through Saturday 11:30 A.M. to 11:30 P.M., Sunday 2 to 10 P.M. Ghirardelli Square open Sunday through Thursday 11 A.M. to 10 P.M., Friday and Saturday 11 A.M. to 11 P.M. Beer, wine. No credit cards. No reservations. Inexpensive.

Vicolo is partially owned by Patricia Unterman, the co-author of this book. But it's a restaurant that's so unique, I want to write about it despite this conflict. The reason: It offers a chance to try wonderful pizza with interesting toppings, and fresh vegetable salads, without having to sit down and eat a long and expensive meal. You stand in line and order by the slice, but you get a chance to sample great versions of the yuppified sort of pizza that's proving so popular in trendy restaurants. A crisp crust that includes cornmeal, a variety of pillowy-soft cheeses, and toppings like a combination of roasted peppers, fennel, and eggplant are what make Vicolo so popular. ■

—Stan Sesser

Vivande
★ ★

2125 Fillmore Street, San Francisco. 346-4430. Open daily 11:30 A.M. to 4 P.M. Beer, wine. Master-Card, Visa. No reservations. Moderate.

Vivande, a delicatessen and cafe run by talented Carlo Middione, gets my vote for the best pasta in town. Vivande makes it fresh once or twice a day, and I've never tasted any that is silkier, more tender, or more flavorful. Middione barely sauces it with fresh vegetables and a little cheese or with *pancetta*, eggs, and cream or with fresh tomatoes and herbs, and it always turns out to be the most delicious plate of noodles you've ever eaten. There's the whole deli case to choose from for *antipasti*, and the most delicate Italian tarts and cookies and ricotta-cheese cakes for dessert. A regularly offered fried oyster sandwich and rotisseried chicken turned over an open fire also bring me back again and again. The spectacular open kitchen practically surrounds the cafe tables, making Vivande one of liveliest spots to eat. ■

—Patricia Unterman

Washington Square Bar and Grill

1707 Powell Street (at Union), San Francisco. 982-8123. Open for breakfast Monday through Saturday 11:30 A.M. to 3 P.M.; for brunch Sunday 10 A.M. to 3 P.M.; for dinner Monday through Thursday 6 to 11 P.M., Friday through Sunday 5:30 to 11:30 P.M. Full bar. Major credit cards. Reservations accepted. Moderate.

The Washbag, as it is fondly called by its wildly loyal patrons, is one of the most popular and beloved establishments in town. Journalists, politicians, magazine publishers, private eyes, and sports commissioners use the bar as their watering hole and club, and the noise level can be maddeningly high, especially with live jazz piano thrown into the fray. While the atmosphere is electric, the food can short out. The menu is incredibly large for the restaurant's small kitchen to handle. However, you might encounter some tasty spinach noodles with creamy clam sauce, a fine tomato and anchovy salad in season, and a satisfying shrimp louie. The point of the Washington Square Bar and Grill isn't just the food, anyway. ■

—Patricia Unterman

Zola's
★ ★ ★

1722 Sacramento Street, San Francisco. 775-3311. Open Tuesday through Saturday 6 to 11 P.M., Sunday until 10 P.M. Beer, wine. Major credit cards. Reservations essential. Moderate.

This charming little bistro is presided over by a dedicated young couple who bring depth and creativity to their jobs. Chef Catherine Pantsios has a way with long-cooked country French dishes like cassoulet, braised chicken legs stuffed with wild mushrooms, and rabbit *confit*. She makes eggplant-and-tomato gratins and leek-and-bacon tarts. For dessert, she pairs a winter fruit compote with cinnamon ice cream. She likes the traditional but transforms it in her own singular, modern style. Her partner, Larry Bain, has gathered together the most interesting wine cellar in town. He pulls out marvelous bottles that he sells by the glass to match dishes on the often-changing menu. Zola's is just the kind of personal, intimate, romantic little restaurant couples are always looking for, but I love it as a place to get something deeply satisfying and original for dinner. ■

—Patricia Unterman

Index

American

Australian

Austrian

Barbecue

Breakfast and Brunches

Burmese

California Cuisine

Hamburgers

Fatapple's ★ 78

Indian

Bombay Cuisine ★★ 25
Gaylord India Restaurant ★★ 230
Himalaya ★★ 97
India Garden ★★ 98
India Palace ★★ 99
The Peacock ★ 166
Royal India Cuisine ★★ 180

Indonesian

Rice Table ★★ 239

Italian

Adriana's ★★ 226
Allegro ★ 15
Buca Giovanni ★★ 227
Cafe Latte ★★★ 33
Cafe Pranzo ★ 37
Caffe Sport ★ 228
Capp's Corner ★★ 47
Circolo 59
Donatello 68
E'Angelo ★★ 73
Enrico's ★ 75
Ristorante Firenze ★ 81
Ristorante Grifone ★★ 231
Harry's Bar and American Grill 96
Il Pollaio ★ 233
La Lanterna ★★ 99
La Traviata ★★ 235
Little Joe's ★ 235
Mamma Tina's Trattoria ★ 132
Ristorante Milano ★★ 236
Modesto Lanzone's ★ 148
Pasta Bella II ★★ 163
RAF Centrogriglia ★★ 175
Rapallo ★ 15
Tra Vigne ★★ 203
Tutto Bene ★ 206
Umberto 209
Vanessi's on Nob Hill ★ 210
Ristorante Venezia ★★ 212
Vivande ★★ 243

Italian Pizza

Blondie's Pizza ★ 24
Caffe Quadro ★★ 41
Calzone ★ 44
Cheese Board ★ 24
Tommaso's ★★ 198
Vicolo Pizzeria ★★ 242

Japanese

Isuzu ★ 102
Ma Tante Sumi ★ 61
Mitoya ★ 147
Moshi Moshi ★ 150
Sanppo ★★ 239

Japanese Sushi

Kabuto ★★★ 233
Oishi/so:too ★★★ 159

Jewish Deli

Brothers Delicatessen ★★ 227
Jewish Community Center ★ 106
Max's Diner ★ 143
Saul's ★ 186

Korean

Korean Garden ★★ 108

Laotian

Lan Xang ★★ 117

Mexican

Cafe Violeta ★ 39
Chevys ★★ 53
Guaymas ★ 91
La Imperial 127
La Mexicana ★★ 235
La Victoria ★ 113
Las Parrillas ★ 118
Los Compadres ★ 127
New Central ★ 155
Tortola ★ 201

Mexican Tacos/Burritos

Middle Eastern

Moroccan

Portuguese

Soul Food

Southwest

Spanish

Thai

Vietnamese

Geographic Index

San Francisco